PENGUIN BOOKS

THE POPE'S ELEPHANT

Silvio A. Bedini, Historian Emeritus at the Smithsonian Institution in Washington, D.C., served for many years as Deputy Director of the National Museum of History and Technology (now the National Museum of American History) and then as the Smithsonian's Keeper of the Rare Books. For many years he has been engaged in research in the Vatican museums, library, and archives. He is the author of more than a dozen books.

Oriens

Quorundam locorum huius

Occaſus   Bel Videre

Palatium p.p̄.

Tiberis flu.

n 2

THE POPE'S ELEPHANT

SILVIO A. BEDINI

PENGUIN BOOKS

PENGUIN BOOKS
Published by the Penguin Group
Penguin Putnam Inc., 375 Hudson Street,
New York, New York 10014, U.S.A.
Penguin Books Ltd, 27 Wrights Lane, London W8 5TZ, England
Penguin Books Australia Ltd, Ringwood, Victoria, Australia
Penguin Books Canada Ltd, 10 Alcorn Avenue,
Toronto, Ontario, Canada M4V 3B2
Penguin Books (N.Z.) Ltd, 182–190 Wairau Road,
Auckland 10, New Zealand

Penguin Books Ltd, Registered Offices:
Harmondsworth, Middlesex, England

First published in Great Britain by Carcanet Press Ltd in association with
The Calouste Gulbenkian Foundation and the Discoveries Commission, Lisbon 1997
First published in the United States of America by J. S. Sanders & Company, Inc. 1998
Published in Penguin Books 2000

1 3 5 7 9 10 8 6 4 2

THE LIBRARY OF CONGRESS HAS CATALOGED THE
AMERICAN HARDCOVER EDITION AS FOLLOWS:
The pope's elephant/Silvio A. Bedini.
p.   cm.
Includes bibliographical references (pp. 261–286) and index.
ISBN 1-879941-41-4 (hc.)
ISBN 0 14 02.8862 7 (pbk.)
1. Papal States—History—Leo X, 1513–1521.   2. Rome (Italy)—History—
1420–1798.   3. Leo X, Pope, 1475–1521.   4. Renaissance—Italy—Papal States.
5. Catholic Church—Foreign relations—Portugal.   6. Portugal—Foreign relations—
Catholic Church.   7. Portugal—History—Manuel, 1495–1521.   8. Manuel I, King
of Portugal, 1469–1521.   9. Hanno (Elephant).   10. Elephants in art.   I. Title.
DG797.8.B44   1998
945'.606—dc21   98-36227

Printed in the United States of America
Set in Bembo
Designed by Kim Taylor

DEDICATION

To the memories of
Dr O.B. Hardison & Dr Joshua C. Taylor
contributors to this work who did not live to see it in print,
and to my wife Gale

ACKNOWLEDGEMENTS

It would be impossible to record my indebtedness to all who have contributed to the preparation of this work over a period of years of intermittent research, and enabled me to bring it to conclusion. Particularly I am indebted to those who have read the manuscript and provided many useful suggestions which have clarified and improved the text: the late O. B. Hardison, Jr., then Director of the Folger Shakespeare Library; the late Joshua C. Taylor, Director of the National Museum of American Art of the Smithsonian Institution; and the late Francis M. Rogers, Nancy Clark Smith Professor of the Language and Literature of Portugal, Harvard University.

To the late Director-General Carlo Pietrangeli, and to the former Secretary-General Walter Persegati, of the Vatican's Monumenti, Musei e Gallerie Pontificie, and to José Pereira da Costa, then director of the Arquivo Nacional da Torre do Tombo in Lisbon, my debt is immeasurable for the assistance and valuable resources which they have provided from the very beginning of my research to the completion of the manucript.

Useful advice and co-operation came as well from others at the Vatican: notably from Monsignor Martino Giusti, Prefect; Monsignor Charles Burns and Monsignor Terzo Natalini of the Archivio Segreto Vaticano; from Dioclecio Redig de Campos, Director-General Emeritus and Mrs Linda Graham, of the Monumenti, Musei e Gallerie Pontificie; from Dr Ing. Gr. Uff. Francesco Vacchini of the Fabbrica di San Pietro, and from Carlo Salerni of the Servizio Pontificiale della Floreria. Elsewhere in Rome Generale C. d'Antonio Severoni, Director of the Museo Nazionale di Castel Sant'Angelo; Elio Lodolini, then Director of the Archivio di Stato di Roma, and Walter T. Cini, former Executive Director of the American Academy at Rome.

In Florence I received special co-operation from Francesco Papafava dei Carreresi, the late Maria Luisa Righini Bonelli, Director of the Instituto e Museo di Storia della Scienza, M. L. Azzaroli of the Museo Zoologico 'La Specola', and the late Ulrich Middledorf. In Lisbon I was fortunate to have the assistance of Maria Helena Pinto and Teresa M. Shedel de Castelo Branca as well as of the late João da Gama Pimentel Barata.

Nelson Minnich and the late Manoel Cardozo, professors at The Catholic University of America, the Reverend Conrad Harkins of Saint Bonaventure University, Henry A. Millon of the National Gallery of Art in Washington, Carlo Pedretti of the University of California at Los Angeles, Frederick Hartt of the University of Virginia, George A. Kubler of Yale University and the late Timothy H. Clarke of London, all provided significant suggestions and information in the preparation of the manuscript.

Translations from sixteenth century Latin documents and writings were provided by O. B. Hardison, Francis X. Murphy, S.SS.R. of Holy Redeemer College, and Josiah O. Hatch III of Washington, D. C.

At the Smithsonian Institution assistance came from several levels: from S. Dillon Ripley, Secretary Emeritus; Theodore H. Reed, former Director of the

National Zoological Park, and Nancy R. Long. Splendid support at the Smithsonian Institution Libraries was provided by Lucien Rossignol, the late Charles G. Berger, Mary A. Rosenfeld Thomas, Carla Coupe, Betty Jean Swartz, the late Ellen B. Wells and Lela Bodenlos.

Most particularly I am indebted to Jacques Barzun, Professor Emeritus of History at Columbia University, and to L.C. Taylor, former Director of the UK Branch of the Calouste Gulbenkian Foundation, for their critiques of the manuscript and the many valuable suggestions for its improvement.

Finally, to my wife, Gale, who pursued the papal pachyderms with me every step of the way from Lisbon to Rome and thereafter, and who compiled the index, my debt is immeasurable.

ILLUSTRATION CREDITS

Archivio Capitolare della Basilica di San Pietro, Vatican City – Figures 65a, 65d; Arquivo Nacional da Torre do Tombo, Lisbon – Figures 11, 28, 55; Archivio di San Spirito, Archivio di Stato di Roma – Figure 17; Ashmolean Museum, Department of Western Art, Oxford University – Figures 44, 45; Biblioteca Apostolica Vaticana, Vatican City – End Papers, Figures 2, 7, 15, 16, 17, 19, 20, 31, 47; Biblioteca Colombina, Cathedral of Seville – Figure 27; Biblioteca de Ajuda, Ajuda – Figure 40; Biblioteca, Real Monasterio S. Lorenzo, El Escorial, Madrid – Figures 33, 34, 39c; Biblioteca Nacional de Lisboa, Lisbon – Figures 11, 13; Bibliothèque Municipale de Besançon – Figure 26d; The British Library, London – Figure 22; The British Museum, London – Figure 26a, 26b; Commisão Nacional, Lisbon – Figure 57; Estudio Mario Novais, Lisbon – Figures 60, 62, 63a, 63b; Estudio Luis Teixeira, Lisbon – Figure 24; The Folger Shakespeare Library – 52; Foto Oscar Savio, Rome – Figures 21, 41; Fratelli Alinari, Florence – Figure 59; Alexis Kugel, Paris – Figure 58a; The Library of Congress – Figures 3, 5, 8, 12, 18, 23, 37, 53, 54; The Louvre, Cabinet des Dessins – Figures 46, 48; Monumenti, Musei e Gallerie Pontificie, Vatican City – Figures 36, 38, 64a, 64b; Museo Correr, Venice – Figure 35; Musée de l'Homme, Paris – Figure 58b; Museum of the Hermitage, St. Petersburg – Figure 58c; Museu Nacional de Arte Antiga, Lisbon – Figures 14, 56; Museo Nazionale di Castel Sant'Angelo – Figure 50; Dott. Carlo Mutignani, L'Aquila – Figure 51; Nationalbibliothek, Vienna, Graphische Sammlung Albertina, – Figure 26c; Preussischer Kulturbesitz Kupferstichkabinett, Staatliche Museen zu Berlin – Figures 32, 39b; The Royal Library, Windsor Castle – Figure 43; Soprintendenza per i Beni Artistici e Storici, Florence – Figures 1, 6, 29, 30, 39a; Sotheby-Parke Bernet Galleries, London – Figure 49; Victoria and Albert Museum, London – Figure 42. Bob Drake drew the map in Figure 4.

CONTENTS

EPIGRAPHS

From ADAM SMITH : An Inquiry into the Nature and
Causes of the Wealth of Nations. 1776

*The discovery of America, and that of a passage to the East Indies by the Cape
of Good Hope, are the two greatest and most important events recorded in the
history of mankind. . . .*

*The discovery of a passage to the East Indies by the Cape of Good Hope, which
happened much about the same time opened, perhaps, a still more extensive
range to foreign commerce than even that of America, notwithstanding the
greater distances. There were but two nations in any respect superior to savages,
and these were destroyed as soon as discovered. The rest were mere savages. But
the empires of China, Indostan, Japan, as well as several others in the East
Indies, without having richer mines of gold or silver, were in every respect much
richer, better cultivated and more advanced in all arts and manufactures than
either Mexico or Peru . . . rich and civilized nations can always exchange to a
much greater value with one another, than with savages and barbarians.*

*In 1497 Vasco da Gama sailed from the port of Lisbon with a fleet of four
ships, and, after a navigation of eleven months, arrived upon the coast of
Indostan, and thus completed a course of discoveries which had been pursued
with great steadiness, and with little interruption, for near a century together...*

From WILLIAM ROSCOE, *The Life and Pontificate of Leo the Tenth*
(1805)

*From the earliest attempts at discovery, the Roman pontiffs had interested
themselves with great earnestness in the result; and no sooner had these efforts
proved successful, then they converted them to the purpose of extending the
credit and authority of the holy see...*

*The exultation which these discoveries occasioned throughout Europe, is
supposed to have been of the most just and allowable kind. The extensions of
the bonds of society to distant nations, and peoples before unknown; the important additions to the conveniences and the luxuries of life, and the great influx
of riches which Europe was to experience, all seem to entitle it to the denomi-
nation of one of the happiest, as well as one of the most important events in the
history of the world. Whether an impartial estimate would confirm this opinion,
may perhaps be doubted.*

PREFACE

IT ALL BEGAN WITH AN OFF-HAND REMARK MADE ONE EVENING AT a reception held at the American Academy at Rome, immediately after my arrival in the Eternal City to conduct research in the Vatican library and archives. Learning of my plans, the Academy's director suggested that I should attempt to determine whatever happened to the rhinoceros at the Vatican. A rhinoceros? At the Vatican? I asked. What rhinoceros? According to legend, I was told, there was once upon a time a pope who had a rhinoceros, but no one seemed to know what had happened to it. A seemingly trivial topic, to be sure, but intriguing.

Later, at the Vatican, the question brought predictable responses. No one whom I asked had any knowledge of such a beast having been on the premises. Perhaps I would do better, I was advised, if I inquired at the zoological park in the Villa Borghese. Just short of tiring of the question, a scholar on the Vatican museum staff recalled that, although he had never heard of a rhinoceros, he had a faint recollection of having once seen a reference or two about an elephant at the papal court, but he could not recall the source. When pressed, the response was 'don't call me, I'll call you.' This seemed to be a beginning, though meagre.

Perhaps it had been an elephant that had been intended, and not a rhinoceros. But what had an elephant been doing in papal Rome, and when? The question remained unanswered during the remainder of my stay. The image evoked by my question always amused, yet there seemed to be sufficient substance to merit continuation of the chase. One official seemed to remember having seen such a beast in one of the paintings of papal processions, but could not be certain. Which painting? How could he remember – there were so many paintings and papal processions! Another had heard of an elephant in Rome that had been covered with gilt paint for a festival, and had died as a consequence, but he could provide no clue to the event. An exhaustive search of inventories of Vatican property and furnishings for the past five centuries yielded no further leads. Yet I departed from Rome with the conviction that where there was smoke there must be fire, and perhaps even an elephant.

It was not until the conclusion of a second visit to Rome later that year that the phantom elephant materialized. A distinguished prelate on the staff of the Secret Archives was not totally nonplussed by my query. An elephant? Strange thing. Perhaps there really had been one, for he recalled that some years previously a British journalist stationed in Rome had published a witty article in an English periodical about just such a beast. At the time he had assumed the story to have been fiction, but it might have been based on fact after all. It was not until some months after my return to the States that a copy of the article in question was at last recovered from the back files of the London publishing office.

In the meantime, another bit of information fell into place while I was reviewing inventories of papal possessions in the Servizio della Floreria Apostolica. Overhearing my perennial question, a young clerk volunteered that a few years previously some dinosaur bones had been recovered from an excavation in the Cortile della Libreria. A dinosaur on Vatican hill? The possibility seemed to be even more preposterous than a rhinoceros or an elephant. Although it was conceivable that dinosaurs once roamed the seven hills of Rome as well as other parts of the world, the recovery of dinosaur bones at this level of Roman civilization seemed remote, particularly after the Vatican's constant construction and reconstruction through the centuries.

As well as the young man could recall, the bones had been unearthed by labourers engaged in enlarging an air-conditioning installation in the Cortile. When approached, library officials disavowed any knowledge of the subject. In hot pursuit on the dinosaur's trail, I discovered the bones in the Vatican museum complex. There, after much persistence, the search for the dinosaur – and the elephant – ended. On the day before my departure, the museum scholar sent a messenger to my hotel with citations of two manuscripts in the Vatican library which related to an elephant. There was no time to seek them out, however, but copies were ordered. Once more I was forced to leave the trail of the phantom pachyderm, this time just as the first tangible evidence was emerging.

The rest of the story – in fact all of the story – gradually unfolded in the course of research pursued in subsequent months. The article in the English periodical provided the clue from which to make a beginning, for it identified the period in question to be the reign of Pope Leo X in the early decades of the sixteenth century. An exhaustive survey of the literature of and about the period not only confirmed the presence of an elephant, but suggested directions for further study, in the Portuguese royal archives in Lisbon, the Vatican library and secret archives, and numerous repositories elsewhere in Europe. These, supplemented with contemporary writings, developed the story more and more.

Then came the most astonishing discovery of all – the presence of the hitherto missing rhinoceros that had initiated the search! Now there was not one but two papal pachyderms, proving that the casual remark passed at the Academy reception had had substance after all. As the story unfolded, all the colour, excitement, intrigue, excesses, gaiety, and literary and artistic achievements of the glorious papal court of Leo X emerged and brought vividly to life the pachyderm and its career as elephant-diplomat in this dazzling ambience. Nothing short of remarkable was the role of the papal pet in this period of political, diplomatic and religious strife, just a decade prior to the sacking of Rome and not long before the beginning of the religious Reformation. Not only had numerous dramatists, poets and poetasters of Leo's court written about the talented little (comparatively speaking) white elephant, but the leading artists of the time had sketched it from life and featured it in many media; some of which works have survived to this day. As for the rhinoceros, it too had its moment of prominence in European history before it fell into oblivion.

In the course of time it became evident that a substantial literature about the papal pachyderms already existed, and that both papal elephant and rhinoceros were known to the world of art from their representation as trophies of Portuguese discoveries. They were noted as well in the history of Portugal, particularly in the chronicle of the reign of King Manuel I by Damião de Goes. It was not until my own research had been almost completed that I realized that had I but approached the subject at the very beginning from the point of view of art history, I would have saved myself considerable effort and time: had I done so, however, I would have overlooked much of the archival resources and some of those aspects and dimensions relating to the papal court of Rome never before fully reported. Parts of the story had been told and retold in other more popular publications, but this is the very first time that all the various parts have been brought together into a whole, and all references to the subject noted.

Inevitably a study such as this one, which crosses the lines of many conventional disciplines, has relied heavily upon the patient assistance of a considerable number of archivists, librarians, museum professionals, art historians, specialists in the history of exploration and discovery, in addition to paleontologists and zoologists, in several countries. To all of them I apologise for my persistence, and express my appreciation of their interest and co-operation. Hopefully the publication of this adventure in historical sleuthing will in some measure justify the efforts of so many others, as well as my own, by bringing to life once more the papal pachyderms.

Silvio A. Bedini *Washington, D.C.*

CHAPTER ONE
The Golden Age

Let us rather pause at the days of Leo X, under whom the enjoyment of antiquity combined with all other pleasures to give to Roman life a unique stamp and consecration. The Vatican resounded with song and music, and their echoes were heard through the city as a call to joy and gladness, though Leo did not succeed thereby in banishing care and pain from his own life, and his deliberate calculation to prolongue his days by cheerfulness was frustrated by an early death.

Jacob Burckhardt : *The Civilization of the Renaissance in Italy*

GAUDIUM MAGNUM NUNTIO VOBIS! PROCLAIMED THE CARdinal-deacon Alessandro Cardinal Farnese, after breaking the seal upon the window overlooking the piazza of Saint Peter and thrusting out his cross to attract the attention of the populace below. 'I bring you tidings of great joy! We have as Pope the most reverend Giovanni de' Medici, lord and cardinal-deacon of Santa Maria in Domnica, and he is called Leo the Tenth!'

The announcement was greeted with a great approving roar from the excited crowd that had been clustered for days in the piazza below. Amid the wild shouts and enthusiastic cries, waiting couriers ran for their horses to take the news to the Italian states and the rest of the world. Immediately, bells began pealing in celebration, first one then another and another, creating a great chorus of sound encompassing the entire city. Heard through the rumbling bombardment of cannon from Castel Sant' Angelo, the medley of sounds overpowered the shouts of 'Palle! Palle!' from the populace, as they welcomed the successful election of a new pope so anxiously awaited.[1]

Pope Julius II, Leo's predecessor, had reigned severely but well, often venturing personally into the field of battle to protect or recover

Church lands. A generous patron of the arts, he had assembled at the Vatican such great masters as Michelangelo, Donato Agnolo called Bramante, and the latter's young protégé, Raphael of Urbino, to work together in decorating the papal palace. Julius had also begun to build the Vatican's collection of antiquities and had demonstrated a respect for literature, although he had little familiarity with it. Unfortunately the reform of the Church which he had initiated terminated with his unexpected death in 1513. The end of his reign and the forthcoming election gave cause for considerable concern and alarm in European courts, for the inclinations of the new pope-elect would materially affect the entire European political structure.

In the last year of his reign Julius II had concluded a Holy League with Spain, England and the Venetian Republic. Following their victory at Ravenna, and after facing the combined forces of the Swiss, Venetians, Spanish and the army of the Duke of Urbino, the French had withdrawn from Italy. Emperor Maximilian I eventually recognized the Lateran Council so that by the time of the pontiff's death, an uneasy peace reigned in Europe. Would the new pope be as militant as Julius had been, and would he agree to the abolition of the traditional simoniacal practices that Julius had initiated? Would he continue to support the arts as avidly as his late predecessor? All these questions were waiting to be resolved by the election that would take place.[2]

As the ceremonies for the election of a successor to the deceased pope began on 4 March, the twenty-five cardinals assembled for the occasion attended the celebration of mass in the chapel of San Andrea, because the basilica of St Peter was under construction. Immediately thereafter they retired into conclave, where they remained in seclusion until a candidate had been selected. As the days passed, discussion followed discussion, for the candidates were many and the conclave had to continue until a single candidate received at least one third of the votes. At first there was little if any mention of the name of the young Giovanni de' Medici. The schismatic cardinals deposed by Pope Julius were not permitted to vote and the younger cardinals were clamouring for a liberal candidate, so that there was no obvious choice. Finally on 11 March the die was cast. Cardinal de' Medici, as senior deacon, although the youngest cardinal ever to become a member of the College of Cardinals, was assigned to count the written votes as they were taken out of the urn. He modestly announced his own nomination, having received the required number of votes, and stated that he would take the title of Leo X if the cardinals approved.

Giovanni de' Medici was selected by his peers partly because he was in such apparent contrast to his recently deceased predecessor. An aesthete, an epicure and a scholar, he represented Florentine humanistic culture at its height. The second son of Lorenzo the Magnificent, born in December 1475, he had been tutored by such great humanists as Angelo Poliziano, Marsilio Ficino and Bernardo da Bibbiena. His father having selected an ecclesiastical career for him, Giovanni was tonsured at the age of six, given an archbishopric at seven, and created cardinal when he was just under thirteen.

Two years later, during Florence's political upheaval, the Medici family had been expelled from the city. Finding himself opposed to the policies of Pope Alexander VI, the young cardinal left Rome to travel extensively in Germany, the Low Countries and France before returning to the Eternal City in 1500. The newly elected Pope Julius II held him in high favour and sent him as papal delegate to Bologna. There he was captured by the French when the Spanish and papal forces suffered reverses, and was taken as a prisoner to Milan. He managed to escape to Bologna and returned to Florence when his family was restored to power. Following the death of his older brother, the young Cardinal Giovanni became in effect the ruler of Tuscany.

Upon learning of the death of Julius II, the young cardinal hurried to Rome to participate in the conclave to elect a successor, reaching Rome on 6 March after an exhausting journey. [1] During his travels

[1] Pope Leo X and the College of Cardinals on his election in 1513. Fresco by Giorgio Vasari in the Sala di Leone X, in the Palazzo Vecchio, Florence.

he had suffered considerably from a stomach ulcer and an anal fistula. Arriving too late to attend the conclave's opening ceremonies including the special mass, an unusual exception was made because of his illness and he was assigned a separate cell in the chapel of Sant' Andrea, and permitted to retain his groom and surgeon with him during the conclave.

The news of Pope Leo's election was greeted with as much excitement in his home city as in Rome. There the celebrations continued for four days during which the incessant tolling of bells and booming of cannon continued to reverberate. Great bonfires brightly illuminated the city through the night and the cries of 'Palle! Palle!' voiced in Rome were re-echoed in Florence. Participants in the procession of the Blessed Virgin, which wended its way from Impruneta into the city, were welcomed with food dispensed from the steps in front of the Medici palace, and wine flowed from gilded barrels upon the balcony of the Palazzo Vecchio.

In Rome the next few weeks following the election were filled with countless ceremonial activities for the pope-elect. Since he was only a deacon at the time of his election, he had first to be ordained a priest, an event which occurred on 15 March. Three days later he was consecrated a bishop. Because of the imminent approach of Holy Week, the date of the coronation was brought forward and scheduled for Saturday, 19 March, instead of the customary Sunday. The pope participated in all of the events of Holy Week, and on Maundy Thursday he actually kissed the feet of the poor and washed them, claiming that the ceremony had been intended to be real and not merely symbolic. Mass on Easter Sunday was celebrated in the Sistine Chapel. He had selected 'Leo' for his pontifical name, it was said, because during her pregnancy his mother had dreamt that she had given birth to a lion. During the short eight years of his reign, the pope made every effort to live up to the image of the king of beasts.[3]

Following tradition, the coronation of the new pope took place on 11 April. Because the ancient basilica of St Peter was almost entirely demolished by this time as the new one rose under construction, the ceremony had to take place elsewhere. A temporary canopied platform was erected in front of the old façade, and it was under this makeshift structure that Leo was crowned with the great triple tiara that had been made for his predecessor.

In accordance with ancient tradition, the master of ceremonies, Paride de Grassi, approached the newly crowned pope and held out before him a bundle of tow tied to a rod. As the lighted tow flared up brightly, Grassi intoned the ancient formula, 'So passes the glory of the world!' It was a rite originating in the days of imperial Rome, when a slave was brought before a victorious general seated in his chariot, to caution him that he was but a man. Then Grassi voiced the next warning which was a part of the tradition, 'Thou shalt never see the years of Peter,' reminding the newly elect that no pope would ever reign longer than Peter's twenty-five years.

Time passed quickly as the new pontiff familiarized himself with his new role. On 11 April, a dazzling procession was formed to conduct the pope to 'take possession' of the Basilica of St John Lateran, signifying that he assumed his position as head of the Church and as temporal sovereign of the Papal States. [2 and 3] In the most splendid entourage within the memory of man, a cavalcade seemingly without end, two hundred mounted lancers led the members of the households of the pope and of the cardinals, followed by bands of musicians, standard bearers of the twelve papal cursors and representatives of the city's thirteen *rioni* or districts. The Teutonic Order of Knights and the Knights of St John were led by Giulio de' Medici, the pope's cousin, wearing the insignia of a Knight of Rhodes. They were succeeded by the papal marshal leading nine white horses and three white mules,

[2] Pope Leo X's procession of possession to the basilica of St. John Lateran. Woodcut from *Cronica delle magnifiche & honorate Pompe fatte in Roma . . . .* by Giovanni Giacomo Penni, 1513.

[3] The procession of possession of Pope Innocent XIII in 1721 from the Vatican to the basilica of St. John Lateran, with each group identified. The pontiff being borne on his *sedia gestatoria* appears at the end of the sixth line of the procession. Engraving by A. Picart, 1722.

followed by the Master of the Horse, chamberlains bearing the mitre and tiara, equerries of the court clad in red silk trimmed with ermine, knights of the Roman and Florentine nobilities, foreign ambassadors... and countless clerics.

Then appeared the Swiss Guard in their gaudy uniforms of green and white and yellow, preceding a white horse bearing upon its back the monstrance containing the Sacrament. The beast moved alone in front of bearers holding aloft a great silk canopy rising over the new pontiff, who was mounted upon the huge white Turkish stallion he had ridden in battle at Ravenna. Behind him walked the *Maestro di Camera* and several other chamberlains, strewing gold and silver coins into the crowd as the procession moved slowly along the route. Although it was still early spring, the rays of a huge throbbing orange sun in a sky clear of clouds fell mercilessly upon the procession. Despite the protection of the canopy it was the corpulent pontiff who suffered most of all from the heat, burdened not only by his own weight but also by that of his jewelled robes.

The entire route had been decorated with great festive arches. One erected by the banker Agostino Chigi was supported by eight columns bearing the inscription, 'The time of Venus has passed; gone also is Mars, and now is the time for Minerva', referring to the prior reigns of Alexander VI and Julius II which were to be eclipsed by that of the learned new pontiff. Statues carved from marble, porphry and alabaster were featured at intervals along the route and the façade of every house displayed wreaths of laurel and myrtle, banners and tapestries. Branches of box and myrtle covered the pavement upon which the great procession moved almost silently.

Arriving at last at the basilica, traditional ceremonies took place in the Council Hall, the Chapel of St Sylvester and the *sancta sanctorum*. The old basilica of St John Lateran had long given up first position in the Church to the basilica of St Peter and the Vatican, upon which succeeding popes had lavished the Church's wealth. During the long absence of the papacy in Avignon, St John Lateran had suffered considerable damage and had been reduced to little more than a ruin. Restoration had been undertaken from time to time, however, and it still retained its sanctity, and the *sacro possesso*, the formal taking of possession of the ancient basilica that was part of each papal coronation, came as a climax to the installation of each new pope.

Following the formal ceremonies, the entourage partook of a great leisurely banquet in the palace of St John Lateran, and then as dusk settled over the city, the procession slowly wended its way back to Vatican hill. The air had cooled considerably by then and many of the celebrating populace remained in the streets to greet the return. It was said that the ceremony cost approximately one hundred thousand ducats, one-seventh of the resources in the papal treasury.[4]

The selection of the youthful Cardinal Giovanni de' Medici was greeted with pleasure on all sides. It was a period of constantly shifting diplomatic and political alliances in Europe, and of continuing corruption and intrigue within the Church of Rome, a situation that eventually would bring it to the brink of ruin and open the way for the Protestant Reformation. It was at the same time a period that produced some of the world's finest and most lasting endeavours in the arts and letters.

Leo succeeded to the papal throne in greatly troubled times. Overhanging Christendom was the threat of Islam. Although we know in retrospect that Christianity and Europe flourished and expanded, that seemed far from certain in 1513. To understand the weakness of the West it is necessary to look at the last years of the Roman Empire. By the end of the third century, such had been the growth of the Empire that two emperors were appointed, western and eastern. In 337, Constantine moved the *de facto* capital from Rome to Byzantium, and with the fall of Rome to the Goths and the death of the last Roman emperor in 476, the dominance of Constantinople, 'the second Rome', became complete. Such was the memory of the power and unity of the Roman Empire, however, that in 962 Otto 'king of the Germans', in hopeful restitution, was crowned by the pope as 'Holy Roman Emperor'. For the next five hundred years an 'eastern' Emperor and Orthodox patriarch amid the splendours of Constantinople co-existed with a 'western' Emperor and a Catholic pope in a dilapidated Rome. The two churches drifted ever further apart: few 'Greeks' knew Latin; fewer Romans knew Greek. With increasing virulence each accused the other of error, even heresy.

Early in the seventh century arose a third inheritor of the lands of the Roman Empire – Islam. By the end of the century, Islam had become the religion of Arabia, and Arabs, Berbers and other converts not only dominated the once-Christianized regions of the eastern Mediterranean but also a swathe of territory right across north Africa, and the whole of Iberia to the Pyrenees. All connection was severed between Christendom in its European heartlands and distant Christian communities, such as those in Armenia, Ethiopia, South India and China. A few individual Christians managed to travel through this Muslim *cordon sanitaire*, including, ostensibly, the 'best-selling' Marco Polo[5]; but for some eight centuries both trade and conversion throughout the known world outside Europe – in Africa, Egypt, Persia, India, the whole Orient – were Muslim monopolies. Precious commodities such as spices, reached the West in small quantities which overland caravans could carry, and at the inflated prices which the consequent scarcity sustained. Such trade was a major source of the wealth of the Muslim powers and an underpinning of their advanced civilizations.

The Byzantine empire, and the Orthodox church, lived for the most part in a mutually profitable accommodation with the Muslim states of the eastern Mediterranean. The attitude of the Roman Church and Western Christendom was wholly different: between 1095 and 1272, successive popes preached nine crusades. The fourth of these never reached Muslim soil; instead, Western Christian forces chose to seize, sack, and plunder Constantinople – 'the Great Betrayal' – thereby fatally weakening the Byzantine empire and leaving a bitter legacy of hatred and Christian division.

For all their dramatic celebrity, the crusades were far less successful in forcing Islamic retreat than the battles fought by Christian princes in Iberia. In 1147 King Dom Afonso Henrique persuaded some shiploads of crusaders on their way to the Holy Land to help him attack Moors nearer at hand: Lisbon was captured and became the capital of 'Portugal'. The country's boundaries were steadily pushed southward until, by 1297, its present borders were secure both against the Moors and neighbouring Castile; the 're-conquest' of the rest of Iberia continued for a further two hundred years.

When the Portuguese had consolidated their state, they took their attacks on the Moors across the straits into north Africa. In 1415 they captured and fortified Ceuta; soon afterwards, they established a trading community at Arguin on the western coast, took Tangier and set about creating a Christian north African enclave. Of greater significance, under the inspiration of Prince Dom Henriques, later known as 'Henry the Navigator', they began to explore the Atlantic and the west coast of Africa. Soon they broke the monopoly of west African trade – mostly in gold and slaves –previously held overland by the Muslims. Portuguese ambition mounted higher: the dominant geography of the period, derived from Ptolemy, believed the Atlantic to be a vast lake, its western and southern shores yet to be established. The Portuguese, encouraged by contact with Arab geographers, thought the coast of Africa continued far to the south and believed that somewhere there might exist a passage through which a sea-route could be established to the riches of the Indies. If that passage could be found, then the Muslim blockade of Christendom, within Europe, would be broken. With many disasters, successive Portuguese expeditions steadily worked their way down a seemingly endless continent, along hazardous coasts, coping with unknown currents, winds, and star patterns, for most of the fifteenth century.

By then, Islam had found a new champion to succeed the Arabs and Berbers – the Ottoman Turks. They occupied almost all the Byzantine empire in Asia, crossed into Europe, routed the Serbs at Kossovo, in 1448, occupied the Balkans and, in 1453, as long expected, besieged Constantinople itself. Even at this extremity the Catholic church offered help only on theological conditions the Orthodox church found intolerable: its leaders preferred the prospect of becoming a largely autonomous *milet* under the sultan to suffering the heresies and intrusions of pope and cardinals. There would have been prelates alive at the coronation of Leo X in 1513 who remembered hearing the news of the fall of the Great City to the Turks – 'the end of the world.' Nor did the threat of Islam from the east end there: during Leo's pontificate and immediately after it, the Turks took Moldavia, the Kingdom of Trebizond, all Persia, all Egypt; in 1521 they occupied Belgrade, in 1526 Buda and in 1529 besieged Vienna. The Turkish fleet

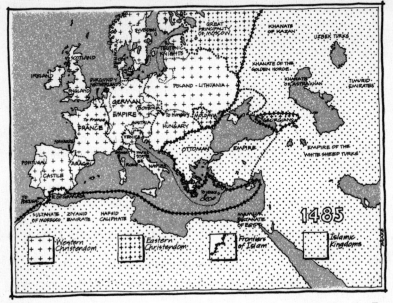

[4] In 1485, catholic Christendom was still confined to western Europe. For eight centuries a ring of Islamic kingdoms had controlled all the land routes from Europe to the rest of the known world – North Africa to Asia – preventing western trade and Christian evangelism.

After seventy years of persistent exploration, the Portuguese in 1487 established that Africa had an end – a sea-route to the Indies was feasible. Then, in six remarkable years, 1492–98, Columbus thought he had found a shorter route, and stumbled upon a continent; and Vasco da Gama finally completed the workable route which opened the riches of the Orient to the West. The long Islamic monopoly of trade and conversion was broken; the world-wide expansion of Europe began.

Of the consequent High Renaissance sense of new discoveries, wealth and opportunity, Leo X, when he became pope in 1513, was the inheritor and epitome.

---

dominated the Mediterranean for the next forty years. Children in far away England were taught to pray to be saved from the fury of the Turk. [4]

Yet in the closing years of the fifteenth century a series of events occurred in rapid succession that gave new hope to beleaguered Christendom. In 1486 Portuguese ships, under Bartolomeu Dias, at last reached the end of the vast African continent and sailed into open water beyond. The cape he had named the Cape of Storms was renamed by King Dom João II 'Bon Esperança' for the Good Hope it offered of the long-sought sea-route to the Indies. Intensive preparations, navigational and in ship design and building, were instituted as part of the King's 'Plan for the Indies'. In 1482, as a part of that Plan, Christopher Columbus – who sailed with the Portuguese, married the daughter of a Portuguese sea-captain and lived in the Madeiras – proposed sailing due west to the Indies, a route that he was convinced (following Toscanelli's erroneous calculations) would prove to be much shorter. Failing to persuade Dom João's council, he had taken his proposal to Ferdinand and Isabella. They had, in 1492, finally expelled the Moors from the kingdom of Granada, the last Muslim stronghold in Spain. Columbus was given some ships and reached what he took to be the Indies, or perhaps the fabled Zipangu (Japan) Marco Polo said he had heard spoken about at the court in Peking. Six years later, in 1498–9, Vasco da Gama led a fleet that reached Calicut, and the true Indies. With their discovery of Brazil in 1500 and of Newfoundland, Labrador and Nova Scotia in 1499-1502, the Portuguese made apparent the existence of a vast new continent. In 1513 the Spaniard Vasco Nuñez de Balboa 'discovered' the Pacific Ocean. In the wake of Vasco da Gama, the Portuguese swarmed through the east, discovering Madagascar in 1500, establishing trading forts at Mozambique in 1501, in Goa in 1510, Malacca in 1511, and Colombo in 1517. In 1514 contact was established with China. Their advanced technology in navigation, shipbuilding and gunnery enabled the Portuguese to dominate both the eastern sea-lanes and also the route back to Europe. The Muslims' monopoly of trade in spices and other riches in the Orient, as well as that of religious conversion, had been thoroughly broached.

Thus began, in the years immediately preceding the pontificate of Leo X, that extraordinary expansion of Christendom, so long on the defensive against Islam and locked in its European heartlands. The discovery of whole new continents beyond the Atlantic, even more (for yet more land was at first of little consequence) access gained to the riches, variety and knowledge of the highly developed East, stimulated a new sense of wonder and of boundless individual opportunities and possibilities: a 'High Renaissance' of the West.

It was one of the most exciting epochs in European history, for the shape of the world then known was undergoing rapid expansion with the discovery and conquest of new lands by dauntless navigators and military commanders of Portugal and Castile. Ships returned to Europe laden with cargoes of spices, gems, new commodities, and riches beggaring description, including live exotic birds and beasts from far-off places such as had never before been seen. All of Europe shared a common curiosity about these new found regions, their peoples, their flora and fauna, and the promise of even greater riches to come. The ambitious lust of the maritime nations conspired with the spirit of ecclesiastical domination of the Holy See, determined to acquire the same acknowledged jurisdiction over the new worlds being discovered as it asserted over the old. It was at this time – during the first months of Leo's reign – that a young white elephant from India entered the scene, a trophy of Asiatic adventurism that was to make a lasting impact not only on the political relations between Portugal and the Holy See, but on Italian arts and letters as well.

When King João II of Portugal died in 1495, he left no direct heir to succeed him. His only son, Prince Afonso, had been killed in a fall four years earlier. The next in line to the throne was the late king's cousin and brother-in-law Manuel, Duke of Beja. Taking the name of Manuel I, he ascended the throne just in time to witness the departure of Vasco da Gama on his great voyage to establish a new sea route to the Indies, a venture which ended successfully with his landing at Calicut in 1498.

This triumph led to the equipping of another, larger, fleet to the Indies under the command of Pedro Alvares Cabral, sent to develop further the base of conquest which had been established. Cabral landed on the coast of Brazil and thus gained yet another territory for Portugal, as in the meantime another expedition under Afonso de Albuquerque set out for India. Albuquerque established a fortress at Cochin and a trading post at Coulan before venturing into the interior. On a second voyage, on which he was accompanied by the navigator Tristão da Cunha, Albuquerque added Brava, Socotra, and the kingdom of Hormuz to his list of conquests.

The costs of geographic expansion were almost as great as the gains, however. A mutiny among Albuquerque's officers, and a rebellion at Hormuz, were followed by the capture and imprisonment of the commander in Hindustan. While Albuquerque had failed in his first attempts to capture Calicut and Goa, he succeeded on a second attempt, and then proceeded to take Malacca. Although again victorious, he suffered a devastating loss of men in the engagement. The Moorish king fiercely defended the city, but was wounded and captured by Albuquerque before he could flee the field of battle on his elephant. In addition to the king's rich stores of silver and arms which he confiscated, Albuquerque also acquired seven of the king's elephants trained for use in warfare and equipped with battle towers.[6]

The Portuguese effectively gained control of the world spice trade, and hitherto unknown and rare commodities were returned with regularity to Lisbon from newly established trading centres in the East

[5] The port of Lisbon in the sixteenth century. From *Civitates orbis terrarum, Liber 50, Urbium praecipuarum mundi theatrum quintum* by George Braun (Cologne, 1581).

Indies and the Indian mainland. From Lisbon they were distributed to other centres throughout Europe. [5] Egypt and the Venetian Republic, meanwhile, became increasingly concerned over this growing competition. Egypt threatened to destroy the holy places in Jerusalem unless the Portuguese expansion was curbed, and an intermediary was sent to Rome to intercede with the pope on Egypt's behalf. These developments only strengthened Manuel's determination to obtain and retain full control of the spice trade, and he dispatched a large fleet to India, sailing under the command of Francisco de Almeida, whom he had named Viceroy of India.

In the course of his journey, Almeida captured hostile Muslim ports on the East African coast and fortified them for Portugal. In an indecisive action off Chaul, he met a large fleet sent out by the Sultan of Egypt which had been strengthened by Venetian support. Almeida later succeeded in destroying it in a major action off Diu, bringing the Indian Ocean entirely under Portuguese domination for many years to come. Returning to Cochin, Almeida was surprised to discover that the king meanwhile had appointed Albuquerque Governor of India in his stead, and he thereupon set sail to return to Portugal. He was not to reach his homeland, however, for *en route* he engaged in a skirmish with the Hottentots in which he lost his life.

Accompanied by Cunha on his return to south-east Asia in 1506, Albuquerque coasted Madagascar, subdued the coastal towns of southern Somaliland, and captured and held Hormuz, while Cunha occupied Socotra. Before sailing on to Cochin, however, Albuquerque was forced to surrender. Needing to consolidate Portuguese victory at sea with land bases at all costs, he stormed and captured four major cities one after another. Making Goa his capital, he took Malacca and established there a colony that became the centre of the spice trade, and then recaptured Hormuz. Albuquerque's exploits led the Sultan of Aussa to send a mission to Lisbon laden with rich gifts to seek the king's protection, and succeeded in establishing friendly relations. News of Portugal's ascendancy over the seas reached deep into Africa, with the consequence that African princes united with Portugal against the Turkish corsairs.

The European world observed Portugal's conquest of the East with considerable interest. Roman pontiffs favoured and encouraged Manuel's activities materially as well as spiritually. A series of papal Bulls and Briefs guaranteed Portuguese possession of their conquests since they provided the Holy See with a means of extending its credit and authority. On the universally accepted assumption that the pope was responsible for all the souls of mankind, Pope Eugene IV had formally granted to Portugal jurisdiction over all lands extending from Cape Naon on the African coast to the East Indies. This grant was subsequently confirmed in Bulls issued by Pope Nicholas V and Pope Sixtus IV.[7]

For many decades – since the mid-fifteenth century – it was customary upon the election of a new pope for European sovereigns to send to Rome an extraordinary ambassador on a 'mission of obedience', as it was called. The practice originated during the Great Schism, when crowned heads of Europe made a choice of which pope they would support. The purpose of the mission was to recognize the new pope formally as Vicar of Christ and successor to St Peter, but even more, as an expression of pride in the achievements of the state, personified in its ruler, by the grace of God. These missions of obedience provided opportunities for unlimited ostentation, and the number of participants and the nature and value of the gifts reflected the importance of the sovereign and his achievements.

The missions were received amidst considerable pomp and ceremony by the reigning pope, attended by the cardinals in full consistory as well as all the foreign ambassadors present at Rome. At the same time the occasion provided the people of Rome with an opportunity for unrestrained celebration. The heads of state preparing such missions took every care to ensure that they would demonstrate, not only to the papal court, but also before the representatives of other sovereigns, all the luxury and splendour of which they were capable.[8]

It was in adherence to this custom that Manuel I had sent a mission to Pope Julius II in 1505. It arrived in the Eternal City on 1 June, headed by the Bishop of Porto, Diogo de Sousa, and the learned jurisconsult Diogo Pacheco. At Rome it was joined by the incumbent ordinary Portuguese ambassador, João de Saldanha. Three days after its arrival, the mission was formally received by the pontiff and the cardinals in a public consistory held in the royal salon of the Apostolic Palace. In a superb Latin oration, the talented Pacheco described the recent discoveries and conquests made by Portuguese navigators, and presented the pope with a silver cross as a gift from his sovereign.

The mission emphasized Portugal's discovery, conquest and traffic in distant lands by the selection of wild life brought as a gift. The diplomat and writer Baldassare Castiglione, who witnessed the event, wrote 'the orators of the King of Portugal have come to make their obedience to the Pope in an orderly and gallant manner; and they have brought to the Cardinals many gifts, large beasts never before seen in Italy, parrots, mandrills, leopards, monkeys of various species which we have not been accustomed to see.' It may not have been the first time that fauna was featured in these ceremonies, but it was undoubtedly the largest display of rare birds and beasts until that time.[9]

The Portuguese king used the occasion to request a number of favours, spiritual as well as temporal, and each of them was granted. The pontiff subsequently presented him with the Golden Rose as a token of the Holy See's favour. The token was accepted in the name of the king by the royal chamberlain Alvaro da Costa.[10]

The exchange of gifts among sovereigns and heads of state as evidence of friendship and cordial intention was a practice that persisted from the earliest civilizations. The nature of the gift and the ceremonial of presentation varied with the times and circumstances, but their purpose as tokens of union and peace remained unchanged. The same custom had been followed by the Roman pontiffs as a continuation of the tradition of the Three Kings from the East. The superior responsibility with which the popes were invested and which they maintained, not only by God's decree as they claimed, but also by man's volition, invested their gifts of spiritual treasures with greater and nobler significance of recompense and encouragement than did mundane princely gifts.

This tradition gradually developed into the practice of compensating Christian sovereigns for services rendered to the Church and Christendom with special honours having symbolical significance. The two most important forms of pontifical recognition were the Golden Rose and the Blessed Sword and Ducal Cap. Selection of recipients for these honours was based primarily on political considerations, often resolved only after long deliberation in secret consistories of the Curia.[11]

The Golden Rose presented by Julius II to Manuel was to be the first of repeated honours the Portuguese royal family would receive from Rome during the sixteenth century. Each of these honours would mark another major military or religious achievement, as one Portuguese victory followed another in rapid succession during the next several decades.[12]

The accession of Leo X to the papal throne effectively ended the pervasive reign of unrest under his predecessor. The papal court and the city of Rome relaxed, while the advent of the new pontiff was received with mixed reactions throughout the Italian states and the courts of foreign countries. The selection of a son of Lorenzo the Magnificent promised a new period of prosperity for the arts and humanities. Yet the election of a pope who was only thirty-eight years of age, at a time when Europe was still faced with a precarious political situation and the Church itself was undergoing a period of unrest, was a cause of concern. For those opposed to a long reign there was hope derived from the nature of his poor health. World events of the next few months, however, confirmed the promise that many had seen in Leo X. [6]

Soon after the accession of Leo X, Rome celebrated a reconciliation between the Holy See and King Louis XII of France, in a peace made also with King Henry VII of England and with King Ferdinand of Spain. This major triumph of the Church was followed by reports of great victories won by the kings of Poland and Hungary against common enemies of the Christian faith.[13]

For Rome, a new period of prosperity had begun, with a constant flow of immigrants from the northern provinces who came with the pope's encouragement and established settlements in the region of the Campo dei Fiori. Lavish palaces for distinguished new residents sprang up all over the city, elegant young men attended by servants began to be seen frequently in the streets, and women went forth better dressed. It was not long after the new pope's election that many of his fellow countrymen flocked to Rome to seek positions in his household and at his court. Within a year the papal court and household numbered 683, many of them representing the most important families of Florence, including his own.

'God has given us the Papacy,' proclaimed the new pope, 'Let us enjoy it!' as he set about to make Rome the cultural centre not only of Italy but of the Western world. [7] The Eternal City soon became a treasure house of talent; the pontiff invited poets, Latinists, men of

[6] Portrait of Leo X shown with his cousin, Cardinal Giulio de' Medici (later Pope Clement VII) at his left and his nephew, Cardinal Lodovico Rossi behind him. Painting in oils by Raphael d'Urbino, *c.* 1514. In the Gallerie degli Uffizi, Florence.

letters, and artists to Rome and they responded in great numbers. Seeing himself as the embodiment of the culture of the age, and the patron of the arts and humanities, the pontiff let no one leave his presence dissatisfied. It was said that anyone gaining the pope's interest was

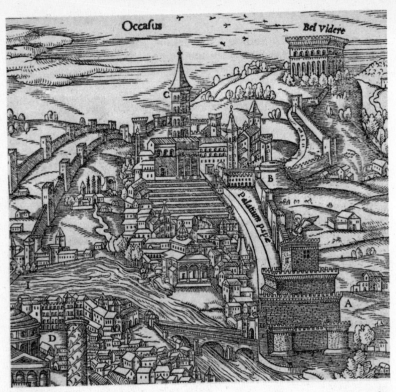

[7] Enlargement from the panorama of 1549, (see endpapers) featuring the Basilica of St. Peter, the Apostolic Palace, the Belvedere in which Leonardo da Vinci lived when the elephant arrived in Rome, and Castel Sant'Angelo, from which Leo X first watched it approach over the bridge. From the *Raccolta Generale Geografica* ... (Rome, 1549) Tomo II, p. 1512.

assured a good living thereafter. Indeed, he often made identical concessions to several, forgetting what he had already done. He never neglected an opportunity to demonstrate his benevolence to the people of Rome. To be admired and loved by all, to be praised and blessed on all sides, were the pope's consuming ambitions. He avoided problems when possible, seeking to enjoy life as much as possible without risk or effort.[14]

The papal court was instantly converted into a centre of creative activity, while Rome, which for centuries had remained a small community, became suddenly transformed into a metropolis without sufficient housing for all who came. The pope selected two distinguished Latinists as his secretaries, Jacopo Sadoleto and Cardinal

Bernardo Dovisio da Bibbiena. He directed his attention to the University of Rome, increasing the numbers of its lecturers and supplementing salaries. Among the artists in residence he favoured Raphael and appointed him conservator of antiquities, arbiter of the arts, architect and painter of the Vatican. A great lover of music, Leo X paid substantial sums for musicians for his own entertainment, and attached greater importance to music in the Church than it had received before. He raised the papal choir to a new state of perfection, imported music books from Florence and instruments from Germany and elsewhere, and expended great sums to hire musicians for solemn public ecclesiastical functions.[15]

Gold flowed freely, chiefly from the reserve which Pope Julius II had managed to accumulate, and Rome had not known such display of wealth since the fall of the Roman Empire. The installation of the new pope and the consequent growth and expansion of the papal court brought fresh activity to the Vatican, where the pope himself was the busiest individual of all. Even prelates of the highest station had to wait four or five hours to see the vice-chancellor, his cousin Cardinal Giulio de' Medici, and as long as six hours before they might be able to meet with the pontiff.

Because of his obesity Leo X moved about with difficulty. He was a late riser, and experienced difficulty in getting up from bed, requiring two servants to lift him. The first to enter his rooms each morning was his secretary, Gian Matteo Giberti, who received instructions on the most important state business of the day. Next came the datary to discuss benefices, after which the pontiff met with the chamberlains. He then attended mass, held audiences, and had his dinner at an advanced hour. He had a single meal a day but it was a hearty one, and he fasted three days a week during which he took only bread, vegetables and fruit.

He rested after his meal and then again held audiences. Often he was joined by friends to play chess. In the afternoon he usually rode through the Vatican gardens. He resided in the Apostolic Palace, but during the summer, to avoid the intense heat, he spent periods of time at the Belvedere, the jewel-like villa in the Vatican gardens, or at Castel Sant' Angelo.[16]

Among the first to seek an audience with the new pope after his installation was the Portuguese ambassador to Rome, João de Faria, who came to offer the felicitations of his sovereign. He was graciously received and the pope expressed his pleasure at Portuguese achievements overseas. He reiterated the assurances of co-operation with

[8, 9] Two contemporary representations of Manuel I: [8] as lawgiver to a prosperous country with far-reaching fleets. Frontispiece of Livro II of *Ordenãçoes de Dom Manuel* (Lisbon: João Pedro de Bonhomini 1514). In the Biblioteca Nacional, Lisbon. [9] as the heroic champion against Islam. From the cover of Amerigo Vespucci's letter *Mundus Novus* in the German language reprint *Von der neü gefunden*, by Michael Furter (Basle 1505).

Portugal he had expressed before the conclave. Faria communicated the results of his audience to his king, who followed his ambassador's advice and initiated a courteous exchange by writing a letter of congratulations to Leo X.

In a second letter written a short time later, King Manuel reported Albuquerque's conquest of Malacca and summarized Portuguese expansion overseas. When the letter reached the Vatican on 3 January 1514, the pope had it read before the Sacred College after solemn high mass on the Tuesday in the octave of the Epiphany.[17]

Greatly impressed by Portugal's successes overseas and determined to acknowledge them appropriately, on the following Sunday the pope, accompanied by all the cardinals at court, proceeded in a brilliant cavalcade to the church of Sant' Agostino to celebrate the Portuguese victories. After a mass celebrated by Cardinal Pompeo Colonna, an impressive panegyric was delivered by Cardinal Camillo Portio.[18] [8, 9]

In an Apostolic Brief of 18 January to King Manuel, Leo conveyed his best wishes, praises, and benedictions, expressing the hope that he would see all of Africa converted to the Catholic faith. The king was greatly honoured by the Brief, which had been prepared by Sadoleto, the pope's secretary for letters to princes. The communication made it evident that the pope acknowledged that the Portuguese motive for conquest was not ambition, nor the acquisition of riches, nor the acquisition of territory, the extension of his lands, but the sincere desire to propagate the law and the knowledge of the faith in those regions.[19]

Despite the lands and riches acquired from the holy wars in which Portugal had been engaging, the consequence of these endeavours was rapidly to disperse the royal income, which could not keep pace with the provisioning of the fleets and armies. There was as yet neither regular taxation nor an adequate system of borrowing. In such circumstances monarchs sometimes appealed to the pope for help to meet deficits or to fund crusading purposes. When the pope agreed, he would waive specified portions of the tithes and other sums paid to the clergy and religious institutions in the monarch's realm. Several of the Spanish kings had, during periods of calamity, obtained munificent distribution of Church resources from the Holy See. This was to be the first time that such a request had been made by Portugal since the reign of King Afonso I, although there had been great and repeated need in Portugal's wars against the Moors. Manuel's intention was to augment the number of ships and war machines for his war against the African Moors, and to deliver the continent to Christianity from Muslim bondage, and, profiting from the alliance with 'Prester John' of Ethiopia, to repulse the Turks. Success would enable him to develop navigation and commerce with the Indies and benefit those regions with missionaries.[20]

Manuel had this scheme in mind when he began planning a mission of obedience to the new pope. He determined that it should be an extraordinary entourage such as had never before been seen in Rome or elsewhere in Europe. Its purpose was to be threefold: to present his obedience to the pope in accordance with tradition; to display a selection of the great riches of those regions of the East and elsewhere that Portugal had commanded and was promised for the future; and finally, to request financial assistance for his endeavours, to be deducted from the ecclesiastical establishment in Portugal. The plan was well conceived, and the king was convinced that it could not fail.

King Manuel had another, unstated, reason for sending a mission to Rome at this time, and it was the most urgent of all. This related to the famous Line of Demarcation established by Pope Alexander VI in 1493 and modified the following year in the Treaty of Tordesillas. As a rule, Portugal kept confidential its overseas activities, with its programme of expansion to the East, in order to avoid creating conflicts and competition with other European nations, particularly Spain. Manuel deliberately informed the pope of the capture of Malacca, however, in order to obtain confirmation from the Holy See that the Spice Islands were within the sphere of Portuguese domain in accordance with the Line of Demarcation. Spain had already claimed that the Moluccas should come under Spanish domination. Furthermore, in 1512 Spain had begun to make plans to present such a claim to the Holy See and to attempt to take possession of the Spice Islands. Consequently, the election of a new pope provided the Portuguese king with an opportunity to confirm his country's priority.[21]

Accordingly, Manuel sent advance notice to the pope of the planned mission, and included a few gifts representative of the successes achieved by his nation in Africa and Asia. The pontiff responded by encouraging the king to continue his war against the infidels, and scheduled 12 March as the date for the mission's entry into the Eternal City. A papal Bull issued on 8 March 1514, *orthodoxe fidel nostre*, called upon all the Portuguese people to support their monarch in this crusade against the Moors in Africa. Thus far, the preliminary communications with the Vatican had proven to be extremely favourable to Manuel's plan.[22]

Meanwhile, the election of a new pontiff in Rome had already bestirred other European crowned heads to present impressive missions of obedience to ensure the Holy See's co-operation in their endeavours. Shortly after Leo's installation several such missions had been quickly assembled and had already come to Rome. First was the embassy from Florence, with twelve representatives of the city's foremost families accompanied by fifty chariots and escorted by two hundred horsemen dressed in crimson velvet. A mission from Poland arrived at the same time, followed in the next few months by missions from Siena, Mantua and Avignon. Other ambassadors came, including one from the Duke of Milan. Cardinal Mattheus Lang, who came to present the homage of Emperor Maximilian I, was escorted by 400 horsemen, ambassadors of other European sovereigns, and a large number of the clergy.[23]

Manuel considered it vital that his mission of obedience should focus attention primarily on the mysterious East, with acknowledgement of Portugal's conquests. He was determined to dazzle the papal court, and by this means, all of Europe, with a display that had no peer in the past and would surpass any in the foreseeable future. He sought advice concerning elements that would most effectively and favourably reflect the image of the Portuguese empire that he wished to portray.

Informed that the pope was a scholar, Manuel selected a Chinese and a Mexican manuscript to be included among the gifts. The pope was said to be an aesthete and a sybarite, and therefore rich pontificial vestments and altar fittings, embroidered and set with quantities of pearls and other gems, and Chinese porcelains were ordered. The pope was known to be a student of nature and particularly interested in flora and fauna, and had in fact soon established his own menagerie as well as a botanical garden in the Cortile del Belvedere. Manuel thereupon determined that when all else was in readiness he would select and include the most unusual exotic birds and beasts from Africa and Asia from his own sizeable menagerie in the royal park of his palace at Ribeira. No cost or effort was to be spared in the preparation of the mission.

For the chief of the delegation Manuel appointed the noted navigator Tristão da Cunha, a member of the king's special council whose military achievements in the East had been well publicized. Cunha had led an expedition to Africa, had discovered the Tristão da Cunha Islands in the far South Atlantic, and in the same year had accompanied Albuquerque on an expedition along the Madagascar coast to Somaliland and the Oman Coast.[24]

Cunha was to be accompanied by his three sons, Nuño, Simão, and Pêro Vaz. The inclusion of the twenty-seven-year-old Nuño was deliberate, for he too had achieved recognition as a military commander in the East.[25]

The renowned jurisconsult Diogo Pacheco was selected to be the second ambassador. His literary and scientific competence excelled those of all other Portuguese savants, and he was assigned to deliver the customary discourse attending the presentation of credentials to the solemn assembly. As previously mentioned, he had performed the same function on the mission sent to Pope Julius II in 1505, and was familiar with the protocol.[26]

The third dignitary to be part of the mission was already in Rome, the Portuguese ambassador extraordinary to the Holy See, João de Faria, a distinguished jurisconsult and an expert on ecclesiastical affairs. He was charged primarily with negotiating the ecclesiastical benefits to be requested by the king from the Holy See. Manuel placed great reliance on Faria's tact and skill and upon his long experience at the papal court. Also to be part of the entourage were the distinguished poet and musician Garcia de Resende, who would serve as the king's secretary on the mission, and the king's equerry, Nicolau de Faria. Others chosen to accompany the mission were Cunha's kinsmen, Garcia de Saa and Manuel de Sylveira. When completed the mission totalled seventy men.[27]

King Manuel then directed his attention to the selection of the gifts. In addition to some trophies representative of the Portuguese conquests in the East, others must reflect the new pontiff's role as the leader of the Church and all Christendom. Accordingly Portuguese artisans set to work to create objects for the pope's use, combining the rarest textiles with precious metals and the most magnificent gems. Among the gifts were a finely wrought gold chalice valued at 12,000 ducats, a tabernacle to contain the Holy Sacrament executed in gold with exquisite worksmanship valued at 54 *marches*, an altar frontal of the finest brocade sewn with countless pearls and precious stones valued at more than 60,000 ducats, and a collection of altar ornaments as well. To these were added vestments, including a chasuble and two tunics made of heavy gold cloth garnished with pearls and unpolished rubies and embroidered with images of Christ and the Apostles. Silver cases to contain each of the gifts were made especially for the purpose.[28]

King Manuel exercised just as much care in the selection of unusual birds and beasts to symbolize the new lands of the East. He surveyed the collections in his royal parks in which the Portuguese monarchy had maintained menageries for several centuries.[29]

Manuel's first choice was a handsome cheetah that had been trained for the hunt; then he added two leopards, numerous parrots and Indian fowl, and some rare dogs from India. He selected a fine Persian horse he had received as a gift from the King of Hormuz, and finally he added a young white elephant that had recently been brought from India. It was four years of age, and had been highly trained to perform, dancing to the music of pipes, and responding to commands in the Indian and Portuguese languages. The elephant would be accompanied by its Moorish trainer or mahout and a Saracen guide.[30]

Manuel was well aware that the members of the Medici family were known for their interest in rare fauna and had imported them from Alexandria across the Mediterranean for the menagerie they had maintained in Florence since the fifteenth century. The pope's great grandfather, Cosimo the Elder, kept at least ten lions, wild boars, wolves, bulls and mastiffs. Later, Leo's grandfather added other animals to the menagerie, which was frequently visited by artists who came to sketch animals in their natural postures. When Pope Pius II and Galeazzo Sforza visited Florence in 1459, Cosimo had staged a famous combat in a specially constructed arena for the occasion. All roads leading to the Piazza della Signoria were blocked off to form the square into a great arena.

Wild boars, horses, dogs, wolves, bulls and other animals were sent into the square, and as the distinguished visitors watched, twenty-six lions were let loose among the captive beasts. As the lions prowled about, the animals shrank and shivered in fear. A bloody battle was expected. Instead the lions took little notice. After a bored walk inside the enclosure, they lay down lazily and went to sleep. Annoyed and embarrassed, Cosimo then had a huge wooden model of a giraffe containing armed men wheeled into the enclosure. The men emerged and used every means to tease and arouse the lions into action, but without response.

Shortly after Leo X was installed at the Vatican, he brought together there a small menagerie of his own with lions, leopards, monkeys, civet cats and bears. These were maintained in cages and other restraining structures adjacent to the papal *gallineria* or henyard in a section of the spacious Cortile del Belvedere.[31] [10]

Manuel accordingly selected birds and animals not already familiar to the Italians and concluded that the elephant was a particularly good choice, since such a beast had not been seen in Rome since the days of the Roman Empire. The elephant as a public spectacle had been a subject of considerable interest from as long ago as the ninth century BC when the King of Assyria, Assurasirpal II, established a zoological garden to contain a number of elephants he had captured in Syria. During the Roman Empire elephants had been first displayed in amphitheatres during the consulships of Marcus Aurelius Antoninus and Albinus Postumius. Thereafter elephants were frequently featured in Rome in public demonstrations until the fall of the empire.[32]

In the course of the next thousand years few elephants were known

[10] The Basilica of St Peter and the Apostolic Palace, view prior to 1590. In the courtyard to the right, an enclosure was built for Hanno. Fresco in the Apartment of Julius III in the Apostolic Palace.

to have been brought to Europe. The first of record was a tamed specimen named Aboul-Abbas sent as a gift to Charlemagne in AD 797 by Haroun al-Raschid, the Abassid caliph of Baghdad. The beast was disembarked at Pisa and sent overland to Lombardy. Charlemagne prized it highly, and took it with him over the Alps into battle. He kept the elephant in a park in Lippenham, Germany, until its death in 810. Four centuries passed before another elephant found its way to Europe; this was an animal brought back from the Holy Land by Emperor Frederick II in the thirteenth century and used in his attack of the city of Cremona. The elephant entered the city in 1214 with the victorious army and was sent to meet Richard, Earl of Cornwall, upon his arrival for a meeting with the emperor.[33]

Little more than a decade later King Louis IX (St Louis) of France brought back an elephant on his return from his disastrous crusade, and it was subsequently memorialized among the chimerae sculpted on the cathedral of Notre Dame in Paris. Soon tiring of the beast, the French king sent it across the English Channel to his brother-in-law, King Henry III of England. The latter added it to his menagerie, which was one of the most important in Europe at that time. In about 1477 the titular king of Naples, René d'Anjou, received the gift of an elephant from King Afonso V of Portugal in addition to two dromedaries, two civets, and several other rare animals brought from the west coast of Africa. In 1497 an elephant, noted by Giovanni Francesco Pico della Mirandola, was presented to Ercole d' Este by merchants of Cyprus, and was ultimately memorialized at Belfiore. None of these had been seen in Rome, however.[34]

The next elephants to appear in Europe were those brought to Portugal from Africa and India during the first two decades of the sixteenth century. Manuel maintained several in a stable specially constructed for the purpose adjacent to his palace at Estãos in the Rosso district of Lisbon. Occasionally manifesting all the characteristics of an Oriental potentate, the king delighted in displaying these unusual beasts. He frequently included as many as five elephants in royal processions from his palace to the cathedral on ceremonial occasions, as well as when he rode through the city and countryside.

During the course of these jaunts, their mahouts made these elephants perform for the people. On special occasions the king also featured in his processions his handsome Persian horse and trained cheetah, attended by a Persian groom. The cheetah, mounted upon a specially made saddlecloth on the horse's crupper behind the groom, attracted almost as much attention from the cheering populace as did the elephants. The proud king, surrounded by his mounted courtiers, would follow some distance behind on his horse, as the entourage was heralded along its route by the sound of trumpets and kettle-drums.[35]

The elephant selected to be sent to the pope was one of four shipped from Cochin to Lisbon by Albuquerque between 1510 and 1514. According to a surviving note from Antonio Caneiro, the king's secretary of state, one of the beasts was a gift to Manuel from the King of Cochin, and another had been purchased by Albuquerque for the king. These were the first Asian elephants to arrive in Portugal, although in an earlier period others had been sent there from Africa.[36]

On 12 January and 19 January Albuquerque in India signed two orders relating to the treatment to be given to one of the two elephants while it was being transported, presumably because it was a beast of particular value or importance. Albuquerque specified that it was to be fed one *paraaos* (approximately twenty litres) of rice per day, as much butter as was required, and that some oil was to be used to anoint its skin. The anointing was a measure required to keep the animal's skin soft and pliable in preparation for its long exposure to salt air during the voyage. These instructions related to the animal that had been purchased, not the one that was a gift from the King of Cochin. Probably the young animal had been maintained in Cochin for the balance of the year in order to fatten it sufficiently in anticipation of the long sea voyage to Portugal.[37] [11]

---

[11] Afonso de Albuquerque's order dated 1 December 1512 for the maintenance of an elephant at Cochin prior to its embarkation on the *nau Santa Maria da Concéiro* bound for Lisbon. *Corpo Cronologico P. II Maço 36, Doc. 181.* In the Arquivo Nacional da Torre do Tomba, Lisbon.

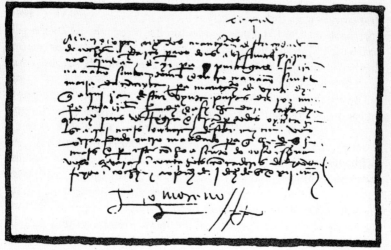

The king's treasurer at Cochin informed his monarch in a dispatch of 20 December 1510 of the forthcoming shipment to Lisbon of the two elephants on the monsoon winds of 1511. He wrote,

They send two elephants, i.e., one which was a gift from the King of Cochin and is for service, the other which was purchased for 101 crusados; and the King of Cochin sends two naires [custodians] to accompany the animals. They [the naires] should be well treated and they go with the hope that Your Highness will recompense them handsomely. They are not to return until the elephants have been well trained, and not before they have trained other men to care for them... Furthermore, these elephants shall not carry any burdens other than men.[38]

The two elephants shipped on the 1511 monsoon arrived in Lisbon early in the summer of 1511. The monsoons are winds which in south and east Asia blow from the north-east to the south-west from October to April and from south-west to the north-east from May to September. Portuguese voyages to and from India were scheduled to take advantage of these winds; a fleet bound for India would leave Lisbon not later than April in order to catch the end of the summer monsoon, and voyages from India to Portugal departed as soon as the winds began in January.

Two more elephants were purchased and shipped from Cochin to Manuel on the monsoon of 1513. These were described as 'small elephants' and were sent by separate *naus* to ensure the safe arrival of at least one of them. The shipment also included cheetahs (*onças*) sent as gifts from the King of Hormuz to Manuel, one of which he later selected to send to Rome.[39]

Inasmuch as the elephant sent to Rome was reported to have been four years of age when it arrived in Rome in 1514, it would have been born in about 1510, and may be identified as one of the two beasts that arrived at Lisbon in the summer of 1511. It undoubtedly was the one that had been purchased and given special care, probably because it had been highly trained to perform.

The weeks passed quickly while the city of Lisbon bustled with preparations for the departure of the mission to Rome. As the gifts were being completed, packed and assembled, the logistics of transport were studied and finalized. In addition to the rare birds and beasts, the mission was to include forty-three other animals, chiefly horses and mules needed for transport, as well as seventy dignitaries with their servants and other attendants, one hundred and forty-three men in all. Provision was made for supplies of food and water required by men and beasts throughout the sea voyage and during travel from landfall to Rome, and the stores were loaded on board the ships designated for the voyage.

Although this was not an unusual enterprise for the Portuguese, who had been sending ships with men and varied cargoes across the seas for some years, the nature of the valuable gifts and live animals and birds required considerable attention. There was to be no stinting, for Manuel was determined that the mission should make the best impression possible. All the birds and animals could be accommodated in cages below deck but the elephant had to be shackled above deck between two masts. Nicolau de Faria was assigned the responsibility for the care of the elephant en route, and in his account he noted that the vessel was a *nau*, a large three-masted vessel of 400 tons or more of a type first developed in about 1450 by the Portuguese for transporting large cargoes from a distance, and that had been used by Vasco da Gama and Christopher Columbus on their voyages.[40] [12]

At first, embarking the elephant constituted a problem, but it was solved by a series of portable bridges. Francesco Chalderia, a Paduan monk who had been living in Lisbon for the past two years, witnessed the embarkation of the elephant and described the event. All went well with the loading of the ships, according to reports, until the time came to conduct the young elephant on board. With everything in readiness

[12] A sixteenth-century *nau* – the sort of ship developed by the Portuguese for bulk transport from distant places. From *Compilaçao de todas las obras de Gil Vicente* (Lisbon: Andre Lobato, 1586).

for departure, the people of Lisbon turned out in great numbers, swarming on the dock to observe the event.

The nervous young beast was conducted from the royal park at Ribeira to the harbour, but when it reached the dock at the water's edge, the animal balked and refused to move further. The Jesuit Augustino Oldoino described the contretemps that threatened to invalidate the mission. Neither force nor soothing coaxing prevailed, and the elephant remained silently obdurate. Finally King Manuel himself was forced to intervene, for he was greatly concerned that the departure should take place as scheduled.

According to an account later circulated among the people of Lisbon, the elephant's obstinacy proved to be a subterfuge of its Moorish mahout to remain in Lisbon. It was said that he had fallen in love with a young girl in the city and was reluctant to leave her, being convinced that a long absence would damage his suit. By whispered conversations in the elephant's ear he informed his charge that it was being taken to a new country that was extremely arid and unhealthy for it. There the beast would be forced to live among barbarians, and its food and its ornaments and all that was necessary for its well-being would be taken away. The keeper appeared to have convinced the elephant that furthermore it would be required to spend many days crossing an ocean to reach its destination, a voyage that was probably as long and wearying as the one it had experienced on its way from India to Portugal.[41]

The story went on to state that when King Manuel learned of the mahout's plot, the latter was summoned to the royal presence. The monarch informed the keeper that he would tolerate no excuses, and that if he did not succeed in getting the elephant on board the ship within the next three days, the king would have the keeper's head. Frightened by the ultimatum, the mahout hastened to the dock to persuade the animal that what he had whispered into its ear previously had been mistaken, in fact absolutely false. He had been led into error by someone who was jealous of the great good fortune that awaited him and the elephant beyond the seas. He assured the beast that the new land to which they were going was in fact beautiful and alluring, and that it would be by the most pleasant road that they would arrive at the capital of the whole world where reigned the Prince to whom all the emperors and kings were subject. For all these reasons he begged the elephant again and again to reverse its decision and to put itself into the hands of God, who would ensure that they would have a happy crossing.

The elephant was convinced at last. Although still afraid, it none the less bravely boarded the ship, and had never had cause to repent its decision. Such was the account reported to the historian Giovanni Piero Valeriano by the Portuguese diplomat Miguel Sylvius.[42]

Another version of the legend claimed that the elephant refused to board ship until it was made clear to it that it would become the servant of the head of the Christian world. Yet another account, reported by Rorarius, related that a solemn promise had been made to the beast that it would eventually be returned to Portugal, and that it was in fact the lack of fulfilment of this pledge that led eventually to its death.[43]

There is some doubt that there was any difficulty at all in loading the elephant. According to Hartenfels, a remarkably similar account was given by a Carmelite monk of St Trinitate, about a Portuguese viceroy who wished to send an elephant on board ship to Spain. And the legend might have had an even earlier basis: Pliny the Younger noted that elephants 'were believed to refuse to [embark on] board ships when going overseas until they are lured on by the mahout's sworn promise in regard to their return.'[44]

The loading of the ships was completed at last and they were ready for departure to Italy. As the mission sailed out of the harbour, it was followed by cries of farewell from the families of the voyagers and the great crowds swarming along the dockside and by the sounds of celebration throughout the city.

CHAPTER TWO

The Road to Rome

In the Belvedere before the Great Pastor
Was the elephant conducted in costume.
It danced with such grace and such love
That a man could hardly have danced better.
And then with its trumpeting so much noise
It made, the entire place was deafened; it then
Turned reverently to the Pope, and his entourage.

Pasquale Malaspina de' Marchesi di S. Margherita :
De l'elefante mandato dal Re di Portogallo a Papa Leone (1533)

AFTER SAILING OUT OF LISBON HARBOUR AMID SUCH WILD festivity, the ship bearing the royal mission bound for Rome set its course along the southern coast of Spain. The first port of call was Alicante, where it was scheduled to anchor for three days. Word of the mission had preceded it, and as the vessel sailed into the harbour, it was met and surrounded by countless small boats overflowing with curiosity seekers.

The ship was immediately besieged and, despite the efforts of the beleaguered crew, the natives kept boarding it throughout its stay, intent upon seeing the Portuguese noblemen and particularly the strange beasts on their way to visit the pope. This overpowering public curiosity had been neither anticipated nor provided for, and was to constitute a major problem all the way to Rome. It came as a great relief to all aboard when the ship finally departed and continued on its way.

The vessel made port again at Ivica (now Ibiza), the southernmost of the Balearic Islands, approximately sixty-five miles off the Spanish mainland. Once again the voyagers suffered an invasion by the natives, who flocked from all sides to board the vessel and gape at the Portuguese and their cargo. Utter confusion reigned, and the little harbour buzzed with frenzied activity until the Portuguese mission departed. Setting sail once more, the ship reached its next port of call,

Palma on the island of Majorca, where a longer stay was planned to enable the horses and wild beasts to be exercised on land. No sooner had the Portuguese vessel heaved into view than it seemed as if the entire island had gone mad. The ship had barely anchored before it again became the centre of utmost confusion. Boats laden with boisterous Mallorcans made for the vessel and their passengers could not be dissuaded from their attempts to climb aboard.

The invaders took over the forecastle and crowded the decks amidst a great display of gaiety, and the crew was helpless in its efforts to cope with them. The ship was forced to remain in port for eleven or twelve days, and throughout this period the natives came and went incessantly. Gentlemen of the wealthiest families of Majorca came with their wives and crowded together with workingmen and peasants, elbowing their way on board, and it was said that there was no one left on the island while the ship remained in port.

The same depopulation occurred again and again in every port, town or city at which the mission called on its route. Upon leaving the Balearic Islands it was decided that in order to avoid similar displays the vessel should head directly for the Italian coast without scheduling any interim stops. While on its way to its ultimate destination, Porto Ercole (Port of Hercules), the ship narrowly escaped a great tempest and humans and live cargo suffered the ship's violent tossing on the choppy seas. It was with considerable relief that the voyagers and crew saw their destination come into view. Porto Ercole was a tiny harbour situated on the south side of Orbetello, lying on a spit of land projecting into the Tyrrhenian Sea.[1]

From that point forward the journey had to be continued on land. After landfall, the members of the mission disembarked, the horses and caged beasts and birds were brought ashore and exercised, until all that remained on board was the elephant. Nicolau de Faria, who had been given the overall charge of the beast, went ashore to obtain a barge or galley of a size sufficient to transport the elephant from deck to shore. Despite many attempts, his efforts failed. It was not that the active little fishing port lacked galleys and barges suitable for the project, but upon learning they were to be used to transship such an unusual cargo as an elephant, the owners of such vessels refused to lend or rent them They were not about to hazard their property, on which their livelihood depended, with the weight of such a large beast.

Faria became increasingly provoked as everywhere he turned he was faced by refusals or uninterested shrugs. Finally, he went determinedly into action. He next approached the magistrates of the city. They were curious about the mission and its purpose, and when word spread that there was also an elephant, nothing could stop their efforts to see it. They offered their full co-operation. With their consent, and provided with a launch from the Portuguese ship manned by fifteen to twenty strong members of its crew, Faria forcibly boarded a nearby galley and commandeered it over its owner's protests. He then ordered special scaffolding to be quickly constructed, and with a heroic mass effort, his men managed to disembark the elephant safely and bring it on to Italian soil by means of a makeshift bridge they had created.

Needless to say, the event was witnessed by countless spectators who had swarmed to the harbour. Every house-top was packed with observers and the waterfront and streets were lined with curious onlookers. The first sight of the frightened little elephant, as it was moved along the ways to the dock, brought excited cries and applause, to the beast's increased distress. News of the disembarkation, and wild accounts of the strangely dressed foreigners on their horses and mules and their collection of wild life, reached far into the countryside around Orbetello, and brought great numbers from all the surrounding towns lying as great a distance away as Siena.[2]

The remaining distance to Rome was seventy miles, and Cunha determined that before the mission proceeded on its land journey, everyone should rest for several days. He was aware that the route ahead would present serious difficulties for the elephant in particular, because it was accustomed to the soft terrain of the jungle and the hard paving of the dusty old Roman roads would soon tire its feet. During their stay it proved to be impossible for the travellers to achieve any privacy, however, for the region continued to be overrun by curiosity seekers. After two days, with the realization that rest had become impossible, the Portuguese mission moved once more, directing its route towards Rome along the ancient Via Flaminia. It was with great difficulty that the cortège was able even to leave the port town. The people from the countryside had formed a caravan that attached itself to the mission, impeding its movement and making progress extremely difficult.

The travellers moved slowly, advancing only small distances each day, for the caravan that was following behind daily increased in size, supplemented by workers from the towns, peasants from the fields, and gentlemen from their villas. All were curious, avidly seeking a view of the great animal and the strangers speaking a strange language who accompanied it. An inordinate amount of time was required to cover the first twenty-two miles of the route, as they continued at an exceedingly slow pace until they arrived at Montalto di Castro, a poor village, where they crossed the Ponte del Abbadia over the Fiora river. There the mission was brought to a temporary halt by the arrival of a group of more than one hundred horsemen who had ridden from afar to observe the foreigners. Eventually they were able to continue along the undulating countryside until they reached the antiquated town of Corneto, which stood on the former Etruscan capital of Tarquin on a chalky plateau overlooking the river Marta.

The Portuguese travellers had little opportunity to take note of the countless towers that distinguished the tiny community, the unfinished Gothic palace of Cardinal Vitelleschi, or the medieval castle of the Countess Mathilda, for to their consternation they found awaiting them two hundred and more horsemen and a great number of men and women on foot. Most of these newcomers joined the swelling caravan as the mammoth procession wound its way painfully towards the Eternal City. By this time the multitude had reached such unmanageable numbers, and such a state of disorder prevailed, that the horde threatened danger to the mission and damage to the countryside.

Disaster struck even sooner than expected. When the mission took shelter at an inn at Corneto, the throngs invaded the premises and even climbed to the roof-tops of neighbouring houses for a glimpse of the elephant and the foreigners. As a consequence, the roof of the inn collapsed. To avoid total destruction of the hostel, and to enable the mission to achieve some rest, Faria found it expedient to conduct the elephant into the centre of the piazza, where it remained exposed through the night for everyone to see. Fortunately the weather was mild and the beast did not suffer from a night spent in the open under the stars.[3]

The next day, as the mission resumed its journey southward to Civitavecchia, there was no abatement of the crowds. Men, and women with children formed deep files on both sides of the road, so that instead of the feeling that they were moving through the countryside, the mission had an impression of moving along an interminable highway in a great sea of bobbing strange faces, engulfed in a considerable confusion of excited cries and chattering that arose all around them. The cortège had just reached Civitavecchia when a heavy thunderstorm broke and torrential rains, thunder and lightning seemed to have no end. The rain continued, to the delight of the local innkeepers, for the travellers were forced to remain for two days in the ancient port, and a large number of the followers forced themselves into the city to share the excitement. Soon there were no rooms to be had anywhere for miles around.

The elephant and its custodians also welcomed the enforced delay, for the beast was already suffering from the long walk, and the constant din and movement of the crowd proved to be distracting and annoying. Unaccustomed to the hard, dry paved road surface of the Via Flaminia along which they were travelling, the elephant's feet had become sorely abraded and calloused. Faria realized that the beast would soon have to have a prolonged rest, and that possibly the Portuguese cortège would have to split into two sections to enable the elephant to travel at a slower pace. Meanwhile the continuing downpour proved to be a beneficial change, for it laid the heavy dust which had beclouded their route, soaking into the hard road surface and softening it to some degree. At the same time, however, the incessant rain created difficulties, shedding a depressing dreariness over the landscape, leaving the road filled with deep puddles, which added to the elephant's discomfort.

The otherwise picturesque route from Civitavecchia to Rome traversed a dreary plain that ran parallel to the ancient Via Aurelia near the sea coast as far as Palo. As the travellers continued on their way, they could see the Alban and Volscian mountains in the distance, with occasional glimpses of baronial castles and groves of dense green foliage. The mission now moved more slowly than before, advancing in short stages to enable the tired elephant to rest as often as possible. Unaccustomed to loud noises and the sight of a moving sea of people, the beast had become extremely apprehensive and weary, but none the less continued faithfully to obey its custodians. It was undergoing an ordeal such as it had never experienced before, but throughout maintained its gentle attitude.

Nor did the situation improve all along the Via Flaminia, for new crowds greeted them amidst much noise and confusion. Many of the wealthy noblemen of the region accompanied by friends and servants rode long distances on horseback for a glimpse of the elephant, and they tried to coerce Faria to interrupt the journey and bring the beast to visit their castles or villas. Despite their repeated entreaties and promises of reward, Faria made excuses that they were not permitted to deviate from their schedule, inasmuch as the pontiff expected them in Rome at a specified time.[4]

The first major halt along the way came at Malagrotta, an old town abandoned by its inhabitants except for a few unfortunates unable to travel. There the foreign travellers settled in as best they could while the downpour continued out of doors. Still more throngs came from every direction to see the fabled elephant. Among them were a dozen noblemen, dukes and counts, who had ventured into the storm from their homes fifteen and twenty miles away. They arrived drenched and chilled by the cold, and with the knowledge that there would be no lodging or refreshment to be had because the boisterous crowds had already taken over the town. None the less, they felt sufficiently repaid for their efforts by having viewed the remarkable beast.

On the same day, a number of monks made their way to Malagrotta. Defying the rain, they celebrated mass in the open for the multitude. Next came several cardinals who had ridden with their attendants all the way from Rome. They claimed they had been out hunting and were just passing by, but they too had been drawn by the news that the elephant was there, and were anxious to obtain a glimpse of it.

Again and again Faria was approached by people from the countryside with requests to delay the journey and bring the elephant to their small towns so that others could see and admire it, but each time he refused. The beast had become so weary and footsore that Faria was forced to remain at Malagrotta for several more days to enable the elephant to rest while the main body of the mission contemplated continuing on its way to Rome. There was little relaxation to be had, however, for even at night noblemen rode out of the Romagna countryside demanding a view of the elephant by torchlight.

Tristão da Cunha [13] and the remainder of the mission resolved to renew their journey just as soon as the rain slackened. On the last leg of their route, just before arriving at the outskirts of Rome, they crossed the Ponte Molle, the ancient Pons Milvius over the Tiber one and a half miles north of the city gate. It was on this bridge that Cicero had captured the emissaries of the Catiline conspiracy; from it the Emperor Maxentius had been thrown into the river during the battle with Constantine. They continued past the bridge along the Via Flaminia until they arrived at the large villa of Cardinal Adriano di Corneto, who welcomed them and offered them shelter.

There the mission rested while awaiting the arrival of Faria and the elephant. They had arrived at the villa on 14 February, almost a full month before the mission was scheduled to make its formal entrance into the Eternal City. The cardinal provided them with every convenience and for the first time since they had left Lisbon they were able to relax and enjoy some leisure.[5]

Cardinal Adriano di Corneto was not only a scholar and a member of the College of Cardinals, but also one of the wealthiest men of Rome with extensive land holdings. He owned two palaces in the city in addition to the villa with its orchards and vineyards. It was claimed that it was to this villa that he had invited Pope Alexander VI and his son Cesare Borgia to dine with him and had then attempted to poison the pontiff. As a consequence, the cardinal had been forced to flee Rome for a time and had just returned in the preceding year, in time

margaritæ Phrygijs operibus intertextæ mirabiliter adornabant. Prorex ſi quidem in India Triſtanus multas ſibi prætioſiores diuitias congeſſerat, præclaris rebus cum grauitate preſtantis ingenij, tum bellicoſa manu geſtis;

[13] Portrait of Tristão da Cunha, the Portuguese navigator. The elephant Hanno is depicted behind him. To be noted also are the headgear decorated with pearls and other gems and the necklace of gems worn by Cunha in the procession of the mission of obedience into Rome in 1514. Engraving from *Elogi virorum bellica virtute illustrium* .... by Paolo Giovio (Basle, 1575).

to participate in the conclave that elected Pope Leo X.[6]

The cardinal's villa was situated just outside Porta Angelica, the gateway that had been built by Pope Pius II and was originally known as the Porta Viridaria, named for the garden (*viridarium*) the popes had maintained behind the Vatican palace. While the main section of the mission rested at the villa, Faria was completing the last stage of his journey with his tired young charge. Once more crowds beset them on their way without consideration for the travellers. Despite the efforts of its keepers to provide the elephant with a means to rest, there was no refuge to be found. The curious stormed the walls of a villa to which the beast had been brought, and so avid were they to see it that they brought down the walls and caused considerable destruction. Greatly alarmed for the safety of his charge, Faria waited until the middle of the night and then stole away with the beast and its custodians to another place where they could hide and avoid the people.

Travelling by night whenever possible, and hiding by day, they made their way to Cardinal Adriano's villa, where Faria felt assured they would find safety at last. Faria recalled that it had been designed as a stronghold and had once served as a Roman fortress. Since it was enclosed with great walls encircling its orchards and vineyards, surely there could be no safer refuge.

Soon after they reached the villa and found shelter there, Faria realized he had made a serious mistake. There was no way to control the crowds, who now swarmed in high glee over the walls into the villa from all sides. It was not long before the orchards and vineyards had been trampled beyond repair, fruit trees and vines totally destroyed, and the shelters damaged beyond recognition. By the time morning came the villa had been reduced to a shambles.

Faria had no recourse but to escape once more with his elephant and its keepers to another building nearby, which was more solidly constructed that those he had previously occupied. It was incredible that the crowds, bent purely on entertainment and not intending rampage, could cause such great damage; contemporary accounts leave no doubt of the extent of the destruction that followed in the elephant's wake. Believing themselves temporarily safe in their new shelter, Faria was soon disillusioned, for it too was ruined by impatient horsemen and newcomers on foot who were determined to see the strange beast. It was a depressing prospect, for the advent of the elephant threatened to become one of the great calamities of the time, promising destruction all along its route and even to the buildings of Rome.

To prevent damage to other villas on the outskirts of the city, the pope himself was finally forced to take action. He sent out a company of archers from the Swiss Guards to protect the travellers. Even their presence did not help much, however, for they had attracted members of the nobility and others from the papal court, who being made curious by rumour and the call for military assistance, became intent on having a preview of the elephant.

Next came the sisters of the pope accompanied by many ladies, Cardinal Marco Corner and the cardinals of Siena and Aragon, as well as numerous bishops and members of the Roman nobility, with many attendants, arriving with an air of great festivity as for a holiday outing. Faria and the elephant's custodians suffered even greater anguish during this period than before, because they had to deal diplomatically with these eminent personalities, making it much more difficult than handling the ordinary crowds.

Problems arose not only from these distinguished visitors. Deprived of a glimpse of the elephant within the confinement of the shelter, curious onlookers brought picks and sledge hammers with which they attempted to break holes through the masonry. They raised ladders against the walls to climb in through windows, and even the strongest doors were shattered.

To the bewildered travellers it seemed as if the whole world around them had gone mad. None the less, they were forced to remain at the villa for four or five days more because frequent storms prevented further progress into Rome. The weather made the crowds even more unruly and intolerable, and the sound of the wind and rain battering the walls further distressed the tired elephant as it kept pacing nervously within its confines.[7]

The date for the mission's entrance into the city was now close at hand, and as soon as the weather permitted, the travellers moved into the papal gun factory outside the city walls. There in one of the rooms Faria had the elephant carefully groomed by its keepers to remove all traces of its exhausting journey in preparation to dressing it in its colourful caparisons. The Pope had designated the first Sunday of Lent, 19 March, as the day for the entry of the Portuguese mission into Rome. On that morning Cunha and the members of his large party dressed themselves in the elaborate formal wear they had brought for the occasion; the birds and beasts were washed and brushed one more time after they had been fed; and then they all waited together at the cannon factory until the time came for them to begin to make their way the short distance to the Porta Flaminia in the Aurelian wall, now the Porta del Popolo, where the procession was to begin promptly at two o'clock in the afternoon.

For centuries tradition dictated that when legations from rulers or princes of republics in the north approached the Eternal City, their entourages were to stop outside the Porta Flaminia and there spend the night before making their formal entry. The next morning they would put aside their travelling clothes, don their state robes, decorate their horses and other mounts with rich caparisons, and dress their familiars and footmen in uniforms. When all was in readiness, they would form a procession which, although hampered by crowds on all sides, would formally begin its promenade through the ancient gate, traverse the Piazza del Popolo, and ride into the city. Upon emerging through the gate they would be met and greeted by the municipal authorities accompanied by cardinals and Roman princes and conducted ceremoniously to the Apostolic Palace. The route prescribed was the Via Ripetta alongside the Tiber to cross the ancient bridge to Vatican Hill. The numbers of the cortège and the splendour of costumes and equipment, the size of the crowds that gathered and ran alongside, all served as measures of the importance of the visitor. This was the road along which the Caesars had marched on their return from their triumphs in the north. Along it had come the young Charles VIII on his way to the conquest of Naples. Only the year before the Portuguese mission's arrival another great procession had conveyed along this same route Federigo Gonzaga, the ten-year-old son of the Marquis of Mantua and Isabella d'Este, taken as a hostage to the pope as a guarantee for his father's future good behaviour.[8]

The Portuguese mission followed tradition and made elaborate preparations for the promenade. As Faria was supervising the covering of the elephant with the magnificent caparison provided for it, he was impressed to discover that the beast had grown since it left Portugal. In a report made to King Manuel a few days later, Faria noted that at this time he was able to touch the elephant's shoulder lightly with his hand, and that upon measurement he discovered that it had grown substantially since its departure from Lisbon.[9]

Finally, when all was in readiness, Cunha gave the signal and the mission began to wind its way through the Porta Flaminia. At that moment, a furious thunderstorm suddenly broke and raged all about them. Drenched, confused, and frightened by the violence of the wind and the downpour, the marchers covered themselves as best they could while frantically seeking shelter, which was nowhere available. No sooner had they passed through the ruined gate in the Aurelian wall, however, than the storm ceased as abruptly as it had begun, and the sun emerged suddenly in all its earlier brightness and splendour. The day remained clear and mild thereafter, and the Roman populace took it as a sign from on high that God looked favourably upon the Portuguese king and his undertakings.

In accordance with custom, the mission was met immediately inside the piazza by a ceremonial party consisting of the governor of the city of Rome and other municipal officials, accompanied by prelates and chamberlains of the papal court, members of the families of the pope and the cardinals, all the ambassadors of foreign powers, and Roman princes.

The governor of Rome formally greeted Cunha and his fellow ambassadors after an exchange of courtesies, and presented an elegant discourse eulogizing the king of Portugal for having fought so unremittingly against the infidel in the name of Christ and the Christian faith. The Portuguese ambassadors responded with courteous thanks, then several of the foreign ambassadors made speeches congratulating King Manuel upon his achievements. Among them were Albert de Carpe representing Emperor Maximilian, the ambassadors of the Duke of Milan and others from Castile, Venice, Lucca and Bologna. All spoke in Latin with great loquacity.

To all of these Cunha responded in the vernacular, while Pacheco replied in Latin to the speeches of the bishops with considerable brilliance so that the honours of the day were equally divided between the two Portuguese envoys. By the time the last of the illustrious gathered there had spoken, the appetite for oratory must have been exhausted: it was two o'clock in the afternoon. It was one of those diaphanous days of spring in Rome that occur nowhere else in the world, the sun limpid against a bright luminescent sky, and a light breeze lending gaiety to the air. The surrounding hills were just becoming covered with a fuzz of new greenery.

Paride de Grassi, the recently appointed papal master of ceremonies, then came forward to organize the cortège in preparation for its entry into the city. The great reaches of the piazza were soon filled with large numbers of the Roman populace milling around the foreigners assembled in its centre, where the papal marshal and his assistants attempted to establish an order of march in accordance with protocol. The confusion of prancing horses, whirling halberdiers and noisy mules created a great din echoed by the exuberance of the crowd. At last the precise order demanded by de Grassi was achieved, and the procession began to move into the Via Ripetta.

As the procession moved forward, the first contingent consisted of members of the families of the pope and cardinals mounted on mules draped in purple. Next came the papal lighthorsemen without lances and the footmen of the cardinals mounted on mules covered with scarlet saddlecloths, bearing the ceremonial hats of their masters suspended around their necks. In accordance with custom, these preceded the chamberlains of the cardinals and those of the pope, eight mounted trumpeters, four pipers and a group of Portuguese musicians with drums and brass instruments.

The Portuguese courtiers assigned to the papal court, totalling about sixty in number and accompanied by numerous clergy, were dressed in long robes of crimson velvet with scarlet hoods and superb golden collars around their necks. They came mounted on horses and mules, each of which was draped with a rich saddlecloth of silk fabric decorated with gold and silver lamé. Then followed the family of the Portuguese ambassador in residence, João de Faria, the families of the visiting ambassadors, Tristão da Cunha and Diogo Pacheco, each mounted on horses draped in velvet, the pope's mounted horse guard and his archers, members of the pope's family, the halberdiers of the Swiss Guard marching in formation, succeeded by the pope's trumpeters and pipers.

The next segment was led by Nicolau de Faria mounted upon a Spanish jennet, preceding the gifts to Manuel I from the King of Hormuz – a black man riding the prized white Persian horse to the haunches of which clung the sleek spotted cheetah. Captured wild in the Asian forests and trained for the hunt in Lisbon, it was a beast such as had never been seen in Rome. Walking proudly behind it came a young Saracen, guiding the young elephant plodding along at a turtle's pace. Its other attendant, the richly dressed Moorish mahout, rode astride its neck, and the beast's back was covered with a saddlecloth of crimson velvet and its head masked in a caparison of gold brocade. Supported in the centre of its back was a great silver coffer, artfully disposed under a handsome brocaded covering which fell almost to the ground and was ornamented in the finest workmanship with the arms of the Portuguese king. Above the coffer rose a silver tower with many turrets. Behind the burdened beast came more trumpeters and pipers, the royal secretary Garcia de Resende, the three sons of Cunha, twenty other Portuguese noblemen, the herald of the Portuguese king richly clad in gold brocade bearing before him his trumpet from which hung the shield with the king's arms, and then the pope's mace bearers.

The third contingent featured the Portuguese ambassadors. The three envoys rode upon splendid white horses with harnesses of gold decorated with Mauresque reliefs, a velvet-clad groom walking on foot at the side of each. They were led by Cunha, who was dressed according to the usage of Portuguese nobility in a costume of velvet and black satin embroidered with pearls. Around his neck he wore a heavy collar woven of pearls terminating over his chest with five large precious stones. On his head he wore a skull cap of gold cloth over which was fitted a velvet hat embroidered with gemstones. Riding on his left was the governor of Rome and on his right the Duke de Barre, brother of the Duke of Milan.

Next came Pacheco accompanied on his left by Albert de Carpe, and the Bishop of Nicosia on his right. Riding behind came the Portuguese ambassador in residence, João de Faria, grouped with the ambassador of France and the Bishop of Naples. Both Pacheco and Faria were clad in superb vestments richly ornamented with gemstones but substantially less elaborate and valuable than those worn by Cunha.

Other foreign dignitaries followed, led by the ambassador of Spain accompanied by a prelate, the ambassador of England with a bishop, then the ambassadors of Poland, Venice, Milan, Lucca and Bologna, succeeded by many archbishops and other ecclesiastical notables, magistrates and other municipal officials. At the end of procession were a dozen fine mules pulling cages filled with parrots and parakeets, Indian fowl, beautiful rare dogs from India and other exotic birds and beasts destined as gifts for the pope.

Of all the unusual and dazzling elements of the great procession, it was the elephant that excited the greatest public interest, not only because of its large size but also by its antics in immediate response to commands. It would lift its trunk, turn and salute from one side to the other, and from time to time it would drink from the great barrels of water situated along the route, always in docile response to the voice of the Saracen guiding it.[10]

The silver tower balanced on the beast's back also brought gasps of surprise from the crowds. The castle-like structure with its numerous turrets featured under the canopy at its centre a large rock containing a gold tabernacle which was executed with such artistry that it was said the workmanship excelled the material of which it was made. A gold chalice was displayed in one of its turrets, and the others contained silver cases displaying holy vestments of gold and silver cloth adorned with embroideries of pearls and unpolished rubies. Notable among them was an elaborate altar frontal of brocade decorated with pearls and precious stones of great value. The Portuguese historian Damião de Goes later commented that it was 'a thing richer in quality than the memory of man will ever see'.[11]

In a letter written to the Emperor Maximilian a few days later, Carpe spoke of the splendour of the occasion, and the exotic character of the foreigners and their gifts as being reminiscent of the accounts of Marco Polo. He described the rich garments, the gifts crafted of gold, and the wild birds and beasts in considerable detail. Another contemporary observer of the procession, Polidoro di Albrizzi, was particularly intrigued by the great jewelled collar worn by Cunha. In a letter to Marino Sanuto in Venice he later reported that there was general speculation that the precious collar was destined to be presented as a gift to the pope, but that some time after the arrival of the mission the presentation had not yet been made.[12]

It is difficult in modern times to visualize Rome as it appeared in the early decades of the sixteenth century at the time that the Portuguese mission arrived. Although still encircled and protected by the crumbling Aurelian wall, only a fraction of the area within its circuit was inhabited. The people built their dwellings close to the water supplies, and the heart of the city spread out from the area of the Piazza Navona, with other clusters of population extending from the Fontana di Trevi on the hill of the Quirinal, which had its supply of water from the Acqua Vergine. Other large groups of dwellings dotted the sluggish Tiber. Of the fabled seven hills, only the Quirinal and the Capitoline were inhabited. All through the region great Roman ruins, such as the baths of Diocletian, Constantine and Caracalla, were surrounded and partially hidden by wild underbrush and loomed like grim and lonely monuments. Cows and goats were pastured in the Roman Forum, while the slopes of the Esquiline and the Viminal hills were dotted with gardens and vineyards as well as groves of olives, and orchards were carved out of the wild growth and ruins of the Coelian and Aventine slopes.

The Via Lata, now the Corso, was the principal thoroughfare through the city. It was then so narrow that a horse was able to pass through it only with difficulty. It was bounded on both sides with low dwellings having wide projecting balconies and exterior staircases clustered so closely together that the sun rarely penetrated to the pavement. From the Via Lata the city spread out on both sides in a jumble of narrow crooked streets punctuated here and there by public squares.

The silt of centuries lay heavy upon the city. Overlaid with dust and the filth of an unconcerned population, it was only when word came that the pope planned to pass through a particular part of the city that any effort was made to clean the streets. Those areas within reach of the Tiber were in worse condition even than elsewhere in Rome, for they were regularly flooded and constantly covered with a residue of mud, often several feet in depth. Despite its limited development and primitive character, Rome none the less had more than fifty basilicas at this time, many containing fabulous ancient mosaics, sarcophagi, paintings and sculptures, housed in structures that were more often than not on the verge of ruin.

Great interest in ancient sculpture had been generated during the immediately preceding reign of Pope Julius II, and the collection of examples from the numerous ruins of the city continued at fever pitch.

Julius had employed agents to scour the bed of the Tiber, and to excavate farm areas in the countryside in search of sculpture. Among the treasures brought to light during this period were the Laocoön, the Torso Belvedere, and the sleeping Ariadne, all of which had been carefully conveyed to the Vatican and installed in the Cortile del Belvedere.[13]

It remained for Pope Leo X later to undertake major improvement of the roads and public areas. Among the first of these was to be the Piazza del Popolo and the 'new road' leading into the city. Inside the Porta Flaminia, the visitor at this time was greeted by a large open space bordered by walls of stone and rude huts scattered along them. From the gate through the square, however, a magnificent view of the Aracoeli became visible through the Arco di Portogallo along the straight length of the Via Lata. Close to the ancient gate at the foot of the Pincio was the Augustinian church of Santa Maria del Popolo, with the Augustinian convent close by. There distinguished visitors were hospiced before making their official entries, and there too the popes returning from the north frequently stopped overnight to rest before entering the city.

The most important feature of the square was the church, which tradition claimed had been situated on the site of Nero's tomb, from which a great walnut-tree had grown. The tree had become the favourite nesting place for crows, which Pope Paschal II dreamed were demons. In his dream the Blessed Virgin appeared to him and ordered him to cut down the tree and erect a church in her honour in its place. This Pope Paschal did, and in the thirteenth century Pope Gregory IX replaced with a church the chapel Paschal had ordered earlier to be built there. Rebuilt two centuries later by Pope Sixtus IV, it became the church of Santa Maria del Popolo.[14]

It was in the adjoining Augustinian convent, which was surrounded by its gardens and vineyards, that two years prior to the Portuguese mission, Martin Luther had lodged upon his arrival in Rome after a journey of six or seven weeks on foot from Germany. The Via Flaminia continued as the Via Lata through the great gateway, passed through the piazza, terminating on Capitoline hill. It was the central of three roads branching out from the old portal, with the Via del Babuino on the left and on the right the Via Ripetta following the Tiber.

As the Portuguese mission moved out along the Via Ripetta, it passed the church of San Giacomo in Augusta at its left, then the pyramidal mausoleum claimed to be the tomb of Nero's mother. Next along the route they sighted the ancient mausoleum built by Emperor Augustus in 28 BC, and converted in the twelfth century into a family fortress by the Colonna princes. The sight and sounds of the long entourage frightened the cattle that had been grazing alongside the tomb, and upon its approach they scattered deeper into the countryside.

The region along the Tiber from the piazza to the Ponte di Ripetta (now Ponte Cavour), was owned by the *compania* of Santa Maria del Popolo and of San Giacomo in Augusta, and in large part remained uninhabited. Portions were ceded in perpetuity by the *compania* to private individuals upon their agreement to erect dwellings and pay the annual census. These buildings were occupied by occasional tradesmen and barge owners and the open spaces were used for pasture.

The procession moved slowly, impeded by the rough condition of the pavement and by the great crowds pressing in from all sides, creating confusion and obstructing their passage. As they approached the bridge leading to Castel Sant'Angelo, the ground was shaking from the vibrations of salvoes from the castle's artillery with which the pope greeted the mission. As these cannonades merged with the sound of the Portuguese and papal musicians and the outcries of the crowd, the sound swelled into a great roar. The birds and beasts in their travelling cages plaintively reacted with alarmed chattering and low roars of concern. The elephant in particular had reached a state of near panic as a consequence of the disturbing ground tremors combined with the assault of sound.[15]

In advance of the mission's arrival, Pope Leo X, accompanied by his cousin Cardinal Giulio de' Medici and a number of other cardinals, had hurried along the secret passageway of the Corridore that connected the Apostolic Palace with the Castel. High in the tower of Alexander VI situated in front of the old fortress was a window that provided a unique vantage point from which the pope could observe the approaching procession. Some of those reporting the event noted that the pontiff watched the approaching cortège with a 'telescope'. This was undoubtedly a *perspicillum* or optical sighting tube without lenses which he frequently used to observe objects at a distance. Besides his several other physical disabilities, the pontiff suffered from myopia and presbyopia and had great difficulty in seeing near or far at all times.[16]

The procession was scheduled to pass in front of Castel Sant'Angelo and then continue back over the bridge into the city once more. The brilliant cavalcade moved slowly along until the young elephant approached the open window from which the pontiff and his party were watching. It stopped in its tracks, folded its knees and knelt to the ground, inclining its head devoutly. Then as the beast arose, it saluted the pope with three great barks, trumpeting 'Bar! Bar! Bar!' according to contemporary chroniclers. The pontiff watching from his vantage point laughed with delight like a child at the performance. The elephant's charming gesture was said to have been not as much an impulsive act of piety as a response to its mahout's command. Perhaps so. Presumably in order to make its intent clearer, the great beast next plunged its trunk into a nearby trough and filled it with water. Then raising its trunk, the elephant sprayed water sufficiently high to reach the pontiff and other nearby watchers, drenching them, to the even greater amusement of Leo X.[17]

Having made its circuit before the Castel, the procession turned back over the Ponte Sant'Angelo, along the Via dei Banchi Vecchi and made its way to the Campo dei Fiori, where the Portuguese mission was to be lodged. The pope's artillery continued its cannonade and his musicians played on until the last of the returning procession was lost from sight. The Portuguese ambassador in residence had arranged for appropriate lodgings at a hostel for Cunha and his distinguished companions, and Faria housed the elephant in a safe building having a stall, where it was to remain until the consistory was held. Dusk had fallen by the time that the various segments of the mission had disbanded and settled into quarters for the night, and once more a steady rain had begun to fall.[18]

Meanwhile, among the spectators observing the procession with the pope and the cardinals, there was said to be a man in his late sixties with white hair and of venerable aspect, shouting and shrieking as the colourful jewelled garments of the foreigners and the exotic birds and beasts passed in review. He was the poet Giacomo Baraballo, the Abbot of Gaeta, and had been a member of the pontiff's personal retinue since the latter had become a cardinal, and had already achieved some local note as a buffoon. It was the elephant in particular that intrigued him, and it was noted that he kept mouthing third-rate verse mixed with Neapolitan interjections concerning the beast's antics until it had passed from view. The Pope was said to have looked back and forth between the elephant and the rotund poet, and it may have been at this time that he conceived a malicious plan for a public spectacle that was to take place later that year.[19]

Even in Rome, the centre of the Christian world, where for centuries the populace had been accustomed to witnessing great processions of successive popes, of foreign conquerors and colourful envoys, the splendid cortège of the Portuguese mission of 1514 surpassed any in the city's annals.

On the day following the procession, the two visiting Portuguese ambassadors were ceremoniously conducted to the Apostolic Palace where they were assigned quarters that had been prepared for them, and where they lodged during the next eight days. It was the custom for foreign ambassadors to avoid appearing in public while preparations for a public consistory were in progress. As chief of mission, however, Cunha was allowed to receive visitors. Many distinguished personages came to call upon him, among them Fabricio Coluna, Marquo Antonio Coluna, the ambassador from Castile Don Antonio d'Estuniga who called himself Prior of San Juan de Castela, the Duke de Barre, and many others.[20]

Monday, the 20th of March, was the day that had been selected by the pope for the public consistory at which the Portuguese envoys would make their formal presentation. Avid as always for public demonstrations, the pope took up his vantage point at a window in Castel Sant' Angelo to watch the colourful display as the Portuguese mission approached the Apostolic Palace. The pontiff then hurried back along the covered passage of the Corridore to prepare himself for the ceremonies and to be present upon the mission's arrival.

Papal emissaries called for the Portuguese ambassadors in their rooms and escorted them to the Sala Regia. The pope, clad in full pontifical regalia, was assisted to his throne, the cardinals took their places, as did the other prelates of the court, and finally the ambassadors from foreign powers were seated. The entry of the Portuguese ambassadors was announced by artillery salvoes from Castel Sant' Angelo, as they proceeded behind the consistory's legal counsels into the pope's presence. The counsels presented the pontiff with a petition, the nature of which was not recorded. The pope reported that he had been informed of the subject of their demand, but that in view of the importance of the subject he could not make a decision immediately.

Grassi, the papal master of ceremonies, noted in his journal that the Portuguese ambassadors surpassed all foreign representatives assembled there with the exactitude with which they observed ceremonial to the smallest detail. This was indeed exceeding praise from Grassi, who could rarely be accused of resorting to superlatives.[21]

After Cunha and his two colleagues had advanced to the throne and kissed the pope's foot in accordance with Roman protocol, Cunha presented his diplomatic credentials. Then Pacheco moved forward and delivered his 'oration of obedience', worded in the bombastic style with many superlatives in the manner of the period. It was, none the less, filled with erudition and elegance of style, and conveyed in a most noble tone.

'*Eloquar an sileam?*' he began, 'Shall I speak or be silent?' With the greatest eloquence he placed India at the feet of the pontiff, whom he said he viewed as he sat with his cardinals around him, as a sun surrounded by stars. They were the representatives of the Church for which the furthest reaches of the world were being explored and conquered. Pacheco went on to tender the obedience of the Portuguese king to the newly elected Pope, and modestly itemized Portuguese successes on sea and on land in the Near East, Africa, and Asia.

[4] Portrait of King Manuel I of Portugal. Miniature painting appearing in the king's copy of the *Livro de Horas*, c. 1517. In the Museu Nacional de Arte Antiga, Lisbon

He then submitted King Manuel's several requests for concessions, and in laconic but well-expressed phrases went on to point out the benefits of the Portuguese achievements to the Church and all Christendom, noting particularly the conquest of new lands and the conversion of African kings and satraps. The orator emphasized also the new, precise geographical knowledge of remote places that had been gained as a result of these endeavours, places which had hitherto been erroneously described, such as the island of Taprobana and the peninsula of Aurea Chersonesum, to which he added the city of Malacca.

Pacheco had carefully planned his oration before his departure from Lisbon, and he had revised and polished it during the mission's numerous frustrating delays and stops on its way to Rome. He had rendered it into Latin, of which he was a master, and his presentation made a deep impression on everyone. Having finished, he stepped back humbly to receive the pope's reply.[22]

To the great surprise of the entire assemblage, the Pope promptly responded in the same language, Latin, without any previous preparation, and spoke with considerable elegance and facility in a manner entirely befitting the occasion. He commended Manuel's devotion to the Holy See, and he praised the virtues of the Portuguese people. He urged the maintenance of peace among the Christian princes, and expressed a heartfelt desire that they unite their arms against the Turkish menace and other infidels.[23]

On the day following the public consistory, the pope, accompanied by all the cardinals, descended from his apartments to the Cortile del Belvedere to inspect the gifts brought by the Portuguese mission. Attending him were the prelates and other members of the court as well as foreign ambassadors. The pontifical vestments, the altar frontal, the tabernacle, chalice, and other gifts were displayed in the conservatory adjacent to the papal gardens.

The richness of the gifts was dazzling, and contemporary accounts competed with one another in the selection of superlatives and estimates of their value. The Venetian ambassador, Angelo Lippomano, reported to Marino Sanuto in Venice that the tabernacle was valued at 54 *marche*, while, in another letter to Sanuto, Albrizzi described 'a cope completely embroidered with figures executed in pearls, as much on the fringe and the hood as the rest... It is so heavy that one can barely lift it with difficulty, and I estimate it to be worth seventy thousand ducats.'[24]

Among other observers, Estevan de Garibai commented on 'a papal mitre, adorned so richly with pearls and precious stones that one of equal value has never before been seen in Rome'. The Franciscan monk, Fra Gratia de Francia, estimated the value of the gifts at more than 80,000 gold ducats, while Sebastiano de Branca Tedallini later wrote that the ecclesiastical garments and altar furnishings alone were valued at 50,000 ducats.[25]

Even though the descriptions and evaluations may have been exaggerated in contemporary accounts, there was no doubt that Leo himself admired the gifts and prized them highly. 'The coffers opened, all of the curious were filled with astonishment,' he wrote to King Manuel, *and in their admiration fell into silence. For it seemed as if one's eyes were not adequate to admire them sufficiently, and the language does not include expressions competent to eulogize them. This is not an exaggeration, for their beauty and their brilliance are surpassed only by their artistic value; nothing similar has been seen, and we never again expect to see such a stream of precious stones. Everyone agrees that the art and variety of design are even more worthy of admiration if one considers the arduous work of the artist who with his skill and elegance surpassed all of the Indian and Arabian craftsmen.*[26]

Space had been provided, meanwhile, in the papal menagerie nearby for the trained cheetah, Indian fowl and Indian dogs, parrots and parakeets, and the elephant.[27]

After admiring the precious gifts in the conservatory, the pope led the party out to the menagerie. A passionate devotee of the hunt, he insisted on assisting at a simulation of the chase to demonstrate the cheetah's prowess. A number of small live animals were brought and let loose in the garden among the beds of flowers, and the pontiff watched with obvious enjoyment each time that the carnivorous beast chased its prey and hurled itself fiercely upon it and tore it apart.[28]

The gift of all gifts, according to every account, which most pleased the pontiff was the elephant. Because the papal menagerie was situated on a slope at the left of the botanical gardens, next to the henyard (*gallineria*), it proved to be extremely difficult to conduct the large beast up the rough terrain into the Cortile. The Pope thereupon determined that more suitable quarters would have to be provided for it as soon as possible.

On 26 March, the Sunday after the mission's arrival, the elephant was made to perform for the Roman populace in the Cortile del Belvedere. It danced to the music of the pipes, trumpeted loudly, performed tricks with its trunk, obeyed a variety of commands given by its mahout in the latter's native language, and acted in other ways to amuse the visitors who thronged to observe it.

In his papal Brief of 11 May to Manuel I, which had been prepared for him by his secretary Sadoleto, the Pope expressed his pleasure and admiration and that of his entire court as well as the people of Rome with the Portuguese mission's elaborate procession of men and birds and beasts, constituting as it did 'prizes from Lybia, Mauretania, Ethiopia, Arabia, Persia and India', as testimonies of the far distant and fabled lands discovered and conquered by the Portuguese in recent years. 'But,' he went on,

it was the elephant which excited the greatest astonishment to the whole world, as much from the memories that it evoked of the ancient past, for the arrival of similar beasts was fairly frequent in the days of ancient Rome.

Through the centuries that followed during which our city lost its dominance, no more were seen. The docility of Annone [the name given to the elephant, which was rendered into English as Hanno] is marvellous, for it is obedient to every order and to every signal of its trainer. One is almost tempted to put faith in the assertion of the idolators who pretend that a certain affinity exists between these animals and mankind. The sight of this quadruped provides us with the greatest amusement and has become for our people an object of extra-ordinary wonder.[29]

The advent of the Portuguese mission and the presence of the elephant in Rome was reported by a number of contemporary writers. Branca Tedallini wrote of the sixty [sic] Portuguese horsemen forming part of the procession 'each with his collar of fine gold', namely, the collar of the Order of Christ, a papal decoration of great antiquity.[30]

The pope's biographer, Paolo Giovio, described Tristão da Cunha as he led the mission 'with honoured greyness of hair, of age still strong, and with robes embroidered with the finest pearls and brilliantly shining with the most beautiful gems, when he entered into Rome by the Porta del Popolo with the elephant before him, as a trophy of the victory he had achieved in India and brought as a gift to Pope Leo X.' Among the observers was also an anonymous Frenchman who had been a resident of Rome for the past several years. He too described the procession and the public consistory held for the Portuguese ambassadors, providing additional details. Other foreigners in Rome reported the event. It was described in glowing terms by a member of the staff of the Duke of Bragança, as well as by the historian Hieronimo Osorio. Writing on behalf of the Portuguese, the latter praised the papal master of ceremonies and his staff for their skill and competence in directing the massive event.[31]

The most extensive description proved to be the one forwarded to Emperor Maximilian by his ambassador. Albert de Carpe described the mission's arrival in great detail in a long epistle in Latin. After noting the splendour of the procession and its participants, he described the rich gifts. Carpe was particularly intrigued by the elephant's caparison and the covering of the tower-like chest it bore on its back. He noted that woven in gold thread on either side of the caparison were the arms of the king of Portugal. He was present with the other ambassadors at the display of gifts, and appeared to be over-whelmed by their richness and value. He wrote about the papal vestments, which he said were woven with gold thread and so heavily laden with pearls and unpolished rubies and other gems that the substance of the cloth was barely visible. Embroideries of the portraits of Christ and the Apostles featured on the vestments were outlined in pearls and gems and the whole ornamented with designs of pomegranates executed in knotwork.[32]

The Venetian ambassador Lippomano reported that the Portuguese mission had entered Rome with greater pomp than had any ambassador before that time. He added that Grassi, the papal master of ceremonies, went so far as to state that the cortège was magnificent. Fabronio, another of the Pope's biographers, proclaimed that there had been no finer event in that epoch.[33]

CHAPTER THREE

The Rose & the Sword

By the end of the fifteenth century... a true menagerie (serragli), now reckoned part of the suitable appointments of a Court, were kept by many of the princes... King Emanuel the Great of Portugal knew well what he was about when he presented Leo X with an elephant and a rhinoceros. It was under such circumstances that the foundations of a scientific zoology and botany was laid.

Jacob Burckhardt : *The Civilization of the Renaissance in Italy*
(1878)

ROME CONTINUED TO RING WITH THE CELEBRATION AND excitement generated by the Portuguese mission for many days after its arrival. The colourful procession, the gifts, and even the diplomatic presentations brought continued favourable comments, and the papal court talked of little else. Pacheco's words were published widely with the consequence that the historic mission of obedience of 1514 became known throughout Europe. So impressive had been Pacheco's oration, in fact, that a number of the most popular poets of the day used the occasion as inspiration for verses extolling the virtues of the Portuguese king and the eloquence of his court orator.

Poets, poetasters, and versifiers of every description flocked around the papal court, some of the foremost writers of the age mingling with others without talent who served the pontiff primarily with their diverting buffoonery. Many of the more talented left permanent evidence in their works of the interest and love which the elephant excited among the people. They wove praises of the royal Portuguese donor and the pope in Latin verses about the beast. Some notable names in Renaissance literature are to be found among them. Marcantonio Casanova wrote 'While the eloquence of Cicero and the shield of Achilles serves him, Manuel sends lightning bolts with his right hand, and his voice thunders.'[1]

Janus Vitalis Panormitanus reduced his record of the event to an epigraph of two simple lines:

> The king is orator, knight, prudent, forceful, spirited,
> He conquers as he moves and battles, with intelligence, with
>   mind and hand.[2]

Others who memorialized the Portuguese king and the elephant included Joachim Cipellus, B. Blosio, Pietro Curzio, Lancellotus Politus, D. Dardanus and Camillo Portio. [*See* Appendix.] Commemoration of the arrival of the Portuguese mission and praise of the elephant Hanno provided subject matter also for the talents of the distinguished poet and member of the Roman Academy, Evangelista Fausto Maddaleni de' Capodiferro. Among his works is an unpublished manuscript describing the event entitled '*D. M. elephanti ad Emmanuele Lusitaniae rege Leoni X pont. max. missi.*'[3]

The most ambitious of the poetic productions was a compilation entitled *Theatrum Capitolium* produced by Aurelio Sereno, in which he added verses by others to his own in praise of the elephant. After his dedication of the work to Pope Leo X, he began

> In the annual games of your pontificate
> Celebrated in the month of March,
> Early in the spring, when the earth is becloaked
> With variegated flowers dispersing everywhere
> Their sweetest fragrance,
> An Indian Elephant, the most sagacious of all beasts,
> Sent to you by the most serene Emanuel, King of the
>   Portuguese,
> By means of the splendid knight, his orator Tristan da Cunha,
> Hitherto unknown and not seen in Italy in our century,
> He was shown throughout the whole city, to a marvelling and
>   admiring populace.
> Such a spectacle had been observed by Pompey, Hannibal,
>   Domitian, and few others,
> And now has been shown in your most august time.
> Thus the gentle animal provided for your public diversion,
> Suppliantly senses your divinity, and adores it.

'How great is the power of the Creator,' rhapsodized Sereno elsewhere in his work, 'which shows to us today this beast, in which are contained so many virtues, that can live for three centuries, that progenitates one time in its life, that respects religion, that salutes our Holy Father, that understands human speech. Such a portent is seen only once, as it was by Caesar and Pompey and Hannibal and a few others favoured by Jupiter in their time, and you, oh Prince, among those few will be numbered.' Sereno added yet another long piece about the elephant, addressed to King Manuel I. As though it were not enough, he wrote, to present a huge animal which though ungainly, did not lack intelligence, the monarch had sent other gifts, which the poet enumerated. Sereno then went from addressing the Portuguese king to speak to the elephant:

> You will not live beneath the poorly built roofs of the Parthian
>   kings
> But under the pennants of heroes and heavenly inhabitants
> When you are stabled on the Vatican hill,
> And feel you enjoy the delights of this world by right.
> In the fertility of its fruits and perennial spring,
> This place outranks the gardens of the Hesperides and Alcinous.
> How shall I recall the sweet airs and serene skies?
> Here you will believe that the Elysian fields have been tilled by
>   the saints.
> If religion, sweet Venus, and glory touch you,
> It is because religion, sweet Venus, and glory reign here.
> If you long for the zealotry of battling Mars, or for your own,
> A martial people inhabit this city of Romulus.
> With such a company, unconquered in your hopes, and led by
>   Leo,
> You will present to the gods of Latium shining trophies.
> You will be led along the joyful path of triumphal pomp
> On the broad piazza sacred to Capitoline Jupiter.
> May you live happily for a long time giving joys to Leo;
> Partake of nectar and ambrosia with your master;
> May you become a tight-rope dancer, and learn to lead in many
>   games
> So that you will relieve your master of many cares.
> Thus he will be able to be most pleasing to Jupiter's Latium
> And win for yourself the ear of the people.[4]

The Florentine copyist, Giovanni Capitone Aretino of Arezzo, attempted to summarize predictions expressed by the poetic troubles in an elegy:

> If you believe, oh elephant, that you serve a lion of Lybia,
> You are deceiving yourself,
> This lion has fallen from the sky.
> This is your master, the chief glory of the earth,
> With the triple tiara crowning his head.
> Among the mortals he is held to be more than mortal,
> It is to him that has been given to open and close the heavens.

> *If to serve God is indeed to reign,*
> *You will reign in serving Leo*
> *For he is a God on earth…*
> *You will become an actor on the scene,*
> *Learn and pursue diverse games or pastimes,*
> *With which to alleviate your master's thousand cares;*
> *In this manner you will become*
> *Most appreciated by the Latin Tonante [Jupiter's thunderer],*
> *And you will gain the favour of the populace…*
> *O, happy beast, born under a favourable star,*
> *With which we have greatly enobled poesy, Rome, Leo…*
> *Do not think of flight; for if you die in this city,*
> *You cannot die by a nobler fate.*
> *You testify to the love of a king for the Supreme Pontiff*
> *Joined in trust by a great holy friendship.*
> *O, happy beast, born under so auspicious a star,*
> *To whom Poesy, Rome, and Leo*
> *Give such great nobility.*

'Live!' exhorted Giovanni Capitone Aretino in another work dedicated to the elephant, 'Live long and contented, auguring prosperous events for Leo, taking nourishment with your master from nectar and ambrosia. Become an actor, learn various tricks with which to amuse him; such will be pleasing to Jupiter of the Latium and you will captivate popular favour.'[5]

Among others who noted the advent of the elephant was Pasquale Malaspina, Marchesi di San Margharita, in a manuscript entitled 'Of the Elephant Sent by the King of Portugal to Pope Leo':

> *In the Belvedere before the great Pastor*
> *Was conducted the trained elephant*
> *Dancing with such grace and such love*
> *That hardly better would a man have danced:*
> *And then with its trunk such a great noise*
> *It made, that the entire place was deafened:*
> *And stretching itself on the ground to kneel*
> *It then straightened up in reverence to the Pope,*
> *And to his entourage.*[6]

Hanno also came to the attention of prominent Portuguese poets of the time. The *Exortaçao da guerra*, an exuberant tragi-comedy by the goldsmith turned dramatist Gil Vicente, reflected the national enthusiasm for Portuguese achievements overseas. It made acknowledgement of the mission to Rome, including a reference to the elephant in an inquiry made by Zebron, one of the stage characters: 'Is the fine elephant alive / That went to Rome for the Pope to shrive?"[7]

Among the events arranged to entertain the visiting mission during their sojourn was the *Comedia Trophea*, a festival-play written by Bartolomé de Torres Naharro, a Spanish poet and erstwhile professional soldier who had joined the Spanish colony in Rome a few years previously. Learning of the scheduled arrival of the mission early in January, when King Manuel's letter to the pope was published, Naharro went to work at once and completed the five-act play in time for its performance by the end of March. In the course of the plot, the Greek geographer Claudius Ptolemy returned from hell to protest Fame's claim that King Manuel had discovered more countries than Ptolemy had ever mentioned, an evocation reflecting the current interest in humanism and the attempt to measure man's knowledge gained from Portuguese discoveries and conquests against current standards.[8]

In the course of the play a dozen kings were assembled together, as well as the rulers of the newly discovered territories, who, being anxious to be baptized, had come to do homage to Manuel and who unanimously supported the Portuguese king's requests to the pope for religious concessions. No mention was made, however, of the request for papal approval of the latest Portuguese conquest, of the Moluccas, which the Spanish would eventually dispute, and of which the dramatist may have been informed.

The performance of the *Comedia Trophea* took place at some time after 20 March and prior to the mission's departure in June. It was held either at the Vatican or in a nobleman's palace; the pontiff was not present. Isabella d'Este may have been a spectator at the performance, for she later obtained a copy of the play for her own library. Naharro became intrigued by the pope's playful elephant and he conceptualized it as a symbol of Portuguese exploration and discovery. So fond did he become of it indeed that he kept a representation of it in his palace in Rome.[9]

Pope Leo had been enthralled with the splendour of the Portuguese mission, which he compared to the lavish events distinguishing the Medici court at Florence, and he was impressed beyond measure by the richness and exotic nature of the gifts so much more dazzling than those he received from other missions. Consequently he was readily amenable to the requests made by King Manuel I. On the same day that the gifts were shown to the papal court, the pope addressed a public Brief to Manuel granting him the concessions relating to Portugal which had been requested by his ambassadors.[10] [14]

Among them was a request for the establishment of commanderies for the Order of Christ, a military papal order established in 1319 by Pope John XXII at the request of King Diniz of Portugal. Ceded to the new Order were all the properties of the suppressed Order of Templars. The first chapter was established at Lisbon in 1321 and the first master of the Order was appointed by the pope. Succeeding masters were required to take the oath of fealty to the Holy See. After the beginning of the fifteenth century, a prince of the royal house administered the Order in place of the master. Henry the Navigator reformed the Order, secured for it spiritual jurisdiction over the islands discovered in the Atlantic, and then used its resources partially to fund successive explorations down the west African coast. He aimed to break into the rich trade of the interior previously monopolized, overland, by the Muslims, and their religious monopoly too. The specially designed caravels which were used to conduct these feats of exploration (in unknown waters, along dangerous coasts, inland up great rivers, without knowledge of currents, winds and southern stars) bore the crusading red cross of the Templars on their sails. The personal insignia of the succeeding Order of Christ was an elaborately wrought wide collar made of gold with enamel medallion inserts, terminating in a great sunburst featuring the Order's symbol consisting of a cross of red and white enamel. It was noted that each of the Portuguese knights of the Order participating in the mission's procession into Rome displayed this collar prominently.[11]

In addition King Manuel had requested that the Lateran Council continue its sessions, which had been suspended following the death of Pope Julius II, and that a definite sanction be given by the Holy See to decrees that had already been formulated. This was readily resolved, for between the time that the preparations for the mission were begun in Lisbon (when the request had been formulated) and the time of its arrival in Rome, the pope had already reconvened the Council.

King Manuel asked also that the secular clergy be required to observe once more the precepts of ecclesiastical discipline and that purity of morals be re-established in their hearts by the suppression of luxuries to which little by little they had abandoned themselves. Finally, Manuel urged that an alliance be formed between Christian princes for the purpose of resolving differences amongst themselves.

While Manuel's requests were receiving favourable consideration from the pontiff and the College of Cardinals, the Portuguese mission had been enjoying its stay in the Eternal City, finding it not only comfortable but extremely pleasant. They had been impressively received by the court and the populace alike, and the envoys and members of their staffs found much to delight them in the city for the next two months and more.

Eventually, however, Cunha became concerned that his mission was in increasingly serious financial straits. No provision had been made in Lisbon prior to departure for the maintenance of his party in Rome beyond the anticipated two months of its stay, and no additional funds were available. He faced the immediate problem of having to provide food, shelter and other needs for an unforeseeable length of time for one hundred and forty men and more than forty horses and mules.

Cunha had been forced to use such personal funds as he had brought with him to provide gratuities (*crociati*) in the form of 'spontaneous' gifts of money to at least four hundred trumpeters, pipers, drummers, grooms and members of the families of the papal household, in accordance with long-established custom. Since such expenses had not been foreseen and could not be delayed, Cunha was required to pay these gratuities from his own pocket. He kept waiting for a solution to come from Lisbon, but to no avail. Finally, after almost two months had elapsed since his arrival in Rome, he was forced to alert Antonio Carneiro, the Portuguese secretary of state in Lisbon, of his plight. The urgency of the problem as expressed in Cunha's letter contrasted sharply with the coarse eloquence describing his circumstances.

'With our entry into Rome,' wrote Cunha to Carneiro on 14 April, *we have made a great appearance, and because of it and the glorious impression it achieved, our King has today become the most illustrious sovereign existing in the world. However, he did not provide us with funds for our maintenance beyond two months of our sojourn, because we believed we would not be detained longer; therefore, I am considering borrowing money on credit and sending the account to be repaid in Portugal, because otherwise I do not know how to continue here. And I recall that there were those in Lisbon who warned me that heading the mission to Rome was neither acceptable nor desirable because too much of one's own money would have to be spent. Now, however, having spent all the money that I have, I have no other hope, but finally to return home.*

Accordingly, he went on, he saw himself as obliged to make use of credit, as King Manuel had authorized him to do in case of need, up to a maximum of 10–12,000 *crusadoes*, which even so would barely suffice for the sustenance of his company. He noted that it would surely be more than the amount required by Duarte Galvão for his intended journey to the land of Prester John [Ethiopia] being planned in Portugal for the following year. His first priority was to raise a certain amount of money on credit, to be given to Garcia de Resende to distribute, and secondly, to take shelter in his house in Xabregas when the funds were exhausted. He noted that he expected to find himself soon in Lisbon once more.[12]

As a consequence of Cunha's plea to Carneiro, King Manuel promptly granted him an annual pension of 250,000 *reis* 'in compensation for the many services We have received from him [Cunha] and more in particular, for the service he has provided us at the embassy of our obedience, with all that We sent to the Holy Father, Leo the Tenth, in which he served us very honourably at great expense and the expenditure of his personal wealth and much to our joy and contentment, in all the things that we ordered him to do in the said embassy.' The emolument was made retroactive to January 1514.[13]

While Cunha was attempting to maintain his large company in Rome, the pope was giving thoughtful consideration to the selection of appropriate tokens of acknowledgement and suitable public honours for the Portuguese king. These were to be in two categories: those of a personal nature to express the pope's pleasure and appreciation, and those that would demonstrate to the world the honours that the pontiff wished to give Manuel I for all his achievements. The latter he could accomplish with papal Bulls and public Briefs providing concessions; and he could also honour Manuel by the gift of the Golden Rose, one of the oldest, most important favours a pope could bestow.

Although the origin of the honour is lost in obscurity, most authorities attribute its initiation to Pope Leo IX (1049–54), who had undertaken the construction of a large monastery for nuns at Bamberg, in the German province of Franconia which then formed part of the Holy See. In recognition of the installation, the nuns were required to render annually thereafter to the pope in Rome a golden rose which he would use in a ceremony to be held each year on Laetare Sunday. If the token could not be rendered in the form of a completely fashioned rose, the nuns were to provide gold of sufficient weight and quantity to make such a flower.

Another version of the story states that when the pope inherited the monastery of Ste Croix in Alsace among his patrimonial properties, he gave it its liberty and it became associated with the Holy See. To perpetuate the memory of this association, he imposed the annual tribute of a rose made of two ounces of gold, to be brought by hand to him and his successors on the fourth Sunday of Lent when it was to be used in a service celebrated in the basilica of Santa Croce in Gerusalemme in Rome. The token was to symbolize the mysterious union of God with the people of Israel liberated from Babylonian slavery, to which reference is made in the offices of that day. Within the next half century this simple tribute was considered to be worthy of princes, and in 1096 the rose was awarded by Pope Urban II to Fulk IV, Count of Anjou, during the celebration of the Council of Tours.

In 1230 the appearance of the token was changed to provide it with the semblance of a real flower; its petals were tinted in red and it was sprayed with musk, and in the next century balsam was added to the musk. The practice of colouring the petals was later abandoned and instead a ruby was set in the centre of the topmost blossom to render it more precious. When in a particular year no reigning monarch merited the honour, the token was awarded by the pope to some noble personage who was present in the congregation during the ceremony of blessing the Rose. Frequently chosen for this honour was the Prefect of Rome.

Until the reign of Pope Alexander VI (1492–1503), the rose was produced in a relatively small size, similar to the flower found in nature, measuring little more than half the width of a man's palm. In the short reign of Pope Callisto III (1455–8), the token had consisted of ten ounces of gold with a sapphire instead of a ruby at its centre, produced at a cost of approximately 110 *fiorini*. In subsequent periods the cost increased considerably. Eventually the addition of a gem was abandoned and the form of the token returned to its earlier version, which is maintained to the present time.

Over the centuries the most celebrated goldsmiths of Rome were commissioned to produce the Golden Rose. It was presented with greater frequency between the fourteenth and seventeenth centuries than before or since, bestowed particularly on reigning princes who had performed signal service to the Church and to Christendom. In later periods it was most frequently awarded to churches and princesses.[14]

Laetare Sunday, the fourth Sunday of Lent, became known as the Sunday of the Rose, and accordingly on 26 March Pope Leo X celebrated the divine office for the benediction of the Golden Rose in the Apostolic Palace. The token had been executed for him by the noted goldsmith Saba di Cola di Giacomo Saba, who had been named among the papal mace bearers since 1489. He was subsequently paid 805 gold ducats for the token he created, a price which included the cost of materials and the sapphire set in its centre.[15]

The ceremony of presentation took place in the Sistine Chapel with a solemn high mass, and Grassi recorded that the pope arrived with appropriate pomp at the Sala dei Parimenti, the room in which the papal chamberlain and prelates were robed during the performance of their customary preliminary functions. For the occasion the pope selected the cope presented to him by the King of Portugal, the first occasion on which it was used. Because of the great abundance of pearls and precious stones and the elaborate embroidery in gold thread with which it was encrusted, it was so heavy that the perspiring pontiff was barely able to seat himself in the *sedia gestatoria* in preparation to entering the Chapel. For this reason he did not wear the chasuble as he normally would have done.

The Golden Rose, which had already been anointed with balsam and dusted with powdered musk, was borne into the Chapel by the master of ceremonies and deposited upon the altar. As the pope approached, the chamberlain of the Holy See presented him with the artificial flower. After he received the Rose, the papal mitre was placed upon his head; he was joined by the assembled cardinals, they then proceeded together ceremoniously to mount the carriages awaiting without, by means of which they were conducted to the church of Santa Croce in Gerusalemme. There the mass was celebrated, and the pope himself sang on this occasion.

The master of ceremonies, following tradition, then asked the pontiff whether he had made a decision concerning the recipient of the token. Leo responded that although it was the custom to announce the name at the beginning of the ceremony, on this occasion he would wait until it was over. It was at this point that a Genovese functionary named Cicotto insinuated that the token might most appropriately be presented to Emperor Maximilian I, possibly with the unvoiced hope that he might be the one selected to deliver it to Vienna. Grassi took this opportunity to remind the pope that just before his death Pope Julius II had indeed voiced his decision to present the Rose on the next occasion to Maximilian. Pope Leo X was not moved by these recommendations, however, for he had already decided that the recipient was to be the King of Portugal. However, since the Portuguese ambassadors were not present at the blessing ceremony, for reasons not stated, he decided to refrain from making his intentions known at this time.[16]

During the following three weeks, rumours in the city affirmed that the token's recipient unquestionably would be the Emperor. Finally, on 17 April, the Monday after Easter, while the pope was present with all the cardinals in the Sala dei Parimenti, he consulted them as a matter of formality concerning the most meritorious candidate for that year's award. He agreed with those who suggested that it should be presented to the Portuguese king.

He ordered the Rose to be brought to the Sistine Chapel from his apartments, where it had been kept since the blessing ceremony, and had it placed on the altar. There the jewel remained during the cele-

[15] The Golden Rose – a special honour presented by Leo X to Manuel I. Nineteenth-century example with arms of Pope Pius IX. Christian Museum, the Vatican.

bration of the mass. After the mass was over, the pope summoned the cardinals and ambassadors and other representatives of foreign powers to approach his throne. With the papal court thus assembled, the pontiff delivered an eloquent discourse on King Manuel I, enumerating his numerous virtues and recounting the many extraordinary services he had rendered to the Christian faith, for all of which reasons he had reached the decision to recognize him with the award of the Golden Rose. [15]

Throughout this presentation, the papal master of ceremonies stood before the pope holding the token. It was true, the pontiff went on to say, that the material value of the Rose was greatly inferior to the grand achievements of the Portuguese monarch, but that one must not lose sight of the value residing in the symbolic significance attached to it.

Summoning the Portuguese ambassadors to step forward, he presented the token to Cunha in the name of his king. The three ambassadors thereupon kissed the pope's foot and withdrew. Accompanied by the prelates and other dignitaries of the papal court, they were then conducted once more to their lodgings in the Apostolic Palace.[17]

On 29 April Pope Leo X issued a Bull, *Providum universalis ecclesiae*, in which he acceded to the other requests made by Pacheco on behalf of the Portuguese king.[18] At the same time the pope offered Cunha the command of a squadron of papal forces to be sent against the Turks, which in itself constituted a singular distinction. While acknowledging the honour, Cunha declined the commission.

In a formal Brief addressed to King Manuel on 11 May, twenty-five days after the presentation of the Golden Rose, the pontiff elaborated further on the points he had made in his discourse before the College of Cardinals and the assembled ambassadors. Referring to the Golden Rose, he asked the Portuguese sovereign to 'kindly accept this gift as witness of the affectionate sentiments and the singular esteem with which His Holiness professes his regard'. In the same Brief the pope conceded the king's request for the privilege of awarding the papal Order of Christ, known also as the 'Militia of Our Lord Jesus Christ'. Leo directed that Manuel in future could award the decoration to those of his navigators and military commanders who had distinguished themselves in the service of Christendom and whom the king considered to be most worthy of the honour.[19]

In response to Manuel's other requests, on 7 June Leo issued yet another papal Bull, *Dum fidei constantiam*. He accorded the administration of the Order to the Portuguese crown during Manuel's reign. Furthermore, he assigned to Portugal spiritual rights to all of the kingdoms, countries, provinces and islands which the Portuguese navigators and military commanders had acquired or would in future acquire in their conquest of infidels. The Pope made note of the Bulls issued by his predecessors, Pope Nicholas V and Pope Sixtus IV, and extended even to the regions noted in those Bulls the protection he had delegated to Manuel and his successors on the throne of Portugal.[20]

By this time Cunha, with the concurrence of the other Portuguese ambassadors, concluded that their mission had achieved its purpose in the most satisfactory manner, and made preparations for the mission's return to Lisbon. He took with him the Golden Rose and the several Briefs and Bulls, including one in which the pope asked King Manuel to confer upon the sons and close relatives of Cunha and Pacheco some of the new commanderies of the Order of Christ to be instituted with the reassigned revenues from ecclesiastical tithes.

The pope added other gifts for the Portuguese king to be conveyed by Cunha. Among these was a costly illuminated volume, described as being not a Bible but a breviary or perhaps a Book of Hours. Tradition claims that the king subsequently presented the volume to Dom Alvaro da Costa, his Keeper of the Royal Wardrobe, with the stipulation that it was to be entailed to his eldest son. Costa was an intimate of the monarch and had served as his envoy to Rome to deal on various matters with Cardinal Jorge da Costa, to whom he may have been related. It was to Alvaro da Costa that Pope Julius had presented an earlier Golden Rose in 1506 for conveyance to King Manuel.[21]

According to legend, it was at this time that the pope conveyed another gift for Manuel by means of the returning envoys. This was described by Mac Swiney de Mashanaglass as 'a chimneypiece of white marble ornamented with admirable sculptures which were attributed to the magic chisel of Michelangelo'.[22]

During the months following the departure of the mission, the pope continued to issue further concessions to Manuel in Bulls and Briefs. In his Bull of 3 November 1514, *Praecelsae devotionis*, Leo X again noted the Bulls issued by his predecessors Nicholas V and Sixtus IV. He allowed Manuel to retain all 'tenths' and 'thirds' normally paid to the Church in his domains, so long as he continued his holy war in Africa. In consideration of the Portuguese king's devotion to the Church and his expressed desire to maintain the purity of the faith, Pope Leo X extended the advowson (the right of presentation to ecclesiastical benefices) which he had accorded to him and his successors in his earlier Bull of 7 June, to all the conquests that the Portuguese would make in the future, not only in the territories extending beyond the Capes of Bojador and Nam to the Indies, but also upon all territories 'or in any region or place whatsoever, even though perchance unknown to us at present (*quam etiam ubicumque, et in quibuscumque partibus, etiam nostris temporibus forsan ignotis*)'.[23]

By the nature of his wording, the pope implied that the Line of Demarcation (370 leagues west of the Cape Verde islands) agreed at the Treaty of Tordesillas in 1494, related essentially to the Western Hemisphere, and that the whole of the Eastern Hemisphere was therefore part of the Portuguese zone for exploitation. However, only the previous year (1513) Vasco Nuñez de Balboa had 'discovered' the 'South Sea', that is, the Pacific Ocean. Although neither the sea-route into that ocean from the west, nor its extent, would be known until the ships of Fernão de Magalhaes ('Magellan' – a Portuguese navigator then in the service of Spain) completed the first circumnavigation of the globe, by 1522, the possibility already existed of explorations from the 'west' into Far Eastern waters. What would happen when the Portuguese, sailing, as authorized, eastward from the Tordesillas line, clashed with westward Spanish explorations somewhere in oriental seas? This was a matter of deep concern to the Portuguese, already in occupation of key points in the Moluccas, monopolizing the rich spice trade by sea to Europe, and exploring (secretly, for lack of secure title) further east and south. It was not until the Treaty of Saragoza in 1529 that the two maritime powers agreed that the Tordesillas line should be projected north to south right round the globe. In the meanwhile, the Bull of 3 November 1514 was received with particular relief and appreciation by King Manuel I.[24]

Although these concessions were considered by many outside Italy to exceed the pontiff's powers, this was not the first occasion on which the papal court had pretended to the right of disposing of states newly discovered or conquered from infidels. Leo had recent precedents in bulls issued by Pope Alexander VI claimed to be based on the exaltation of the Church and propagation of the Christian faith.

In addition to the several Briefs and papal Bulls, Leo X continued to seek out honours and awards to shower upon the Portuguese monarch, a process that continued long after it had seemed that the reciprocal actions of giving and receiving had achieved a balance. The pope recalled that although he had presented a Golden Rose to Manuel, the latter had already received one in 1506 from Pope Julius II, so that his award of the same token could not be considered in itself a unique distinction. The only papal honour that had never been conferred upon a Portuguese monarch was the 'Papal Sword and Ducal Cap'.

This honour, known also as the *Gladius et Pileus* or the 'Stocco e Berettone Ducale', was presented on rare occasions to a king, prince, head of state, or distinguished warrior in recognition of a brilliant achievement in armed combat or diplomatic negotiation. It was the highest distinction bestowed by the Holy See.

The practice of awarding 'the sword of honour' had its beginnings in at least the ninth century. The blessing of the sword traditionally took place in a special ceremony on the morning of Christmas Day. The sword or rapier was similar to those worn by wealthy knights in the Middle Ages, a two-handed weapon having a gold pommel encrusted with gems, and a polished steel blade bearing an inscription. The phrase normally used for the inscription was taken from the Old Testament in the Second Book of Maccabees, which belongs to the Apocrypha. The phrase read *Accipe sanctum gladium munus a Deo, in quo deijcies adversarios populi mei Israel.* The scabbard was generally covered with red velvet having gold mountings chiselled with reliefs and mounted with gems.

From the fourteenth century the sword was accompanied by a baldrick or belt and a ducal cap, the latter called in Latin a *pileus* or *capellus* and in Italian a *berettone.* The baldrick was of a richness consistent with that of the sword and scabbard. The form and colour of the ducal cap changed frequently over the centuries. From time to time it was either black or violet, but generally it was made of red velvet, surmounted with the image of a dove embroidered in pearls or in silver filigree. The cap, encompassed by a golden crown, ended in two flaps, the tips of which were trimmed with ermine, and which fell upon the shoulders of the wearer like those of an episcopal mitre. The gift was a costly one, for the sword was always produced by one of the foremost goldsmiths employed at the papal court. [16]

The custom of awarding the sword was said to replace an earlier practice of bestowing the golden and silver keys containing filings from the chains in which St Peter had been imprisoned. Other sources claim that the award of the Papal Sword and Ducal Cap replaced a yet earlier custom of sending the standard of St Peter with the papal keys to a prince or sovereign who was about to take up arms against an enemy of the Church. Among the earliest recorded instances of the award of the Papal Sword and Ducal Cap are the sword and cap presented by Pope Alexander III in 1177 to the Doge of Venice, Sebastiano Ziani, and a similar presentation made in 1202 by the legate of Pope Innocent III to William the Lyon, King of Scotland.[25]

An explanation of the symbolism of the Papal Sword and Ducal Cap was provided by the seventeenth-century historian, Theophilus Raynauldus. The sword, he stated, was the most perfect symbol of supreme command and of sovereign power, for it was used to compensate the good and to correct the bad. Consequently it was considered to be the most appropriate representation for Christ Himself, he went on, and the Lord had conferred omnipotence on it and for this reason it was called the *Gladium Domini.* In this manner it became the symbol of divinity and qualified as the *cultores gladii.*

The scabbard, Raynauldus wrote, recalled the human nature in which the Divine Word was clothed; the perfections which could ornament human nature were represented in the precious stones mounted on the scabbard. The sword inside the scabbard could thus be considered to be the image of Christ appearing in human form. The baldrick or belt also possessed mystical meaning, according to Raynauldus, representing the hypostatic union between the human

[16] *Gladius et pileus*, the papal sword, ducal cap, scabbard and balderick – further gifts of honour to Manuel I. Nineteenth-century examples. Christian Museum, the Vatican.

nature of Christ and His Divinity.

The Ducal Cap featured the symbol of the Holy Spirit represented in the form of a dove, in order to remind the recipient that he must not make arbitrary use of the gifts, but instead must apply them in conformity with the precepts of reason and following the desires of the pontiff awarding them.[26]

The blessing of the Papal Sword and Ducal Cap was accomplished by the pope himself, and always on Christmas Day immediately before the beginning of the divine office. The only exception was when the illness of the pope prevented it, and it was then blessed on the following morning before the celebration of mass. The sword and cap thus blessed were presented during the following year to that head of state within the realm of the Church considered to have most deserved them.[27]

Having determined to honour King Manuel I with this special award, the pope made appropriate preparations. The sword prepared and blessed by the pontiff at Christmas 1514 was extremely rich in decoration. It had been made during the autumn months by 'Mayestro Santus Cole', a goldsmith in the pope's employ, who on 28 November received 100 gold ducats in payment for his labour and the precious metals employed. On 18 December he received a further payment of 303 gold ducats for the cost of other materials he had used.[28]

The presentation was made in the Sistine Chapel during the celebration of mass on the feast day of St John. The ceremony began with the master of ceremonies, Grassi, formally reminding the pope that the moment had come to name the recipient of the Papal Sword and Ducal Cap. The pope ordered the items to be brought into the Chapel and placed upon the altar. He then directed the Portuguese ambassador in residence, João de Faria, to be brought into his presence. Leo did not make a discourse upon this occasion but merely instructed Faria to take the sword and cap to his sovereign so that he could use them in his war against the infidels.

Faria, holding the sword and cap in his hands, kissed the pope's foot and retired. After all the cardinals had taken leave of the pontiff, Grassi and the Master of the Apostolic Palace, who was at the same time Commander of the Holy Spirit, accompanied Faria, one on each side, followed by the chamberlains and equerries of St Peter, although the other prelates remained behind. The ambassador was conducted in this manner through the city to his palace. Each of the masters of ceremonies was presented with gratuities of twenty-five ducats by Faria on behalf of his king.[29]

In the Brief accompanying the award of the Papal Sword and Ducal Cap, the pope did not fail to compliment the role played by Faria in winning approval of the requests made to the pontiff by the Portuguese king. He noted that it had been Faria who had been responsible for obtaining the Bull *Dum fidei constantiam*, which established Manuel's ultimate authority in the East, and with 'having completed his long mission with extreme prudence and tact.'[30]

During the Portuguese mission, João de Faria had been greatly overshadowed by the presence of Cunha and Pacheco. He was described by Resende as 'a magistrate having great merit well versed in civil and canonical jurisprudence who, not permitting himself to be seduced by the utopias which exist only in books and which constitute in general the failings of wise men, was considered to have been endowed with one of the finest intellects in Portugal.'[31]

Meanwhile the pope still remained uncertain whether he had fully acknowledged the Portuguese king's contributions. Being reminded that Manuel had the reputation in his own country of being a connoisseur and protector of the arts, Leo realized that no particular consideration of this royal interest had been represented by any of the papal gifts. A solution was ultimately found. On 10 January, 1515, Cardinal Giulio de' Medici sent Manuel a volume of music. In the accompanying letter he noted that it was sent with the intention that it would bring him surcease from the heavy burdens of state through the joys of song. In a later communication to the Cardinal, Manuel acknowledged the gift and stated that it was much appreciated.[32]

In Lisbon once more, Cunha and Pacheco and the other members of the returned mission were received by the king on Trinity Sunday, 3 June. Their success in Rome was celebrated with a great procession that moved solemnly from the church of Nossa Señhora da Conçeico Velha. It was led by the king himself and attended by all the prelates of the church, the nobility of the court and the lower clergy, followed by the populace of Lisbon.

The papal Bull was displayed by the Bishop of Safi and then the document was placed on exhibition upon the principal altar of the church. Dom Diogo Ortiz, the Bishop of Viseu, offered up prayers for the success of the king's crusade against the Moors. On the same day were confirmed the Bishop of Funchal and the offices given to the Bishop of Lamego and the Bishop of Guarda in a mass celebrated by the Bishop of Viseu.[33]

On 16 June, the feast day of the Body of Christ, King Manuel formally received the Golden Rose and the Papal Sword and Ducal Hat. Tristão da Cunha was absent from the ceremonies due to illness, but he was represented by his oldest son Nuño. Officiating at the ceremonies were five of the highest dignitaries of the church in Portugal – the bishops of Viseu, Funchal, Safi, Lamego and Guarda – as well as the Count-Prior Mordomo-Mor, the Count of Vila Nova and of Barão, Dom Pedro de Castro and Dom Fernando de Castro, Dom Nuño Manuel, and numerous other noblemen, accompanied by heralds-at-arms, footmen, mace-bearers and the court musicians. Following the celebration of mass, the king emerged from behind a curtain and waited on the top step of the main chapel. There, with his son beside him and surrounded by the nobility, King Manuel received Nuño da Cunha, who presented him with the Golden Rose and the Bull relating to it. Taking the Rose, the king handed it to the Bishop of Lamego. Then João de Faria came forward to present the Papal Sword and Ducal Cap, holding the sword upright with the Cap placed upon its point in the traditional manner of presentation, together with the papal Bull of award. Faria then pronounced the words that he had been told by the pope to say concerning the sword's significance and the use to be made of it to achieve victories for the faith.

Costa, the king's chamberlain, thereupon came forward to take the Cap from the sword's point and placed it upon a tray. Artur de Brito, son of the king's head chamberlain, then took the Sword from Faria's hand and the king returned to his position behind the curtain.

The Golden Rose was carried to the altar by the Bishop of Lamego and the sword and cap were brought to the king and placed beside him. The ceremony ended with the king's return to his palace with the sword carried ceremonially before him, while the other participants followed.[34]

CHAPTER FOUR
The Elephant-Diplomat

*That a mind, which, like that of the pontiff, could discrim-
inate all the excellences of literature and of art; as we are
told was the fact, also stoop to derive its pleasures from the
lowest species of buffoonery, is a singular circumstance, but
may serve to mark the diversity and range of intellect
which distinguished not only Leo X but also other
individuals of this extraordinary family...*

William Roscoe : *The Life and Pontificate of Leo X* (1805)

IMMEDIATELY UPON THE ELEPHANT'S ARRIVAL IN ROME, IT BECAME the particular pet of the pope and the papal court, and of the people of Rome as well. The pontiff often visited the elephant in its enclosure, intrigued by the high degree of intelligence demonstrated by the young beast, and its playful antics never ceased to delight him. It must also have amused those bystanders who observed the ungainly, corpulent, near-sighted pontiff clumsily playing with the equally rotund pachyderm. The beast would genuflect when the pope appeared, open its mouth and trumpet loudly, it was reported, and would appear to cry like a woman and shed tears.

Obeying its mahout, it would walk a short distance to fill its trunk with water which it then released like a cannon to shower upon everyone present. It was said to understand both the Portuguese and Indian languages. Wishing to share his new pleasure with everyone, the pontiff ordered that the Roman populace was to be permitted to visit the elephant at its enclosure every Sunday.

Soon after the mission's arrival, Sanuto had noted in his diary, 'The Pope kept his elephant in the Belvedere courtyard where he was accustomed to keep the chickens [*gallinarium*].' The original plan to house the large beast in a separate shelter as part of the menagerie on the slope of the Belvedere proved to be impractical, however. The area was too remote to enable the public to visit it conveniently. Of even greater concern, the elephant experienced considerable difficulty traversing its uneven sloping terrain. Finally, the pontiff wished to have Hanno close by, where he could visit it more frequently.

Accordingly, a new site had been selected, at the end of the Borgo Sant' Angelo where it adjoined the actual portico of the piazza of St Peter, just inside the ancient wall called the Corridore that connected the Apostolic Palace with Castel Sant' Angelo. The pope ordered a small building to be erected in that location to protect the elephant from the elements, enclosed on three sides and constructed up against the wall of the Corridore and surrounded by a spacious yard. [17]

An entry in the *Diversorum Cameralium* of 1522 noted 'the [elephant's] new house measured thirteen paces by fourteen [approximately eleven metres by twelve]' and that the location was subsequently converted into a habitation for people. Later, in words

[17] Detail from a late sixteenth-century map by Leonardo Bufalini, clearly showing where the elephant was housed between the piazza of St Peter and the Corridore. From *Roma, Edita per Magrm. Leonardum Die XXVI Mens. Mai A.D. MDLI.*

attributed to the elephant in its last will and testament, the site was described as being situated in such a manner that the lions [menagerie] were to the east of it, and 'the house of the Carmeniccaria', which has not been identified, was to the north. Because of the elephant's presence, that section of Borgo Sant' Angelo later became known as the 'Borgo dell' Elefante'.[1]

The delighted Romans immediately devised a name for the papal pet, calling it 'Annone'. Historians have generally assumed that originally the beast had been named 'Hanno' and that the name had been italianized to 'Annone.' The reverse is at least as likely: when the Roman spectators first saw the great beast during the procession of the Portuguese mission into Rome, they probably inquired from its Moorish mahout or trainer what it was called; the attendant would presumably have replied that it was an '*aana*', the word for 'elephant' in his native Malayalam language, spoken in the Kerala State. According to zoologists, elephants do not respond to 'pet' names as do domestic pets; they are given names only to distinguish one from another in a herd, which tends to support the name's derivation from '*aana*'. The beast's considerable size may have induced the Roman populace to add the augmentative suffix and to devise the name 'Annone.'[2]

The earliest contemporary mention of the elephant's given name occurred in the published eyewitness account of the mission's arrival by the distinguished Latin poet in the pope's service, Giovanni Piero Valeriano. In the introduction to the second book of his *Hieroglyphica*, he wrote: 'While the pope watched from a window of the Vatican palace, the elephant, to which the name "Anno" had been given, genuflected three times…' ['*Quam Pontifex e fenestra (Palatii Vaticani) spectaret, Elephantus, Anno nomine accessit, ac ter genibus flexis…*']³

The elephant's name has been rendered into English as 'Hanno', derived from the sound of the Italian word. This has led to conjecture as to whether the name derived from Hanno, a common name among the Carthaginians. Possibilities included Hanno, the Carthaginian navigator who first reported the presence of elephants on the west coast of Africa in the fifth or sixth century, Hanno the Great [Hannibal], the third-century Carthaginian warrior and politician, or possibly Hanno, the animal lover and lion tamer mentioned by Pliny the Elder. All such attributions appear to be without basis, and 'Hanno' to be no more than an anglicization of the elephant's true Italian name, 'Annone'. At any rate, as 'Hanno' the little elephant has been memorialized in English and other languages.

The persistent description of Hanno as a 'white' elephant (by contemporary writers who had observed the beast, as well as by later historians of the papacy including Ludwig von Pastor), indicates that it was at least of a sufficiently light colour, for the writers had no means of comparison. The distinction was probably first made by members of the Portuguese mission of obedience, who would have been aware of this unusual characteristic in comparison with other elephants in the Portuguese king's menagerie.

White elephants generally differ from others by a lighter colouring, the presence of ginger-coloured hair, and often of patches of white skin. The degree of albinism varies from one animal to another, and a true albino is extremely rare. In India and Ceylon all beasts that were categorized as 'white elephants' received special treatment. Oriental rulers frequently provided such pachyderms with their own retinue of servants, and throughout their lives these animals were maintained in a manner befitting their special status.

Whether Hanno was the elephant presented as a gift to King Manuel by the King of Cochin, or whether it was the one purchased in the same year by Albuquerque for a substantial price, it is certain that it was particularly prized as a white elephant, a fact confirmed by contemporary artistic representations. Based on statements of contemporary writers, Hanno was four years of age when it came to Rome, indicating that it was born in 1510. At the time of its arrival in Rome, it measured between five and six *palms* [approximately 50 inches] at the shoulder, having grown a full *palm* since its departure from Lisbon.

Elephants of that age consume a considerable amount of fodder, from 75 to 100 pounds each day. They ingest from 35 to 50 gallons of water daily. In its native habitat an elephant's diet consists of coconuts, mangoes, plantain stems, maize and sugar cane. In captivity its natural diet is supplemented with root vegetables and grain such as bran and oats when available. It is accustomed to feed at frequent intervals during at least sixteen hours daily, and it sleeps lightly, usually half the sleeping time of humans. The elephant is accustomed to dozing for short spells while standing, and even then its jaws continue working. In their efforts to cope with the massive amounts of vegetation ingested, the digestive juices create a constant dull rumbling sound.

A domesticated elephant is remarkably docile and gentle and demonstrates a considerable aptitude for obedience. It has an innate instinct for its own safety, and a fair ability to think. Its intelligence potential is estimated to be equivalent to that of a horse. The elephant prefers solitude and has a great dislike of noise and confusion. It lives in friendly harmony with other beasts and there is little if any basis for the contention that it fears dogs, horses and rhinoceroses. The training of elephants is a highly specialized skill which was perfected in India long ago. An elephant prefers to have a single master and consequently one mahout or trainer is assigned to each beast being trained, and he remains with the animal permanently. The mahout has the privilege of naming the elephant for purposes of identification.[4]

There is little resemblance between the Cortile del Belvedere of the time of Leo X and its appearance today. The corridor or wing from the Apostolic Palace to the palace of the Belvedere had already been completed by Bramante, except for the topmost loggia on the right side of the courtyard towards the city. The death of Julius II, followed shortly by that of Bramante, interrupted the construction of the corridor or wing at the left towards the wooded area. Furthermore, the urgency imposed by the late pope on Bramante to complete the work as quickly as possible led to faulty construction, with the consequence that part of the completed work crumbled. It was not until the middle of the sixteenth century that the left portion was completed. Meanwhile the lower portion of the courtyard had been levelled for staging bullfights and other events, and it was to this segment of the courtyard that the elephant was occasionally brought for viewing.[5]

The menagerie assembled by Leo X was no makeshift housing of birds and beasts haphazardly collected. It was in fact one of the most advanced and professional installations in Europe at that time. Nor was it the first such collection at the Vatican. The formation and maintenance of menageries had been, from the earliest civilizations, the traditional avocation of princes. The great collections assembled by Roman emperors were reflected in those of medieval European monarchs; as for the popes, after their return from Avignon, where they kept a number of lions, they restored the menagerie habit to Rome. Notable among the unusual wildlife featured at the Vatican were two ostriches brought to Pope Benedict XII by a Florentine named Varino in February 1337 'from the kingdom of King Robert', probably Sicily. He received ten florins as his reward for the unusual gift.

At first, after the papal court's return from Avignon to the Vatican hill, the presence only of house pets and birds is recorded. In 1418 Pope Martin V paid a gold florin to two servants who accompanied him on a journey with the assignment of carrying the papal parrot in a cage. In 1462 Pope Pius II paid five ducats to 'the custodian of the parrot' Maestro Gachetto, and later in the same year he paid a certain Gabazzo for cloth with which the cage of the pope's parrakeet was to be covered. Later still, in December, a Florentine craftsman named Domenico received three and a half *écus* for materials required to repair a bird cage at St Peter's.

Pope Pius II also kept stags. Near the end of the same century Pope Sixtus IV maintained a live eagle and a parrakeet at the Vatican at a cost of two *bioques* a day for the purchase of meat with which to feed them. During his reign Pope Alexander VI kept bulls and restored the practice of public bullfighting in the Belvedere. Although birds and beasts were maintained at the Vatican for the purpose of observation as well as diversion, it was not until the early sixteenth century, in the reign of Pope Leo X, that the true menagerie or *seraglio* evolved in Rome. By then it had become a fairly common adjunct to royal courts. 'It belongs to the position of the great,' pronounced the Perugian chronicler Francesco Matarrazzo, 'to keep horses, dogs, mules, falcons, and other birds, court-jesters, singers and foreign animals.' Among those who already had menageries were King Henry I of England and Emperor Frederick II.[6]

Pope Leo X was accustomed to having exotic birds and beasts about him, for the Medici family menagerie in Florence was one of the best known in Europe. The relatively easy means of transport from the Mediterranean's southern and eastern ports and the mildness of the Tuscan climate made it feasible to purchase unusual specimens, to which were added countless others brought as gifts from heads of state and other dignitaries who came to Florence.

The pope's great-grandfather, Cosimo the Elder, kept lions in a lion house at the Palazzo Vecchio, and as already noted, featured them in a great festival held in honour of the visit of Pope Paul II and Duke Galeazzo Sforza. The pope's father, Lorenzo the Magnificent, had an even greater preoccupation with wild animals, and from time to time imported new specimens from Alexandria. Lorenzo used trained cheetahs for hunting, and kept bears, tigers and lions in cages, and he frequently engaged them in programmed contests with bulls, horses, monkeys and mastiffs.[7]

Soon after Leo X was installed at the Vatican, he brought together there a small menagerie of his own, particularly featuring lions, and including leopards, monkeys, civit cats and bears. Some beasts were maintained in cages built for them and kept in restraining structures adjacent to the papal henyard [*gallineria*] in a section of the spacious Cortile del Belvedere. The interest of Pope Leo X in his menagerie was reflected in his household accounts. On 2 October 1513 he paid six grand gold ducats to 'the man who brought the lions from Florence to Rome'. On 26 October payment was made to Francesco Ferrara, 'guardian of the leopard of His Holiness', six gold ducats for the beast's maintenance and four more as a month's salary for the keeper. On 29 June of the following year he paid eighteen gold ducats 'to the Hungarians for the [purchase of] the bears'.[8]

In addition to these beasts, an area of the pope's menagerie situated on the plantation along the slope of Vatican hill adjacent to the Cortile del Belvedere contained spotted leopards, panthers, apes and parrots he had received as state gifts, as well as several lions sent as gifts reflecting his pontificial name. A contemporary account mentioned 'a multitude of parrots, of diverse colouring... a quantity of monkeys, of apes, of civets, and of other bizarre animals...'[9]

Little information has survived about papal menageries in general, and the subject has been largely ignored by historians of the Vatican palaces. Ironically, the specimen which received the most notice other than Hanno was the smallest in the compound – Pope Leo's chameleon. It was mentioned by the artist Giorgio Vasari and noted also in a volume owned by Fabrizio Delfini de Nobilibus, the humanist jurisconsult of Acquasparta. In his copy of the work *De situ orbis terrarum* by the third-century Latin writer, Gaius Julius Solinus, Delfini had added a handwritten note opposite a reference to a chameleon, 'I remember having heard from a Florentine man that Pope Leo X had for his delight a chameleon.' The Florentine from whom Delfini obtained his information is not identified. In this period of renewed interest in the natural sciences, the chameleon was rare and a curiosity which had not yet been fully studied. The pope's exotic novelty was depicted by Giovanni da Udine in a frieze in the Sala dei Chiaroscuri in the Apostolic Palace, of which regrettably only a small fragment has survived.[10] [18]

With the arrival of the Portuguese mission, more space, new cages, additional food supplies and bedding materials had to be provided for the specimens brought from Portugal, and particularly for the elephant. The pope assigned the responsibility for the care of the great beast to one of his intimates, his privy chamberlain Giovanni Battista Branconio dell'Aquila. Whereas the Moorish mahout and Saracen attendant were responsible for the day-to-day maintenance of the elephant, Branconio was charged with overall supervision, the provision of shelter, the purchase of fodder and other needs. In his comedy *La Cortegiana*, Pietro Aretino took the liberty of referring to Branconio as 'the pedagogue of the elephant' to the amusement of the court, amusement not shared by the prelate so labelled.[11]

Of the countless appointments made by Pope Leo X, that of Branconio was one of the most curious. Scion of an ancient but now

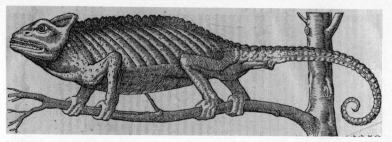

[18] Sixteenth-century drawing of the chameleon. From *Historiae animalum* by Conrad Gesner 1555-1557.

penurious noble family of Aquila in the Abruzzi region, Branconio had been well educated before he made his way to Rome to learn the arts of the goldsmith and gemologist from a master in that city. He subsequently joined the service of Galeotto della Rovere, Cardinal of San Pietro in Vincola, who was related to Pope Julius II. The death of Julius and the convening of a conclave to select a successor provided Branconio with the opportunity to traffic in votes for the new pontiff. For his support he had been promised many benefits from the assembled cardinals, including Giovanni de' Medici. When the latter was elected, he selected Branconio as one of his domestic prelates and then appointed him to the powerful position of privy chamberlain with the title 'Member of the College of Apostolic Protonotaries' (*Protonotario Apostolico partecipante*).

The pope conceded to Branconio and his natural heirs the old castle of Collebrincioni and named him abbot of the monastery of San Silvestro in Aquila. In addition to other favours, he also assigned him the abbacies of Bominaco and of San Clemente in Pescara which yielded lucrative rents. Later Branconio was sent as ambassador to France, and there were plans to appoint him legate to Avignon when Leo's own death intervened. Branconio's important position in the Vatican hierarchy, his increasing wealth derived from papal favours, and his skills with gold and gems, established him as an important personage at court. Consequently he developed associations and friendships with many princes of the church and artists working in the palace. He became an intimate friend of the artist Raphael Sanzio, who designed the palace that Branconio built opposite the basilica of St Peter. His responsibility for Hanno was not meant as a chore, as Aretino implied, but evidence of the pope's trust and reliance.[12]

In addition to the Moorish mahout and the Saracen, a further custodian was assigned to the care of the beast, probably for the maintenance of its habitat. He was named Francesco Parisiano, and the position was considered to be a most honourable one because of the pope's personal interest in the beast. Parisiano was Portuguese and originally named Francisco. He was a monk of the Archifraternità del Santissimo Corpo di Christo, an order based in the church of San Giacomo Apostolo in the Borgo outside the Vatican. He died soon after the elephant's arrival, for the records of the order noted that, following the establishment of the Archiconfraternità in 1509, among the first of its members to die was 'Francesco Parisiano *Governatore* [custodian] of the Elephant of Our Holy Father Pope Leo'.[13] Fra Francesco is identified with greater certainty near the end of the rolls of the papal court for the year 1514 in a listing of the elephant's custodians, which read:

> For the Elephant, as reported officially by the Most Excellent
> Baron [Branconio]:
>> Julius al-Farab
>> Domenico, from Lorraine, 6 December 1514
>> Francesco, from Portugal
>> Pietro, a Spaniard

[*Pro Elephante, referente ex.mo [?] Barone / Iulius Alpharabius / Dominicus, lorenus 6 decembris 1514 / Franciscus, portugallensis / Petrus, hyspanus*].[14]

The first of the names, 'Iulius Alpharabius', is interesting. It was noted by observers of the Portuguese mission's arrival that during the procession the elephant was attended by two men: a black man or Moor, and a Saracen. The appearance of the name 'Alpharabius' confirms that the Saracen remained with the beast in Rome after the mission had returned to Lisbon. The name as it appears on the rolls is the latinized form of Julius or Giulio al-Farab, a Moslem. The cognomen means 'the man from Farab', which was a region in Turkestan inhabited by Saracens.[15]

The custodian named 'Dominicus' is identified as a native of Lorraine, while 'Petrus' was a Spaniard. Also listed in the rolls during the same period under the *Scutiferi* or honorary 'shield-bearers' was *D. Alfonsus superstans Elefanti*, whose armorial bearings depicted a man mounted upon an elephant and attended by a servant, suggesting that he too was one of Hanno's keepers. The same rolls identified, among other employees of the palace, Petrus Scarella *gallienensis* and *D. Albertus gallinarius*, presumed to have been the keepers of the papal henyard which was adjacent to the menagerie. The custodian of the Cortile del Belvedere was *D. Antonius de Rubeis*.[16]

Because it seemed as if the people of Rome were unable to see enough of their pet, the pope arranged to have it paraded through the city on occasion or brought to one of the piazzas. There the beloved beast could perform for the public and be admired as it danced merrily to the pipes, shed tears, playfully sprayed the observers with water from the fountains and bowed and kneeled and performed various tricks in response to commands of its mahout.

News of the pope's elephant and its talented performances soon travelled beyond the walls of the Eternal City to other Italian capitals, particularly Florence. Shortly after his election, the pontiff had appointed Balthassare Turini da Pescia to serve as Papal Datary or secretary under his cousin Cardinal Giulio de' Medici. His primary function was to keep Lorenzo de' Medici, the pope's nephew in Florence, informed of all events that transpired at the papal court. Turini reported not only public transactions but anything that might relate to the private concerns of the Medici family. His letters from Rome spanned only a brief period, from March to September 1514, but provided an intimate view of the court and its personalities. Four of his letters related to Hanno.

In June 1514, scarcely three months after the Portuguese mission's arrival in Rome, Lorenzo de' Medici wrote to his uncle the pope requesting a loan of Hanno for festivities being planned in Florence to celebrate the annual feast of the nativity of St John the Baptist, the traditional 'Triumph of Camillus'. The presence of the performing elephant would make the occasion even more splendid and significant, Lorenzo informed his uncle. Turini responded to Lorenzo on the pope's behalf with graciousness and warmth, but in the negative. The elephant's feet were still extremely sore as a consequence of its long overland journey to Rome, and they would be injured further by having to walk on paving. If only Lorenzo had made his request earlier, the pope regretted! It was now too late to make suitable arrangements to get the elephant to Florence in time for the event; with such short notice it was impossible to make the preparations required to ensure Hanno's well-being on a long journey 'because of his great size and weight, and because of the unfamiliar route from Rome to Florence, and particularly because of its weak feet, which are offended by the stones' of the paved highways. The journey would require at least a month, the pope estimated, yet the feast day was only fifteen days away. As Lorenzo would understand, the pontiff as a matter of 'parental' concern could not permit the beast to be again exposed so soon to the perils of extended travel such as it had recently suffered.

None the less, Leo assured his nephew, he was most anxious to please him, and had even considered whether it might be practical to construct some form of footgear for the beast, as he had been told were made for dogs, or whether it might be feasible to ship the elephant by sea or by some other means. Should the elephant become ill, however, or have to be left *en route*, the pope warned Lorenzo that such a prospect would displease him immeasurably, and that he felt certain that his nephew would find the prospect unpleasant. The pope went on to claim jokingly that Lorenzo would have to pay a huge tax on the elephant at the city gates of Florence. However, in place of Hanno, the keeper of Castel Sant' Angelo was sending two wolves.[17]

In a letter dated two days later, Turini informed Lorenzo on the pope's behalf that he had looked into the matter further. He was informed that Hanno could walk only ten or twelve miles a day, and needed to rest two or three days each time after such an exertion, hence it would require more than a month for the elephant to reach Florence. The pope was willing, however, to send the elephant to Florence in some other year.[18]

The expressed concerns of Leo X for Hanno were sincere, for he prized the great beast above all his other diversions, and he was unwilling to tolerate its absence for the period required. Furthermore, it is likely that by this time he was already plotting to utilize the young elephant in one of the burlesque spectacles featured at the Vatican for his delight. Little more than a week later, the pope's brother, Giuliano de' Medici, wrote requesting the pontiff to send to Florence the two trained leopards and the lion he had received from King Manuel I. The pope agreed and the animals were dispatched that very day, together with the beasts's Persian keeper.[19]

While praise was being heaped upon the pleasure-loving pontiff and his elephant in Rome by the court poets, an occasional cold wind of criticism blew into the Eternal City from the north. The German humanist Ulrich von Hutten, who, after serving in the imperial army, had just been crowned court poet by Emperor Maximilian, took the pope's preoccupations and pleasures severely to task. A letter published by von Hutten, supposedly written to him by Wilhelm Lamp, a Master of Arts in Rome, reported that at the papal court there was nothing new to be seen except 'an animal as large as four horses and having a trunk as tall as a man, and that the pope treasured the beast above all things'.[20]

A new era in arts and letters was dawning in Rome with the reign of Pope Leo X. Humanists achieved greater influence in his time, and rhetoric was idolized at the court to such a degree that it led to a new form of entertainment, featuring disputations and literary contests. Himself an extremely well-educated man, the pontiff surrounded himself with such notable writers as Baldassare Castiglione, Pietro Aretino, Filippo Beroaldo, the elegiac poet Marcantonio Flaminio, Bernardo Accolti, Palladio Blosio, the Sicilian poet Gian Vitalis, the illustrious and wealthy poet and antiquarian Angelo Colocci, the canon Camillo Portio, among many others, in addition to his erudite secretaries Pietro Bembo and Jacopo Sadoleto and his librarian Tommaso Inghirami called 'Fedra' or 'Fedro'.

The pope particularly loved music and his household accounts record numerous payments for the purchase of instruments and the service of musicians. He enjoyed listening for hours to performances on stringed instruments, and in the evenings he played on instruments he kept on the walls of his bedroom. He used his gardens as settings for banquets and concerts, and he set aside a circle within the shadow of the woods for a secular court to which ladies were admitted and in which poets recited their compositions. Next to music the pope loved the art of improvisation and he often participated personally in these poetic exercises. He frequently assigned themes for such contests scheduled on special occasions, and served as judge of subject, language and metre.[21]

In addition to his affinity for the arts, the pope demonstrated a great love of buffoonery. Historians have claimed that this pleasure in vulgarity, which was not prevalent in royal courts of the period, derived from Florentine taste and custom. Others have suggested that the vulgarity developed and was emphasized because the absence of ladies at the papal court resulted in greater licence and grosser expression. There were also those who viewed these proclivities as evidence of the pontiff's efforts to combat spells of melancholy, which beset him with increasing frequency in the face of the endless problems of his holy office. There is no doubt that he lavished rich rewards and benefices on those who could amuse him. He sought to enjoy life without effort or risk and he abhorred boredom.[22]

One of the pope's favourite haunts was Castel Sant'Angelo, and like his predecessor, he frequently lodged there, often using the fortress for the staging of banquets and other festivities. Cardinal Cibo, his official master of special events, lived in the Castel as did the castle keeper and assistant keeper. The cardinal frequently arranged elaborate theatrical performances in the fortress, featuring a staff of musicians on a curtained stage designed by Raphael. Great dinners followed the performances.

On occasion the moat surrounding the castle was drained and demonstrations of physical skill were held therein, as well as such sporting events as the *pallio*, races of the *bufale*, tournaments with canes, and bull fights with men acting the part of bulls. In one such contest three men were killed and four others wounded. The Castel served also as the papal prison, and from time to time the heads of executed prisoners were prominently diplayed on spikes along the castle bridge in accordance with ancient custom.[23]

The curious contrasts in the pope's personality were reflected in the papal court. Mixed in with the great literary figures were such versifiers as the already noted Bernardo Accolti, the self-styled 'l'unico Aretino'; the burlesque Abbot of Gaeta, Giacomo Baraballo; Fra Mariano Fetti; Giovanni Gazoldo; the stammering Cinotto; Girolamo Brittonio; and Camillo Querno, all of whose only claim to fame was their performance as buffoons. Vain and parasitic poetasters, petitioners, jesters and buffoons were employed in occupations ranging from carvers and courtiers to domestic prelates. By means of the banter and parody which diverted the pope they sought to gain access to his purse. Some of them had been the pope's servants and familiars in Florence and had come to Rome following his election.

The best known and most notorious was Fra Mariano of the Fetti family of Florence, who had been the barber of the pontiff's father and had later joined the Dominican order and become a follower of Savonarola. His total lack of mannerliness was matched only by his enormous appetite. His major distinction was his ability to consume twenty chickens or forty eggs at a single meal, as well as pies prepared especially for him containing ravens cooked complete with feathers and beaks. Incredibly, Pope Leo X appointed the uncouth Fra Mariano keeper of the papal seals to succeed Bramante after the latter's death.[24]

The pope delighted particularly in the role of the buffoons, and favoured especially Querno and Baraballo. Corpulent and with long flowing hair, Querno's constant hunger and thirst made him the butt of any assemblage. The most famous of the buffoons, however, was undoubtedly Giacomo Baraballo, Abbot of Gaeta. His verses were tinged with madness, and he was so easily impressed with praise given him in mockery that he claimed the right to be crowned arch-poet on Capitoline hill as the re-born Petrarch.

Baraballo had already been well-known at the Medici court in Florence before the pope had come to Rome. Early in his career he had been imprisoned by Pope Alexander VI in Castel Sant' Angelo together with the protonotary de Spiritibus and the abbot of Alviano on charges of complicity in the falsification of certain papal bulls and briefs. However, it was frequently the case in that period that imprisonment was for causes other than those noted in the formal charges, so that the true nature of Baraballo's misdemeanour cannot be ascertained. Fortunately for the abbot, during the period of the *sede vacante* between the death of Pope Alexander VI and the election of Pope Julius II, possession of Castel Sant' Angelo was taken in the name of the College of Cardinals by the Cardinals Santa Croce, Cesarini, and de' Medici, later Pope Leo X. The cardinals opened the prison and released the prisoners. The abbots of Gaeta and Alviano were required to pay heavy fines, however, for which funds were provided by Bishop Nolano and Bishop Mariano Ususmaris. There was no further mention of the incident.[25]

Baraballo came to public notice again after the triumphal re-entry of the Medici family into Florence when he took part in the festivities celebrating the Medici return to power. Since young Cardinal de' Medici was known to patronize the poets of his time, Baraballo claimed to be one and wrote extravagant verses honouring the cardinal. He accepted the ironic and exaggerated praises others showered upon him, which led him to believe that he was in fact the peer of Petrarch, or perhaps even greater. Finally, amidst the noise and confusion of the Medici court, and the derisive laughter of the courtiers, Baraballo was mockingly proclaimed arch-poet and took an active role in festivities in Florence prior to his arrival in Rome.

Fra Mariano had been summoned from Rome to Florence to participate in the poetic frolics, but then the unexpected death of Pope Julius II and the convening of the conclave to elect a successor demanded Cardinal de' Medici's immediate presence in Rome. The frolics none the less took place in his absence. After the event Fra Mariano wrote to the Marquis of Mantua that among the caprices featured in the festivities were 'comedies and moresques of the abbot of Gaeta, prince and inventor of a new madness'.[26]

The election of the young Medici cardinal to the papal throne brought Baraballo hastening to Rome to join his court, and he was duly registered among the *scutiferi* or shield-bearers. Perhaps the most memorable entertainment of the period took place at the conferring of Roman citizenship upon Leo's brother, Giuliano de' Medici, in September 1513. For the occasion a great wooden theatre in the classical style was erected on the Campidoglio and decorated with paintings by the major artists in Rome. One of the featured events was the reading of poetry and recitation of the *Penulo* of Plautus. Seventy-two poets were convened to comment on a poem entitled *Epulum* by Simone Seculo; notable among them was the Abbot of Gaeta, who signed himself modestly 'Baraballo, arch-poet'.[27]

It was inevitable that sooner or later the pope's elephant would become involved in one or other of the major festivities scheduled so frequently at the papal court; and when it was, the event was to prove one of the most memorable events of Leo's reign. Traditionally the patron saints of the Medici family were Cosmo and Damiano and, after becoming pope, Leo determined that henceforth their feast day would be celebrated in perpetuity at the Apostolic Palace with suitable festivities. The cardinals were so informed in a public consistory and advised furthermore that the occasion, to be held each 27 September thereafter, would be known as the 'Cosmalia'.

Accordingly, in the following year preparations were begun long in advance of the date with discussions of what would constitute a suitable event to mark the occasion. The programme eventually selected was a burlesque coronation of Baraballo as arch-poet to be celebrated with an appropriate triumphal procession. Inspiration for the theme of the occasion may have come from Leo himself, as he recalled the ageing poet's earlier excitement at Castel Sant' Angelo when he witnessed the procession of the Portuguese mission of obedience. Or it may have been suggested by Cardinal Bibbiena, a man noted for his peculiar wit.[28]

Some days before the coronation was scheduled, Sier Vetor Lippomano sent notice of it to a friend in Venice. 'On the feast day of Saint Cosmo,' he wrote,

the pope will have a celebration and has arranged that the Abbot of Gaeta, who from a good courtier has become mad, will be dressed in green velvet, the pope will crown him with laurels like a poet, and he will go on the elephant that day into Rome, and the pope will give permission to have masks, and there will be recited many verses which all the learned men of Rome are composing to be recited, and he [Baraballo] will respond to all of them, and demonstrate his erudition.[29]

'The incoronation of our Abbot of Gaeta,' reported Balthassare Turini da Pescia to Lorenzo de' Medici in Florence,

is at last prepared, and the robes of green velvet, of crimson satin ornamented with ermine, and other fine decorations for him and the elephant all are in readiness; and many fine recitations to be presented before His Holiness are in preparation, and our friend [Bernardo Accolti] is preparing one of certain stanzas into which are interwoven Petrarch and Dante as being ragged and sad, etc., and it will be nothing if not worth seeing.[30]

Baraballo's delight with having been selected to be featured as the principal of the Cosmalia knew no bounds, and he was particularly pleased to learn that the pope planned to have him mounted upon the elephant and conducted to be crowned to the Campidoglio, the seat of city government. Word of the sumptuous preparations being made in Rome and the spirit of ridicule which pervaded anticipation of the

[19] Contemporary satirical caricature depicting Baraballo as an ass mounted on Hanno's back. Woodcut, early sixteenth century, artist not known.

event reached the respectable Baraballo family in Gaeta. They were appalled by the news and promptly dispatched family representatives to Rome to attempt to convince the abbot that participation in the event would bring shame and embarrassment not only to him but also to his entire family. [19]

It was all to no avail, however, and the family's pleas fell upon deaf ears, for the abbot remained obdurate. Baraballo accused his relatives of being envious of the recognition and glory that had come to him; furthermore, the pope was not one to renounce his plans for anything on earth once they had been made. The abbot continued with his preparations, to his relatives' mounting frustration.[31]

27th September came at last and found the Vatican in an exceptionally festive mood. That morning vespers were sung in the minor chapel at St Peter's, with the pope joining in, and a solemn mass was celebrated by Cardinal Raffaello Riario, Bishop of Ostia. Almost the entire membership of the College of Cardinals in their brilliant red capes was in attendance, in addition to the conservators of the city government, foreign ambassadors, numerous Roman princes and noblemen in sumptuous robes of velvet, brocade and satin. A plenary indulgence followed the mass and the chapel remained open for anyone who wished to visit it.

Without exception the distinguished assemblage accepted the pope's invitation to a great banquet honouring the special guest, the Abbot of Gaeta. Having finished dining, they retired to the pope's apartments where they formed small groups in active discussion to await the main event. At last the sound of bagpipes and trumpets announced the entry of Baraballo, preceded by a triumphant escort of courtiers. He was approximately sixty years of age at the time, of venerable aspect, having a deceptively wise and sedate mien. For the occasion he was impressively robed in a gold and purple *laticlavus* and a *toga palmata* of green velvet with a surplice of crimson satin adorned with ermine.

The pope invited him to present an example of his lyrics before proceeding with the coronation, and the abbot readily responded. His improvised verses in Latin and Italian were received with great bursts of applause and laughter from all sides. Finally he was prevailed upon to be seated, and one after another of the court poets arose to read their compositions, all of which mockingly praised Baraballo. The first to speak was Angelo Colocci, and he was followed by Filippo Beroaldo the Younger, Giovanni Francesco Filomuso, Jacopo Sadoleto, Bernardo Accolti, and numerous others.[32]

Colocci made his presentation in verses of Catullian flavour, extolling autumn as the best of all seasons, not because it was a time for hunting, but because its breezes were reminiscent of spring. He addressed the sun:

> But as you have brought forth and extolled
>> so brilliant a new poet
> By your single light, for these cosmic dwellers
>> on this most perfect of days,
> This poet is a solar flower
> Blooming at dawn, dying at evening![33]

Accolti, who was then considered to be the most illustrious poet in Rome if not in all Italy, depicted Dante and Petrarch as lamenting that Baraballo had stolen from them their glory of language and beauty of poetry.[34]

Beroaldo had written a comedy for the occasion, in the prologue of which the aged Baraballo was invaded by Bacchanalian fervour and turned to versifying. In addition to being a poet, Beroaldo claimed, the abbot was at the same time a musician, politician, lover, dancer, jurisconsult and physician. He was learned in the rights of domestic fowl, proclaimed Beroaldo, he could counsel on the use of wine in preference to noxious water, which was harmful to the stomach; he was aware that the song of the warbler was more salubrious than that of the starling or the crow. To reward such knowledge, the gods and goddesses, like Cybele and Eternity, decreed that the great Baraballo was to be crowned with seven crowns, as arch-poet, arch-architect, arch-musician, arch-politician, arch-lover, arch-geometer, arch-lyre player, and in fact, arch-everything.

The arrangements called for Baraballo to be dressed in the *laticlavus*, mounted on the highest arch-beast, the turreted elephant with which the King of Calicut had triumphed over the Indian pygmies, to be preceded by two carts. Upon entering the city of Rome he was to be met by the senators, the mounted nobility, and the Roman populace and would be greeted with great applause and hilarity. The keynote of the occasion, sounded by Beroaldo was to be 'stay healthy, drink and remember me.'[35]

In his presentation, Filomuso played on words in making a comparison of the glory and fortune of this Cosmo, Baraballo, with that of the cosmos, and of the universe that had generated him. Hanno he addressed with derisive Latin magniloquence. 'O, great elephant,' he declaimed,

only in habits and sentiments inferior to men, you see what a sacred charge Rome entrusts to your back; with what faithfulness you must jealously preserve it. This poet is the delight of our Prince, of the courtiers, of the populace and of our fathers [priests] and the public – the love of our city. This cheerful babe his parents tossed laughing in their arms, saying 'O sweet child, sacred to the liberal arts of Bacchus and Phoebus, take the name of Cosmo and enjoy it; your metres and songs ornament the universe and the universe already knows your name.' Equal to the cosmos is your name; nor are you inferior in achievement: the resplendent light of Phoebus and of Bacchus and the stars are like your songs of the Muses. It is appropriate, therefore, that you, Cosmo, should be surrounded by clear stars, and that you should be raised upon the elephantine rock. And it is appropriate that to you, O elephant, should be awarded honours equal to those of the great Atlas… Proceed with sure steps, do not let slip from one side to the other your legs and your hoofs… this charge that presses upon your back is the greatest.[36]

Then followed a presentation of the *Carminum* of which only the Latin prologue by Beroaldo survives. The poet spoke of the genius of the Latins and the revelry of the Greeks, and recorded the extravagances and the nonsense that entertained the leisure hours of the popes. Speaking after Beroaldo, Proto Mariano, Catelaccio, Ceccone, Cecetto, Cecchino, Gian Manente, Romanello, Cristoforo… all expounded on the art of comedy. By universal acclaim 'all the gods and goddesses, Apollo, Jupiter, Pallade, Mercury, Cibele, and all Eternity, judge and sentence Baraballo most worthy of the crown…'[37]

Ja. Mamus Philenus produced a quatrain in Latin verse for the occasion:

> *Those whom it behooves the Capitoline theatre to remind*
> *Of what kind have been the deeds of men of old;*

> Let them approach hither, and re-read the monuments of the
>   learned Serenus,
> And they will see the things as though before their eyes.[38]

The poet Vitalis presented another, somewhat obscure poem, noting that 'So well has this good poet succeeded in Sicily, that he merits the name and fame of Succuli.'[39]

After the recitations had been exhausted, the investiture of the arch-poet took place. Although the pope had been a spectator throughout the preliminaries, he did not wish to be the one to crown the poet, and consigned the task to Cardinal Mattheus Lang, Archbishop of Gurk and representative of Emperor Maximilian at the court. The austere German, who had come to Rome only two years after the completion of the league formed between the pope and the emperor, was not pleased with the assignment but he was unable to find any way to avoid it. As he placed the large cap surmounted with a triple crown upon the old abbot's head, Lang spoke a few words, urging the poet to place his lyrics at the service of the Church.[40]

With all of this, Baraballo could hardly contain his joy. Resplendent in his rich robes, he minced down the steps of the Vatican to the sound of pipers while trumpeters marched before him amidst a hubbub of increasing volume from the distinguished guests and the public crowding around him. He was loudly acclaimed as he attempted to mount the elephant. Experiencing extreme difficulty, he tried again and again until finally he had to request assistance. He was hoisted up somewhat unceremoniously and seated upon a throne attached to the elephant's pack saddle which had been specially designed for the occasion. The throne's arms terminated in great carved gilt heads of griffins, and below the chair over the beast's back was draped a rich lustrous robe embroidered with the words *Poeta Barabal.*

Finally esconced upon his precarious seat, Baraballo beamed all around upon the assemblage, holding his arms rigidly in front of him with a branch of laurel in his grasp. The doubtful stability of his heavy headpiece worried him so that he held his head stiffly straight and with the greatest dignity, intensely aware of this, his greatest moment of glory. A cavalcade formed itself in the cleared area behind the elephant and two carts took their place in front of it. Guided by its mahout, the patient beast slowly led the procession forward into the city in the direction of the Campidoglio on Capitoline Hill. There the senators and masses of the populace had assembled to await it.

The pope watched the departure of the entourage first from the loggia of the Apostolic Palace; then he hurried along the passage in the Corridore to Castel Sant' Angelo to observe the arrival of the

[20] Sketch of Baraballo mounted on Hanno's back *en route* to the
Campidoglio from the Vatican. The hand-written legend in Italian states 'This
was executed in intarsia on a door of the hall near that of Constantine in the
Vatican palace, of which mention is made in Giovio's *Elogia*.' Water colour,
artist unknown, sixteenth century. From *Cod. Barb. lat. 4410*, fol. 32ᵛ. In the
Biblioteca Apostolica Vaticana.

procession in the city from his favourite window by means of his sighting tube. The procession surrounded by the great bustling crowd moved slowly and clumsily as it descended the Borgo, its progress announced by the din of chanting and shouting as the people laughingly observed the spectacle of the rotund old poet bouncing uncomfortably on his mount over the elephant's back, his expression one of pride mixed with fear. As the procession proceeded along the Via Alessandrina, it was greeted by a renewed uproar of greeting and shouting from the masses that pressed along the route, mixed with the sounds of the heralding trumpets, clashing cymbals and piercing pipes, resulting in a deafening onslaught of sound.[41]

Paolo Giovio noted the occasion in his writings. 'I should scarcely have believed,' he wrote,

unless I had myself been present at the sight, that a man not less than sixty years of age, of an honourable family, and venerable by his stature and his grey hair, should have suffered himself to be decorated with the toga palmata, *and the* latum clavum *of the ancient Romans, and bedecked with gold and purple, to be led in a triumphal procession before the public, with the sound of trumpets.*[42]

The raucous clamour of the crowds, the persistent clash of cymbals and the braying of trumpets, the dulling beat of the drums, the pervasive high-pitched wail of the pipes, and the pressure of the crowds on both sides of the procession, increasingly confused and frightened the elephant, so that it was fast attaining a state of panic by the time that it approached Ponte Afriano (now Ponte Sant' Angelo) which spanned the Tiber at this point. In the early sixteenth century the Vatican and the Borgo were not part of the city of Rome and were under papal, not city, jurisdiction. Passing over the bridge from Castel Sant'Angelo, it was common to say that one was 'going into Rome.'

As Hanno arrived at the bridge it was greeted by an increasing crescendo of noise, and abruptly balked, unable to deal with the sound and the shifting columns of excited bystanders. For the first time it refused to continue, despite the urging of the worried mahout. Shouted encouragement from the crowds only increased its confusion. Finally, shaking itself mightily, with one great heave it cast its precious burden – poet, throne and all – onto the dusty bank at the edge of the river. Baraballo, frightened by the fall but perhaps secretly relieved at being so summarily displaced from his precarious mount, quickly scrambled away. Dusting himself off, he found it prudent to disappear quickly through the crowds as the elephant was led back to the Vatican and to serenity, despite the disappointment of the crowds. Most disappointed of all, however, was the pontiff on the balcony from which he had been observing the procession.[43]

Donato Poli, a Florentine professor at the Accademia Romana, who was an observer of the incident, composed a sonnet to commemmorate it, which was published anonymously:

> Our archpoet Baraballo
> Mounted on this great beast, whither seen from far
> Or near, appears to be so fine a captain
> That he makes the butterflies burst into laughter.
>
> With the four lightning bolts placed upon his shoulders
> He would resemble Alexander;
> Place a flask in his hand
> One would say he was Bacchus, an Indian prince.
>
> Through one eye, one might mistake him for Hannibal.
> Nominating him 'arch poet' is insane, –
> A modern Donatus, so to speak,
> Who travesties the ancient wisdom.
>
> He is not most happily called Petrarch:
> If he is accorded this honour from the past
> The present hour then becomes as illustrious
> As radish leaves.
>
> And then if such license exists
> I shall hope next year
> To see Giovanni Manente a theologian.[44]

The fame of the great bacchanalian carnival to crown a buffoon held at the Vatican spread throughout Italy, and continued to be noted by writers long thereafter. Years later Pietro Aretino, in his comedy *La Cortegiana*, recalled the event noting about one of his characters, 'he had the style of the Abbot of Gaeta crowned upon the Elephant.'[45]

Baraballo was mentioned also in the writings of Niccolò Macchiavelli. In his *Asino d'Oro* (The Golden Ass), Macchiavelli presented the figure of a poet seated upon the back of an elephant as a decoration over the doorway of an enclosure in which were maintained the lunatics and simple-minded fools who had been changed into beasts by Circe:

> A figure that seemed alive stood sculptured in marble above the
>   great arch that sheltered the entrance,
> Like Hannibal, he seemed to ride on an elephant in triumph;
> His clothing was that of a dignified man, renowned and
>   eminent.

A garland of laurel he had on his head; his face was very
*   pleasant and happy;*
Around him were people to shower him with honour.
'He is the famous abbot of Gaeta,' said the lady, 'as I am sure
*   you know, who was once crowned as a poet.*
By the gods of Heaven, as you see, his image was put in this
*   place along with the creatures shown at his feet,*
So that anyone passing by, without further information,
Could judge what sort of people are shut up in there.
But now let us try not to waste so much time in looking at this
*   man*
That the hour of returning overtakes us.'[46]

The event represents an excellent example of the sharp contradictions
that prevailed during the reign of Leo X. Buried beneath the open
merriment and enjoyment of the pontiff, the cardinals and the literati
who witnessed the rise and fall of the abbot of Gaeta, is the cruel
humour which devised the lavish, contemptuous ceremonial. It exem-
plified the pontiff's ever-present need to laugh to hide his recurrent
melancholy, regardless of the expense to others.

At the same time it reflected the pathos of the sad image of the
ageing Baraballo. So strongly convinced of his own achievements and
the acknowledgement they deserved, he had become blind to the
cruel wit behind the ceremonial and the shameful universal mockery
at his expense. There is no doubt that by the time the mock 'coronation' had taken place he no longer had full command of his senses, and
the ignominious ending to his journey of glory must have destroyed
his mind entirely. Shortly thereafter, Baraballo disappeared into obscurity: the register of the pope's expenses for 28 July 1516 does not
include his name. Writing to Equicola on 1 October 1519, the
archdeacon of Gabbioneta spoke of Baraballo as having been dead for
several years.[47]

It was typical of the pope to want a permanent record of the event,
and in due course he ordered that the coronation of the arch-poet be
depicted on one of the doors between two rooms of the Stanze di
Raffaello in the Apostolic Palace. These were the Camera della
Segnatura, in which Raphael had painted the Dispute of the
Sacrament and the School of Athens, and the Stanza in which he had
depicted the Fire of the Borgo. Raphael was given the assignment and
selected one of his young assistants, Giovanni Barile, for the task.

A capable sculptor, architect and engraver, Barile had decorated the
other doors and stalls of the papal apartments with scenes executed in
intarsia [wood mosaic inlay]. Working from a sketch, probably

prepared by Raphael, Barile produced a scene depicting the triumphant poet upon Hanno's back in vari-coloured woods, reproducing the effect of the coloured raiment with remarkable success. The doors were restored in 1702 by the artist Carlo Maratta, and survive to the present. The event is memorialized also in an unsigned drawing in watercolour in the collections of the Biblioteca Apostolica Vaticana which represents the same scene that appears on the door; it seems to be contemporary but is dated after the creation of the door panel.[48] [20]

Because of the pope's absence from the city on the feast day of Cosmo and Damiano for the next several years, the Cosmalia was not held again until 1519. It then involved similar buffoonery featuring the amateur versifier Camillo Querno from Monopoli. He looked less than prepossessing, being permanently disfigured with a wound on his face as a result of the savagery of the amused courtiers after a reading of his work.

Probably the most outrageous of the Cosmalia occurred in another year when a bullfight was scheduled in the piazza of St Peter as a prelude to the poetry readings. Three men were killed and four others wounded. A reading of poetry by an unnamed monk that evening was deemed insufficiently entertaining so he was tossed in a blanket and the pope ordered his servants to cut the cords of the monk's trousers. Mortified, the monk bit several of the footmen; in retaliation he was tied upon the back of a horse and beaten so severely on his back and buttocks that a number of cupping glasses were required. For a long time bedridden, he received two ducats in compensation for the entertainment he had provided.[49]

It was inevitable that Hanno and the abbot of Gaeta should eventually become subjects of the acerbic verses of Pasquino, the 'talking statue' which was first installed in 1501 and which survives to the present. [21] This fragment of a sculpture of the third century BC is believed to have originally represented either Hercules or Menelaus. During the modification of the Orsini palace, now Palazzo Braschi, undertaken by Cardinal Oliviero Carafa at the turn of the fifteenth century, the fragment was uncovered in the ground nearby. A suitable pedestal was built for it and the mutilated statue was erected upon its present site at the corner of the Palazzo Braschi in a triangle that has come to be called the Piazza di Pasquino.[50]

The origin of Pasquino's name is uncertain. One legend states that it was derived from the name of a neighbouring blacksmith, another claims that it was a barber and yet another that the original Pasquino was an ill-fated tailor whose shop was nearby. The tailor became the

[21] The statue of Pasquino as it appeared in the sixteenth century in the Piazza di Pasquino. Copper engraving, from *Speculum Romanae Magnificentiae* by Antonio Lafreri (Rome 1564–1584).

most generally accepted figure. According to the popular story, his employment at the papal court led him and his apprentices to share the nuggets of scandal he learned there with neighbouring shopkeepers and other clients. It became a common practice to attribute to the court tailor — and after his death to the mute sculpture — the court gossip rendered into verse by the students and faculty of the nearby university and by the courtiers and poets of the court as well. These anonymous writings, called *Pasquinati*, were posted on the statue or its pedestal where all of Rome sought them out and read them with considerable glee.

In about 1509 the students and faculty initiated an annual celebration of Pasquino that took place thereafter on 25 April, St Mark's Day. At about this time Cardinal Carafa went to the trouble of having the missing parts of the statue restored with plaster-of-paris casts and of dressing the statue to represent one of the classical divinities. A lecturer at the university who was assigned the annual task, conceived the idea of scheduling a competition of Latin epigrams as part of the event, and the practice was continued in later years. A selection was published each year in a pamphlet entitled *Pasquilli* produced by the printer Giacomo Mazzochi of Bergamo, who was at the same time university librarian. As many as three thousand verses were pasted on to the statue and adjacent walls on each St Mark's Day, and from these a selection was made for publication in the pamphlet. In between anniversaries, the statue served as a convenient billboard for displaying edicts, decrees, indulgences, and other public notices.[51]

The particular divinity the statue was made to represent each year depended upon the political and cultural climate of the moment. In 1510, for example, the statue represented Hercules, and the following year it was draped with mourning to commemmorate the passing of its donor, the Cardinal. Thereafter the cost of restoration was undertaken by the new owner of the palace, Cardinal Christopher Bainbridge. When he was absent from the city, the responsibility fell upon the Bishop of Camerino, master of the Apostolic Palace under Pope Julius II.

To celebrate the recent military victory of Pope Julius II at Ravenna in 1512 Pasquino assumed the guise of Mars. In 1513 the major event was the election of Pope Leo X; for that occasion the statue was draped as the naked Apollo of Belvedere and was so represented on the cover of the *Pasquilli* published that year. In 1514 Mercury was featured, with a great purse to signify the generosity of the new Pope and the prosperity that would undoubtedly ensue during his reign. It was in this year that the elephant was first mentioned in the pasquinades. The arrival of an elephant in Rome brought a characteristic observation in Latin verse from Pasquino's sharp tongue:

> Rome produces its monkeys and wild goats

> *And every type of wild beast, more even than*
> *India and Africa.*
> *And now that Leo has become their king,*
> *All the animals , even the very grand elephant,*
> *Must hold him in honour.*[52]

Thereafter the elephant was featured in Pasquino's published verses during all of the years that Hanno lived in Rome. In 1515 Pasquino assumed the mask and form of Oedipus to celebrate the muse of poetry and music. Nor did Pasquino ignore the mock musician of the papal court, Gian Manente:

> *All of you, run! Why do you linger, oh poets?*
> *Marone [a crude exclamation], mount upon the elephant,*
> *Is it not a marvel that, after so many centuries,*
> *Orpheus is reborn, and demonstrates it with plectrum and with*
> *   the melodious zither;*
> *In this very age Baraballo, multi-talented,*
> *Is crowned upon the back of an elephant...*
> *Oh, how much more beautiful is this age than that which,*
> *Wretch that I was, I inhabited.*
> *Oh, with how many Orpheuses it is filled, among which*
> *The chief one is my friend Manente...*[53]

Epigrams honoured the poet Baraballo, and at one point Pasquino commented:

> *And if you pursue the profession of poet*
> *And hold many competitions with people*
> *Why is not the Abbot of Gaeta among them?*
> *And if you play and sing thus so sweetly*
> *Why is your harmony so indiscreet*
> *That you are not disposed to Giovan Manente?*

To which Orpheus was made to reply:

> *Ho, there, you, if by chance you are there*
> *Staying with Baraballo,*
> *Come hither, let each sing to our lyres.*[54]

The same volume included another epigram in which may be detected the ascerbic pen of the military and militant Ulrich von Hutten, who was then about to leave Rome to return to his native Germany:

> *Farewell, Rome, I have seen you,*
> *And I am ashamed of having seen you.*
> *Farewell, buffoons, elephant, prostitutes,*
> *Procurers, male prostitutes,*
> *Heralds, odious ones, rapists, perjurers, thieves,*

> *The sacrilegious, the incestuous,*
> *Godless Rome, farewell.*[55]

A curious piece of prose writing addressed to Pope Leo X in the name of Pasquino was included at the end of the little volume of *Pasquilli* published in the following year (1516). It claimed to have been written on behalf of the servants and clerics in the service of the pope and of the cardinals who went roaming about the city. It stated that in the following month there must be conceded to them the favours previously given by other pontiffs, on pain of losing the elephant, lions and other beasts [of the papal menagerie], and of postponing the procession for the Abbot of Gaeta. Otherwise, there would be much grumbling, the citation warned. It was signed by Marforio and bore also the name of Gian Manente.[56]

Other contemporary writings memorialized the elephant. In 1514 a curious eight-page pamphlet was published in Rome by an anonymous writer using the pseudonym of Philomathes. The work described Hanno as well as other elephants in history. It was entitled *Nature, Intellect and Habits of the Elephant Extracted From Aristotle, Pliny and Solinus: several other examples of the Elephant: together with a Chapter on the defects of nature: in Rhyme.* The work extolled the virtues of King Manuel I and the Portuguese achievements in the conquest of Africa and the East and with the Christianization of infidels. It reported the Portuguese mission of obedience in some detail, listing the gifts and particularly the elephant. The author then proceeded to discourse on the general subject of elephants in history and in nature. The cover of the pamphlet featured a woodcut of an elephant with pack saddle intended to depict Hanno. The single known copy of the pamphlet is in the British Library. An ink sketch from which the woodcut is believed to have been made appears in a manuscript among the Chigi papers in the Biblioteca Apostolica Vaticana.[57] [22]

In its lifetime Hanno's fame was not limited to Rome and Florence, and it attracted the attention also of the celebrated Marchioness of Mantua, Isabella d' Este. She was intrigued by the events occurring at the papal court and had an insatiable curiosity about its social functions and bizarre celebrations, word of which frequently filtered back to Mantua. Above all, she was interested in papal politics, and found it expedient to maintain a pleasant relationship with the pope's cousin, Cardinal Giulio de' Medici, who was at the centre of court activities and could keep her informed. As a consequence, she obtained several accounts of the dazzling Portuguese mission and the rich and unusual gifts from such correspondents in Rome as the poet Guido Postumo Silvestri, the Bishop

[22] Woodcut of Hanno featured on the title-page of the pamphlet entitled *Natura, Intellecto & Costumi de lo Elephante ...* by Philomathes (Rome, *c.* 1514). In the British Library, London.

of Nizza, and particularly from her own agent at the court, Francesco Chierigati.[58]

Probably the most exciting and detailed account of the mission was one that Isabella received from an individual named Grossino, who as assistant to the Cardinal of Ferrara had participated in the formal ceremonies on that occasion. Grossino described Pacheco's oration that had lasted one and a half hours, and the pope's own lengthy response. He wrote about the jewelled gifts which he estimated to be worth 60,000 ducats, and then went on to describe at great length the elephant and its behaviour. He reported that the Moor who attended it commanded the beast to kneel and 'made it perform various acts so that the pope laughed very loudly; he made it open its mouth and made it bark and trumpet so that it appeared to be arrogant, and then he made it move ahead a short distance into the garden to drink water, which it then sprayed out as if it were a cannon and drenched everybody nearby.'[59]

When Isabella arrived in Rome on 18 October 1514 for a prolonged visit, there can be no doubt that she asked to be shown the elephant. Probably she observed it also during papal processions and celebrations on other occasions during her sojourn before she returned to Mantua. At this time she made the acquaintance of Raphael and commissioned him to execute a painting of Hanno for her. At the instigation of their mutual friend Baldassare Castiglione, Raphael apparently accepted the commission. Castiglione's parents had been in the service of the Gonzaga family for many years and as a consequence he had long maintained a close association with Isabella's court. His friendship with Isabella was somewhat obsequious, and he memorialized her in his work *Il Cortegiano*. On her behalf he had induced Raphael to paint a portrait of her son Federigo.[60]

Overburdened with projects as always, however, Raphael was unable to produce the elephant's portrait at that time. No further mention was made of the project until some months after the Marchioness returned to Mantua. Then in a letter of 16 March 1516, her agent in Rome, Carlo Agnello, advised her 'of the portrait of the Elephant. I hope that Your Excellency will be well served, because Raphael d' Urbino, an excellent man, has taken the impression [preliminary sketches] to make his portrait and he gave me the measurements.'[61]

Raphael persisted in his promise to produce the painting in personal communications with Isabella and later with Agostino Gonzaga, her agent in Rome, as well as with Castiglione. It would probably have been an allegorical composition to serve as a pendant to other paintings in the Grotta in the Gonzaga palace at Mantua. Although he had made the preliminary sketches, however, there is no evidence that Raphael completed the commission.[62]

Meanwhile the Gonzaga fortunes had reached a new low, and it was probably due to lack of funds that the project was not pursued. None the less, Mantua was to have its image of Hanno. Following the death of Francesco Gonzaga, his son Federigo installed his own government with advice and guidance from his mother Isabella and of his uncle Cardinal Sigismondo. Having been exposed to the artistic activities and splendours of the papal court where he had been held hostage of Julius II for several years, he sought to add some of the same artistic quality to Mantua. He attempted to bring Giulio Romano from Rome, finally succeeding in 1524 with the aid of Castiglione. In the Palazzo del Te, Romano created a world of sensual fantasy, including a stucco medallion on the ceiling of the Sala di Fetonte, the bedchamber of the young Marchese Federigo. It represents Hanno with two young cherubs riding on its back. Surviving is Romano's sketch on which the medallion appears to have been based.[63]

Hanno was scheduled to be featured also in the great welcoming celebration being prepared for the arrival in Rome of the pope's favourite brother, Giuliano de' Medici, called 'the Magnificent' like his famous father. He had been married recently, on 25 January 1515, to Filiberta of Savoy, sister of the late King Louis XII of France, and the pope had named him Captain General of the Church. He was to receive the states of Parma, Piacenza, Reggio and Modena as his marriage portion. The Duke of Milan and the new King Francis I had in the meantime laid claim to Parma and Piacenza, however, and the matter had to be resolved by a coalition subsequently formed between the Holy See, Emperor Maximilian I, the King of Spain, the Swiss, Genoa and Milan.[64]

In March the newly-weds and their elaborate wedding party set sail in three galleys from Provence to Ostia. It was the pope's custom to send members of his own family and distinguished nobles of the court to meet important visitors. On this occasion, when Giuliano disembarked he was greeted by three cardinals who were relatives, and by numerous courtiers. Giuliano had brought a large entourage and they formed an impressive spectacle as his escort defiled on horseback, followed by the ladies in silks and satins in their carriages, in a procession which stretched seemingly for miles along the route.[65]

Giuliano's visit had been anticipated with great excitement in Rome, and as was the custom triumphal arches had been erected along the route he was to follow from the Porta del Popolo to the Campidoglio. Fifty Roman nobles on horseback escorted him with a great cortège of grooms, pipers, drummers, and trumpeters. He was met by Senator Giacomo Bove of Bologna, the Rome conservators Mario Scappuduccio, Evangelista Torquato and Giacomo del Nero, the priors of the Caporoni and the two Perpetual Chancellors and the Orators of Rome, to the deafening sounds of a bombardment of welcome from the artillery of Castel Sant' Angelo and the shouts and cries of the populace crowding the route.[65]

The event was marred by a most unfortunate occurrence, however. It was reported by the Venetian diarist Marino Sanuto, who had obtained his information from the Deacon of Treviso, Domino Bonin. All had gone well as the stately procession progressed slowly into the city until, in the words of Sanuto, 'there was sent to meet him the elephant, being the one that had been sent as a gift by the King of Portugal. Upon its back was a turret with armed men inside. It seems that by accident, or by evil design, the said structure fell.'[66]

As Hanno was being conducted along the route, the beast was made increasingly nervous by the pressing crowds and the constant din, and it had reached a state of near panic before it had arrived at its destination, despite the efforts of its custodians to calm it. Suddenly startled by another discharge of cannon, it stampeded. As it was attempting to turn, the turret capsized and was thrown towards the Tiber. The men inside it were cast to the ground and some of them, as well as many nearby spectators, were injured. This was taken to be a bad omen for the distinguished visitor, and had a sobering effect on the festivities.[67]

The observers of the procession that day undoubtedly included Raphael's assistant, Giulio Romano, who captured the moment of the capsizing turret in a sketch that survives in the Ashmolean Museum's collections, and which was later featured in a drawing by Raphael for the fresco of the 'Battle of Scipio'.[68]

This was not the only accident to beset Hanno during its sojourn in Rome. Because of the unflagging desire of the Roman people to observe the strange beast at close quarters, and the large crowds of visitors who thronged the Vatican to obtain a glimpse of it, the pope determined that the people deserved a better opportunity to view Hanno and its antics. Accordingly, on one occasion he had the elephant conducted to the large open space inside the Baths of Diocletian, which was of sufficient size to accommodate large numbers. The crowds exceeded the pope's expectations, however, reaching alarming proportions.

The spectators were jammed tightly together and the presence of many of the Roman nobility mounted on horseback created an additional hazard as everyone strained for a glimpse of the elephant. The inevitable happened, and people were crushed under the feet of the horses and there was considerable bloodshed. The accident was reported in an official record maintained by an unknown court chronicler of deaths and mortalities occurring in Rome. It noted that thirteen were killed in the mêlée but the date of the occurrence was not given in the account.[69]

The same source added a confusing statement, noting 'This was the great beast' donated to the King of France by the pope during the final conference which took place in Bologna, when Leo went there to discuss the league with him.' Upon his succession to the French throne in January 1515, Francis I made plans to mount an expedition to Italy immediately, to recover the city of Milan. This move was strongly opposed by Leo X, who suggested instead an alliance between the Holy See, King Ferdinand of Spain, and Emperor Maximilian I. The French king, undeterred by this threat, went on to achieve victory at the battle of Marignano and then to capture the city of Milan.

Pope Leo X had planned a visit to Florence in that period and arranged to meet King Francis I at Bologna upon his return from Florence. A great reception was prepared in anticipation of the pope's visit to his native city. Two thousand men had been put to work in churches converted to workshops to make decorations, construct obelisks, trophies and triumphal arches to greet the pontiff at a cost, it was said, of 700,000 *florins*. To provide attractive vistas along the route, houses were demolished, the cathedral was provided with a new façade and a castle supported on twenty-two columns was erected in the Piazza Santa Trinità for the occasion. Since the pope arrived earlier than expected, he agreed to wait several days at the villa of Marignole before entering the city so as to not disappoint those working on the preparations. Finally, on St Andrew's Day, Leo entered Florence through the Porta Romana followed by a huge train of cardinals, men at arms and attendants – a memorable day.[70]

Following the festivities, the pope travelled to Bologna, arriving on 8 December 1515 and then held a meeting with the French king three days later. The meeting was in considerable contrast to his reception in Florence. The king was abrupt in his demands and the encounter fell far short of Leo's hopes. He returned to Florence where he remained until 17 February, when he was recalled to Rome by the death of King Ferdinand of Spain. In Florence once more, he found that the Arno was in flood, there was a food shortage in the city, and that his brother Giuliano was seriously ill. He died a month after the pope's departure.

The statement that the pope planned to give the elephant to the King of France is puzzling, particularly in view of his great love of the beast. One is led to assume that the statement, if made, was in response to a request from the king, and was not the pontiff's voluntary offer. In any case, fate was to intervene to annul any plans to transfer Hanno, if ever they existed.[71]

CHAPTER FIVE

The Ill-Fated Rhinoceros

...the sly Rhinocerot,
            Who (never with blinde furie led) doth venter
Upon his Foe, but (yer the Lists he enter)
            Against a Rock he whetteth round about
The dangerous pike upon his armed snout;
Then buckling close, doth not (at random) hack
On the hard Cuirass on his Enemies back;
But under's belly (cunning) findes a skin,
Where (and but there) his sharpned blade will in.

Revd Alexander B. Grosart, ed : *The Complete Works of Joshua*
Sylvester (1876)

WHILE THE ELEPHANT HANNO WAS PLAYFULLY DISPORTING itself before the public in Rome, to the amusement of the papal court and the people, events taking place in the Portuguese colonial empire were setting the scene for the delivery of another papal pachyderm to the Eternal City. Although the successful conquests in the East had made it possible for Portugal to assume control of the world spice trade, there was concern over its ability to maintain this valuable commerce exclusively for Portugal. It was Afonso Albuquerque, the founder of the Portuguese empire in the East who had been appointed governor of the Portuguese Indies by King Manuel I, who conceived a grand scheme by means of which he thought this could be accomplished. A critical factor was, of course, the protection of Portuguese shipping lanes and trading posts. As part of this necessity, Albuquerque determined to establish a fortress on the island of Diu.

This important site lay in the territory of the kingdom of Gujarat, ruled by Sultan Muzafar II. In the sixteenth century Cambay, the name given to Gujarat by Muslim and Portuguese writers, was considered to be one of the major kingdoms of India. Bounded on the north by Dival and Sind, and confined in the interior by Malwa and Sanga, its coastal territory extended from Magalor on the south-east coast of Kathiawar as far as Chaul, with the seat of Muzafar's court at Champanel, also known as Ahmadabad. In 1512 King Manuel authorized Albuquerque to seek Muzafar's permission to construct a fortress at Diu and to obtain assurance that in future the Gujarat traders would be permitted to engage in commerce only with the Portuguese at Goa, and no longer with Egyptian and Turkish traders as before.[1]

Albuquerque determined first to test the sultan's response before planning his next move. His proposal for a meeting having met with encouragement, he proceeded to select the members of the mission with great care. They included Diogo Fernandes de Beja and Jaime Teixeira as ambassadors, Francisco Pais as secretary; as interpreters he included Duarte Vaz, Pero Queimado, and a native named Gamapatin, all of whom were familiar with the language.

Albuquerque personally chose the gifts to be presented to Muzafar. Featured among them were a fine dagger with a handle set with rubies, Persian and Chinese brocades of great richness, silver and gilt toilet articles including a wash basin, ewer, blanching cup, vases, a small chandelier, and a gold and enamel chain, all items designed to appeal to Muslim tastes.

The Portuguese mission departed from Goa in February 1514 and arrived at Champanel early in April. From there they made their way to Mondoval, where the sultan was staying, arriving two weeks later. The visit proved to be much shorter than anticipated. The sultan received the visitors graciously and admired the gifts they had brought. He then gave them gifts to take back to King Manuel, including a balustered chair encrusted with ivory. As a gift for Viceroy Albuquerque, he sent a live rhinoceros of monstrous size that was being kept in the sultan's park at Champanel. After the preliminary exchange of amenities, the Portuguese emissaries proceeded with their negotiations – which soon came to an abrupt halt. The sultan was unwilling to permit a fortress to be erected on Diu for the obvious reason that it might be used as a base from which his mainland could be attacked. Instead he offered other sites, none of which suited the Portuguese. Failing to change the sultan's decision, the mission departed on 26 April and made their way to Surat once more.

At the same time the sultan arranged to have the rhinoceros conducted from Champanel to Surate, where members of the mission were to take possession of it. They reached Surate on 16 May and the animal arrived two days later. For the convenience of the new owner, one foot of the beast had been fitted with an iron shackle and chain. The onset of severe weather forced the mission to remain at Surat for the balance of the summer, despite Albuquerque's order that there should be no delay in their return. The mission was finally able to leave for Goa by sea in three *zamboucs*, arriving at Goa in mid-September. Although the ambassadors had had no choice in the matter, upon their arrival at Goa the viceroy took them seriously to task for the delay in schedule. They remained in port while Albuquerque held a council of war to determine whether or not he should attack the sultan and take Diu by force. The final decision was in the negative.[2]

After viewing the sultan's gifts, Albuquerque concluded that it would be impractical for him to attempt to maintain a live rhinoceros in Goa. Finally he reached a satisfactory solution – he would send it to his monarch as a gift for his menagerie. It happened that the flotilla of Captain Cristovão de Brito which had sailed from Lisbon arrived in port at just that time. Albuquerque commandeered one of the five ships scheduled for the return voyage for shipping his rhinoceros, probably the *Nossa Señhora da Ajuda* under the command of Francisco Pereira Coutiñho.[3]

The rhinoceros accompanied by its keeper, an Indian named Ocem, was brought on board and Albuquerque assigned Jaime Teixeira to be the beast's custodian for the voyage. He then ordered Francisco Corvinel, agent of the port and secretary of the trading post, to provide Ocem with a coat and cloth costume from the clothing in stock 'which I am having given to him in the name of the King'. Teixeira was also made responsible for bearing communications from Albuquerque to King Manuel as well as gifts for the Portuguese queen, the Princess Isabella and the young prince Dom João.[4]

The flotilla, burdened with its ponderous live cargo, left Cochin for Lisbon at the beginning of January 1515, sailing between Madagascar, then called the island of St Lawrence, and the African mainland, touching upon the coast of Mozambique and then doubling around the Cape of Good Hope to St Helena. From St Helena the ships proceeded to the Azores and entered the mouth of the Tagus River, having touched upon only three ports of call during the long and hazardous journey lasting 120 days.

It was an extremely dangerous route because of sudden tempests at sea, uncharted reefs and rocks, and islands still unlisted on the nautical charts of the period. Furthermore, the Portuguese vessels were relatively small for such a long voyage, weighing not more than 100 tons. The ship's food provisions were easily perishable, their supply of water not always drinkable and the holds, as always, overloaded with merchandise, the weight of which added to the danger.

During the long dreary days at sea the rhinoceros was deprived of its customary nourishment of grass, although it was amply provided with hay, straw and cooked rice. Despite this limited diet, the beast maintained a relatively even temper. It was still in fairly good health when it was disembarked at Lisbon on 20 May 1515, making landfall off the Tower of Belem, on which its image was later to be featured. [23, 24]

[23] The Tower of Belem constructed in the reign of King Manuel I, with gargoyles in the form of rhinoceroses. From *Die Baukunst der Renaissance in Portugal* by Albrecht Haupt (Frankfurt, 1890).

[24] Enlarged detail of a gargoyle representing a rhinoceros, now greatly worn by the elements, at the base of a turret of the Tower of Belem.

As the large beast was being brought off the ship, the unexpected sight caused considerable commotion, and great crowds flocked to the waterfront from all parts of the city and the surrounding countryside, avid for a glimpse of the remarkable animal, which they greeted with great clamour and confusion. This was the first live rhinoceros to appear on the European continent since the third century.[5]

The presence of the rhinoceros excited considerable interest not only with the Lisbon populace but also among the naturalists of the time. All that was then known about the species was what had been written on the subject by chroniclers of the ancient world. Pliny the Younger had copied his information from Agathachides, who had written about the African, not the Indian, rhinoceros; consequently the known information did not apply to the Indian variety. For example, the Indian rhinoceros does not use its somewhat short horn as a weapon of attack or defence, as does the African. Instead, it uses the triangular razor-sharp tushes in its lower jaw, which can inflict painful and serious if not mortal wounds on another large opponent.

Rhinoceroses had formed part of the menageries of several Roman emperors. Domitian had two-horned rhinoceroses among his wild beasts and Commodus also had several. In the third century AD Caracalla and Heliogabalus each owned a rhinoceros and there was another in Rome in the first century.[6]

The king was pleased with the surprise gift and the rhinoceros was added to his menagerie and maintained in the royal park of his palace at Ribeira. [25] There the king had installed numerous cages with iron grillework, each designed to accommodate the needs and nature of the beast it contained.

Menageries had been a pastime of the Portuguese kings for several centuries. The first is traditionally attributed to Dom Diniz who had captured a great bear while hunting near the city of Beja in 1294. He kept the animal on his estate at Fuellas, and later added a live wolf. In the mid-fifteenth century King Afonso V imported a large number of unusual beasts which he kept at his castle at Pena near Sintra, high in the mountains several leagues outside of Lisbon, in a region that featured castles and summer villas. It was at Sintra that Afonso had been born and there he spent the major part of his life. Eventually he established a menagerie at Sintra, staging exhibitions there, and from time to time he selected some of the wild animals to present as gifts to friends, courtiers and heads of state. In 1475, for example, he sent a number of wild beasts he had imported from Guinea to King Louis XI of France, and two years later he presented René d'Anjou with a collection of assorted marmots and monkeys as well as an elephant.

[25] The royal palace at Ribeira, Lisbon; the rhinoceros was first lodged in its menagerie. Eighteenth-century view from *Le Roiaume de Portugal* by Van der AA. Pierre (Leyden, N.D.).

Profiting from the Portuguese commerce with western Africa, Afonso's successor, João II, imported large numbers of rare birds and beasts from that region for his palace preserves.[7]

Portugal's active commerce not only with Africa but also with Asia enabled King Manuel I to import a great variety of exotic birds and beasts for his several royal parks. He stabled elephants and other large beasts at his palace at Estãos, and built another menagerie for smaller species in the palace park at Ribeira. Among the first of the creatures to be accommodated there were gazelles, antelopes, lions and a large collection of African birds, in addition to the trained cheetah.

The king decided to house the rhinoceros at Ribeira to keep it separated from the elephants at Estãos. Accommodation of a four-ton wild animal required special new construction which was promptly undertaken. In the interim the rhinoceros was stabled in one of the outbuildings near the Casa da India. With the great beast so close at hand, the king could not resist adding it to his royal entourage as he did the elephants when he rode through the city or out into the countryside. He now featured the rhinoceros, led by its keeper Ocem by means of a long chain, well in advance of the five elephants with their mahouts and the king's mounted party.[8]

The ancient royal palace at Ribeira was surrounded by great terraces and gardens, covering that part of modern day Lisbon occupied by the Ministry of the Interior at the intersection of the Street of Gold and the Street of the Arsenal. Nearby, on a slight plateau, was the Casa da Mina, built long before the palace, which King Manuel later had enlarged by adding to it the Casa da India. A courtyard which opened in front of these buildings was enclosed with a high crenelated wall pierced at intervals with grilled windows. A passageway from the courtyard which provided a means of communication with the apartments of the king and queen was decorated along both sides with ornamental tapestries.

The arrival of a rhinoceros reminded the king of the claims made in the classical writings by Roman historians that the elephant and rhinoceros were natural enemies and would fight each other to the death. Now at last he had an opportunity to test the legend and resolve the question for all time, in what would be an encounter between humanistic scholarship and the reality of the animal world. The event would provide an unusual diversion for the court, and would serve as a distraction for the queen; who had been ailing and morose for some time since the death of her last infant.

After careful review, it was determined that the most suitable arena for the encounter was the long courtyard extending between the royal apartments and the Casa da Mina. The king selected 3 June, Holy Trinity Sunday, for the event, and ordered wooden fencing to be erected at one end of the courtyard to block off one of the promenades into the city. It was through this passage that the contesting beasts were to be conducted to the site of encounter being prepared for them.

Holy Trinity Sunday dawned with clear skies and pleasant weather. As the hour for the great contest approached, the makeshift theatre area of the courtyard was thronged with courtiers, ladies of the queen's entourage, and invited guests, while many others clustered at the windows and on the terrace. The king and queen and their favoured guests assembled on platforms in the courtyard constructed for the occasion. The days of the Colosseum and the Roman Empire seemed to have returned. The spectators chattered somewhat nervously amongst themselves as they waited expectantly for the bloodshed they had been promised, aware of possible danger to themselves and uncertain of what would occur.

The first contestant to arrive was the rhinoceros accompanied by

Ocem, who led his charge by the chain attached to its foot. The beast appeared calm and docile as it was conducted behind a makeshift screen of rugs draped to extend between the royal boxes. It was considered desirable to conceal the rhinoceros from the elephant until all preparations had been completed.

The youngest of several elephants maintained in the state stables of the palace at Estãos had been selected to be the second contestant. As the designated hour approached, its Indian mahout conducted it through the city to the palace. The streets along the route were filled with townspeople, clamouring and shouting in the holiday atmosphere of the day. Unaccustomed to noise and fearful of so many people approaching it from all sides, the terrified young beast finally arrived at the entrance to the courtyard in a state of considerable nervousness.

All was at last in readiness, and the king gave the command to raise the barrier of rugs at the end of the passage. As the screen was removed, the rhinoceros turned and began to move forward at a deliberate pace towards the elephant. Ocem relaxed the chain but kept the end of it tightly in his hand. The great beast lowered its snout towards the ground and began to breathe heavily, the wind from its nostrils making the dust and bits of straw on the ground fly about him as if he were in the centre of a whirlwind. A sense of great power and danger emanated from its slow, deliberate movement.

Meanwhile, as the rhinoceros began to move, the elephant was turned from the opposite direction by the mahout riding on its back, and for the first time it saw the great brute advancing slowly and deliberately in its direction. The young beast instantly panicked. Turning confusedly around and around, it sought to escape the path of the rhinoceros, trumpeting hysterically and flaying its trunk from side to side.

As the rhinoceros continued to approach menacingly with measured tread, the elephant lost its courage and its head completely. In addition to its lack of experience, its youth and much smaller size were undoubtedly factors contributing to its reaction, for it was no more than eight palms (some five feet) in height.

Now totally out of control, the elephant turned abruptly, and raced towards one of the grilled openings in the wall near the door of the courtyard at the corner that overlooked the palace buildings. Without pausing an instant, it thrust its great head against the iron grill with such force that the iron bars snapped and twisted, two at a single stroke. This was no mean feat, for the bars were made of wrought iron each eight inches thick.

The bewildered and terrified mahout mounted on the elephant's back acted with an instinctive sense of self-preservation. He threw himself to the ground behind the beast, otherwise he would have been crushed in the elephant's thundering charge. As soon as the poor young animal, crazed with fright, had created an opening in the wall, it charged through the falling rubble and made its escape amidst thick clouds of dust and the sound of the crumbling barrier.

Emerging violently from the courtyard, the elephant took a disordered course along the streets, instinctively directing itself towards the royal stables at Estãos. Startled horsemen and pedestrians scrambled out of its way, but the beast took no notice of them as it rushed along with great leaps and bounds. Its occasional distressed trumpetings brought curiosity seekers in numbers to witness its escape through the barrage of street dust it stirred up and which rose behind it.

Meanwhile in the courtyard the rhinoceros roved the enclosure with an air of assurance, Ocem trailing watchfully behind it. From time to time the beast looked up to gaze curiously at the spectators, who were laughing uproariously and applauding the lone victor in a battle won by default, without striking a single blow.[9]

It was a richly symbolic moment; the reality of animals which had been described centuries ago brought into a face-to-face encounter. The event, arising from morbid curiosity, illustrates the casual cruelty of the times. That, however, was to be frustrated: the unhappy elephant managed to escape, to the disappointment of those who had come to witness its bloody death.

The excitement in Lisbon caused by the advent of the rhinoceros and the discussion on all sides of the inconclusive tournament of the pachyderms brought news of the great beast to other parts of Portugal and filtered to other countries by word of visitors to the court and through the commercial sector from traders in the city. At this time a number of German merchants and other businessmen formed a sizeable foreign colony in the Portuguese capital. Not long before it had included the German navigator and cosmographer Martin Behaim. There was a regular flow of commercial communication between Lisbon-based German or Portuguese traders and commercial centres abroad, such as Nuremberg and Antwerp and other cities of the Low Countries.

A notable member of the German community in Lisbon was Valentim Fernandes, a native of Moravia who had performed a number of important services for Portugal. In a letter written between 3 June and 1 July 1515, less than six weeks after the arrival of the rhinoceros, Fernandes furnished an account of it in German to an unidentified merchant in Nuremberg whom he addressed as 'my dearest brother'. He described the disembarkation of the rhinoceros, and then went on to include descriptions of India and the kingdom of Cambay from which the beast had been brought, as well a number of other cities in India, and of the Portuguese achievements in that land. The original letter does not survive, but a copy translated into Italian was preserved and later published. This letter provides the exact date of the rhinoceros's arrival and an account of the combat with the elephant:

On the 20th of this month of May 1515 there arrived here in Lisbon, the most noble city of all Portugal, an animal called Rhynoceros by the Greeks and Ganda by the Indians sent by a powerful king of India of the City of Cambay as a gift to this most serene king of Portugal, which animal at the time of the Romans as Pliny has said, Pompey the Great in his games, demonstrated in the circus with other diverse animals; this Rhynoceros which is said to have a horn on its nose and to be the enemy of the elephant, and having to fight it is said to sharpen its horn on a rock and in battle attempts to wound its enemy in the stomach since that is the most weak and tender spot, and it is said to be as long as an elephant but having shorter legs and to be of the same colour as boxwood.

And this is what Strabo says which is in accordance with what we have seen and mostly about its enmity for the elephant. On the feast day of the Holy Trinity an elephant was confined in a certain area near the King's palace and the above mentioned Rhynoceros being led to the same place; I observed immediately that when the said elephant first saw the Rhynoceros it began in a great furor to escape, and running towards a window barred with great iron rods as thick as a man's arm it took them between its teeth and shattered them...[10]

At about the same time, a second letter was sent from Lisbon to the merchant community in Nuremberg describing the rhinoceros and enclosing a sketch of it. Although the writer and recipient are unidentified, it is probable that the writer was a Portuguese writing in German:

On the first of May 151- [year unreadable] there was sent to our King of Portugal coming from the East Indies to Lisbon, a live animal, called a rhinoceros. In order to give you an idea of the strangeness of this beast, I am sending you a sketch. It has the colour of a toad, it is extremely massive and covered with scales. It has the shape of an elephant, but lower in some parts, and is its mortal enemy. On the anterior part of the muzzle it bears a horn which is strong and sharp, and when it approaches an elephant to fight with it, it sharpens its horn on the stones and in running towards it, puts its head down in front of its paws where the elephant has the skin least protected and where it can rend it. The elephant greatly fears the rhinoceros because it can always wound it, and it is on the other hand well protected, and is very agile and malicious. The animal is called Rhinoceros in Greek and Latin and Ganda in India.[11]

Although there are pronounced similarities in both letters, they were none the less independent communications. The sketch enclosed with the second letter was the work of an unidentified competent artist of Lisbon. Both the second letter and sketch came into the hands of the noted Nuremberg artist Albrecht Dürer, who at this time had reached the peak of his career. It is not known whether the letter was addressed directly to him; it is more than likely that it was passed along to him with the sketch by an acquaintance. In any case, Dürer made a pen-and-ink copy of the original drawing and copied the relevant descriptive passage in German on the border of his copy:

In the year 1513 [sic] upon the I day of May there was brought to our King at Lisbon such a living Beast from the East-Indies that is called a Rhinoceronte. Therefore on account of its Wonderfulness I thought myself obliged to send you the Representation of it. It hath the colour of a Toad, and is close covered over with thick Scales. It is in size like an Elephant but lower and is an Elephant's deadly enemy…[12]

The error in date which occurred in the original letter was perpetuated in the text copied on the sketch. Dürer proceeded to make another drawing from the original, inscribing it 'Rhinoceron 1515'. He subsequently produced a woodcut in which he reversed the position of the beast and changed the inscription to '1515 / Rhinoceros'. This woodcut was to become the classic representation of the rhinoceros for the next several centuries and was widely reproduced and copied by other artists. [26a and 26d]

At approximately the same time, another woodcut of King Manuel's rhinoceros appeared. It was the work of the contemporary Augsburg painter and engraver, Hans Burgkmair. His representation is considered more realistic than Dürer's because the detail included (such as the rope and chain with which the beast's forefeet were tied) lends plausibility. [26b]

Whether Burgkmair received a sketch of the beast from a correspondent in Lisbon as had Dürer, or whether he personally viewed the rhinoceros, cannot be determined. Fernandes had communicated with the humanist Konrad Peutinger as well as merchants in Nuremberg. Burgkmair was in frequent communication with Portuguese traders and voyagers to the Indies, as demonstrated by the series of woodcuts he had produced in 1508 depicting the peoples and domesticated animals of Africa and Asia. Burgkmair's woodcut of the rhinoceros apparently received little circulation, however, for only a single copy has survived.[13]

A third contemporary and equally interesting drawing of the

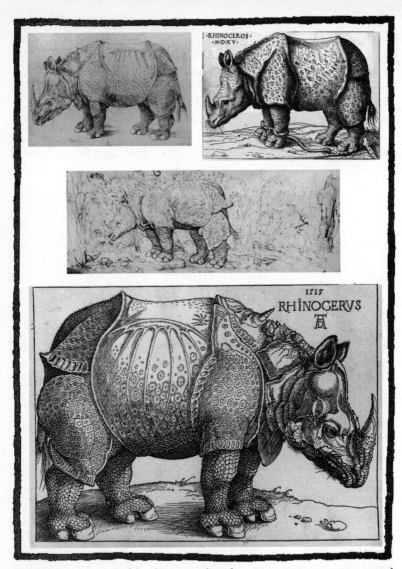

[26] Representations of the rhinoceros based upon contemporary reports and drawings received from Lisbon: [a] drawing by Albrecht Dürer, Nuremberg, 1515. Pen and ink on paper. In the British Museum. [b] Woodcut by Hans Burgkmair, Augsburg 1515. In the Graphische Sammlung Albertina, Vienna. [c] Sketch, probably by Albrecht Altdorfer, appearing at the bottom of a page of the prayer book of Emperor Maximilian I. Red ink on paper. In the Bibliothèque Municipale de Besançon. [d] Woodcut by Albrecht Dürer, 1515. In the British Museum.

Lisbon rhinoceros is known, an original sketch executed in red ink at the bottom of one of the marginal illustrations in the prayerbook of Emperor Maximilian I. The beast is standing on a flat rock, its forefeet apparently shackled with chains, shown against a background of plants and an old tree stump.[14] [26c]

In an inscription obviously of later date, is the monogram of Albrecht Altdorfer of Regensburg, one of the 'little masters'. Although Altdorfer's style generally resembled that of Dürer with whom he had studied, the prayerbook drawing of the rhinoceros has much more in common with the woodcut by Burgkmair.[15]

It was not long after its arrival in Lisbon that the presence of the rhinoceros became known in Italy. Less than two months after its disembarkation, a four-page pamphlet in verse was published in Rome on *The Form, Nature and Habits of the Rhinoceros which was brought to Portugal by the Captain of the King's Fleet and other beautiful items brought from the islands newly discovered*. It was the work of Giovanni Giacomo Penni, a Florentine physician and poet of indifferent talents who had come to Rome at the time of Leo's election. The pamphlet reflected the considerable interest in the exploration and exploitation of the new worlds and the treasures they contained which flourished throughout Europe and particularly in Italy.[16]

Penni's rhymes first described 'the victory of the most serene and invincible Manuel, King of Portugal, against the Moors, and the capture of Azamor and of Almedina and other lands in the kingdom of Morocco', apparently based on Pacheco's oration and using the same title. Penni seemed to be well-informed of details concerning the Portuguese fleet that arrived at Lisbon at the end of May 1515 with its three shiploads of spices. He noted that Albuquerque had sent gifts not only to the Portuguese queen but also to the prince and princess, and he described them, as well as gifts for certain courtiers.

Penni had not personally observed the rhinoceros, however, nor was he familiar with the woodcut by Dürer, although the woodcut drawing appearing in the pamphlet bore a certain resemblance to it. His poetry left much to be desired, but apparently he had no illusions about his talent, for he wrote:

> Some may say that these verses in hand
> Have been fashioned without ingenuity
> And that I vituperate the Muse and Pegasus
> Showing my talents to be vile and inept.
> Perhaps someone may be persuaded
> That I with my verses do something worthy…[17]

The pamphlet has a remarkable resemblance to the eight-page publi-

[27] Woodcut of the Lisbon rhinoceros on the title-page of the pamphlet entitled *Forma e natura e costumi de lo Rinoceronte*, artist not known (Rome, 1515). In the Biblioteca Colombina, the Cathedral of Seville.

cation in verse on *The Form, Nature and Habits of the Elephant* which had appeared in Rome at the same time or shortly before, even to the same format and type style and the inclusion of a woodcut of the beast being described on the title-page. [27] A most unusual feature of the pamphlet is that it was published so quickly after the arrival of the rhinoceros in Lisbon in May, appearing on 13 July 1515, less than two months later. It did not include an account of the contest between the rhinoceros and the elephant, however, which had taken place on 3 June. Apparently it was produced in an extremely limited edition, because like the pamphlet about the elephant, only a single copy is known to survive. This copy was originally purchased by the distinguished scholar and bibliophile, Fernando Colón, the natural son of the explorer Christopher Columbus. As was his wont, Colón carefully noted on the pamphlet the place and date of purchase, Rome 1515. It is now part of the Biblioteca Colombina, the library which he bequeathed to the Cathedral of Seville.[18]

The increasing number of successes in Portuguese discovery and conquest in the East required that more declarations of exclusive right to the new found lands be obtained from the Holy See. Accordingly, King Manuel sought new ways to ensure the pope's goodwill and to obtain papal acknowledgement of Portuguese accomplishments, in order to maintain the seagoing ascendancy over Spain which Portugal had achieved in past decades. As the king contemplated the selection of new gifts for the pope, he reflected on his own good judgement in having sent an elephant with the Portuguese mission the previous year. Because of its rarity and unusual size, the beast had proven an extremely attractive gift, and its talented performance made it an ambassador extraordinary, a constant reminder to the pope and his court of the identity of its donor. There could be no doubt that the presence of the elephant at the Vatican was an important factor in maintaining the continued excellent political and diplomatic relations between Portugal and the Holy See.

Now the Portuguese king felt that there was need for another mission, or its equivalent. It was perhaps as much a matter of vanity as of diplomacy. Born in obscurity as the ninth son of Dom Ferdinand, Duke of Beja, fate had cast Manuel upon the Portuguese throne as successor to King João III. Good fortune continued to smile upon him and enabled him to extract the greatest benefits possible from the combination of internal, foreign, and colonial politics of his time. His ships in great numbers continued to travel to and from his Asian colonies laden with riches and commodities of every description, making the court at Lisbon the most ostentatious and glittering of all Europe. Only the papal court of Leo X in Rome surpassed it for pomp and pageantry, and then only in the arts and letters and humanities, not in riches and exoticism.

It is also possible that by now there may have been some concern at the Portuguese court about the costly maintenance of the rhinoceros, which further inclined the king to send it to Rome as his second 'ambassador extraordinary'. At just about this time, when King Manuel was contemplating the sending of other gifts to Rome, the historian Paolo Giovio suggested that the king might provide the pope with an opportunity to match the rhinoceros against Hanno in a tournament.

Having reached a decision, with or without Giovio's suggestion, Manuel then made a selection of other gifts to symbolize the opulence of the East. His choice was a selection of rare spices combined with objects of gold and silver. Accordingly, on 9 October he ordered his royal treasurer Rui Leite to provide João da Pina, 'a nobleman of our House,' with fourteen silver items from the royal treasury. He specified two casks, two small jugs, two shallow basins, two ewers and six cups, all of silver. These were ordered to be gilded and prepared for shipment with cloth wrappings, packed into individual containers. The whole was then to be placed in an *arche*, a container made of wood which in turn was to be wrapped with packing cloth to protect the contents from the sea air.

The six cups were decorated with images of animals in relief adorned with enamel and finished in silver gilt. One weighed seven *marcos* seven *onças* and four and a half *oitavas;* another four *marcos* and six *oitavas*, and the remaining four were of various lesser weights. The two silver ewers were decorated with *bastiaes* or embossing and together they weighed fifty-four *marcos* seven *onças* and four and a half *oitavas*. A large embossed and enamelled urn with silver gilt chains weighed half as much. Another large embossed vase was studded with enamel medallions, and a hollow basin was embossed and inset with an enamel medallion. The other pieces were of comparable design and quality. A detailed list of the papal gifts forms part of a volume of the king's receipts and expenses for the period 1514 to 1517. Regrettably missing are folios 8 through 17, which reported the expenses of the Portuguese mission to Rome.

Entries noted on five folios occurring later in the volume, however, provide considerable detail about the other gifts to accompany the rhinoceros. Notable among these was a silver cup purchased from Admiral Vasco da Gama and two other cups purchased from Barão [Baron] de Alvito. The inclusion of objects purchased from private owners instead of those produced by the royal silversmiths, suggests that they were of exceptional quality, possibly antiquities, admired by the king. Each of these objects was to be provided with its own fine leather-covered case lined on the interior with velvet.[19]

A postscript added to the royal order in the king's name by Barão de Alvito directed Leite to include 'the chain of gilded iron and the green velvet collar with roses and gilded eyelets which we ordered you to have made for the aforesaid rhinoceros [*ganda*], to be decorated with a fringe'. A fringed collar of green velvet was certainly a frivolous accoutrement for such a large savage animal, but the king may have thought that the contrast would emphasize its great size and strength.[20]
[28]

Another part of the king's gifts stored in the ship's hold consisted of 5,000 hundredweight (*quintal*) of pepper, more than 1,000 each of cloves and cinnamon, almost 16 hundredweight of ginger, and another 6 hundredweight of aromatic nutmeg, almost 700 of ordinary nutmeg, more than 1,000 hundredweight of kevel pepper, and almost 500 of benzoin. This collection of spices represented at least as great a value as the silver gilt items. Although the total worth of this shipment was modest when compared with that brought to Rome by the

[28] Order from King Manuel I to his silversmith relating to the selection of gifts to be sent to Pope Leo X, dated 9 October 1515. In the *Corpo Cronologico*, parte I, Maço 19, document 2. In the Arquivo Nacional da Torre do Tombo, Lisbon.

Portuguese mission, the monarch no doubt concluded that the uniqueness of the rhinoceros would compensate for the difference.[21]

The precious gifts and the rhinoceros were finally brought on board and preparations were made for departure. The ship was under the command of João da Pina. When all was in readiness, it sailed out of the Tagus River in December 1515 *en route* to Rome.[22]

The first part of the journey was uneventful. The ship entered the bay of Marseilles in January, at the moment King Francis I and Queen Claude arrived there. They were on their return journey to Paris from Sainte Baume in Provence where the monarch had travelled 'to render graces to God' for the victory he had achieved over the Swiss at

Marignano and the conquest of the duchy of Milan. The entire city of Marseilles turned out to greet the sovereigns with great manifestations of joy and festivity. On the morning following their arrival, the king and queen attended religious services in the cathedral. Later the king boarded the galleys that had been prepared for him and observed a great mock battle, in which oranges were used as missiles, that had been staged for him by the captain-general.[23]

Learning that a Portuguese ship had arrived in the bay with a rhinoceros on board, the king expressed a desire to see the beast. Captain Pina was informed and he sailed his vessel to one of the several islands in the bay two leagues seaward, either Pomeges (now Cagastracia) or Rataneau (now Lila), and there he off-loaded the animal so that the king could observe it more conveniently. The next day Francis I boarded a galley and led a large entourage of other galleys and brigantines to the island. The visit was eminently successful and Pina reportedly presented the French king with an extremely beautiful horse which he had on board. Grateful for the gift, the king rewarded Pina with 5,000 gold *eçus*.[24]

Shortly after his return to Paris, King Francis dispatched Antoine de Conflans to Lisbon for the express purpose of purchasing elephants and other exotic beasts for his court. He had written in advance to King Manuel requesting his assistance in facilitating the purchase *iusto pretio* of a male and a female elephant and certain oriental products 'which exist in great abundance in Lisbon, habitually being provided from India'.[25]

The French king had a serious interest in wild beasts, now reinforced by the recent sight of the rhinoceros. Pierre Belon noted 'in the same manner that we keep some small dog for company which we have sleep at the foot of our bed for pleasure, Francis I has had from time to time, a lion, panther, or other such fierce beast which he had made endeared to him as some tamed animal in the homes of peasants.'[26]

After a brief anchorage in the bay, Pina again set sail at the end of January or early February. Passing through the straits of Porto Venere, they were suddenly surprised by a violent storm that arose a little north of the port at the entrance to La Spezia. The small Portuguese vessel was helpless in the turbulent seas, and was tossed again and again against the rocks of the perilous steep coast. It was totally wrecked and sank with all hands on board. Although the rhinoceros would normally have been able to swim to safety, it was restrained by the shackles and chains that bound it to the deck, and it too was drowned. Later writers speculated on the cause of the wreck. One claim was that the chained rhinoceros had become frightened and enraged during the storm and had caused the capsizing of the vessel by shifting its weight.[27]

According to several contemporary writers, during the next several weeks the wreckage of the vessel and remains of the cargo were washed ashore, as well as the carcass of the rhinoceros, which was recovered on the shore near Villefranche on the French coast. 'It was not possible that such a beast could save itself, being chained,' Bishop Giovio wrote, 'albeit it swam miraculously among the sharp rocks which are along the coast...' The recovery of the dead rhinoceros was reported to King Manuel and he ordered the beast to be mounted.

Whether this was undertaken at Genoa or whether the carcass was skinned and the hide returned to Lisbon was not recorded, but the latter is the more likely. The art of taxidermy was still in its infancy in the sixteenth century. The procedure then used consisted merely of removing the animal's skin intact by slitting it along the stomach to the hind legs first, lifting it off carefully and then proceeding in the same manner up the animal's back. The skin was cured and preserved, probably by means of an arsenic compound, then dampened and shaped into the animal's form. The skeleton was not used. The hide was stuffed with straw until it was tightly filled and had assumed the appearance of the living animal. The filled hide was then carefully sewn together and the mounted beast was ready for display. In the Italian language of the period, the name for this type of mounting was *impagliato*, literally meaning 'filled with straw'. The mounted rhinoceros was placed on board another ship and sent off to Rome a second time, much as if the shipwreck had not occurred.[28]

The earliest published account of the fatal voyage formed part of the first unillustrated edition of Bishop Giovio's posthumous work on decorative emblems and mottoes, published in Florence in 1551. Following an account of the elephant Hanno, the writer noted that the rhinoceros 'arrived at Rome in its true form and size, and this was in the month of February 1515 [*sic*] with the information about its nature according to Pliny the Second, and as narrated by the Portuguese...' This was accompanied by a poem of twelve lines in Latin by the Franciscan Antonio Sanfelice, which Giovio quoted in full:

> I am the rhinoceros, brought hither from dusky India,
> From the vestibule of light and the gateway of the day.
> I boarded the fleet bound for the west, its bold sails undaunted,
> Daring new lands, to see a different sun.
> Once my city watched the battles within the walls of the circus
> There I was pitted in the arena against

My enemy the elephant.
He brought to bear his ancestral rage, the eternal
Battles with my kind, trusting in the bulk of his huge body
But we are armoured with a threefold skin and in our weapons
Mightier than the sword, and with a horn unconquered by the
tooth.
The elephant [Barrus], himself falls when he is pierced in the
belly with my weapon.
Skilful prudence fights brute force.[29]

The poem, recounting as it does the journey of the rhinoceros from India to the Western world, its contest with the elephant in the royal park of Ribeira, and its 'conquest' of the elephant, might well have served as the descriptive label to accompany the mounted beast when it was sent to the Pope. The Portuguese historian Damião de Goes wrote that as Pope Leo X received the mounted rhinoceros, 'it was with great surprise, and sadness for the loss of the crew that went down with the ship, and of the gifts that the King Dom Manuel had sent to him…'[30]

The arrival of the mounted beast in Rome was noted also in Angelo Fabronio's biography of Pope Leo X. He implied that the public reaction to the arrival of the huge gift would have merited more attention had it been a living rhinoceros. He reported 'the spectacle would have been even greater, if the rhinoceros, an animal not seen in Italy for many centuries now, which the King had also ordered to be brought to Rome, had not suffered shipwreck (since, hindered by chains, it could not swim) on the reefs of the Ligurian coast.'[31]

The first words concerning the loss of the vessel and its crew and cargo that were exchanged between Lisbon and Rome appears to have been a letter of 11 August 1516 from the Portuguese king to his ambassador at Rome, Dom Miguel da Silva, who had succeeded João da Faria to that position. The king wrote:

We are extremely sorry about the total loss of the vessel we sent to Rome, which was carrying on board an Indian rhinoceros as well as other gifts for our Holy Father, and which has caused us great displeasure. You are to tell His Holiness that it was only a few days ago that we received this news, and of the great unhappiness which we feel, because the animal at the time it was brought to us was so novel, never before seen in these parts, and hardly to be found in books, and because of the manner in which it was sent to us, we appraised it, and the estimated value was more than one hundred thousand doubloons… We thought that His Holiness would accept with pleasure what we were sending with such good will and love and that such had never before been presented to any pontiff, nor seen in those parts. But by reason that fortune had ordered things in this manner, we hope that His Holiness believes that the presents were intended for him. They were so novel and from such distant countries that His Holiness would have been amused to see them. It is not customary, and in fact not imagined, that we request an indulgence of His Holiness, but now we humbly ask the Holy Father to accept at least our love and the greatest pleasure we had in sending him these things, and that we are always and in every way at his service. Knowing that His Holiness will receive you as we have asked Him, we hope he will understand our sorrow over the fact that he was unable to see such great novelties.[32]

This letter raises several questions and answers as many others. As noted by Giovio, the mounted beast did not arrive at the Vatican until February 1516, during the time when the pope was absent from the Eternal City. Following his meeting with King Francis I at Bologna, the pontiff had travelled back to Florence and did not return to Rome until the end of February, after the arrival of the rhinoceros. The confusion attending his absence and return, and the complicated nature of political and diplomatic developments at that time, may well have been responsible for the pope's failure to acknowledge promptly the gift from the Portuguese king. Presumably King Manuel postponed writing about the matter because he had been awaiting some acknowledgement from Rome concerning his unusual gift and, receiving none, was finally compelled to approach the Pope through his ambassador.

The question that remains unresolved is the king's request that the pontiff be told that Manuel had been informed of the loss of his ship, crew and cargo 'only a few days ago', when in actuality six months had passed since the disaster. It is possible that the king's letter was deliberately intended to counteract rumours then current that he had not in fact sent the rhinoceros and other gifts to Rome after all, despite his claim to have done so.

These rumours were perpetuated even to the end of the century. In 1582 Filippe de Caverel, secretary of the embassy to the Portuguese court from the states of Artois, wrote that a rhinoceros was being shown in Lisbon which appeared to be one and the same that King Manuel had brought into combat with an elephant in 1517 [*sic*]. He believed that it was the same beast because the rhinoceros was known to live to a considerable age.[33]

Rumours that the rhinoceros had never been sent as claimed were circulated also in Rome at the time of the shipwreck. Three centuries later, speculation on the cause of the shipwreck was revived by the eminent French naturalist Baron Georges Cuvier in his published writings on the species of living and fossil pachyderms. He described

the arrival of the rhinoceros in Lisbon in 1515, and its subsequent shipment to Rome, noting that the beast 'having an excess of fury, caused
the loss of the ship which was transporting it'. Cuvier provided no
source for this interesting supposition, and his comment was presumably based upon one of the earlier accounts of the shipwreck.[34]

Despite the scanty contemporary references, the arrival of the
rhinoceros in Rome in February 1516 should have merited comment
from members of the papal court and others in the city because of its
size and rarity. It is true that it was a time of great confusion in Rome.
The pope's late return was followed almost immediately by news sent
from Florence of the death of his favourite brother, Giuliano de'
Medici. The pope grieved deeply for his brother; at the same time he
was experiencing considerable physical incapacity due to his fistula, in
addition to a malarial attack. These distractions were further
compounded by the Holy See's political and diplomatic difficulties,
and all were soon to be eclipsed by the turmoil caused by the arrival
in Rome of Fra Bonaventura (to which we shall later return).

Although for all these reasons the pope apparently failed to send an
acknowledgement to King Manuel, the rhinoceros was not totally
overlooked by artists working at the Vatican. Giovanni da Udine was
to assign it equal importance with the elephant Hanno in a ceiling
decoration at the Palazzo Baldassini, and Raphael incorporated its
image in a painting in his Loggie at the Vatican.

The saga of the rhinoceros seemed to have terminated with its
arrival in Rome, and art historians have sought in vain for some trace
of its disposition thereafter. The missing rhinoceros continues to
intrigue many merely because of its sudden disappearance. A search of
the collections of the Vatican and all the museums of Rome proved to
be unproductive, nor did sixteenth- and seventeenth-century inventories of their collections provide any clues. It was presumed to have
been destroyed in the sacking of Rome in 1527, if not earlier. Still,
another possibility offers itself: Pope Leo X, or perhaps his cousin
Giulio de' Medici after he was elected Pope Clement VII, may have
sent the mounted beast to Florence to become part of the natural
history collection maintained by the Medici family. Or it may have
been acquired for his museum of natural history by the leading Italian
naturalist of the succeeding period, Ulisse Aldrovandi of Bologna.

What appears to be a reference to one of these possibilities came to
light in an obscure footnote in a scholarly article on scientific taxidermy for museums, published as part of the annual report of the
United States National Museum of the Smithsonian Institution for the
year 1892. The reference stated that George Brown Goode, then

director of the National Museum, having travelled widely in Europe, informed the writer of the article that 'probably the oldest museum specimen in existence is a rhinoceros still preserved in the Royal Museum of Vertebrates in Florence. This was for a long time a feature of the Medicean Museum in Florence, and was originally mounted for the museum of Ulisse Aldrovandi in Bologna. It dates from the sixteenth century.'[35]

There can be no doubt that the reference relates to the rhinoceros sent to Pope Leo X, for no other example of the rhinoceros appeared in Italy in the sixteenth century. The notice of the survival of the mounted animal written 370 years after it was sent to Rome was a most promising lead. However, a search of the records and of the present collections of the five natural history collections in Florence failed to bring anything more to light.

La Specola, the museum of the University of Florence, still proudly displays the mounted hippopotamus acquired by the Medici family in the mid-eighteenth century, but not a rhinoceros. The journal of the Medici natural history collections published in 1775, *Saggio del Reale Gabinetto*, described the arrangement of the collections of natural and physical sciences, 'for the larger animals, such as the Elephant and the Hippopotamus, there are large stations on the first floor for displaying and maintaining them', without mention of the rhinoceros. Nor is any mention of the beast to be found in the correspondence on natural history topics between Aldrovandi and the Medici princes of his time.[36]

It was reported by one source that the rhinoceros did in fact appear in inventories of 1589 and of 1737, but a recent review of those records failed to find such listings. Nor does it appear in the inventory made in 1782 of the museum's surviving specimens. The search was continued in the museum collections in Bologna assembled by Aldrovandi, again without result. His numerous publications on natural history likewise yielded no clues. A survey of more than 300 of Aldrovandi's surviving unpublished manuscripts revealed a hand-written description of the rhinoceros in the first volume of *Degli animali*, without mention of the Lisbon specimen. In the same volume, however, is included a previously overlooked wash drawing of a rhinoceros which seems to bear a substantial resemblance to the Dürer woodcut.[37]

Despite the apparent absence of any written evidence of the presence of the rhinoceros in Florence, it is depicted in a painting executed for the Borgherini palace by Francesco Granacci in 1517 – just at the time of the great beast's arrival in Rome. As a youth Granacci had been

[29] 'Joseph Introduces His Father and Brothers to the Pharaoh'. Painting by Francesco Granacci, which includes the Lisbon rhinoceros – see detail, [30]. Commissioned in 1517 for the Borgherini palace in Florence. Oils on a wood panel. In the Gallerie degli Uffizi, Florence.

a fellow student with Michelangelo Buonarotti in the studio of Domenico Ghirlandajo, and the young men became fast friends as they continued their art studies together. When Michelangelo was summoned to Rome in 1508 by Pope Julius II to paint the ceiling of the Sistine Chapel, he invited Granacci to come to Rome to work with him. Granacci accepted and worked with Michelangelo in the chapel for a time. Becoming dissatisfied with the quality of the work of his assistants, however, Michelangelo kept them away from the project, and finally they returned to Florence in great disappointment, Granacci among them. Thereafter Granacci was employed at various times by Lorenzo de' Medici, who commissioned him in late 1515 to make preparations for the visit of Pope Leo X to Florence, for which Granacci executed a triumphal arch.[38]

Also, in 1515 Silvio Borgherini, a wealthy gentleman of Florence, commissioned a series of paintings to decorate the master bedroom of his palace, now the Roselli del Turco in Borgo Ognissanti, in preparation for the marriage of his son Francesco to Margherita Acciaiuoli, daughter of the prominent statesman. The paintings consisted of wooden panels (*spalliere*) painted in oils which were then fitted to the walls at eye-level. The connecting theme of the eight panels was the biblical account of Joseph in Egypt. Four of them were executed by Jacopo da Pontormo, two by Andrea del Sarto, and the remaining two by Granacci.

For one of his panels, Granacci chose the subject 'Joseph introduces his father and brother to the Pharoah', which is sometimes entitled 'Joseph and his brother in Egypt'. The artist transmuted Cairo into a north Italian Renaissance town. In front of the steps to a large public

[30] Detail, greatly enlarged, from [29], showing the rhinoceros and its custodian. In the Gallerie degli Uffizi, Florence.

building in the background, there appears a one-horned Indian rhinoceros with its two front feet shackled and joined by a short chain, held by an attendant walking behind it. Although executed on a small scale, the beast is depicted in considerable detail.

In view of the date of the painting, 1517, this animal can have been none other than the Lisbon rhinoceros, which, in all likelihood, Granacci had seen. This probability is reinforced by the fact that his drawing is clearly based neither on the Dürer woodcut nor the engraving by Burgkmair, although it has a slight resemblance to the latter. If not painted from personal observation, it appears to have been copied from another source which had been executed from 'life', if the term can be applied to a mounted beast. [29 and 30]

The question that arises is why the rhinoceros should have been included in a scene depicting Egypt, since it had no relationship to either the subject of the panel or the region. It can only be assumed that, knowing of the Medici association with the beast, Granacci added it as an amusing item, as it would have been if indeed Pope Leo X had sent the mounted rhinoceros on from Rome to Florence at about that time. The rhinoceros painted by Granacci has a marked resemblance to the crude woodcut appearing on the title-page of Penni's publication. Although this work was published in Rome, Penni was a Florentine and there may be a link between the two depictions of the beast, leading one to wonder whether Granacci may have been the artist who produced Penni's woodcut.

With a scene shift to Florence, an exhaustive survey of the inventories of the Medici collections was undertaken but with inconclusive results. If the rhinoceros had in fact been sent to Florence by 1581 to become part of the Medici collections, it would probably have formed part of the display in the Arsenale of the Palazzo Vecchio when Grand Duke Francesco began to make a systematic organization of the collections. It would have remained there at least until some time between 1772 and 1775, when the collections of the Arsenale were dismantled and dispersed.

In conflict with the apparent lack of evidence of the presence of the rhinoceros in Florence is the statement by George Brown Goode reported in 1892 that the rhinoceros was the oldest mounted specimen from the sixteenth century existing in European collections. Had Goode observed the mounted beast on his travels, or was he reporting it from earlier documentary sources? The question remains unanswered and the ultimate fate of the rhinoceros unresolved.[39]

CHAPTER SIX

'The Wheele of Change'

What wonder that men of the time, carried away by the impression made on them by the capital of the world, spent their whole lives there? However great the evil which may have lurked in the society of those days, still they contained not a little of what was good, which, by the very nature of things, was less spoken of than what was bad...

It is a characteristic of the Eternal City that it possesses the power of attracting all that is prominent in the way of intellect, knowledge, and art. But never before or since have her walls contained within them a more brilliant society.

Ludwig von Pastor : *The History of the Popes From the Close of the Middle Ages* (1891)

AS THE SAD SAGA OF THE RHINOCEROS WAS UNFOLDING TO A mournful conclusion, the elephant Hanno continued to enjoy the unabated love and enthusiasm of the papal court and the people of Rome. Throngs clustered constantly about its enclosure, with papal permission, observing its antics in the new quarters constructed for it. They were occasionally favoured also with glimpses of the great beast as it was being paraded through the streets on state occasions and during festivals.

All went well until May 1516, when heresy fell upon Rome, enveloping it like a heavy dark cloud and threatening not only the pope but Hanno as well, and adding a particularly distasteful element to life at the court. This was a period when astrology and the occult sciences were achieving great popularity, particularly in European courts. Horoscopes were drawn up to govern political and military actions as well as public events, which were permitted to take place only on auspicious days. Prophecies were greatly respected and Pope Leo even encouraged the impression that he shared the current enthusiasm for astrology.

This concern with prophecy and its derivatives lent force to critics of the Church, particularly among the mendicant orders that had fallen into disrepute and disfavour over a long period. They took advantage of the general state of ferment and credulity in men's minds, and linked their criticism of luxury and corruption to prophecies of imminent doom – unless major reforms were immediately forthcoming.

Although Pope Julius II had begun to plan for reforms by convening the Lateran Council, the sale of ecclesiastical offices and benefices by the Church had continued, as had the scandalous behaviour of the clergy, and excessive luxury within the Church at all levels. Although Girolamo Savonarola had been burned at the stake in Florence in 1498, his influence persisted and his adherents and disciples continued to travel about the country preaching their opposition and heresy. Shortly after the election of Pope Leo X, twelve Franciscan monks roamed over a large part of Italy preaching apostasy and bringing terror to the people with their dire prophecies. When one of these, Fra Francesco da Montepulciano, appeared in Florence, his public sermons caused great consternation, heightened by his sudden death immediately after having delivered one. It was in an effort to restore a sense of equanimity among the people disturbed by these fearsome predictions that Giuliano de' Medici had arranged a particularly great festival on the feast day of St John in 1514, for which he had wished to borrow Hanno.

Pope Leo X had been forced to take action against one after another of these fanatic monks. He was particularly pleased by the manner in which one of them, Teodoro of Scutari, had been stilled by the Archbishop of Florence in the spring of 1515. Then, early in the next year Hieronymus of Siena, a Tuscan hermit, who may have been one of Savonarola's disciples and was said to have worked miracles, established himself in the pulpit of the cathedral of Milan from which he denounced the hierarchy of the Church. This frequent occupancy continued for months as he defeated all efforts to dislodge him. At last the disruption he was causing the cathedral clergy with his interruption of ordinary services resulted in the doors of the cathedral being closed permanently against him.[1]

In May 1516 another of these itinerant preachers, Fra Bonaventura, created an even greater furore. Described as 'a Franciscan monk of the fourth order', he was a follower of the Portuguese friar Amadeo Menez de Sylva, who had founded a Franciscan reform movement in Italy in the mid-fifteenth century called the *Amadeiti* or *Amadeans*. The group had been favoured by Pope Sixtus IV and enjoyed partial autonomy until the year following Fra Bonaventura's visit to Rome, when Pope Leo X combined all the Franciscan reform groups into a single entity which became known as the Observants.

Fra Bonaventura was originally from Subiaco and had travelled through northern Italy, loudly announcing himself to be the Angelic Pope whose coming had been foretold by Savonarola and had been expected and sought since the days of Joachim of Fiore in the twelfth century. Proclaiming the views of the Joachimites as well as of Telesphorus, whose prophecies had been published in Venice in that same year, Fra Bonaventura had attracted more than 20,000 zealots who followed him everywhere, kissing his feet and worshipping him as their saviour.

The apostate monk had written an inflammatory paper addressed to the Doge of Venice in which he described the Church in Rome as the scarlet woman of the Apocalypse and himself as 'chosen by God to be the Pastor of the Church in Zion, crowned by the hands of angels, and commissioned to be the Saviour of the World'. His paper announced that he had excommunicated the pope and all the cardinals and prelates of the Church in Rome, and warned all the faithful to disassociate themselves from it. All Christian kings were admonished to support him, and the government of Venice was urged to ally itself with the King of France, because that monarch had been selected to reform the Church and convert the Turks. Fra Bonaventura's original paper had been forwarded by the Venetian government to Pope Leo X before the monk's arrival in Rome, so that the pontiff anticipated the disturbance that was sure to follow in his wake.[2]

Immediately upon his arrival in Rome at the beginning of May with his enormous entourage, Fra Bonaventura preached to the Roman populace, assembling in large crowds and curious to see the famous apostate and hear his sermons. Not only did he tell the people that he had summarily excommunicated the pope and the cardinals, and urge them to leave the Church, but he also thundered forth a terrifying prophecy: the pope would die, he predicted; so would five cardinals whom he identified by name, all of which deaths would take place before the following 12 September. Furthermore, the pope's elephant and its keeper would die in the same period![3]

It will be recalled that this was a particularly unhappy period in the pope's life. He was still mourning the recent death of his last surviving brother, Giuliano, and he was tortured with pain and discomfort from his fistula which had troubled him most of his life. More recently he had become afflicted with a bout of tertian fever. This malady, known also as *vivax malaria*, was caused by a malarial parasite and its victims were wracked with paroxysms which recurred at intervals of forty-eight hours.[4]

As a consequence of this compilation of ills, the pope had sunk into a state of deep depression. Lost in spells of melancholy even before the arrival of the monk, he was now constantly preoccupied with his future and possible imminent death. When Fra Bonaventura began preaching to the Roman people and causing disturbances in the city, the pontiff was in no mood for toleration. He promptly ordered that the monk be arrested and incarcerated in Castel Sant' Angelo.[5]

The occurrence was described in some detail in a curious letter from a certain Bernardo in Florence addressed to the Venetian ambassador to Rome, Nicolo Zorzi (or sometimes Giorgi), who in turn communicated it to Marino Sanuto in Venice. Bernardo reported that when he first arrived in Florence he was told that there had come to Rome a Franciscan monk of the fourth order who had predicted that the pope would die in September, and that as a consequence of the prophecy the pontiff had ordered the monk to be imprisoned in the Castel. Bernardo admitted having received this news with some incredulity.

Since then, a traveller arriving in Florence from Rome had brought more details of the situation. He reported that in Rome there was an elephant with two custodians, only one of whom exercised his responsibility. It is assumed that he meant that it was the mahout who was responsible for the beast's activities. According to the account, when the monk observed this, he said 'Poor man! You had better tend more to your soul than to this beast, because on [a given day] you will die and the beast will die as well!' The traveller went on to relate that on the date specified both the elephant and its keeper had died. The magistrates of Rome, wrote Bernardo, upon learning what had happened, sent for the monk and demanded an explanation. They questioned him as to whether it was he who had foretold the deaths that had occurred. The monk admitted that he was the one, and added also that the pope and five cardinals would be dead before 12 September.

The questioning magistrate received the reply with considerable consternation. During this period the pope was employing Dominicans, the Order of Preachers, to serve as inquisitors to maintain the integrity of the faith, so the magistrate immediately sent for the superior of a Dominican convent to act as inquisitor. He commanded that the monk be put to the rack to force him to reveal the source on which he based his prognostications. Thereupon Fra Bonaventura turned to the magistrate, saying, 'You think to do me ill, but it would be better if you attended to your soul, inasmuch as you too will die and it will occur on [a specified date]!' And then turning back to the inquisitor who was about to strike him, the monk said to him, 'Oh, miserable one! You think only to torture me, and do not realize that on such a day [a date was specified] you too will die!'

He spoke in such a manner and with such conviction that the inquisitor, instead of striking him, became frightened. Then upon an order from the pope, the monk was imprisoned in Castel Sant'Angelo. 'And it came to pass,' wrote Bernardo, 'that on the day specified death came to all those he had predicted. Until now among the cardinals that have died have been the Cardinals of Senigaglia, Alborensis and Sanseverino; meanwhile the Cardinals of San Zorzi and Soderini are lying ill in such a state that it is said they cannot survive. The pope has tertian fever and is a man of great obesity: with the entry of this illness into his body, concern is expressed that it [the prophecy] may indeed come true.'[6]

The major occurrences up to this point were summarized and verified also in an official report of 12 May sent to Prince Karl Gurcensem for the attention of Emperor Maximilian I from his agent or solicitor at the papal court, D. Stephen Rosin. He wrote:

After paying my humble respects, I am reporting to the Holy Roman Emperor that Fra Bonaventura who in the first year of Pope Leo's reign (at the time that the Emperor was in the city), drew huge crowds of people, was on last Wednesday led captive to Castel Sant'Angelo after having proclaimed himself to be the shepherd angel chosen by God in His mercy, and the saviour of the world appointed over all mankind, whose head was the Church of God in Zion. And more than 20,000 persons flocked to him and kissed his feet, as if he were the true vicar of God. He wrote a book which he sent to the Doge of Venice and to the city's Great Council, which he entitled The Venturian Book Concerning the Church of Rome, Cast Down As An Apostate and Cursed By God As a Whore.

At the beginning of this book was a letter having this preamble:

'Bonaventura, of the Church of God in Zion, pastor chosen by God and crowned by bands of angels, destined for the salvation of the world for all the faithful of Christ, sends salutations and apostolic benediction.' In this volume he deprives and excommunicates and curses Pope Leo and all the cardinals, and enjoins all Christian prelates under penalty of eternal excommunication and a blanket sentence of excommunication and deprivation, that they not obey the mandates of the Roman Church. At the same time he preaches that he will be anointed Emperor of the Romans, and that the power of the Church will be transferred to the Church in Zion. He exhorts all Christian kings to take up arms and come to his aid; chiefly, he exhorts the Venetians that they should

immediately put themselves in league in arms and friendship with the King of France, since that sovereign was chosen by God as the agent for the transferral of the Church of God to Zion and for the conversion of the Turks to the Christian faith. He also exhorts the Venetians to make copies of his book and send them to the King of France and many others. I have not seen the book myself, but the Emperor's orator Lord Capen saw a certain part of it, the pope himself having shown it to him (the Venetians had sent him the original), and Capen related these things to me when I was at dinner with His Illustrious Lordship, not without wonder that such things touched the very heart of the Church.[7]

The continued incarceration of Fra Bonaventura resulted in the gradual dispersal of his followers. Little by little they disappeared from the city. Bonaventura's prophecy, however, came to public attention again within the next two weeks, when one day early in June the elephant Hanno was found to have suddenly become extremely ill. The beast was unable to move about and lay listlessly in its pen despite the mahout's efforts to rouse it. It was obviously in pain, and was experiencing great difficulty in breathing.

The privy chamberlain Branconio was immediately summoned, and he in turn informed the pope with expressions of considerable concern. Pope Leo, burdened as he was with mounting public problems and his own illness, became greatly alarmed and distraught. Nothing must happen to Hanno! Obviously Fra Bonaventura's prophecy had been preying on his mind, and here was another evidence of its apparent basis in truth. The pontiff accompanied Branconio to Hanno's pen and gazed upon his great pet lying so helpless and in such agony. This was the first time that the elephant had been ill since its arrival in Rome and the pontiff was uncertain how to cope with the new problem. The situation was obviously extremely serious.

The pope immediately directed that the finest physicians in Rome, including his own, be brought immediately to the Vatican. The puzzlement of the men of medicine when so summarily summoned was quickly dispelled: indeed the pope was ill but they were not to attend the pontiff; their patient was, to be sure, an important member of the court – in fact the elephant. The pope directed that they attend the beast at once. To heal it neither effort nor cost should be spared. Veterinary medicine had not yet been developed except to some degree for the care of horses and farm animals, and even if it had, there would have been little experience in Rome with large jungle beasts. Consequently the medical men could not do else than treat Hanno as if he were a human. First, its urine was tested, and then its blood was let, but no clue to the nature of the illness could be found in either. Inevitably the next step was to prescribe the universal remedy of the time when a cause could not be determined or no other solution offered: a purgative was called for, a strong one in view of the size of the patient.

But which purgative should be selected, and what should be its proportions? How could they judge the quantity required for such a massive body? As these questions were hotly debated in one consultation after another, the physicians were left with as many answers as there were debaters. Inasmuch as the beast was evincing intense pain with spasms that shook it periodically, and was having extreme difficulty in breathing, the doctors agreed that its malady was 'angina'. This was scarcely progress, for it meant merely that Hanno was suffering from suffocative pain, without identification of either cause or remedy. Furthermore, it became evident that the elephant was constipated. Eventually the physicians reached an agreement on the nature of the purgative and the size of the dose. In accordance with the practice of the period, the purgative contained a large quantity of gold.

What was considered to be an appropriate dosage was given to the patient, with the expected difficulty in forcing the beast to take it. Far from improving its condition, however, the additional pressure of the purgative upon a system already badly constipated caused the beast to expire. The date was 8 June 1516.[8]

From the moment he had learned of the elephant's illness, the pope rarely left its side. He waited watchfully and impatiently as the doctors argued amongst themselves and finally ministered to it, and meanwhile tried to find ways to comfort the suffering beast, but all to no avail. The pontiff became inconsolable when Hanno was finally pronounced dead. He would gladly have given a heavy price, he said, for the preservation of so magnificent a beast.

The pope's sorrow was shared by Branconio and many others at the court who had become fond of the large pet, and for a time the demise of their favourite threw a great shadow of sadness over the entire papal family and the business of the court. The shock of Hanno's death and the personal grief of the pontiff overshadowed the death of one of the elephant's keepers, which occurred simultaneously, just as the clairvoyant monk had predicted. So little attention did the keeper's death generate at the time, in fact, that he remains unidentified.

What arrangements could possibly be made in the confined space of the Vatican for the burial of such a large animal which now lay where it had expired? The pope provided a simple answer, to everyone's relief: Hanno was to be laid to rest in the Cortile del Belvedere, where it had first been displayed after its arrival in Rome, for it must remain at the Vatican where it had spent its life. And such a short life it had been! Two years, two months, and twenty-six days in all in the Eternal City, and less than seven years in life.

Although Hanno was gone, the pope determined that it was not to be forgotten. He instructed Branconio to make all necessary arrangements. The elephant was to have a permanent monument to inform future generations of its presence in Rome and of its role at the papal court. Although the fates had decreed that the people of Rome were to be deprived of the elephant in life, the pope would make certain that they would be provided with a lasting reminder of the pleasure it had brought them.

Accordingly, the court painter Raphael was summoned from his other assignments. What was required, Raphael was told, was a large painting of the elephant to be executed in the animal's full size and natural colouring, marked with the measurements of its main members. The portrait was to appear on the wall at the entrance to the Vatican adjacent to the old clock tower. Furthermore, the pontiff insisted that it was to be executed by none other than by the gifted brush of Raphael himself.[9]

The artist responded willingly, as was his wont, and he assured the pope that he would have his wish. At that time Raphael was engaged in the decoration of the third of the palace stanzas, the Stanza del Incendio del Borgo Vecchio, which featured the glorification of the papacy as its theme. He had been at work on the project for two years and it was not to be completed until yet another year had passed. At the same time he had been assigned by Pope Leo X to the project of designing the cartoons for a set of ten large tapestries to decorate the lower portions of the walls of the Sistine Chapel.

As he had always done in the past with the pope's numerous and unusual commissions, Raphael promptly accepted them, produced the designs and then divided the work among his several talented assistants, providing them with sketches and specifications, and they executed the work in his style.[10]

In the matter of the elephant's memorial, however, there is considerable doubt that he could have followed his usual procedure. The pope had specified that it was to be executed by Raphael personally, and his direct involvement with the project became well known. Art historians are divided, some proposing that Raphael assigned the execution of the memorial to Giulio Romano. It is certain, however, that Raphael designed the memorial fresco. He also may have worked on it assisted by Romano, or it may have been executed entirely by

Romano from Raphael's design. Both had made drawings of the elephant in life at one time or another, as confirmed by sketches that have been preserved.

The great mural, which no longer survives, was completed to the pope's satisfaction at last. When it was revealed to Leo and his court, it seemed as if Hanno lived again, shown with its bell and its two custodians, and the sun and moon visible in one corner. In accordance with the pontiff's instructions, Raphael had added the measurements of the elephant's height and length of the main members of its large body from measurements made before the beast's burial. While the painting of the mural was in progress, it attracted considerable public attention, and many of the court joined the pope and his familiars as they came to watch the artists at work on their scaffolding, applying first the wet plaster and then the colours.

Pilgrims arriving at the great basilica from distant parts of Italy and Europe were undoubtedly startled to be confronted by the fresco of an elephant at the entrance to the most important shrine of the Christian world, for it was indeed as large as life and more vivid than any circus poster could have been. Even in the Forum, the Colosseum or in Diocletian's Baths, such a display would have been impressive, but in the piazza of St Peter it was overwhelming. The pope had achieved his wish, for not only was the mural a reminder for the Roman populace, but remained a memorial for all the world to see.

Meanwhile, as the pontiff ruminated over the loss of his pet, he determined that it should be remembered also with a fitting epitaph. He himself composed the words, which reflected his fondness for Hanno:

> *Under this great hill I lie buried*
> *Mighty elephant which the King Manuel*
> *Having conquered the Orient*
> *Sent as captive to Pope Leo X.*
> *At which the Roman people marvelled, –*
> *A beast not seen for a long time,*
> *And in my brutish breast they perceived human feelings.*
> *Fate envied me my residence in the blessed Latium*
> *And had not the patience to let me serve my master a full three*
> *years.*
> *But I wish, oh gods, that the time which Nature would have*
> *assigned to me, and Destiny stole away,*
> *You will add to the life of the great Leo.*
>
> *He lived seven years*

He died of angina
He measured twelve palms in height.
Giovanni Battista Branconio dell'Aquila
Privy chamberlain to the pope
And provost of the custody of the elephant,
Has erected this
In 1516, the 8th of June,
In the fourth year of the pontificate of Leo X.

That which Nature has stolen away
Raphael of Urbino with his art has restored.

Pope Leo X composed the first segment of the epitaph, to which Branconio added the account of the beast's career. This elegiac composition, conceived in sorrow, was submitted by the pope to the court poet, Filippo Beroaldo the Younger, to render into Latin hexameters. It was in this form that it was inscribed either on a marble plaque affixed to the wall below or beside the mural, or inscribed directly on the wall itself. Beroaldo's rendering, in its original Latin as it appears in one of his surviving manuscripts, is provided in the Appendix.[11]

Bishop Giovio later confirmed that the epitaph was to be found near the tower of the gate to the Vatican, and that its author was Beroaldo the Younger. He wrote 'He [the pope] ordered the gate [entrance] next to the Vatican tower to be painted and on it this epigram of Beroaldo the Younger to be inscribed – together with a pictorial representation of the elephant.' Beroaldo's Latin version of the epitaph, exists in an unpublished manuscript and is included also in his collected works. [31] That Raphael personally executed the mural on the wall to the Vatican entrance is adequately confirmed by the epitaph, although he may have been assisted by Giulio Romano or Giovanni da Udine or both.[12]

Some historians are of the opinion that four sketches of Hanno in red chalk in the collection of the Ashmolean Museum at Oxford, which were unquestionably drawn from life, may have served as the basis for the Vatican mural. Others are convinced that no relationship exists between the sketches and the mural. It is much more likely, in fact, that the mural was based on a pen-and-ink sketch drawn from life, originally attributed to Raphael but more recently to Giulio Romano. The original drawing, or a copy of it made by an unknown artist, is in the von Beckrath collection of the Kupferstichkabinett in Berlin. The elephant is shown in full profile with its mahout seated over its neck

Monte sub hoc Elephas ingenti contegor ingens
Quem Rex Emanuel devicto oriente Leoni
Captivum misit Decimo: quem Romula pubes
Mirata est animal non Longo tempore visum.
Vidit & humanos in bruto tempore sensus.
Invidit Latiy Sedem mihi parca beati.
Nec passa est ternos Domino familiarier annos.
Ah Quae sors rapuit naturae debita nostrae
Tempora. Vos Superi magno Accumulate Leoni

    Vixit ann. septem
    Obijt Anginae morbo

Altitudo erat palm Duodecim
Jo. BB Branconius Aquilanus
A cubiculo & Elephantis curae Prefectus
    Posuit
Leonis Decimi Pont Anno Quarto

Raphael Urbinas quod Natura abstulerat
    Arte Restituit.

[31] Handwritten draft of Hanno's epitaph in *Cod. Ottob. lat. 2967*, fol. 94r. Author unknown. In the Biblioteca Apostolica Vaticana.

and the Saracen on the ground with an *ankush* (elephant prod) in hand holding the beast's trunk.

    The drawing is executed in black crayon on grey paper with pen-and-ink detail and cross-hatching, and highlighted in white. The

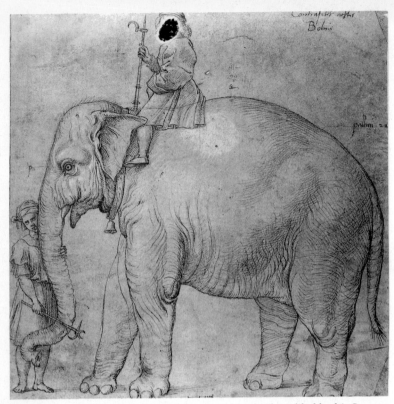

[32] Hanno with its Moorish mahout astride his back and led by his Saracen guide holding its trunk, with notations of the elephant's measurements. Attributed variously to Raphael and to Giulio Romano, *c.* 1514-16. Pen and ink on paper. In the Preussischer Kulturbesitz Kupferstichkabinett, Staatliche Museen zu Berlin.

mahout appears to be a Caucasian while the trainer standing beside the elephant is obviously an Oriental. The outer edges of the drawing bear the elephant's measurements, as had been requested for the mural by the pontiff. The inscriptions '*palmi 22*' appears over the beast's buttocks and '*p. 10 2/1*' over the highest point of its back. At the elephant's eye-level is noted another '*p.*' without notation of the number of palms. A scale is included under the image of the elephant, and the words '*Contrafetet achter Bolini*', added later in the sixteenth century by an unknown hand, are in brown ink. The words, meaning 'Likeness after Bolini', constitute somewhat of a puzzle inasmuch as Bolini has not been identified.[13] [32]

The sketch for the mural, attributed to Raphael or Romano, whether it was copied from the one presently in the Kupferstichkabinett or another from which that one was copied, is considered to be an excellent example of scientific naturalism. This and the other surviving representations of Hanno drawn from the live model brought a new dimension to the depiction of the elephant as a species, (and indeed that of other animals) throughout the remainder of the sixteenth century. Earlier drawings or depictions of the elephant had tended to fantasize the beast.

Another version that appears to have been made from the same original, or which may in fact be a copy of the drawing in the Kupferstichkabinett, is a wash drawing in the collections of the Fogg Art Museum at Harvard University. It is remarkably similar to the one in Berlin in content and arrangement, although lacking in many of its minute details and lifelike feeling. Whether the drawing in Berlin is an original by Raphael or a copy, that and the one at Harvard appear to be contemporary. On the other hand, one or the other may have been copied from the mural itself.[14]

That the two drawings relate to Raphael's cartoon for the mural seems to be confirmed by a sketch made some twenty years later from the mural itself. In 1538 the Portuguese artist and architect Francisco d'Ollanda travelled to Rome to study its antiquities. He remained in the city for several years, during which time he became a friend of Michelangelo. D'Ollanda was a competent miniaturist and visionary artist and had achieved renown as one of Portugal's leading humanists. During his long sojourn in the Eternal City he recorded many ruins and architectural features in his busy sketchbook.

Included was a quick sketch of Hanno's mural, of which d'Ollanda probably took particular note inasmuch as the elephant had been a gift to the pope from his sovereign's father. His hurried sketch clearly delineated all the major features represented in the two drawings in the Kupferstichkabinett and the Fogg Art Museum, as well as several other details which the drawings do not include. His sketch was divided into two parts, each appearing on one page of his sketchbook, now in the library of El Escorial in Madrid.[15]

On one page d'Ollanda sketched the mural of the elephant and its attendants. He added a feature which undoubtedly existed in the mural, a representation of the sun and moon at the upper left. Pliny the Elder had written,

the elephant… has a religious respect also for the stars, and a veneration for the sun and moon. It is said by some authors, that, at the first appearance of a new moon, herds of these animals come down from the forests of Mauretania to a river, the name of which is Amilo; and that they there purify themselves in solemn form by sprinkling their bodies with water; after which, having thus saluted the heavenly body, they return to the woods, carrying before them the young ones which are fatigued.

It is this legend that was mentioned in Hanno's epitaph, and the sun and moon obviously had been included in the mural as well.[16]

D' Ollanda's sketch of the mural shows the sun and moon (marked *sol* and *lua* – for *luna* – respectively) combined in what appears to have been a lunar eclipse with the smaller body of the moon obscuring the larger orb of the sun. By including this feature, Raphael may have intended to imply that the moment of the passing of the elephant brought darkness to his world. Hanno's epitaph was copied by d'Ollanda on a separate page, revealing a distinct variation from the original text in Beroaldo's manuscript. (See Appendix). The discrepancies may be due to the epitaph's not having been rendered in its final form exactly as Beroaldo had originally written it. Or, during the course of the quarter century since it was first installed, it may have suffered damage and parts of it may have been inaccurately restored. Or d'Ollanda may have copied it inaccurately. [33 and 34]

The elephant's untimely death gave rise to various rumours concerning the cause of its death. It was suggested in some quarters that the humid air of Rome disagreed with the beast and caused the malady from which it had expired. Others believed that Hanno had become homesick for its native land, and had pined away in sadness. Others, more malicious, or perhaps more knowledgeable, whispered that the elephant had died from malnutrition. It was implied that its high and mighty chief custodian, the self-serving, ambitious and avaricious chamberlain, Giovanni Battista Branconio, had been stinting on the allowance he provided for the elephant's hay and vegetables and other dietary needs. It was common knowledge at court that the monthly cost of the elephant's maintenance was more than one hundred gold ducats, which was a considerable expenditure.[17]

One report led to a legend created by later historians that the beast had died as a consequence of having its entire body gilded for a public occasion. This legend grew as the result of a misunderstanding of Burckhardt's mention of the coronation of Baraballo, during which the mock poet was mounted upon 'a gold harnessed elephant'. Hecksher quoted other sources as having stated that the beast 'was all dressed up in gold' and rendered the phrase as meaning that the elephant had been gilded, causing its suffocation.[18]

Meanwhile, the people of Rome, although undoubtedly appreciative of the pope's thoughtfulness in having provided them with the life-size representation of Hanno by Raphael to keep its image in mind, memorialized the beloved beast in their own way. The elephant

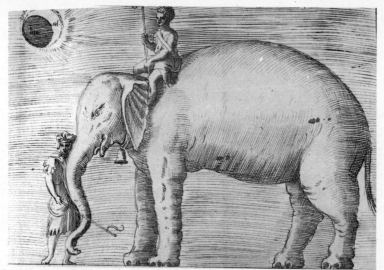

[33] Representation of Hanno – part of his memorial (see also [34]). Drawing by Francisco d'Ollanda made during his visit to Rome in 1538 in his sketchbook, now in the Biblioteca del Real Monasterio San Lorenzo, El Escorial, Madrid. Pen and ink on paper.

[34] Epitaph for Hanno – part of the huge memorial placed on the wall at the entrance to the Vatican. Drawing by Francisco d'Ollanda, in his sketchbook in 1538. Pen and ink on paper.

D M

MONTE·SVB·HOC·ELEPHAS·INGENTI·CONEGOR INGES
QVEM·REX·EMANVEL·DEVICTO·ORIENTE·LEONI·
CAPTIVVM·MISIT·DECIMO·QVEM·ROMVLA·PVBES·
MIRATA·EST·ANIMAL·NON·LONGO·TEMPORE·VISVM·
VIDIT·ET·HVMANOS·INBRVTO·PECTORE·SENSVS·
INVIDIT LATII·SED·MIHI·PARCA·BEATI·
NEC·PASSA·EST·TENEROS·DOMINOS·EMVLARIER ANNOS·
ATQVAE·SORS·RAPVIT·NATVRAE·DELITA·NOSTRAE·
TEMPORA·VOS·SVPERI·MAGNO·ACCVMVLATE·LEONI·

VIXIT·ANNOS·VII·

OBIIT·ANGINIE·MORBO
ALTITVDO·E RAT·PALM·XII·
IO·BAPTISTA·BRANCONIVS·AQVILANVS·
A·CVBICVLO·ET·ELEPHANTIS·CVRAE·PRAEFEC·
P O S V I T·
M·   D·   X VIII·I VNII·
LEONIS·X·PONT·ANNO·QVARTO·
RAPHAEL·VRBINAS·QVOD·NATVRA·ABSTVLERAT
ARTE·RESTITVIT ⸗

had been housed in a shelter built for it at the junction of the Borgo Sant' Angelo between the Corridore and the later addition of the Bernini portico of St Peter's – actually the Via del Corridore and what became the Largo del Colonnato. During the reign of Pope Leo X, the short street which connected Piazza of St Peter with the Corridore became familiarly known as the 'Street of the Elephant' (*Via dell' Elefante*). At the same time the section between the Borgo Sant'Angelo and the edge of the piazza was renamed 'Village of the Elephant' (*Borgo dell'Elefante*). Shortly after Hanno's death a tavern in that section was renamed 'Hosteria del Leonfante'. This tavern also appears in contemporary records as 'Hostaria del Leonfanti' and 'Casa del Liofante'. These place and street names were created after the elephant's arrival in Rome and unquestionably commemorated the papal elephant.

In 1526 the artist Raffaello del Montelupo wrote, 'I have returned to staying in the Borgo opposite the Inn of the Elephant [*Hosteria del Leonfante*] in a small house which furthermore belonged to my master [Lorenzetto Lotti].' The census of 1526 for the district (*rione*) of Ponte registered as a newcomer to Rome 'Niccolo, host of the Elefante [tavern or inn]'. In 1555 the inn was still operating, as noted in a record of 'the house rented to Bernardino the lute player... [which] is in the Borgo and is called the Inn of the Elephant.' In 1567 a house in the Borgo, probably the selfsame inn, was noted to be situated '*prope signum elephantis*'. Descriptions and building plans of the elephant's shelter are maintained in the Archivio di San Spirito, a short walking distance from where Hanno lived. According to an entry in the *Atti Bonavena* on 3 August 1566, 'The location of the house is placed in the Borgo of Saint Peter at the junction called seventh to the [street of the] Elephant from the location of the Inn at the Sign of the Elephant.' These place names continued to be used in the Borgo until almost the end of the sixteenth century, then disappeared entirely.

Hanno's death and the pope's sincere mourning for his pet provided the critics of the Church with new opportunities to ridicule the great affection the pontiff had demonstrated for the elephant and the many attentions he had lavished upon it. The subject formed the basis for one of the first published criticisms levelled against him by German supporters of Martin Luther. An account of the elephant's demise appeared in one of the letters written by an anonymous correspondent in Rome to Ulrich von Hutten in Germany, which the latter included in his publication, *Opera quae extant omnia*. It was written in the particularly poor Latin von Hutten affected when writing such 'letters' from the monks in order to satirize them. The correspondent wrote:

You will have heard that the pope has a great animal that was called an elephant, and he held him in great honour and loved him much. Now, therefore, you must know that this animal is dead. And while he was ill, the pope suffered great sadness and called in many doctors and said to them, 'If it is possible, cure the elephant for me.' Then they all used great diligence and examined his urine and gave him a purgative, that contained five hundred grams of gold, but they were not able to cause the elephant to eliminate, and so he died, and the pope mourned greatly over the elephant. And they say that he gave a thousand ducats for the elephant, because it was a remarkable animal, having a long trunk and great size. And when it saw the pope, it knelt down to him, and cried with a terrifying voice, 'Bar, bar, bar.'[19]

Several of the writers at the papal court took note of the death of the elephant in their writings, attributing various dates to it. Sebastiano de Branca Tedallini reported the event under the date of 18 June 1516. His editor later noted that Branca Tedallini had erred in many dates in his diary of the court, and he changed the date to 16 June, which is also incorrect.[20]

Marino Sanuto in Venice was informed of the beast's passing in letters from Nicolo Zorzi in Rome dated 14, 17 and 19 June. Zorzi also noted that at this time Rome was undergoing a devastating heat wave, as a consequence of which few of its people were to be found at home in the city. Subsequent communications from Zorzi confirmed that Fra Bonaventura's awesome prophecy was rapidly coming true, for he reported on 23 June that the Cardinal of Senigaglia had died and that the Cardinal of Sanseverino had become seriously ill. In the first week of August he informed Sanuto that the pope also had become ill. Later he noted that the Cardinal of Sanseverino was *in extremis*, and had died on 1 or 2 August.[21]

Some of the same events were commented upon by the stern chronicler Paride de Grassi in his papal court diary. 'During this period,' he wrote, 'there was a widespread rumour concerning the serious and perhaps incurable illness of the pope, especially in the light of the fevers, which are said to have been acute (so much so that thought was given to the preparations necessary for holding a conclave). Even the pope is deeply concerned for himself...'

Elsewhere Grassi mentioned that at the time the pope had learned of his brother's death, he had not demonstrated any grief or sorrow, 'since he himself was now not among us as a man, but as a demigod, and ought not to appear to anyone to be grief-stricken or sorrowful.' In a more charitable vein, however, Grassi added that the demigod suffered greatly from 'a fistula on the buttocks having five openings' [*fistula in natibus cum orificiis quinque*], and that throughout the month of August the pontiff talked of nothing but of his own approaching demise, 'wherefore he was shaken with repeated sobs'.[22]

Pope Leo X's concern with his health and his fear of death throughout much of his life has been commented upon by several who knew him. Giovanni Piero Valeriano, one of his intimates, wrote that the pope was happy only in appearance; that contributing factors to his unhappiness and melancholy were the deaths in his family which had followed one after another in rapid succession, the illness which racked his body for long periods of time, and his concern for his own forthcoming death, so that he scarcely ever had a period of quietude. This pervasive melancholia, disguised under a publicly happy mien, was often given as a reason for the pope's apparent delight in the carnival-like atmosphere he maintained at the Vatican.[23]

Notable among the principal contributors to court gaiety was the poetaster Giovanni Gazoldo, who distinguished himself primarily as the refined glutton of the court. It was in fact this celebrated buffoon who became the butt of a joke about Hanno after the elephant's death, because he surfeited himself with food and drink at the pope's banquet table so frequently and in such outrageous quantity. In the burlesque vein which was their habitual style, the men-about-town among the courtiers thought to amuse the pope by conceiving a great banquet to honour Gazoldo with a repast so rare that the pontiff himself would be unable to provide it at his table. Amidst great merriment they suggested that Gazoldo be made to dine on the flesh of the dead papal pet, to be prepared and served in boiled and roasted forms.

As official court poet, Beroaldo, who had already written about Hanno in the prologue to one of his comedies and had latinized its epitaph, went so far as to compose an ode for the occasion of Gazoldo's great dinner. In words purportedly spoken by Hanno, the elephant was made to say:

I am sepulchred in the living body of Gazoldo, as I wished my destiny to be because I was sent from India to satisfy the voracious appetite and the bard's vast stomach, which is always hollow and sonorous. Finally now that profound chasm has been filled. Thirty times a day and often during the night he waters me with odorous Greek wine. Oh! if only he had been my custodian during the voyage, I would not have so frequently suffered thirst...

While alive, I bore the poet Baraballo; dead, I am now borne by a poet no less important, laden with laurels and with floggings. But I will be completely happy when he, obsessed or possessed by the trumpetings and the elephantine spirit, belches forth the thundering verses which will send my name on to posterity. He is no less than my Baraballo, whether in the composition of tetrameters, trimeters, or iambic pentameters, or in the singing of the verses of Virgil in the company of heroes.[24]

Far greater impact than Beroaldo's exercise in poor taste was derived from the presumed last will and testament of Hanno. This satire, which equally amused and perturbed the court, was widely circulated not only throughout Rome but in other Italian cities within a month of the elephant's death. Vicious in its intent and effect, but amusing in its skilful weaving of known facts and current gossip, the testament summarized the calumnies, buffooneries, court scandals and corruption of the court of Pope Leo X as voiced in the streets of Rome.

The testament contained a total of twenty-nine legacies, each featuring an individual part of the elephant's anatomy, interior as well as exterior, bequeathed in each instance with apparent particular justification, cleverly matching each legacy with the foibles of its legatee. The testament followed the legal form in common usage in Italy since the Middle Ages. The satire was presumably produced between 8 June, the date of the elephant's death, and 18 July 1516, inasmuch as some of the individuals named as legatees were no longer living after the latter date.

The document was directed specifically and uniquely against the ecclesiastical establishment and reflected public sentiment not only of the people of Rome but of Italians in general about the Curia's corruption. It commented directly and with clinical precision on the scandals arising in the papal court and it echoed the reactions of those who had been offended as a result of personal anger or partisan antipathy. In some instances the bequests are puzzling and the meaning obscure because they relate to characteristics or events which can no longer be traced.

The satire was often witty, frequently vulgar and sometimes ferocious, but always clever. Following upon the public criticisms and dire predictions voiced by the apostates Teodoro of Scutari and Fra Bonaventura, the testament was inflammatory and was potentially very harmful to the Curia if not the Church itself. It exploded in the papal court like a bomb, and the memory of its claims and accusations lingered on in Rome for many years.

The testament opened with a statement about the presumed testator, which reflected to a substantial degree the words of the epitaph composed by the pope. It claimed, or pretended, to have been drawn up by Mario de Peruschi, a noted but universally disliked fiscal counsel of the consistory of cardinals at that time. It read in part as follows:

The Indian elephant which Emanuel, King of Portugal, sent to Leo X,

Pontifex Maximus, having lived in Rome approximately four years [sic], under the supervision of Zuan Batista Aquilan [Giovanni Battista Branconio dell'Aquila], has become ill, either from the varying temperature and air of Rome or as a result of the avarice of the said Zuan Batista; and considering that, no matter how great our prudence, nothing is more certain than death, the elephant, inasmuch as he is of infirm body, has deposed on me various legacies and last wishes. Notary Maria dei Previchi [sic] counsel of the consistory, who must write this his last testament with the legacies therein inscribed and upon me deposed, makes the testaments that follow.

Settled therefore in his new habitation — on the east side of which are confined the lions, with the Tower of Pope Nicholas to the south, the Carmeniccaria house [which cannot now be identified] at the north, and to the west the former abode of the elephant — and having first sought leave verbally to attest, (which is not conceded easily even to cardinals) those present being the two nearby lions Castor and Pardo, together with the Most Reverend godforsaken Cardinal de Costanza of the family of Boisi [Adriano Gouffier de Boissy, archbishop of Costanza, who had been created Cardinal of SS. Marcellino and Pietro], protector of drunkards in hypocrisy and ignorance of all France, and the Most Reverend Andrea Corner, Venetian bastard, inept, presumptuous, and inconsiderated Archbishop of Spalato, and the Most Reverend Lord Jacopo de Ameria [Jacopo di Nino di Amelia], Bishop of Potenza, jurisconsult of matter, misery, abuse, malignance, and mendacity, and Lord Pronotary Beltramo [Girolamo Beltrami, Spanish Jew convert] Spanish annotator of the Catholic faith in Hebraic letters, made the notation of the witnesses, admonished the above-mentioned elephant which to me revealed in a happy spirit the expression of its last wishes, and which with its trumpeting voice spoke thus:

Write that first of all I commend my soul to the sun, which rises to worship each day, and I order that my body be buried in the Vatican among the ruins of Bramante [in the Cortile del Belvedere], and that I constitute as my general heir, although he does not merit it, Zuan Batista Aquilan [Giovanni Battista Branconi of Aquila]. [35]

My dear heir, I wish to have as executors of this my testament the abbot of Bariabale of Gaeta [Giacomo Baraballo], who treated me well when he achieved the laurel for the poetic arts, and of one or another matter, the learned Fra Mariano [Mariano Fetti] — once a barber from the Florentine diocese — and the Most Reverend Jacopo de Ameria [Jacopo di Nino di Amelia], jurisconsult of misery, malignance, mordacity and prevarication, who by the disgrace of God is the Bishop of Potenza.

... you are to give my gold blanket, which I wore only on the most solemn days, to the Fabbrica of St Peter [the administration responsible for the construction and maintenance of the basilica] on this condition, however, that in the

[35] Page of a manuscript copy of the purported last will and testament of Hanno, a satire composed and circulated in June or July 1516. Venetian manuscript version, *Cod. Cicogna 2673*, fols. 240r-241r. In the Museo Correr, Venice.

charity of the said Fabbrica it not be converted to profane uses.

… you are to give my hide to Leo, Supreme Pontiff, in order that he can stretch it over an elephant constructed of wood in my size, so that at least my shape can be recognized, until the arrival of another new elephant to take my place.

… my ivory [tusks] you are to give to the Most Reverend Cardinal of San

Zorzi [Raffaello Riario, created Cardinal of San Giorgio ad Velum Aurum] so that his persistent thirst, which tantalizes him with the perpetual expectation of achieving the pontificate, will be more easily stilled and moderated [referring to Riario's participation in the plot to eliminate Pope Leo X and take his place]...

... my knees you are to give to the Most Reverend Cardinal of Santa Croce [Bernardino Carvajal, schismatic cardinal] in order that he may imitate my genuflections and ceremonial formalities, with this condition, however, that he no longer prevaricate in the council, so that for another time he will not be constrained with head uncovered to ask pardon for respect of the hat.

... give my prudence to the Most Reverend Cardinal Volteranno [Francesco Soderini, Cardinal of S. Susanna, involved in attempt to poison the pope] so that he may use it in the exercise of his unwonted liberality.

... my eyes you will give to the Most Reverend Cardinal Aginense [Leonardo Grosso della Rovere], so that with them he may continue to mourn the death of the Bishop of Saluzzo [Sisto Gara della Rovere of Lucca] and the life of the Prior of Rome.

... you are to give my nerves to the Most Reverend Cardinal of Accolti [Pietro Accolti, Cardinal of S. Eusebio], with the condition, however, that twice a week he has himself bound in an extended position while continuing harmony with his brother Bernardo [Bernardo Accolti, called 'l'Unico Aretino'] for many reasons which I am unable to express, filled with illness and grave paroxysms.

... my testicles you are to give to the Most Reverend Cardinal of Senegaia [Marco Vigeri, bishop of Senigallia, known for his sensuality and addiction to pleasures of the flesh] so that he will become more fruitful in progeny, and in the more merry procreation of the Antichrist with the Reverend Julia of the nuns of [the monastery of] Saint Catherine of Senegaia [Senigallia].

... you are to give my member [penis] to the Most Reverend Cardinal di Grassi [Achille Grassi, Cardinal of San Sisto, who fathered several children with Adriana de Scottis of Bologna], so that he can become more active in the incarnation of bastards with the help of Madama Adriana [Adriana de Scottis] of Bologna.

... my affections you are to give to the Most Reverend Cardinal Adriano so that he learns to reconcile wife with husband [Adriano Castellesi di Corneto took part in the plot to assassinate Pope Leo X; his earlier marriage had to be annulled].

... you are to give my tongue and my fortunate manner of speaking and my eloquence to the Most Reverend Cardinal of San Pietro in Vincula [Sisto Gara della Rovere, noted for his ignorance and ineptitude], with the condition that it be used to make a funerary oration with a hot tongue.

... my drumstick is to go to the Most Reverend Cardinal de Monte [Antonio Maria Ciocchi del Monte, ridiculed for his high-pitched, out of *tune voice] so that his resounding, exhorbitant voice at last finds and holds the truant tonic.*

… you are to give the medulla of my legs to the Most Reverend Cardinal de Sauli [Bandinello Sauli, whose limp was well known], and so that having alerted him in my name he will use them by the conjunction of his legs one time in life and at the last gasp of death.

… my ears are to go the Most Reverend Cardinal de' Medici [Giulio de' Medici], so that they can be prepared to listen to the simpletons of all the world.

… give my jawbones to the Most Reverend Cardinal di Santi Quattro [Lorenzo Pucci, accused of thefts and embezzlement], so that he can devour all the money of the entire republic of Christ and consume licitly and illicitly [fas aut nefas] every convent and church through the invention of new taxes.

… give my liver to the Most Reverend Cardinal of Santa Maria in Porticu de Bibbiena [Bernardo Dovisio da Bibbiena, accused of attempting to depose Francesco Maria I della Rovere from the duchy of Urbino] to induce him to divest himself of the benefits received in the time of his extreme calamity and to fill his cornucopia with March cheeses [refers to the Dovisio's arms and cheeses from the papal Marches or marzolini] from the diocese of Casentina.

… you are to give my other intestines to the Cardinal of San Severino [Federico Sanseverino, Apostolic Pronotary, notorious pleasure-seeker, often represented among his dogs, who took part in the schismatic council of Pisa] on condition that, in accordance with common usage, they are kept to excessively fatten the dogs, and diminish the nobility and the advice that he abstain from the furtive gathering of shady characters…[25]

The testament went on to list bequests to each of the remaining cardinals of the Curia. There was considerable agitated speculation concerning the identity of the author of the scurrilous document, and it was generally concluded that it was the work of the famous satirist, Pietro Aretino. Certainly the most loquacious spokesman of the period, Aretino was a master of such barbed insights as the testament revealed. Protégé of Pope Leo X, and later of the pontiff's cousin Pope Clement VII, Aretino had been given the nickname 'the scourge of princes' for his attacks upon his powerful contemporaries.

At the time that the testament appeared, Aretino is believed to have been employed as a servant of the Sienese banker in Rome, Agostino Chigi, who brought him to the attention of Leo X. Attribution of the testament to him is supported to some degree by the fact that the 'document' was mentioned in two of his published works. In the first edition of his comedy *La Cortegiana*, published in 1534, Aretino noted in the argument that among things most strange was 'the testament of the elephant.' In the second scene of the third act, the loquacious Alvigia, while prattling with the monk who is the guardian of the

Aracoeli, comments that the souls of men are like lies or illusions for they occupy no space. He explains his contention in the following manner:

'Assuming that you are confined in a small room or space, and you would say that the elephant made its testament before its death. Would this not be disconnected?'

'Yes, my father,' the other replied.

'Nevertheless,' the monk went on, 'the small room will prove nothing of its own account, not even for a thousand lies that you might say hereafter.'[26]

Besides these references to the elephant's testament, another contributing factor to the suspicion that Aretino was the author of the piece was that in 1529 he was suspected of having penned a similar testament demonstrating loathing for Pope Clement VII and Emperor Charles V. Aretino defended himself against the accusation, and later in La Cortegiana reminded his readers that 'the fact of the matter is that the Elephant made its testament before its death…'[27]

Although it had become common practice to attribute satires of that period to Aretino as a matter of course, students of literature claim that stylistically the elephant's testament does not resemble Aretino's work, and that he could not have been its author because he had not yet come to Rome; he could not have been so intimately informed of the scandals and gossip of the court as was demonstrated by the legacies. The authorship of the damning piece of writing remains a subject of conjecture for scholars.[28]

Hanno was featured in another classic work, the Dialogues of Torquato Tasso, the Italian poet from Sorrento who had learned about the papal pet on visits to Rome as a young man. During the latter part of his life he was confined in an asylum, and it was in this period that he produced his series of Dialogues. Describing Hanno therein, he praised the elephant for its mental abilities, and commented 'It could have figured with the rhinoceros in battle, but most likely wished to demonstrate its gentleness rather than its ferocity…' In the second chapter of Il Conte, o vero l'Imprese, he noted 'We believe, therefore, that the animals do not have distinct voices, as we have been taught by Aristotle in his book, the Interpretations, although each with an inarticulate voice can signify the effects of the soul: and by chance in this guise, [Annone] Hanno, splendid elephant sent by Emanuel as a gift to Leo X, was heard by his master.'[29]

Tasso also found occasion to mention the papal elephant in his major work, Jerusalem Delivered:

Then from the mansions bright of fresh Aurore
Adrastus came, the glorious king of Inde,

A snake's green skin spotted with black he wore,
That was made rich by art and hard by kind;
An elephant this furious giant bore,
He fierce as fire, his monture swift as wind;
Many people brought he from his kingdom wide,
'Twixt Indus, Ganges, and the salt sea side.[30]

It was not until a few years after the death of the pope's elephant, that it was memorialized also by Portuguese poets. In 1519 Diogo Velho da Chancellaria extolled the role of Portugal in gathering riches from foreign parts, noting that in the new world centre that Lisbon had become,

Gold, pearls, stones,
Gums and spices…
Tigers, lions, elephants,
Monsters and talking birds,
Porcelains, diamonds –
All now are quite common.[31]

Garcia de Resende, the courtier and poet who had accompanied the Portuguese mission to Rome as its secretary, also mentioned Hanno and the ill-fated rhinoceros, if somewhat obliquely. The reference occurs in one of the poems that formed part of the *Miscellania* he compiled during the last few years of his life, several decades after the mission had taken place. It was not published until 1534, after Resende's death, as an appendix to his chronicle of King John II. In a review of the flora, fauna and other riches from the East, he wrote:

We have seen elephants brought here,
And other similar beasts
Brought from India by sea
And we have seen them sent by sea
To Rome in great triumph.[32]

Valeriano provided an extensive description of both the pope's elephant and the rhinoceros in addition to descriptions of elephants and rhinoceros derived from the works of ancient writers. An entire book of his *Hieroglyphica*, in fact, concerns itself with the significance of the elephant throughout history.[33]

As the sixteenth century advanced, Hanno was not totally forgotten: some decades after its death the Roman poet Pasquale Malaspina dedicated some of his work to it:

A live and natural elephant
Was sent as a gift to the Holy Father

By the King of Portugal. Liberal,
Magnanimous, genteel, learned and courteous:
To this day his name remains immortal
Clearly resounding in every community;
And he reigns happily in his nation,
Like a truly virtuous blessed man.
In the Belvedere before the Great Pastor
Was the elephant conducted in costume.
It danced with such grace and such love,
That hardly could any man have danced better;
And then with its trumpet so much noise
It made, that the entire place having been deafened,
It stretched forward, bent front knees to the ground,
Then stood reverently before the pope and his entourage.[34]

CHAPTER SEVEN
Remembrance & Reflection

The Rome of Leo, as described by Paolo Giovio, forms a picture too splendid to turn away from, unmistakable as are also its darker aspects — the slavery of those who were struggling to rise; the secret misery of the prelates, who, notwithstanding heavy debts, were forced to live in a style befitting their rank; the system of literary patronage, which drove men to be parasites or adventurers; and lastly, the scandalous maladministration of the finances of the State.

Jacob Burkhardt : *The Civilization of the Renaissance in Italy*
(1878)

Hanno's presence in Rome had impact equally on the arts of the period as it had on *belles lettres*. The elephant was featured in the works of Raphael, Giulio Romano, Giovanni da Udine, Giovanni Barile, Francisco d'Ollanda, and Maarten van Heemskerck as well as others. Few of the artists working in Rome during that period escaped its spell and failed to sketch it. There appear to have been two major exceptions: while at work at the Vatican Michelangelo must have observed the animal, but he is not known to have sketched it; another who undoubtedly saw Hanno, although no sketches of it by him are known, was Leonardo.

Despite the passage of more than four and a half centuries since the elephant romped on Vatican hill, at least four contemporary representations of Hanno remain on public view on the Vatican premises, though rarely recognized, and at least two other drawings of the animal exist in its collections. The best known is the intarsia panel executed in rare coloured woods decorating the great door between the Stanza della Segnatura and the Stanza del Incendio del Borgo in the Stanze Raffello of the Apostolic Palace. This mosaic in wood depicts the fat Abbot of Gaeta seated complacently if precariously upon his gilded throne, borne by a thoughtful Hanno with the Indian mahout seated on its neck.

The mock coronation of Baraballo took place in September 1514, just when Raphael and his assistants were at work in the Stanze, a project that included the decoration with carvings and inlay of all the doors and ceilings and other woodwork. Inasmuch as the work was already in progress, the pope seized this unusual opportunity to memorialize the event in one of the door panels. Raphael undoubtedly provided the original sketch from which the intarsia specialist worked. As Giorgio Vasari noted, Raphael 'commissioned Giovanni Barile to adorn all the doors and ceilings [of the Stanze] with a good number of carvings, which he executed and finished with beautiful grace'.

Forming part of a Latin manuscript in the Vatican Library is a sketch in water colour by an anonymous artist depicting the scene, with Baraballo poised on Hanno's back on his way to the mock coronation. [see 20 on page 97]. It is identical in all details with the intarsia panel except for the ground and background: the intarsia includes low green hills and a rock ledge in the background, while the sketch depicts the elephant walking on relatively level terrain with clumps of grass cropping up at intervals. Written below the drawing is the statement in Italian, 'This is to be found inlaid in a door of the Hall near that of Constantine in the Vatican Palace, of which mention is made by Giovio in his *Elogii*.' This work was published in 1551, confirming that the sketch postdates the execution of the panel.[1]

The image of Hanno appears in three separate works in the loggie of Raphael in the Apostolic Palace. The loggie are arcaded galleries, or open-air corridors, built on three storeys, which provide access to the Vatican apartments. It was the loggia of the second storey that was decorated by Raphael and his assistants between 1515 and 1518 for Pope Leo X. This loggia is divided into thirteen arcades, each with a vaulted ceiling and each of which features four paintings executed in fresco. Forty-eight of these depict scenes from the Old Testament and the remaining four scenes are derived from the New Testament. Each of the paintings is surrounded by elaborate arabesques executed in coloured stucco work, and the same treatment is given to the supporting pilasters and the wall spaces below them.

Raphael is believed to have produced the overall design and to have prepared the preliminary sketches in the form of wash drawings for the scenes as well as for the decorations. Raphael turned over his wash drawings in sepia to his chief artist, Romano, who developed cartoons for each in full size, and then assigned them to the other assistants in accordance with their special skills. Among the assistants were Giovanni da Udine, Gianfrancesco Penni, Pierino del Vaga, Polydoro da Caravaggio, Pellegrino da Modena, and Raffaellino del Colle. Inasmuch as Giovanni da Udine was the most adept at executing birds and animals, it is probable that he was assigned to paint 'The Creation of the Animal Kingdom' on the ceiling of the cupola of the first arch, in which the Eternal God is shown walking on earth with a lion at his side, to symbolize Pope Leo X, and calling into being birds and beasts of all descriptions. According to Vasari, it was Romano who was responsible for that painting, but it is probable that he only produced the cartoon from Raphael's design and then was assisted by Udine in the final work.

The artists were fortunate to be able to use live models from the pope's menagerie nearby for most of the painting's subject matter. Clearly distinguishable is one of the bears acquired by the pontiff from Hungary, the elephant Hanno, monkeys, panthers, deer, a variety of exotic birds, and even a unicorn derived from the artist's imagination. An interesting behavioural note is the presence of magpies sitting on the bull's head at the right rear of the painting, apparently searching for ticks or other insects. [36]

[36] 'The Creation of the Animal Kingdom'. Fresco in a vignette on the ceiling of the first cupola at the base of the colonnade of the Loggie di Raffaello in the Apostolic Palace. Visible in the painting are an elephant and a rhinoceros. Attributed to Giovanni da Udine from a design by Raphael c. 1515-17.

Particularly puzzling in the scene is the presence of the Lisbon rhinoceros. Only part of the animal is visible, including the head, most of the neck and forelegs. The set of this head in profile is to be found again in the works of later artists. Where did Raphael or Udine find a model for this beast? It is a matter of conjecture whether Udine based his representation of the rhinoceros on observation of the mounted specimen from Lisbon after its arrival in Rome, inasmuch as it bears no resemblance to the Dürer woodcut. Could his source have been the same as had served Penni and Granacci?

Hanno made its second appearance in the loggie in a tripartite decorative panel designed by Raphael and executed by Giovanni da Udine. Featured in a medallion of the left section, the elephant is depicted with its mahout astride its back and wearing its bell. The posture of the animal and rider suggests that it may have been based on the sketch in the Kupferstichkabinett attributed to Raphael or a derivative of it. The panel was reproduced in the late eighteenth or early nineteenth century by Conte Cav. Carlo Lasinio in a volume of engravings of 'Ornamental Designs of the Loggie of the Vatican' [*Ornati delle Loggie del Vaticano*], published in Rome between 1786 and 1839, the date of the author's death. Lasinio, a professor of art at the academy of Florence, was distinguished for having introduced into Italy the process of engraving on multiple plates for colour printing. The panel underwent considerable damage from weather in the course of the years, and only the central section remains today.[2] [37]

Hanno's third appearance in the Loggie is in a stucco bas-relief situated at eye-level in one of the first bays. Somewhat the worse for wear, it reproduces the Kupferstichkabinett drawing or a derivative of it. The elephant wearing its bell is shown facing left, with the Moor astride its back and the Saracen at one side holding its trunk. Each man has an *ankush* in hand. In the relief the elephant's tusks are shown to be somewhat larger than in the sketch but the postures of the animal and the men are similar. The relief was probably produced during Hanno's lifetime and executed by Giovanni da Udine from Raphael's design. Hanno appears to have been a favourite theme with Raphael, for it is represented on at least two, or possibly three other stucco bas-relief panels in the Loggie.

Raphael had great respect for Giovanni da Udine's talent for depicting fauna in particular, and recognized the young artist's command of zoological and botanical subject matter, which surpassed that of any of his other assistants. Raphael enjoyed browsing through Giovanni's sketchbook, and master and assistant frequently took walking excursions together in Rome in search of artistic subjects. It

[37] Decorative panel in three parts in the Loggie de Raffaello, including Hanno in a medallion, the design attributed to Raphael and execution to Giovanni da Udine. From *Ornati delle Loggie del Vaticano* by Carlo Lasinio, (Rome, early nineteenth century). Figure II, part iv.

was on one of these excursions to the Baths of Titus, the ruins of which had recently been discovered, that both were impressed by the apparent freshness of the stucco and the coloured ornamentation, despite the passage of centuries.

Giovanni copied some of the designs from the Baths, analysed the composition of the materials, and later succeeded in duplicating them with a combination of travertine, chalk and marble. With Raphael's encouragement, he utilized the ancient techniques in the execution of some of the decorative elements of the Loggie, including the several stucco bas-relief panels of Hanno. He also applied some of the techniques later in the construction of the elephant fountain at Villa Madama.[3]

The stucco bas-relief, the now missing medallion of the decorative panel, the sketch in the Kupferstichkabinett, the version in the Fogg Art Museum and the sketch of the mural by d'Ollanda all feature a bell around the elephant's neck. The stance of the beast, the poses of the attendants, as well as the presence of the bell, confirm a relationship between the five representations of Hanno and show that it did indeed wear a bell; it was not a gratuitous elaboration of the artists.

Hanno may also have been featured among the exotic birds and beasts which formed a frieze in the Sala dei Palanfrenieri, or Sala dei Chiaroscuri as it also was known, which Pope Leo X commissioned Raphael to embellish after the artist had completed work on the loggie. Raphael selected the saints and apostles as his theme, and himself executed the figures in the tabernacles in sepia [*terreta*]. Vasari reported that Giovanni da Udine then decorated the interstices with arabesques, cherubs, lions, papal arms and grotesques, birds and beasts, divided by panels of various marbles, all of which he finished in a variety of techniques similar to the ancient encrustation found in Roman baths and temples. In an adjacent room in which the *cubiculari* stayed, the young artist executed a cornice or frieze featuring the pope's menagerie.

Raphael assigned Giovanni da Udine 'to paint all the animals that Pope Leo possessed,' according to Vasari, 'such as the chameleon, the civet cats, the apes, the lions, the elephants [*sic*], and other beasts even more strange.' So pleased was the pope with the imagination and artistry displayed that he invested Raphael with the overall responsibility for the improvements to be made thereafter in the Vatican. The handsome room was short-lived, for it was drastically altered by Pope Pius IV. He had it divided into four rooms, and relatively little of the original decoration survives except for the head of Saint John the Baptist as a child executed in chiaroscuro, and two parrots flanking it.

[38] 'The Adoration of the Magi', elephant apparent. Tapestry of the 'New School', originally designed for the Sistine Chapel. Tapestries Museum, the Vatican.

Later in the century Pope Gregory XIII wished to have the room restored to its original form and Taddeo Zucchero was employed to reproduce the images of the apostles. He was forced to repaint them in their entirety because of the state of disrepair and permanent alteration the originals had undergone.

Despite the familiarity of Raphael and his assistants with Hanno, the elephant was not included in the first set of tapestries, 'The Acts of the Apostles', which Raphael produced for the Sistine Chapel. Hanno is to be found, however, in what is generally known as the second Vatican series, 'of the New School'. They were designed by Raphael's assistants after his death, and are displayed in the long corridor of the Vatican Museum approaching the Sistine Chapel. The figure of Hanno is perpetuated in the tapestry of 'The Adoration of the Magi'.[4] [38]

During the elephant's lifetime, or certainly within the next several years following its death, Giovanni da Udine was commissioned to execute a fountain for Cardinal Giulio de' Medici, to be set into a grotto in the gardens of the Villa Madama on the slope of Monte Mario. The villa is claimed by some art historians to have been designed by Raphael and executed from his designs by Antonio da Sangallo the Younger. The villa and grounds were decorated for the most part by Giulio Romano and Giovanni da Udine. Although it was already under construction in 1515, more than a decade elapsed before the villa was completed.[5]

As the feature of the fountain, Udine selected the head of Hanno carved in white marble, its protruding trunk serving as the spout for the water. The head is not stylized: it is an impressively realistic portrait of the elephant Hanno. It was said that white marble was selected because the beast was a white elephant from Ceylon. [39a, 39b and 39c]

Stucco featuring sea shells and various other elements of marine life decorated the grotto of the fountain, in imitation of the temple of Neptune which had been discovered in the recently excavated ruins of the Palazzo Maggiore. Udine's work, it was reported, far excelled the original in quality because of his fine execution of the animals, shells, and similar items.

Planned for the grounds was a series of waterfalls, fishpools and fountains to be featured in a systematic manner to relate to the architectural, floral and landscape elements of the villa in the same manner as those of the Villa d'Este in Tivoli. The elephant fountain, which was to be a part of all this, has survived to the present, although in poor condition, standing in the central niche of an ivy-covered buttressed wall of the terraced garden. Embellished by a small vaulted ceiling decorated with marine motifs, it is supplied with water by a perpetual spring high in the hills above the villa. Vasari suggested that Giovanni da Udine worked from an original design made by Romano for the fountain.[6]

Several entries in the account books of Cardinal Giulio de' Medici relate directly to the villa's fountains. In May 1524 the Cardinal made two payments totaling 150 ducats to 'Maestro Antonio di San Gallo' for 'the construction of a fountain in the vineyard', and Giovanni da Udine was paid for his work on the fountain in the following year.[7]

While the Villa Madama was under construction, Romano was being sought by the young Duke of Gonzaga to work at his Palazzo del Te in Mantua. At the same time Michelangelo was in Florence working on the Medici library and he, too, urgently sought the services of Giovanni da Udine to assist with the construction of the new vestry for the church of San Lorenzo. Correspondence between

[39] Three views of the elephant fountain at Villa Madama, Rome: [a] Sketch made by Maarten van Heemskerck during a visit to Rome in the early sixteenth century. From his sketchbook in the Preussischer Kulturbesitz Kupferstichkabinett, Staatliche Museen, Berlin. [b] Sketch made by Giovanni da Udine. In the Gallerie degli Uffizi, Florence. [c] Sketch made by Francisco d' Ollanda during his sojourn in Rome between 1538 and 1540. Ink and water colour on paper, from his sketchbook in the Biblioteca del Real Monasterio San Lorenzo, El Escorial, Madrid.

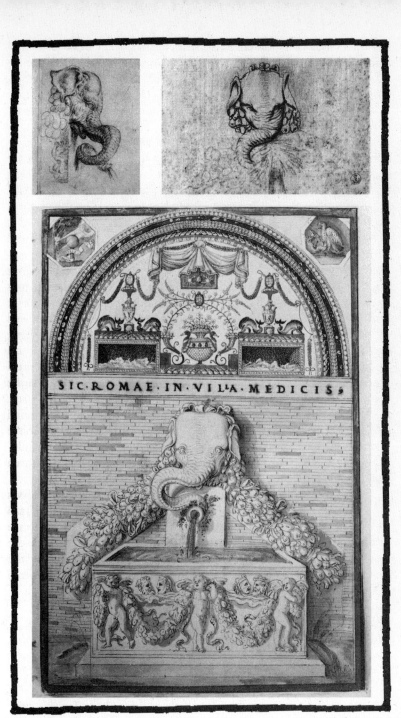

SIC·ROMAE·IN·VILA·MEDICIS;

Giovan Francesco Fattucci, Pope Clement VII's agent in Rome, and Michelangelo, reveals that the pope had decided to make Giovanni available to Michelangelo but that he would have to wait until the project in progress was completed. In his letter of 18 April 1526, Fattucci warned, 'I do not believe that the vault will be finished in six months, and certainly not in two.'

Later Fattucci reported to Michelangelo that the pope had informed Giovanni that he was to proceed to Florence after he had completed the design of certain banners for Andrea Doria, but that first he was 'to finish a fountain of mosaic [the elephant fountain] in the vineyard [of the Villa] which should be completed by the end of August'.[8]

When completed, the elephant fountain became a popular subject with foreign artists visiting Rome. Maarten van Heemskerck of Haarlem travelled to Rome in 1534 to study the works of Michelangelo and remained for three years. During that period he sketched many of the Roman ruins and other architectural sites. Intrigued by the elephant fountain, he produced at least two sketches of the elephant's head, in profile and full face, with details of other decorative elements.[9]

As already noted, four years later the Portuguese architect and artist, Francisco d'Ollanda, visited Rome and sketched the great mural commemorating Hanno. In addition, among his sketches of Roman ruins is an elaborately detailed drawing in colour of the elephant fountain, including details of elements of the structure which have not survived. The drawing provides a unique record of the fountain's appearance in its prime, a decade after it was completed, before time and the elements wrought slow destruction.

Hanno remained an inspiration for d'Ollanda, for after his return to Portugal he incorporated elephants in sketches for the fountains at the Agoa Liure at the royal palace of Rossio, featuring the portrait bust of the king surrounded by four elephants, spouting water from their trunks to fill the basin. A design for another fountain, not built, for the grounds of the royal palace at Ribeira to be viewed from the harbour, featured a single monumental elephant supporting its mahout and a battle tower on its back.[10] [40]

Hanno was memorialized in Rome outside the Vatican precincts and the properties of the Medici popes. When the Palazzo Baldassini was restored several decades ago, two representations of the pope's elephant and one of the Lisbon rhinoceros were discovered therein, executed within Hanno's lifetime or a few years after. The palace was built in about 1514 or 1515 for the jurisconsult Melchiore Baldassini

Da Fonte e lago de Agoa Liure.

Lembrança da fonte dagoa Liure trazida ao Resio.

[40] Sketch made by Francisco d' Ollanda after his return from Rome, of a fountain then proposed for the royal park at Rossio, featuring a portrait bust of King Manuel I with four elephants. Ink on paper. In the Biblioteca da Ajuda, Lisbon.

in the Via delle Coppelle, or street of the cask makers, one of Rome's main arteries at the time. An intimate friend of Pope Leo X, Baldassini served as counsel of the consistory and of the poor. In the same year that the palace was begun, the pope appointed Baldassini professor of civil law at the University of Rome. The counsel was extremely wealthy and determined that no cost be spared in the construction of his palace. He employed Antonio di Sangallo the Younger to design and supervise the project, and for its interior decoration he selected two artists who had been working in the Apostolic Palace, Pierino del Vaga and Giovanni da Udine.[11]

During the recent restoration, a magnificent fresco was discovered on the vaulted ceiling of the first floor. This remarkable work depicts a veritable bestiary, executed in individual panels separated by arabesques and floral decorations. Featured among them are a rampant leopard, a griffin, a goat, a bull and an ape sharing equal space with unusual birds, and yet other creatures featured among festoons and arabesques along the side walls. Outstanding are the two largest beasts depicted on the panels at one end: the first is the pope's elephant, shown in somewhat the same position as it appears in the drawing in the Kupferstichkabinett but without its attendants; the second, in the panel opposite, is none other than the Lisbon rhinoceros, facing to the left. It is clearly not derived from Dürer's woodcut, but appears to have some affinity to Granacci's representation of it. The work on the vault has been attributed by some authorities to Pierino del Vaga, and by others to Giovanni da Udine. Both artists were at work in the palace at the same time, and the vault of grotesques presumably was painted prior to but not later than 1519, the year in which both Pierino and Giovanni were working in Raphael's loggie in the Apostolic Palace.[12]

The vaulted ceiling of the Palazzo Baldassini is decorated in a style similar to that of Raphael's loggie, and most resembles the *uccelleria* [aviary] which Giovanni da Udine executed in the frieze of the Camera degli Palanfrenieri. Until now no one has attempted to explain the presence of the rhinoceros in this collection of birds and beasts, but it tends to confirm the arrival and presence of the stuffed beast in Rome.

Hanno appears to have become a symbol of the period, for it exists in yet another form in the decoration found in the Palazzo Massimo alle Colonne. The edifice was built by Baldassare Peruzzi for the brothers Luca, Piero and Angelo Massimo, on the site of an earlier palace destroyed in the sack of Rome in 1527. Featured along the cornice of the palace loggia are bas-reliefs in terracotta depicting books, musical instruments and the Massimo family arms. Notable among them is the finely sculptured image of Hanno, shown without its mahout and harnessed to a four-wheeled chariot filled to over-flowing with armour, shields and other accoutrements of war. The

[41] Chariot being drawn by Hanno. Stucco bas-relief by Giovanni da Udine on the ceiling of the atrium of the *portinaria* of the Palazzo Baldassini in Rome, *c*. 1515-20. In the Palazzo Baldassini, Rome.

reliefs are the work of Giovanni da Udine, produced after the completion of the Palazzo Baldassini.[13] [41]

Throughout the entire period that Hanno lived at the Vatican, it must have been observed frequently by a resident of the Belvedere palace that overlooked the Cortile del Belvedere. Attracted to Rome by the excitement and promise of 'the golden age' that a Medici pope would bring to the Eternal City, and the prospect of rich commissions that were anticipated due to the encouragement of the arts evidenced by the new pontiff, Leonardo set forth from Milan on the way to Rome in September 1513 with four of his pupils. Meeting with the pope's brother, Giuliano de' Medici, who was also on his way to Rome, they travelled together. Leonardo did not receive the warm welcome from Leo X that he had expected; however, Giuliano came to his rescue. He arranged to have rooms modified and set aside for him in the Belvedere, the summer palace at the top of Vatican hill. Giuliano also hired a German artisan to assist the master with his work while in Rome.

It was not an unpleasant prospect for the ageing artist. From his rooms on one side he could see the plains of the Campagna with the ragged line of hills on the horizon. On the other side he had a magnificent view of the botanical gardens, and on the plantation along the slope he could see the papal menagerie. From these rooms he must often have heard the roars and growls of the large cats, the shrill cries of the caged birds, and the occasional trumpeting of the elephant from the other side of the piazza of St Peter.

Leonardo is likely to have spent many long and bored hours of his frustrating sojourn in Rome by sketching not only the rare botanical specimens with which the pope had filled his gardens, but also the wild birds and animals in the menagerie on the adjacent slope, including that most unusual and largest of these denizens in its special shelter adjacent to the piazza of St Peter, for Leonardo da Vinci was greatly interested in wild beasts. Alas, although his botanical drawings of the period have survived, any drawings of animals have not. It seems inconceivable the ever-curious Leonardo did not sketch so rare and celebrated a neighbour as Hanno.

Leonardo's disappointment over his failure to obtain the patronage of the pope, with whose family he had been associated most of his life, made this one of the most unhappy periods he had yet experienced. The courtiers who favoured the great Michelangelo or the brilliant young Raphael, both then employed in the Vatican palace, may have set the pontiff's mind against Leonardo, with claims that age had dulled his talents; furthermore he had a reputation for never completing his commissions.[14]

Much of Leonardo's sojourn in Rome remains clouded in obscurity, which biographers and art historians have attempted unsuccessfully to dispel. Particularly puzzling is his association with Branconio. Because of his high position and his intimate relationship with the pope, Branconio was able to dispense and control favours to the advantage or disadvantage of the artists working at the Vatican. As a very close friend of Raphael's, he would not have been favourably inclined towards Leonardo.

Perhaps among Leonardo's lost papers there may have been sketches of the elephant and other beasts of the papal menagerie, executed during the two and a half to three years of his Vatican sojourn. He could hardly have avoided witnessing the procession of the Portuguese mission in 1514, with its variety of fauna.[15]

From time to time there has been speculation among art historians as to whether Hanno may have provided the inspiration a century later to Gian Lorenzo Bernini for his design of the sculptured elephant supporting an obelisk in the Piazza della Minerva in Rome. Although Bernini may have been aware of the saga of Hanno, it would have been more likely that the source of his inspiration was the elephant reported by Gigli to have visited Rome in 1630. It was soon thereafter that Cardinal Francesco Barberini, nephew of Pope Urban VIII, was considering the installation of a small obelisk designed by Bernini in the 'secret garden' of his palace. The plinth was to be supported upon an elephant's back, but the project was never fulfilled.

More than three decades later, the elephant-supported obelisk of the Piazza della Minerva was developed as a consequence of co-operative efforts of Bernini and his patron, Pope Alexander VII. The source of their inspiration proves to have been neither Hanno nor Gigli's elephant but a singular work, *Hypnerotomachia Poliphili*, published in 1499 by the Dominican Francesco Colonna. Heavily illustrated throughout with engravings depicting the dreams of Colonna's hero, Poliphili, one is of an elephant bearing an obelisk upon its back. When an obelisk was discovered in excavations of the Piazza della Minerva, the reigning pontiff proposed to Bernini that it be erected in the square. Bernini turned first to the drawings he had made several decades earlier for Cardinal Barberini. Required by Alexander VII to follow as closely as possible the engraving in the *Hypnerotomachia*, however, the artist then produced new drawings similar to the illustration in Poliphili's dream. The pope approved and Bernini's assistant, Ercole Ferrata, was commissioned to sculpt the figure of the elephant, and the monument was installed in 1667.[16]

Particularly puzzling is the fresco of an elephant depicted with its custodians far removed from the scene at Rome. It is featured in the Portico dell' Elefante on the first floor of the Cortile Ducale in the Castello Sforzesco, the great fortress that dominates the city of Milan. The composition and the poses of the beast and custodians are almost identical with those in the drawing of Hanno in the Kupferstichkabinett. Existing documentation, however, now attributes the work to an unidentified artist, although at one time it was believed to have been the work of Bonifacio Bembo executed in about 1472, during the reign of Galeazzo Maria Sforza, in a space reserved for the purpose by the castle's architect, Benedetto Ferrini, the '*magistro fiorentino*'. The image of the elephant was mentioned in a listing of 1497, '*Quando se ornarà el cortile de mezo se ricorda essere bene pingere uno ducale onorevole in testa depso cortile cioè sopra la sala dello elefante.*'

The fresco was brought to light in the late nineteenth century during a restoration of the portico. There appear to be faint traces of what may have been another, perhaps earlier, fresco. It depicts a group of mounted horsemen and pages visible in the distant background, among whom may have been Galeazzo Maria Sforza. Curiously, the elephant appears to be painted in black. Although this may have been the original colouring, it is possible that the original colour changed chemically with the passage of the years because it was exposed to the elements out of doors. Could the elephant in fact originally have been painted white? The documentation is inconclusive, suggesting that the original fresco may have been of the horsemen, with another fresco painted over it in the following century.[17]

It has been speculated that the pope's elephant may also have provided the inspiration for the gigantic sculpture of an elephant in the Park of Monsters which formed part of the sixteenth century 'wonder villa' at Bomarzo. Duke Corrado Orsini, called Vicino, undertook the project in about 1552, following his second marriage. The task was entrusted to Pirro Ligorio, who was assisted in the design of the gardens by Giacomo da Vignola. Eight years were required to complete the palace in the rockbound little medieval town upon the slopes of the volcanic Monte Cimino near Viterbo. After the palace building had been completed, Orsini began to convert the adjacent valley into a pleasure garden. The only certain connection that can be made between Hanno and the monstrous stone elephant in the park, however, is that the duke was a relative of Pope Leo X.[18]

The presence of numerous extremely large boulders which could not be moved made the project appear hopeless at first, until Orsini conceived of a means to utilize them. He ordered that they be carved into the forms of fantastic monsters. The undertaking required years to complete. As the work progressed, Orsini, often inspired by his friend Cardinal Madruzio of Venetia Tridentina, developed innovative ideas for the subjects to be included, and gradually the park assumed a distinctly Far Eastern character. One of the most arresting of the great sculptures is a larger than life elephant, bearing a great battle turret on its caparisoned back with a mahout astride its neck. The beast is holding a Roman soldier in its trunk. Its large ears suggest that it was modelled after an African elephant, however, and not Hanno.[19]

Seemingly there was no limitation to the variety of forms and media in which Hanno was represented during its lifetime and memorialized after its death. Fresco, oils, water colour, chalk, crayon, pen and ink, stucco, marble, intarsia – and these were not all. It was to be permanently memorialized as well in an Italian maiolica platter, which was produced during its lifetime in about 1515 at the maiolica manufactory at Caffaggiolo, a short distance outside Florence. The manufactory was established in about 1506 by two Croatian brothers to supply the requirements of the Pierfrancesco de' Medici family, a younger branch of the ruling family of Florence.

The platter depicts Pope Leo X being carried in procession on his

[42] Papal procession featuring Pope Leo X on his *sedia gestatoria* preceded by the elephant Hanno. The pontiff blesses the people with one hand and holds a rose in the other (the Golden Rose?). Surrounded by mounted cardinals and courtiers, musicians and members of the Swiss Guard, Maiolica platter, Caffaggiolo factory, *c.* 1516. In the Victoria and Albert Museum, London.

sedia gestatoria, held shoulder high by the bearers, amidst a cavalcade of cardinals and other prelates mounted on mules, followed by noblemen and soldiers on horseback. Halberdiers of the Swiss Guard march in front to the music of pipers and drummers. In the background a standard bearer holds high a gonfalon bearing the Medici crest while an ensign of the Swiss Guard carries another. The procession is shown passing before a high wall, which may be the Leonine wall of the Vatican, above which are visible birds in flight and the tops of trees, possibly on the Gianicolo. The procession is led by the elephant Hanno, adorned with its rich caparison decorated with embroidery, its mahout in European costume astride its neck. In one hand the pope holds a rose and the other is raised in benediction. [42]

The platter may have been produced at about the time of the pope's visit to Florence following his meeting at Bologna with King Francis I in November 1515, or as a result of it. The presence of the elephant confirms that the locale depicted is Rome and not Florence. Inasmuch as the pontiff apparently holds a Golden Rose, the scene may have been intended to depict his procession from the Sistine Chapel to the church of Santa Croce.[20]

[43] Drawing for 'The Adoration of the Magi' in the style of Giulio Romano but in a technique more closely resembling the work of Viagio Pupini. In the Royal Library, Windsor Castle.

[44] Four sketches of Hanno drawn from life and widely copied by other artists. The drawing, originally attributed to Raphael, is now credited to Giulio Romano. Red crayon on grey paper. In the Department of Western Art, Ashmolean Museum, Oxford University.

A drawing of 'The Adoration of the Magi' in the collection of Windsor Castle resembles the composition of the tapestry of the New School of the same subject at the Vatican. Although some of its features are in the style of Romano, its technique more closely resembles that of Viagio Pupini. An elephant and camels are shown behind the three kings approaching through an opening at the right.[21] [43]

During the succeeding decades Hanno was utilized again and again as the subject or inspiration of other works of art, its image frequently based upon a sheet of red chalk sketches. Originally attributed to Raphael, the sketches are now considered with some certainty to have been the work of Giulio Romano, although there are also claims that they were drawn by Giovanni da Udine. The elephant is shown in four positions presumably drawn from life. It appears to have been an attempt to capture various poses of the unusual beast on one of the public occasions in which it appeared, probably the festivities marking the arrival of Giuliano de' Medici in Rome.[22]

This drawing – now in the Ashmolean Museum in Oxford – with its four red chalk sketches of Hanno, [44] can be identified in several major works for which they served as inspiration. The fourth head was probably the basis for the representations of the elephant included in the tapestry of 'The Adoration of the Magi'. Although the original

[45] Drawing for 'The Adoration of the Magi' featuring an elephant. School of Raphael. In the Department of Western Art, Ashmolean Museum, Oxford University.

cartoon for the tapestry has not survived, copies of it exist in the Chatsworth Collection and in the Ashmolean Museum in Oxford.[23] [45]

The same Oxford drawing is related also to a drawing for 'The Triumph of Bacchus' begun by Raphael but which remained unfinished. On 21 March 1517 he accepted a commission from Alfonso d'Este of Ferrara to execute a fresco of 'The Triumph of Bacchus in India' as soon as he had completed his current project of a painting of St Michael. He designed the scene and sent it to Alfonso, only to learn on 11 September that Alfonso had had the painting executed from Raphael's sketch by Pellegrino de San Daniele. In subsequent correspondence, Raphael asked that another subject be assigned to him, and accordingly another 'Triumph' was selected.

Although the painting by Pellegrino was subsequently lost, two other renditions from Raphael's sketch have survived. One is a painting by Benevenuto Tisi called Garofalo, now in Dresden, and the other is a fresco by Girolamo da Carpi which survives in a small room adjacent to the garden lodge in the castle at Ferrara.

Time passed, and despite numerous solicitations, Alfonso had not yet received the painting of the new 'Triumph' promised by Raphael. On 30 April 1519 Alfonso wrote to Paulucci in Rome that 'we are expecting with great anticipation a painted work by Raphael of Urbino, who has reported many times that he would have it finished soon.' He urged that every effort be made to obtain it from the painter, as it was the only painting in the series that had not yet been completed.[24]

The painting was never delivered, and after Raphael's death in 1520, Alfonso gave the commission with somewhat different instructions to Titian, who produced a painting of Bacchus and Ariadne for the duke's study. Apparently it included some of the motifs from Raphael's sketch. A design in the Museum Albertina in Vienna has been claimed to be Raphael's original, but most authorities consider it to be the work of his workshop and not of the master. Through all these versions stalks the figures of one or more elephants, derived from the image of the papal pachyderm.[25]

Components of the four sketches in the Oxford drawing were subsequently elaborated into a composition entitled 'The Battle With the Elephants' painted by Giulio Romano, which is known also by the title 'The Battle of Scipio Against Hannibal.' [46] It features a battle of the Romans against Pyrrhus in which war elephants are featured prominently. The finished drawing by Romano was for many years in

---

[46] Engraving by Antonio Lafreri, after a drawing by Raphael for 'The Triumph of Scipio', second half of the sixteenth century. To be noted are the similarity of the poses of the elephants to those of Hanno in Giulio Romano's drawing [44]. In the Cabinet des Dessins, The Louvre, Paris.

[47] A menagerie featuring two camels, a giraffe and five elephants; the poses or features of four of the elephants closely resemble those of the elephants in Giulio Romano's drawing [44] and in Lafreri's engraving [46]. Copper engraving from *Speculum Romanae Magnificentiae* by Antonio Lafreri (Rome, 1582).

the collection of a M. Gatteaux in Paris, and is now lost. An engraving was made from the drawing in about 1567 by Cornelis Cort as an 'invention' of Raphael. The engraving was to serve as the prototype illustration of the elephant for many years to come.[26]

The first version of Cort's engraving, entitled 'Repetition of the Battle of Scipio Against Hannibal' after Romano, was in fact the first version of the work, despite the confusing title. Mariette noted that the engraving was made from the lost original by Raphael. Passavant reported a legend that there was in France a cartoon for a tapestry of 'The Battle of the Elephants', but was unable to trace the legend's origin.[27]

The selfsame sketches of the Oxford drawing appear to have served also as the source of yet other works featuring elephants. In the late sixteenth century Giovanni Battista Franco produced two etchings, in one of which the elephant is represented in three positions shown together with a leopard. Two of the elephants are of the African variety, while the third, depicted with a mahout, clearly resembles the one depicted in Cort's engraving inspired by Raphael.[28]

In 1582 the Roman printer and engraver Antonio Lafreri produced a copper engraving of a menagerie featuring two camels, a giraffe, and five elephants in various poses. [47] It is readily apparent that four of these, from their postures and accoutrements, were copied either directly from the Oxford original or from drawings now in the Kupferstichkabinett in Berlin and in the Fogg Art Museum derived from it.

The posture of the elephant, the bell around its neck, the presence of the mahout, all are features repeated in the two drawings noted. The combining of the two sketches is most unusual and suggests that Lafreri based his work on these other drawings, and possibly on Raphael's mural which still existed in his time, as well as on the Cort engraving of 'The Triumph of Scipio' after Raphael.[29]

Polydoro da Caravaggio, another who had worked as Raphael's assistant at the Vatican, produced a design for an elaborate cup or bowl

[48] Sketch for a *tazza* supported upon the back of a caparisoned elephant, probably based on drawings of Hanno. Attributed to Polydoro Caravaggio, early sixteenth century. In the Cabinet des Dessins, The Louvre, Paris.

featuring the Medici arms supported on the back of an elephant. In all likelihood the figure of the beast was modelled after the live elephant Hanno, which Caravaggio undoubtedly observed while working at the Vatican.[30] [48]

There can be no doubt that Hanno provided inspiration and ample opportunity for sketching by artists working at the Vatican during its brief residence, and Romano in particular appears to have found it to be an intriguing subject. A sketch executed lightly in pen with brown ink of the great beast wearing its bell and bearing two putti on its back was formerly in the Ellesmere Collection. [49] It was a preliminary drawing for a stucco medallion executed probably by Francesco Primaticcio in the Sala delle Aquile, the bedroom of Federigo Gonzaga in the Palazzo del Te in Mantua, which was completed in

---

[49] The elephant Hanno bearing two *putti* on its back, one of them holding a torch. Pencil sketch by Giulio Romano, c. 1514-16, which appears to have been the basis for a ceiling medallion in the Palazzo del Te in Mantua. Formerly in the Ellesmere Collection, now privately owned.

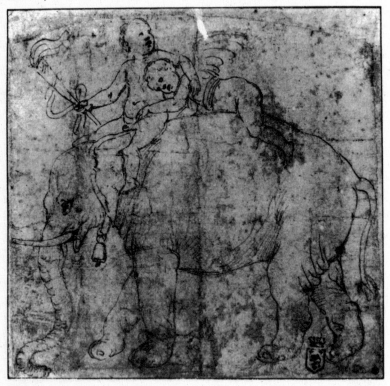

[50] Fresco panel depicting a battle with elephants. Attributed to Sicciolante da Sermoneta, 1545–48. On a vaulted ceiling in Castel Sant'Angelo, Rome.

1527 or 1528. Former owners of the drawing are believed to have been King Charles I of England and later Sir Thomas Lawrence.[31]

It is eminently appropriate that Hanno was memorialized as well in Castel Sant'Angelo, in front of which it had made its memorable obeisance to the pope upon its arrival in Rome. One of the ceiling frescoes of the Sala Paolina depicts a battle of elephants, dominated by the figure of the great beast. The work is attributed to Sicciolanta da Sermoneta, painted between 1545 and 1548.[32] [50]

The papal elephant was remembered also outside the Eternal City, and was most appropriately featured in a fresco decorating the Cappella Branconio, the Branconio family chapel in the church of San Silvestro in Aquila, Giovanni Battista Branconio's native town and the church in which he was buried. Forming part of the frieze is a scene depicting Hanno as a white elephant standing beside the 'poet' presumed to represent the Abbot Baraballo, although in fact it more resembles Francesco Petrarch. [51] The chapel with its elaborately painted decoration is claimed to have been designed for Branconio by his close friend, Raphael. The painting of the frieze as well as the ceiling and walls of the Cappella Branconio was commissioned in 1625 by Girolamo Branconio, the privy chamberlain's great-nephew, on the centenary of Branconio's death, and was executed by Giulio Cesare Bedeschini.[33]

[51] Portrait of Giovanni Battista Branconio with Hanno in a frieze in the Branconio family chapel in the Church of San Silvestro in L'Aquila dell'Abruzzo. Family tradition is that the chapel was designed for Branconio during his lifetime (i.e. prior to 1520) by his friend Raphael. The frieze was executed by Giulio Cesare Bedeschini in 1625, the centenary of Branconio's death.

Depictions of Hanno appeared in the same period in published form. The earliest, already noted, was a contemporary woodcut on the title-page of a pamphlet on the nature and habits of elephants published in Rome in about 1514. It was derived from a drawing which formed part of a manuscript in the Chigi family archives in the Vatican Library.

A similar woodcut was featured in a horoscope compiled for Pope Clement VII in a work by Sigismondo Fanti, a mathematician of Ferrara. *The Triumph of Fortune* (*Triompho di Fortuna*) was published at Venice and although the title-page bears the date 1526, it was not distributed until January 1527, less than six months before the sacking of Rome. It was reprinted later in the year. Described by bibliophiles as the most sumptuously illustrated fortune-telling book of the Renaissance, the *Triompho* contained seventy-two answers to questions calculated according to a complicated astrological system devised by Fanti. Each horoscope is given an individual name, such as 'The Wheel of Love', etc.

The woodcut of Hanno appears at the centre of the horoscope entitled 'The Wheel of the Elephant'; it is depicted with a howdah strapped to its back. [52] Dedicated to Pope Clement VII, for whom the horoscopes were compiled, the work reflected the preoccupation of the period with and reliance upon astrology at the highest levels of government and society.[34]

[52] 'The Wheel of the Elephant'. The elephant Hanno featured on the page of the horoscope of Pope Clement VII in *Triompho di Fortuna,* a volume of horoscopes of the Medici family, by the Ferrara mathematician, Sigismondo Fanti (Venice, 1526).

The pope and his menagerie, as well as his well-known preoccupation with astrology and prophecy, continued to provide entertaining subject matter for the satires of Pasquino, even after Hanno's death and the disturbing prophecy of Fra Bonaventura had been forgotten. Following the death in 1514 of the English cardinal who had paid the costs of the annual Pasquinade, the pope made himself the patron of Pasquino. Believing that such a tradition should be maintained, he paid the annual expenses of the festivities thereafter from the papal treasury. As the pontiff had anticipated, this action provoked praise for his patronage from the university students and the people of Rome, and was frequently reflected in the verses produced by students and pedagogues for the event. The pope's weaknesses were universally recognized, and it was well known that praise was the way to gain his favour.

The pontiff's generosity in supporting Pasquino did not deter his critics, however. In 1518 the published *Pasquilli* presented Pasquino in the guise of an astrologer. The unknown versifier could not forgo the opportunity to attack another of the pope's weaknesses which had become common knowledge, his fear of impending death. The *Pasquilli* predicted the pope's imminent demise with the prophetic words, 'When the lion from the heavens ceases to lend its customary warmth to the earth, the lion will die!'

The papal menagerie was featured prominently in the prediction, for Pasquino was made to say, 'the chameleon, the elephant, the Indian goat, the rhinoceros, all are dead: it is undeserving that the lion should outlive them.' The prophecy could not have been viewed lightly at the court, and the pope was undoubtedly greatly disturbed by it, for it revived the memory of Fra Bonaventura's prophecy, and provided fuel for his continuing contemplation of his fate. Elsewhere in the same pamphlet Pasquino commented, 'Rome has many monkeys, goats, every type of beast, recently come from India and Africa. It also has a monstrous elephant; and while the lion reigns as their king, it is proper and inevitable that the beasts are honoured.'[35]

Although the rhinoceros from Lisbon was not destined to be displayed at the Vatican in life or after death, the presence of a rhinoceros is to be found in the Vatican gardens, depicted in mosaic in the vestibule of the jewel-like Casino of Pope Pius IV. Construction of the building, begun under Paul IV, was completed in 1563 and modified several times under succeeding popes. Its decoration was chiefly the work of the Neapolitan architect, archaeologist and painter Pirro Ligorio. He frequently copied his themes from Roman originals so that it is likely that the mosaic image of the rhinoceros was based not on knowledge of the gift from Lisbon but on a Roman source.[36]

After the rhinoceros had been featured in Dürer's woodcut and the engraving by Burgkmair, it was depicted as part of a Medici symbol devised in 1536, exactly twenty years after its demise. The symbol was adopted by Duke Alessandro de' Medici, the illegitimate son of former Cardinal Giulio de' Medici, who upon election to the papal throne had taken the name Pope Clement VII. The pope was determined to give his son the rule of Florence despite the legitimate claim to the ducal throne of Ippolito, the son of Giuliano de' Medici and nephew of the late Pope Leo X. By continued and ingenious scheming, in July 1631 Pope Clement VII managed to set Ippolito aside and to install Alessandro as head of the Florentine republic.

In the following year the republic was abolished and Alessandro was declared Duke of Florence and continued to rule. His reign was memorable only for his outrageous injustice, cruelty and bestiality. It was said that during a reign that was a continuous orgy, he proved to be a creature who would have disgraced even the most shameful epochs of Roman villainy. Following the death of Ippolito, Alessandro married the emperor's daughter, Margaret of Austria.

In an effort to distinguish himself in military activities, he deliberately sought conflict in which he boasted that he would either win or die. He asked the historian Paolo Giovio to devise a suitable symbol for his coat-of-arms that would reflect this attitude, and the historian accordingly selected the rhinoceros. Later in his published works he reported the story of the ill-fated career of the Lisbon rhinoceros, stating that nevertheless it 'came to Rome in its veritable effigy and size, in the month of February MDXV [sic] with information about its characteristics as described by Pliny.' This curiously phrased comment has been taken as further confirmation that the rhinoceros actually arrived in Rome after it had been recovered and mounted.

Giovio then went on to relate that Duke Alessandro ordered covers or trappings to be made for the wild Barbary horses he raced in Rome. He commissioned the cloths to be richly embroidered with his motto, *Non buelvo sin vincer Io non ritorno indietro sin vittoria*. This motto, rendered in a combination of Spanish and Italian, may be translated, 'I shall not return without victory', and was derived from the verse *Rhinoceros nonquam victus ab hoste redit* ('The rhinoceros never returns from the enemy defeated'). The image of the beast was richly embroidered below the motto, and the ornate trappings were offered by the duke as the prize to the winner of the *palio* held in Rome. [53]

So pleased was Alessandro with his new motto that he had the rhinoceros carved in *agima* work on the sides of his chariot as well as

[53] The emblem of the rhinoceros and the motto *Non Bvelvo Sin Vencer* adopted by Alessandro de' Medici. From *Dialogo dell'impresse militari et amorosi...* by Paolo Giovio (Venice, 1557).

on his breastplate. An engraving of the Medici armour in the collection of Schloss Ambras, near Innsbruck, depicts Giovanni de' Medici holding a shield featuring the rhinoceros. The courageous motto and the fearsome symbol were not to bring Alessandro the fame and fortune he had anticipated, however. He had little opportunity to make use of them, for he had adopted them shortly after his marriage in June 1536, and he was brutally slain in January of the following year.[37]

A little more than three decades after King Francis I of France ventured into the bay of Marseilles to see the Lisbon rhinoceros, the same beast was featured as a royal symbol in the monuments erected to welcome his son as King Henry II on his triumphal entry into Paris in 1549. Having succeeded to his father's throne in 1547, at the age of twenty-eight, the young monarch had been prevented from visiting Paris until almost two years later. Elaborate preparations were made to honour him, and the most prominent artists of the time co-operated in the design and production of triumphal arches and monuments to mark salient points along the route of entry from Porte Saint-Denis to the royal palace.

Among those thus employed was the noted sculptor Jean Goujon, often called 'the French Phidias'. He designed a great obelisk which was erected in front of the Church of the Sepulchre on the Rue Saint-Denis. It rose seventy feet in height from a rectangular base and had the figure of a rhinoceros supporting the plinth; it was surrounded by dead lions, bears, wild boars and wolves. The sides of the obelisk were carved in hieroglyphics and it terminated in a golden globe upon which stood the female figure of a victorious France shown sheathing her sword after successful combat. [54] The base featured the inscribed quatrain: *'For a long time has lived and will live the memory of Hercules, who has overcome so many monsters. People proud and strong which through me France has dominated, are and will be my enduring glory.'*[38]

[54] The rhinoceros obelisk designed by Jean Goujon and erected in front of the church of the Sepulchre in Paris for the triumphal entry into the city by French King Henry II in 1549. From *C'est l'ordre qui à tenu a la nouvelle et joyeuse entrée…* (Paris, 1549).

The Lisbon rhinoceros also found its way into French literature. It occurs, for example, in the work of François Rabelais. In the thirtieth chapter of the Fifth Book of *Pantagruel*, Rabelais described the famous country of Satin, inhabited by a considerable number of animals presented as rare, or unknown in some instances. 'There I saw a rhinoceros,' he wrote, 'looking exactly like that which Henry Clerberg showed me at another time, a little different from a boar I have seen at Limoges except that it has a horn on its nose, as long as a cubit and pointed, with which it dared to engage an elephant in combat, and which it plunged into its stomach (which is the most tender and weak part of the elephant) rendering it dead on the ground.'[39]

Rabelais's account appears to have been derived from Pliny's *Natural History*. Clerberg is readily identified as Johannes Kleberger, a German merchant from Nuremberg living in Lyons during the period that Rabelais was a physician in that city. Amateur of the arts and wealthy benefactor of the poor, Klerberger was not a collector of zoological specimens as Rabelais suggested in the passage quoted. However, he had had his portrait painted by Dürer in 1526, at which time he may have acquired a print of Dürer's woodcut and later shown it to Rabelais. Rabelais was writing in a period when menageries were first coming into being throughout Europe. In 1536 he visited the one maintained by Filippo Strozzi in Florence, and the subject of rare beasts obviously intrigued him.[40]

Probably no single work of art has been more plagiarized or copied more often than has Dürer's woodcut of the Lisbon rhinoceros. To begin with, there were substantial discrepancies between his own drawing and his woodcut block. The original drawing was acquired by the English physician and collector, Sir Hans Sloane. When his collections were purchased in 1754 by the British Crown, the drawing became part of the holdings of the British Museum, now the British Library.

Apparently the space limitation imposed by the width of Dürer's wood block caused him to reduce the body of the beast and make it shorter and heavier and thus less realistic. In the first stage of his woodcut, hairs appear on the rhinoceros's chin and neck, greater emphasis is given to the shading of its plates, the dorsal horn is more prominent, and there are other variations as well.[41]

The Dürer woodcut served as an illustration accompanying descriptions of the rhinoceros in several editions of Sebastian Münster's *Cosmographia universalis* published in 1550. In this work the animal's appearance and characteristics were described, in addition to a brief account of the specimen sent to Lisbon and its contest with an elephant.[42]

Joachim Camerarius also reproduced the Dürer woodcut in a work published in 1590, in which all the illustrations of the elephant and rhinoceros appear to have been based on the work of earlier artists.[43]

Dürer's woodcut is again to be found in works by Paolo Giovio, Giovanni Piero Valeriano, Ambrose Paré, Marcus Cheeraerts the Elder, Antonio Tempesta and various others during the next two centuries. It was included in the *Historiae Animalium* by Conrad Gesner, a five-volume work published at Zurich between 1551 and 1558. From Gesner's compilation the representation of the rhinoceros was borrowed for other works on natural history and zoology, including the *Historia Naturalis* of Johannes Johnstonus published in Amsterdam in 1657, which also was based on Gesner's pioneering work, and *The Historie of Four-Footed Beasts, Serpents and Insects...* by Edward Topsell, which appeared in London in 1658.[44]

More surprising is to find the Dürer woodcut of the rhinoceros to have been the inspiration as well for a relief on one of the west doors of the cathedral of Pisa, probably executed by Angelo Scalani in about 1600, as a replacement for the decorations destroyed in a fire in 1595. During the seventeenth and eighteenth centuries the image of the rhinoceros proliferated into a great variety of decorative forms and objects, including Dresden porcelain, gilt bronzes, and Liverpool delft.[45]

It is curious that, as has been mentioned, but a single copy of Burgkmair's depiction of the rhinoceros has survived. It has been suggested that his representation may be linked directly to the original sketch of the beast by an anonymous Portuguese artist from which Dürer's work was derived, for it included none of the embellishments which had been added by Dürer to his woodcut, and Burgkmair's rendition was more accurate and realistic than Dürer's. If it was not inspired by the same original Portuguese drawing, then its basis may have been another sketch emanating from Lisbon at the same time.[46] It is doubtful whether Burgkmair had an opportunity to observe the Lisbon rhinoceros himself although it is known that he maintained contact with Portuguese traders and voyagers to the Indies. This is demonstrated by a series of woodcuts he produced in 1508, depicting African and Asian peoples and their domesticated animals.[47]

A single version of the rhinoceros copied from Burgkmair's engraving is known, carved three-dimensionally upon an oak-choir stall in the church of St Martin at Minden in north Germany. It was probably produced a few years after the appearance of Burgkmair's engraving. The roping of the animal's forefeet, the trefoil hoofs and the absence of the second dorsal horn clearly identify the carving with Burgkmair's engraving and not the Dürer woodcut.[48]

Dürer's woodcut made considerable impact outside the European art world as well. The rhinoceros was prominently featured in a late sixteenth-century ceiling fresco of a jungle group depicting three elephants and several natives in a palace at Tunja, in the highlands of Colombia in South America. The representation is believed to have been inspired by an illustrated work on measurement by Joan de Arphe y Villafane, published at Seville in 1585, in which the rhinoceros was described in prose and verse. The author noted that he had selected the rhinoceros because it had come to form part of the *coetaneous corpus* of exact knowledge, and that he had omitted reference to other horned animals because there was insufficient information about them.[49]

During the sixteenth century the Lisbon rhinoceros appeared in several other applications. Among them were a tapestry *feuille d'aristoloche* manufactured in the Low Countries in mid-century and presently in Krönberg Castle at Elsinore, Denmark. Dürer himself included a reduced version of his rhinoceros in 'The Triumphal Arch of Maximilian' first published in 1517. The Parmesan artist Enea Vico produced a woodcut in 1548 which closely resembled the one by Dürer, except that the image was reversed and a tail was added.[50]

The rhinoceros also was featured in several sculptures, including a fountain in the Piazza Pretoria in Palermo executed in Florence by Niccolò Pericoli called Tribolo, and then shipped to Palermo where it was completed and installed by Callilani. Pericoli also installed a sculpture of the Dürer rhinoceros in the Grotto of the Unicorn at the Medici villa in Castello which was completed in 1568.[51]

A rhinoceros carved in relief in marble inspired by the Dürer model is now in the Museo Nazionale in Naples. This may be identified with 'the rhinoceros without a head' which in 1556 had been in the collection of Metello Varro Porcari. The collection later became part of the Museo Borgiano before it was acquired by the Naples museum, to which the head was restored at a later time.[52]

Despite the proliferation of images of the pope's elephant throughout Italy and of the Lisbon rhinoceros in European art, until recently no representations of the pope's elephant were known in Portugal. Although King Manuel's mission of obedience and his gift of the elephant to the pontiff received substantial notice in Portuguese literature and histories of the period, apparently it did not attract the attention of the country's major artists, except for d'Ollanda's sketches

[55] Miniature sketch, (See page i of prelims) here much enlarged, depicting King Manuel I riding a young elephant, possibly Hanno, which appears on the title-page of the manuscript 'Livro octavo do Odiana' of the monarch's own copy of the *Leitura Nova*. Preserved in the *casa forte* of the Arquivo Nacional da Torre do Tombo, Lisbon.

made in Rome several decades after the event.

However, Hanno appears in two royal bibliographic treasures once owned by King Manuel I. The elephant is depicted on the title-page of the manuscript 'Livro Octava da Odiana' of the *Leitura Nova*, presently in the *casa forte* or vault of the national archives of Portugal. This collection of sixty-one codices was initiated by King Manuel I at the beginning of the sixteenth century and is one of the richest and most important holdings of the early archive, not only because of its literary and historical content but also because of the outstanding quality of its calligraphy and the inspired miniature paintings it contains.

Within the decorative border of the title-page is a charming tiny pen-and-ink sketch of a very young elephant romping, with the crowned king seated on its back. [55] The animal is a young male Indian elephant as distinguished by the high point at the middle of its back, the rounded forehead, and the small muscular ears; the rider's crown is that of King Manuel I. Presumably the drawing was made shortly after Hanno's arrival in Lisbon and before it was sent to Rome in early 1514. The king may well have disported himself in the royal park with his new acquisition, the occasion being memorialized by one of the court artists.[53]

Other sketches of Manuel's elephants as well as the rhinoceros appear in another manuscript, the king's copy of the *Livro de Horas* *(Book of Hours)*. This small codex of several hundred pages of Latin text is lavishly decorated with numerous miniature paintings. The work was initiated in 1517 and the paintings attributed to Domingos Sequeria, while the calendar is identified as the work of António da Holanda. Other miniature paintings in the volume are credited to Gregorio Lopes and Christavão de Figuiredo.

Of particular significance are the drawings of 'The Good Shepherd' and 'The Flight Into Egypt'. In the former an elephant is featured with other animals in the border decoration, while an elephant, a rhinoceros and several camels are included in the border of the latter. [56] Both of the little paintings reflect the king's continuing preoccupation with exotic fauna from the lands discovered and conquered by his navigators and military commanders.[54]

A recent discovery in Portugal has revealed that Hanno's passage had not gone totally unnoticed by some country artist, for in 1975 a remarkable wall-painting was discovered in a little church in the village of Montemor-O-Novo, in which clearly depicted are the elephant Hanno and its two attendants.

Situated near the river Almançor in an agricultural community known for its cattle raising, the tiny isolated church of San Pedro da Ribeira, facing west in the traditional spiritual context of the Middle Ages, appeared to be just another of the numerous places of worship dotting Portugal's countryside. According to an inscription dated 1511 found in its foundations, the church had been erected upon the ruins of a thirteenth-century church already existing in the reign of King Afonso II. Early local records confirm the existence in circa 1220 of the small church of 'S. Pedro da Ribeira'. At a date not recorded, in the early sixteenth century, the present edifice consisting of a single nave was erected upon the foundations of the earlier structure, or remodelled from it, and it became the hermitage of a religious order called the Brotherhood of the Faithful of God *(Irmandade dos Fiéis de Deus)*.

Until recently the wall of the apse, behind the altar, was covered with a large retable painted in 1550 in oils on wood in the style of the Portuguese Renaissance, its theme featuring St Peter. In 1975, when

[56] An elephant, rhinoceros and camels depicted in the border painting of a page relating to the Flight Into Egypt of King Manuel's *Livro de Horas*. In the Museu de Arte Antiga, Lisbon.

the retable was removed for restoration by the Instituto José de Figueiredo, the wall-painting was revealed, still in a reasonable state of conservation. The fact that it had been covered by the retable and apparently forgotten for four centuries had protected the painting from variations of climate and changes of ecclesiastic administration

that might have resulted in redecorating the church interior.

The wall-painting consists essentially of three distinct parts: on the left, St Peter, the first pontiff, sits upon a damask-covered papal throne. His countenance is severe and he holds in his left hand (the pigmentation now damaged) the two keys that denote his god-given authority. To each side of the throne stands a tree; at the foot and round about, paths run through rocky outcrops. At the opposite side of the painting, on the right, stands an Indian elephant, our Hanno, with its attendant. Between pontiff and elephant, the middle of the painting depicts a landscape which portrays the life of rural Alentejo: near St Peter stand two horses and two oxen; two women *aquadeiras* in long skirts, scarves and hats, carry jugs on their heads; a shepherd in his heavy coat, accompanied by a spotted dog, tends a flock of sheep; a man and a woman sow seeds; two men, each shouldering a hod, gaze transfixed on all this rustic animation... The pictorial arrangement implies that the elephant is on his way, traversing the countryside, to the pope in far-off Rome. [57] The whole painting is framed by intertwining clusters of grapes and vine leaves in a manner familiar from book illustrations in the fifteenth and sixteenth centuries. The painting has a luminous, almost transparent, quality, in a palette of soft ochres and sepias typical of southern Portugal.

[57] Sixteenth-century fresco [a] in the apse of the church of San Pedro da Ribeira in Montemor-O-Novo, Portugal [b] The fresco has faded unevenly; of the elephant – detail [c] – little more than an outline remains.

[57d] The village church of San Pedro da Ribeira, Montemor-O-Novo, site of the elephant fresco [57a–c].

The little church, which had long since ceased to be used for religious observances, slumbered in quiet neglect. Then, two decades ago, arrangements were made to restore the retable. Antonio Alberto Banha de Andrade reported, 'the painting, which was discovered in 1975, on the back wall of the apse, until then covered with a retable of the sixteenth century, is in need of restoration. Very rich in colour, with a rustic theme, it becomes even more valuable due to the rare appearance in Portuguese paintings of that period of an elephant from India, which then (1513) was sent to Rome, in the embassy of Tristão da Cunha.'[55]

It is even more surprising to find the papal elephant featured in carvings of ivory objects brought back to Europe from Africa by Portuguese traders in the sixteenth century. In the course of recent studies of carved African ivories, several representations of elephants were discovered that apparently had been based on European images of Hanno, on decorated oliphants – hunting trumpets carved of ivory – produced by the Sapi peoples of the Portuguese colony Sierra Leone.

After having completed exploration of the African coast during the late fifteenth and early sixteenth centuries, the Portuguese established a number of permanent commercial bases and trading posts in Benin and Sierra Leone as well as in the Congo. Serving as intermediary between Europe and the newly discovered lands, Portugal transmitted

Western artistic values to these alien cultures and the resulting inter-action was reflected, for example, in certain items of African art executed in ivory.

A greater taste for luxury developed among the upper levels of Portugal's society during this period as a consequence of the country's increasing riches and power. Art in many forms was commissioned by the Portuguese in other European countries, particularly Germany, Flanders and Italy. At the same time Portugal's contacts with its bases in Africa and the Far East had developed a new taste for the exotic. Accordingly, Portuguese traders commissioned local artists to produce a variety of objects in ivory decorated with carvings which they then exported in great numbers to grace the tables of European princes and prelates.

Ivory was plentiful and inexpensive during this period of early contact, and the presence of extremely talented artists among the carvers of ivory encouraged Portuguese traders to commission a wide range of products in this medium. Among the most popular were forks, spoons and knife handles, salt cellars, oliphants, religious objects such as ciboriums, and similar items. The carved ivory surfaces gener-ally featured subject matter copied or modified from European engravings. Among favourite themes were fantastic animals, mytho-logical subjects and heraldic topics including the arms of the House of Aviz, then reigning in Portugal.

Hunting scenes with animals were also frequently to be found in decorations of oliphants. Professor Ezio Bassani, who has made an extensive study of African ivory carvings, has been able to relate some of the carvings depicting pachyderms to European artistic sources. He noted that in each instance these elephants sculptured on the oliphants were Indian in origin, not African, as distinguished by the size of the ears. The Indian origin is further confirmed by the fact that the carved images of the beast appearing on African oliphants depict it with human attendants or attachments such as a howdah; the elephant was never domesticated in Africa.[56]

Three depictions that purport to be of Hanno have been identified by Bassani carved on oliphants produced by the Sapi population of the Portuguese base in Sierra Leone. The Sapi were ancestors of today's Bulom, Temne and other peoples of Sierra Leone. In an oliphant owned by the Paris antiquarian J. Kugel, an elephant is shown with its howdah. Although representations of an elephant bearing a howdah occur in European works as early as the late fifteenth century, none have been found in Indian miniatures prior to the beginning of the seventeenth century. It must be presumed, therefore, that the Sapi-

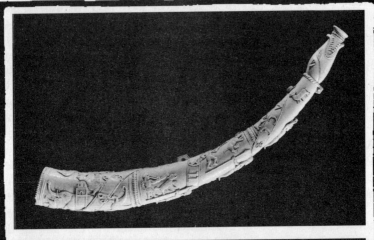

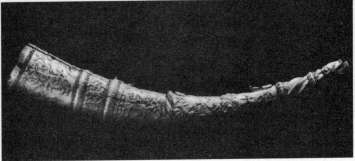

[58] Ivory oliphants, Sapi-Portuguese, from Siera Leone, 1490–1530: [a] Carving depicting an elephant with its howdah (near the wide end). Private collection. [b] Carving depicting the elephant Hanno with its keeper astride its neck holding an ankush and led by its guide by means of a chain. Musée de l'Homme, Paris. [c] Detail of carving depicting a confrontation between a young elephant and a rhinoceros. Hermitage, St. Petersburg.

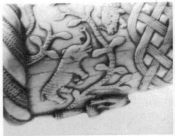

Portuguese carving was based upon a European drawing or engraving of the period, probably generated from Giulio Romano's sketches.[57]

The carving on another oliphant, in the Musée de l'Homme in Paris, represents an Indian elephant being led on a chain by a guide and bearing its keeper, who is holding his *ankush*. There is a close link between this carving and the drawing in the Kupferstichkabinett in Berlin in which both of Hanno's attendants are present. It is more likely that it was based upon the sketch made by Francisco d'Ollanda of Raphael's fresco of Hanno at the entrance to the Vatican. This may have been copied in Portugal and sent to Africa as a model to be used in the carvings. If so, the artist made some modifications and took liberties with the original, changing the position of the trunk, lengthening the tusks, omitting the bell around the elephant's neck and substituting a chain for the cord held by the guide.[58]

Particularly interesting is a carving on another ivory oliphant from Sierra Leone in the collection of the Hermitage Museum in St Petersburg. It depicts an Indian elephant in combat with a beast resembling a unicorn, but which more probably is an Indian rhinoceros. The scene may have been based on accounts of the contest between the two pachyderms staged by King Manuel at his palace at Ribeira; that the rhinoceros is from India and not Africa is confirmed by the presence of a single horn instead of two.[59] [58a, 58b and 58c]

There could be no doubt that these carved representations were based on similar images appearing on European drawings, such as a group of three elephants is the famous *Triumph of Caesar* of 1500–6 by Andrea Mantegna, and two contemporary engravings by Giulio Campagnola and Giovanni Antonio da Brescia, in which the elephant depicted was of African origin. The presence of these images in the carvings of ivory oliphants indicates that they post-date the death of Hanno, probably produced not earlier than the mid-sixteenth century.[60]

The proliferation of illustrations of the two papal pachyderms in such a great variety of artistic media and literary forms throughout the remainder of the sixteenth century and even later leaves no doubt of the impact they made as symbols of the short but eventful reign of that cheerful melancholic Pope Leo X.

Without question the elephant, and the rhinoceros as well, must take their place in papal history together with the notable artists and writers, buffoons and poetasters, who distinguished the papal court by their presence as the golden age reached its apogee before its abrupt and disastrous decline.

CHAPTER EIGHT
The Prey of Time

Thou stranger, which of Rome in Rome here seekest,
And nought of Rome in Rome perceiv'st at all,
These same olde walls, olde arches, which thou seest,
Olde palaces, is that which Rome men call.
Behold what wreake, what ruine, and what wast,
And how that she, which with her mightie powre
Tam'd all the world, hath tam'd herselfe at last,
The prey of Time, which all things doth devowre.
Rome, living, was the world's sole ornament,
And dead, is now the world's sole moniment.

Edmund Spenser : *Complaints* (1591)

THE EXCHANGE OF GIFTS AND COURTESIES BETWEEN KING Manuel I and Pope Leo X continued actively to the ends of their respective reigns, which occurred almost simultaneously. The communication instituted with the mission of obedience flowered into a continuing correspondence on a variety of subjects, ranging from the Portuguese achievements overseas to religious concerns and arts and letters. Traces of the influence of this exchange can occasionally be found in Portuguese art and writings.[1]

Meanwhile, elsewhere, Pope Leo X was encountering increasing difficulties. The contest for the duchy of Urbino had been extremely costly, severely draining the papal treasury. The pope, despite his many good qualities, proved to be a less than efficient manager of finances. He attempted to meet the demands for money from all sides by negotiating loans from every possible source, pawning Vatican treasures, selling ecclesiastical offices, diverting funds assigned for other purposes to pay immediate debts, even borrowing from funds set aside for the construction of the basilica of St Peter, and by increasing duties and taxes. When in 1517 the conspiracy of a number of cardinals against the pope's life was exposed, Pope Leo X took advantage of the situation to demand excessive sums from the conspirators as part of their punishment. All of these elements, reflecting as they did the immorality of the papal court, were later made significant issues by the wrathful words of Martin Luther which contributed to the religious Reformation.[2]

It may be said that in some ways the death of the elephant Hanno marked the beginning of the end of the Leonine Age, in which it had figured so prominently. The High Renaissance, which had flourished as brilliantly during the reign of Leo X as during that of Julius II, had begun to dim, in the Eternal City and elsewhere in Italy.

In retrospect, the election of Cardinal Giovanni de' Medici to the papacy as Pope Leo X proved to be in some ways as unfortunate as it was at first considered desirable, for he represented the worst as well as the best features of the Renaissance. Although unremittingly active in politics, he was generally less than successful. He is best remembered as a supporter of the arts and letters, of music and learning in general, and as the most erudite man to have worn the papal tiara up to his time and for long thereafter. He was generous to a fault at a time when the Church finances required strong economic control, and it was his fate that so many of his qualities for good appeared to work to his disadvantage. Despite the criticisms that were levelled against him by contemporary detractors and later historians, Pope Leo X nevertheless emerges as a charismatic figure, who contributed greatly to the flowering of the Renaissance in Italy.[3]

The pontiff often lacked discretion in his selection of intimates and his support of individuals. Although his two secretaries, Bembo and Sadoleto, were counted among the foremost scholars of the age, he rarely sought their advice in matters of letters. Too frequently he permitted himself to be deluded and imposed upon by the numerous buffoons and would-be poets perched like scavenger birds at the court in Rome. When presented with manuscripts of their work by these writers, Leo often surveyed them quickly with his hand lens while reaching into his purse to reward them. He was extremely lavish in his gifts. Valeriano described the situation in one of his sermons, *Simia*, in which he likened the pope to a lion being teased by a flock of monkeys.[4]

When Paolo Giovio read to him from a volume of his stories, the pontiff promptly had his name added to the rolls of the Studio Romano and placed him under the patronage of Cardinal Giulio de' Medici. For a poem praising him, the pope gave Angelo Colocci 400 (some sources said 4,000) *scudi*. Benedetto Lampridio was compensated generously for his Greek studies and Pindaric odes, and Antonio Tebaldo received 500 ducats for a laudatory ode. Leo repeated this practice throughout his reign. News of the pontiff's liberality succeeded in bringing Italy's finest artists and writers to Rome, where they flourished under his patronage. Unfortunately the same liberality also brought droves of versifiers seeking honours and compensation. It was small wonder that the reign of Leo X was known as the Golden Age, for never was gold more freely distributed. He gave his name to his age, and for the past three centuries his reign has been praised – by artists and men of letters. In his own time he was praised by Erasmus not only for his kindness and humaneness and love of peace, but also for his magnanimity and learning and support of the fine arts.[5]

The pope's leisure was spent in a variety of peaceful pursuits. As has been noted, he enjoyed playing chess and cards, and listening to music in his private rooms. A weakness for which he was severely criticized was his love of the hunt, which he was convinced was necessary for his health. He was often absent in the field for weeks at a time, with large numbers of his courtiers. He devoted a substantial amount of time to the company of goldsmiths and jewellers, ordering expensive new baubles for his own adornment, and planning festivals and other events for the amusement of the court, while attempting to raise money to meet his overwhelming debts.

The pontiff's liberality extended to these festivals and public events as well. During the carnival season of 1519, the pope announced a battle to be held between his chamberlains and his heralds or shield-bearers (*scutiferi*) to take place under the battlements of Castel Sant' Angelo. Twenty-five contestants for each side were selected. Elaborate preparations for this unusual event were made, including special liveries of satin for the participants ordered at great cost at the pope's expense. The day of the whimsical tournament arrived, and the ammunition of the contestants flew hot and heavy on all sides – oranges![6]

Obese, slow in movement, speaking rarely, always smiling, laughing often, Leo's primary mission in life appeared to be to promote pleasure for himself and his associates. He willingly endorsed every pomp that would amuse his fun-loving court. Abstemious with food and drink, he enjoyed arranging sumptuous banquets at frequent intervals for his familiars, simply for the pleasure of watching them gorge themselves like beasts and behave like fools. The choice of his two principal ministers was representative of his attitude. Among his closest associates were Giovanni Lazzaro de Magestris known as Serapica, and Fra

Mariano. The former, an ugly brutish individual formerly employed as a dog trainer by the Cardinal de Sanseverino, was placed in charge of the papal treasury by the pope. Fra Mariano, formerly barber to Leo's father, had come from Florence; he succeeded Bramante as the Keeper of the Seals. Another of Leo's favourites was the one-time jeweller who became his privy chamberlain and custodian of the elephant, Giovanni Battista Branconio.

On the other side of the coin, Pope Leo's expenditures served better ends than frivolities. He expended great sums for major improvements in the city of Rome, continuing the reconstruction of the Apostolic Palace and the rebuilding of the basilica of St Peter and renovating the church of Santa Maria in Dominica. He provided a new outlet from the congested central part of the city towards the Piazza del Popolo by building the Via Ripetta. Concerned with drainage of the Pontine Marshes, he developed a plan which he asked Leonardo da Vinci to undertake. He added immeasurably to the Vatican library by sending out agents far and wide to find and purchase classic literary works. He continued the programme initiated by Julius II for the preservation of Roman sculpture and other treasures recovered from the ruins in Rome and the surrounding countryside.[7]

As we have seen, Pope Leo X was extremely superstitious; he maintained his own astrologers at court. One of these was Luca da Borgo, on whom he relied for advice on all personal and official actions to be taken. The pope also favoured various other astrologers and alchemists who were among the hangers-on at the court, and he went so far as to institute a course in astrology at La Sapienza, the University of Rome, conducted by another of his astrologers, Francesco Priolo. He also consulted the well-known Luca Guarico. In this preoccupation Leo reflected the wide interest in astrology which prevailed throughout Italy. Even his predecessor Pope Julius II had relied on astrology to such a degree that his astrologers selected the day of his coronation and the date of his triumphal return to Rome after his expedition to Bologna.[8]

For more than a century prior to Leo X's election, there had been a great outcry throughout the Christian world demanding a reform of the Church because of the increasing excesses and abuses in ecclesiastical life and in the administration of the Holy See. Attempts were made time after time to resolve the situation, but no tangible results were achieved. Equally scandalous was the behaviour of the Roman nobility. The state of the Church and the need for its reform were presented in a classic statement at the close of the Lateran Council in

1517 by Count Giovanni Francesco Pico della Mirandola, in the presence of the then pontiff and the assembled College of Cardinals. No corrective action resulted, and it became clear that no substantial reform would be initiated by the new pontiff.[9]

The wealth and power of the Church made its excuses the more disturbing. In Leo X's time, the Church is reckoned to have owned at least a third of the wealth of Christendom. It accumulated great quantities of gold and coin at a time when the money in the economy was limited. This it did from its property and church taxes –'annates', 'thirds', 'tenths'; from pious benefactions, the sale of dignities and fees for ceremonies; from payments as penance and as absolution – 'God,' said Cesare Borgia, 'desireth not the death of a sinner but rather that he should pay and live.' Then there were special taxes, whether for holy warfare, specific crusades, or the building of St Peter's and the Vatican to Julius II's vast expectations. For this, Leo promoted the sale of Indulgences: the Church held the key to a 'treasury of merits', accumulated from the surplus earned by the saints, which the Church could sell to rescue the living and the dead from their just deserts in Purgatory. Against the disreputable selling of Indulgences in Germany, an Augustinian monk – professor of theology at the university of Wittenberg – named Martin Luther protested. He held, as had others before him, that 'the only true treasury of merits is the grace of God'; the Elector of Saxony refused to let the Dominican Johann Tetzel and his agents indulge their salesmanship in his domains, and the Emperor Maximilian declared that the Church took from the people of Germany more than a hundred times the amounts he could.

In Germany religious doctrine, financial extortion, politics and a nascent nationalism had begun to combine in an explosive mixture. All over Christendom, a network of bishops and clergy – ultimately responsible to the pope – exercised a degree of independence and influence over the people which many rulers found offensive, the more so when the papacy became increasingly the plaything of Italian princely families. To make matters worse, Italian popes – for the benefit of their legitimate relations or illegitimate offspring – became involved in the constant wars between the north Italian city-states, and between Valois and Hapsburg contenders for control over them. The papacy had become worldly in its preoccupations, and its Italian character undermined its claim to universality. When Luther nailed his 95 Propositions on the church-door in Wittenberg in 1517 – the normal way to propose a public debate – Leo dismissed the whole affair as a 'monk's quarrel'; only four years later, his legate at the Diet of Worms could report: 'nine-tenths of Germany shouts for Luther.'

Luther had at first argued for a General Council of the Church to consider the theological arguments in dispute. Such an appeal to some other authority as superior to the pope, however, had been declared in the Bull *Execrabilis* of 1460 to constitute heresy. Having taken little action for three years, Leo decided to take an uncompromising stand: as heir of St Peter and Vicar of God, the pope had absolute supremacy; through his cardinal legate he demanded Luther's unconditional retraction. In a public letter, Luther declared Leo himself only 'a Daniel in Babylon', but 'the Roman Church, formerly the most holy of churches, is become the most licentious den of thieves, the most shameful of all brothels, the kingdom of sin, of death and of hell, the wickedness of which not anti-christ himself could conceive.' Leo he portrayed, in the tract 'On the Papacy of Rome', as indolently catching flies while his pet elephant cavorted. Hanno, it seemed, had become sufficiently established in the popular mind to act, for years after his death, as a telling symbol of Leo's irresponsibility and negligence in the midst of a stew of ecclesiastical luxury and abuse.

In another tract of 1520, an 'Address to the Nobility of the German Nation', Luther advocated German control over all ecclesiastical matters in Germany, and appealed to the German princes to help effect the reformation of the church in their states. He reiterated the Augustinian doctrines that led to a belief in Predestination and Justification by Faith alone, doctrines which undermined the edifice on which papal control and papal finance was founded – the doctrine of merit earned by 'works', including donations. Then at the Diet of Worms in 1521, Luther attacked papal control still further, even in matters doctrinal, by expounding the 'priesthood of all believers, the supremacy of individual conscience': 'for I cannot rely on the authority of popes and courts alone, since they have frequently erred, and contradicted each other, and unless my conscience is subdued by the word of God, I neither can nor will retract anything; seeing that to act against my conscience is neither safe nor honest. Here I take my stand; I can do no other.'

Luther's indignation at papal abuses and his doctrinal position quickly became entangled with German politics – which is why his reforming movement did not die with him, as did that of John Wycliffe, Jan Huss, Girolamo Savonarola, Fra Bonaventura and the rest. Luther's original notion of an appeal to a General Council of the Church had won some support from the Emperor Maximilian, for tension between emperor and pope was constant. Leo, urging the emperor to issue an imperial ban on Luther, made play with the possibility of papal forces supporting the French against the emperor.

However, Luther's extreme position at the Diet of Worms – his elevation of the authority of individual conscience – alarmed the new young emperor, Charles V, who promptly issued the ban: 'I have therefore resolved to stake upon this claim all my dominions, my friends, my body and my blood, my life and my soul.' The rulers of the German states still found Luther's preference for state control in ecclesiastical matters attractive, contributory to their wish for greater independence from both emperor and pope: Luther, returning from Worms, was 'seized' and put into the castle of Wartburg in protective custody by the Elector of Saxony. Thence he wrote the tracts, began the translation of the Bible, wrote the hymns and issued the denunciations which laid the foundations of a new church. Leo, on the day the emperor issued the ban on Luther, signed an alliance by which the papal forces supported the Hapsburgs in their running battles against the Valois, an alliance crowned quickly with the recovery of Milan and other cities.

Leo had shown masterly ability in the political game, but his natural amiability, indolence and reasonableness made him ineffective against the rough and impassioned Luther. As William Roscoe, historian of Leo's pontificate, wrote: 'the conduct of Luther, in enforcing his own peculiar dogmas, and silencing those who opposed his tenets, may justify the assertion that if he had been pope instead of Leo X he would have defended the Church against a much more formidable adversary than the monk of Wittenberg.'

Leo's successor, Adrian, tried to reform the notorious abuses of Rome and the Church: 'Let the pope and the Curia do away with the errors by which God and man are rightly offended... If the Germans see this done, there will be no further talk of Luther.' In less than two years Adrian was dead; another Medici – Leo's cousin Giulio – became pope. Reform languished; the traditional political game continued. Within three years of Leo's death the emperor and the princes of southern Germany had formed a Catholic Alliance: those of northern Germany formed one of 'Protestant' states. Despite Luther's denunciations, the 'Reformation' was propelled to further doctrinal extremes by the Swiss reformer Huldreich Zwingili and the French theologian John Calvin, and caused yet more numerous divisions in a once catholic church. It was Leo's unhappy lot to be identified with the fragmentation and bitter quarrels within western Christendom, the effects of which remain to this day.[10]

News of the recapture of Milan from the French reached the pope in a dispatch from Cardinal Giulio de' Medici two weeks after the event, while Leo was hunting at his country villa, La Magliana. Although he was recuperating from surgery, the pontiff had gone to the villa for a day's outing. The day proved to be extremely hot and humid while the night turned cold with strong winds. Hot and tired from the chase, Leo caught cold standing at an open window observing a bonfire below which had been lighted to celebrate the day's hunt.

Upon being carried back to Rome two days later, the pontiff was informed of the capture of Piacenza and Parma. His condition worsened rapidly, and on Sunday 1 December at seven o'clock in the morning, Pope Leo X breathed his last. His doctors had claimed that he was only slightly indisposed from the cold he had caught at La Magliana, and neither he nor his associates had been informed that his illness could be mortal.

The mournful tolling of the major bell of the Campidoglio on the morning of 2 December, with the counterpoint of fifty salvoes of the artillery of Castel Sant'Angelo, announced to the populace the death of their pontiff, followed by the intermittent dolorous sounds of the bells from all the other churches of the city. The stupefying news brought throngs to the piazza of St Peter and the streets of the city were soon alive with people. The twenty-nine cardinals resident in the city, mounted on horseback and attended by secretaries and servants, rode to the Apostolic Palace as quickly as possible. There was some suspicion that Leo had been poisoned, but it was never proven.[11]

Although Leo had been ill for years, all had expected that he would have a long reign because of his youth; his death came as a shock to the papal court. It was an even greater shock to the ranks of his intimates and hangers-on. Suddenly their whole world had disintegrated, and all their ambitions, expectations, hopes, and calculations vanished into thin air. The pope's death found the papal treasury totally empty; there was no money to pay even for the customary ceremonial burial of the pontiff. The papal household then numbered 663 people and the household expenses alone were approximately 100,000 ducats a year – double those of his predecessor. Salaries had long gone unpaid, and many of the pope's intimates had made loans of substantial sums to the pontiff. Serapica, for example, had lent Leo X 18,000 ducats; now there was no possibility of collecting it.

Following an age-old tradition, the pope's relatives and intimates seemed to be motivated by a single thought when news of his death reached them. They surged like madmen through the papal chambers, searching for anything that was negotiable, stealing gold and silver, jewels, books, musical instruments, clothing and furniture, in fact anything that had value.[12]

After all the pomp that had distinguished his reign, and in fact because of it, there was no pomp for Leo X in death, and his funeral ceremonies were mean. Because the basilica of St Peter was under reconstruction, it was not possible to bury him there. When Pope Julius II had died, Fedro, called the Cicero of his time, had presented a great funeral oration fitting for the occasion. For Leo, none of the major literati he had supported at his court could find time for the ceremony. The funerary oration was delivered by an obscure familiar named Antonio da Spello. He delivered a brief and hurried eulogy of the pontiff who had given his name to the epoch, and whom history was both to revere and to criticize. With Leo's death, Rome had a rude awakening from its golden dream and faced the stark reality that the Golden Age had ended.[13] [59]

Upon the announcement of the pope's death, the cardinals were hastily summoned for a conclave, but only thirty-nine were able to reach the city in time. Two of their number became extremely ill and had to be carried from the proceedings. The conclave lasted for fifty days. Before the main business could begin, the more prominent poets and versifiers who had thrived so long upon Leo's patronage found occasion to voice belated eulogies of Leo X. Theirs was a contest for visibility, because one of the cardinals assembled for the conclave would become the next pope, and hence their potential patron. Although ostensibly honouring the memory of the departed pontiff, some of the sonorous sonnets which assaulted the assembled conclave were exercises in satire, sometimes witty and frequently vulgar, notably those by Antonio Lelio Romano and Pietro Aretino. Sixteen days passed before it was considered that the late pope had been properly eulogized and that the conclave could begin in earnest.[14]

The selection of a successor found the cardinals greatly divided, and eleven votes were taken during the next month. It was necessary to select a cardinal having no known political association, to ensure that his election would not create political problems. The final choice was sixty-three-year-old Adrian Florenz, Cardinal of Tortosa, who had been tutor to Emperor Charles V. Stern, aloof and almost anti-social, he was at the same time plain and soft-spoken. He brought a welcome, sobering influence to the papal court. One of his first actions was to reduce the papal payroll to an absolute minimum. He promptly dismissed most of the artists, poets, musicians and other appendages of Leo's court. He initiated an economizing programme by reducing fees for all services to the Vatican, limiting the income of cardinals, and eliminating pomp in every form. Opposed by nature to the spirit of the Renaissance, his reforms were trenchant and thorough.[15]

[59] Monument erected to the memory of Pope Leo X in the church of Santa Maria Sopra Minerva in Rome. Commissioned by Ippolito de' Medici, it was designed by Alfonso Lombardi based on Michelangelo's sketches, and erected by Baccio Bandinelli. The statue of the pontiff was executed by Raffaello da Montelupo.

Inevitably the reforms initiated by the new pope, who had taken the name of Adrian VI, made many enemies in the Curia, but he knew what was required and demonstrated a strong determination to correct the problems he had found. He had begun an investigation of the financial accounts of the cardinals when suddenly death overtook him, a little more than one and a half years after his election. There was dancing in the streets of Rome when his death was announced, and the College of Cardinals lost no time in assembling a conclave to elect a successor.[16] The selection of Cardinal Giulio de' Medici, who took the name of Pope Clement VII, brought great rejoicing to Rome because it was anticipated that he would follow in his cousin's footsteps and bring another golden age to the papal court. He was known to have many good qualities. He was abstemious, pious, temperate, erudite and a patron of the arts. Despite these fine characteristics, however, he soon brought disappointment to supporters and opponents alike. He had poor judgement of men, lacked any ability for ruling and was incapable of making decisions; above all, he lacked Leo's flamboyance and style.

During his reign the Church lost millions of its adherents. He quarrelled with King Henry VIII, and was unable to take steps against the Spanish Charles V's domination of the Church. Although aware of the growing 'protestant' defections occurring in the north, he was unable to take positive action to prevent them. Lacking skill in statesmanship, he made the error of trying to play off the King of France against Emperor Charles V, with the consequence that he brought the latter's armies to the gates of Rome. There, on 6 May 1527, they mutinied. For three days and three nights the Eternal City was swept by flames and horror as German and Spanish mercenaries tortured and massacred the people, raping nuns and daughters of senators and nobility, stripping the churches of their treasures, desecrating altars and burning a great number of houses. Order was not fully restored for nine months, in February 1528.[17]

Pope Clement VII escaped just ahead of the invaders by fleeing along the secret passage in the Corridore to the questionable safety of Castel Sant'Angelo, where for many months he was to remain a prisoner with the thirteen cardinals who had also found refuge there. Huddled within the confines of the fortress were some 3,000 noncombatants, including diplomats, scholars, priests and servants, and less than 500 soldiers. From the battlements they could see the devastation of the city, with 13,000 houses burned and 30,000 inhabitants slaughtered in the holocaust.

The devastation was beyond measure. Tombs in churches were

broken open; jewellery and garments, if they were of precious cloth, were stripped from the corpses, the remains left abandoned to add fuel to the plague that followed. Cesspools and sewers were searched for hidden gold and jewellery, and left open. The tomb of Julius II was broken open by Spanish troops, the corpse dragged out and plundered. The heads of St Andrew and St John were kicked about by the soldiers in the streets. The great golden cross of Constantine, featured in the basilica of St Peter for 1200 years, disappeared, as did the gem-encrusted tiara of Pope Nicholas V and the Golden Rose presented by Pope Martin V to commemorate the healing of the Schism; they were never to be seen again. The Prince of Orange had taken up residence in the Vatican library and made every effort to save it from the invaders. He posted guards to save the Raphael Stanze and the Sistine Chapel from the marauders.

The Frenchman Grolier reported 'Everywhere cries, the clash of arms and the shrieks of women and children, the crackling of fire and the crash of falling roofs. We were numb with fear and held our ears, as if we alone were preserved by fate to look on the ruin of our country.' Francesco Guicciardini, who was there, wrote of this terrifying period:

Many were suspended for hours by the arms, many were cruelly bound by the private parts; many were suspended by the feet high above the road, or over water, while their tormentors threatened to cut the cord upholding them. Some were half buried in the cellars; others were nailed up in casks while many were villainously beaten and wounded; not a few were burnt all over their persons with red hot irons. Some were tortured by extreme thirst, others by insupportable noise and many were cruelly tortured by having their good teeth brutally drawn. Others again were forced to eat their own ears, or nose, or their roasted testicles and yet more were subjected to strange, unheard of martyrdoms that move me too much even to think of, much less describe.

Hard on the heels of the sacking of Rome came a raging plague that brought even greater distress and devastation among those who had survived.[18]

Just as the Golden Age of Pope Leo X and the brilliance of his court terminated its short meteoric career and was brought to a miserable impoverished conclusion, so the major figures associated with it died one after another within a short period. Bramante, who had served both Pope Julius II and Pope Leo X as architect of the Vatican, had died in 1514; Hanno, elephant-symbol of happier times, died in 1516; Leonardo da Vinci, who had been more of an observer than a participant at the Vatican during part of Leo's reign, died at Cloux in 1519; and in 1520 Raphael died unexpectedly in Rome; Pope Leo X passed away in 1521; Pope Adrian VI in 1523, and Pope Clement VII in 1534. Of the major artists employed at the Vatican, Giulio Romano died in 1546 and only Michelangelo and Giovanni da Udine survived into the second half of the sixteenth century.

After reaching the zenith of its success in conquest and colonization during the reign of Pope Leo X, the Portuguese empire began a decline initiated imperceptibly with the death in 1515 of its great military leader, Afonso de Albuquerque. The supremacy which he had achieved for Portugal in the East was never surpassed or even matched by his successors. Meanwhile, on 20 December 1521, King Manuel I of Portugal died, three weeks after the death of Pope Leo X. [60] Manuel left his mark not only on his own country but upon the world. One of the wealthiest monarchs of Europe in his time – his court swelled to include some 4,000 courtiers and retainers – he had used the riches derived from Portuguese endeavours materially to improve the nation as well as to pursue his own interests. One of these was public works: at least sixty-two architectural and engineering projects, including churches, monasteries, castles, palaces, cathedrals, town

[60] Sarcophagus of King Manuel I, supported upon the backs of two Indian elephants carved from solid blocks of marble. In the Mosteiro dos Jeronimos, Lisbon.

walls, bridges, arsenals, fortifications, and marsh drainage projects, were undertaken and paid for by Manuel. In these were developed the architectural style to which was given his name 'Manueline' (*manoelino*). Most of these projects came to a halt when he died and was succeeded by his son, Dom João III, nicknamed 'the Pious'.[19]

Portuguese nautical adventures continued for a time, and included the 'discovery' of Japan in 1543 and the establishment of a base in China at Macao in 1557. However, King Dom João III's dominant concerns were religious. Whereas Manuel had accommodated the Jews, many of whom had fled the Inquisition in Spain, João admitted the Inquisition to Portugal – a disaster for Portugal as well as for the Jews: control of the onward traffic of foreign commodities shipped to Lisbon, the greatest *entrepôt* of the period, passed from Portuguese-Jewish factors to those of many European countries, notably those from England. Much of the profit from Portugal's trade abroad enriched those countries rather than Portugal. More constructively, João III invited the Jesuits to Lisbon, only two years after the founding of that Order by a group of friends in Paris, and gave them charge of evangelizing all the peoples outside Europe with whom the Portuguese had established contact. Trade, colonization, missionary activity and education became closely interwoven. Over a thousand Jesuits, of many nationalities, radiated throughout the Orient from their base in Goa; St Francis Xavier, 'Apostle of the East,' was reputed to have walked 100,000 miles and to have made 300,000 converts; in time, over 500 Jesuits were based in Brazil.

King Dom João III was succeeded in 1557 by his grandson, Sebastião. Surrounded by piety, the boy grew up to believe that his destiny was to drive Islam from north Africa. When of age, he led in person 17,000 men in what should be called the tenth (and last) crusade: in the desert sands half were killed, including the king, and half taken prisoner at the disastrous battle of Alcáza-qui-vir in 1578. The great Aviz dynasty was, in effect, extinguished; Portugal passed to Philip II of Spain. During the sixty years of Spanish domination that followed, the enemies of Spain and of Catholicism were able to seize some of the Portuguese forts and settlements, especially in the Orient, and to usurp her long-held trading monopolies. Although Portugal's fortunes revived with the development of Brazil, and the finding of gold and diamonds there in profuse quantities, the country never again rose to that position of distinction its navigators and soldiers had won for it in the first half of the sixteenth century.

First had come the demise of the brilliant papal court of Pope Leo X, followed by the sacking and ruin of Rome. The passing of each decade of the sixteenth century slowly but surely eroded every vestige of the magnificent mission of obedience that had forged such a strong link between Portugal and the Holy See, and every memory of the talented young elephant that had become the symbol of this association and of the erudite and brilliant courts of Lisbon and Rome.

Raphael's great fresco and Leo's whimsical epitaph for his elephant, prominent memorials which had greeted foreign ambassadors and pilgrims alike arriving in Rome, fortunately survived the sacking of Rome, apparently with little damage. Amid the vicious despoilment of the basilica of St Peter and the Apostolic Palace, these memorials to Hanno remained in sufficiently good condition to enable visiting foreign artists to make detailed sketches of them a decade after the ravage of the Eternal City.

Both the fresco and epitaph were eventually destroyed, however, almost exactly a century after their installation, not by time nor by enemies of the Holy See, but by order of Pope Pius V. During the first two decades of the seventeenth century, he commissioned the architect Carlo Maderno to undertake a remodelling of the entrance to the Vatican. The original wall was replaced with the Porta Horaria to provide a new main gateway. This in turn was destroyed half a century later by Gian Lorenzo Bernini to make way for his massive colonnade.[20] [61]

Although the great mural and epitaph at the entrance to the Vatican survived for a full century, and other depictions of the elephant remain on public view to the present day, the passage of the years gradually erased their identity and significance. The coronation of the arch-poet Baraballo alone evoked some remembrance two centuries later, in the works of the English poet Alexander Pope. In the second book of his *Dunciad*, a satirical poem against dullness, Pope described the games of the poets, critics, and booksellers to celebrate the anointment of Bayes (Colley Cibber) as poet laureate:

> So from the sun's broad beam, in shallow urns,
> Heav'n's twinkling sparks draw light, and point their horns,
> Not with more glee, by hands pontific crown'd,
> With scarlet hats wide-waving circled round,
> Rome, in her capitol, saw Querno sit,
> Throned on sev'n hills, the Antichrist of wit.[21]

Pope may have confused one arch-poet with another in these lines, citing Querno instead of Baraballo, who was actually the one featured in the pageant to which he alluded. Or, perhaps he was unable to fit the longer name into the verse.

[61] The front of the Apostolic Palace, post 1680, by which time the entrance façade, once dominated by the memorial to Hanno, had been replaced by Gian Lorenzo Bernini's massive colonnade (compare [10]). Fresco in the Appartemento of Julius III in the Apostolic Palace.

Even Hanno's marble fountain in the grounds of the Villa Madama, saved in the sack of Rome that destroyed the rest of the villa, defied deterioration for centuries while remaining neglected amidst the dense tall weeds of the vineyard. It evoked only faint memories of the papal favourite it commemorated, however, while the frescoes and stuccoes of the Palazzo Baldassini awaited the present century to be rediscovered.

Of the mounted rhinoceros, as noted, all trace was lost after its arrival in Rome. Despite its rarity and great size, in its preserved state it apparently failed to stir the interest of the artists and writers other than Granacci, and no sonnets were penned to its memory. Its unexplained disappearance continues to constitute a mystery which future scholars may succeed in resolving. There will always remain a lingering hope that in some forgotten storeroom or basement of a palace in Rome or Florence, long after the straw with which it was filled has rotted and turned to dust, the carcass of the lonely beast awaits recovery.

Following the advent of Hanno, elephants became increasingly common on the European continent, and several others made their appearance before the end of the sixteenth century. In about 1545 Gabriel de Luitz, Baron d'Aramont, the French ambassador to Constantinople, arranged to have an elephant sent from Persia to the French king, but the beast died during the journey, at Berrhoea

(Calep) in Syria. The death of the elephant was witnessed by Pierre Gilles, who rescued most of the carcass and published a description of it at Lyons in 1562.

On 14 April of the same year King João III of Portugal arranged for an elephant to be brought to Vienna as a gift to King Maximilian II of Bohemia and Hungary, who later became Emperor of the Holy Roman Empire. The beast was transported from Spain in Doria's fleet and disembarked at Genoa. It travelled overland to Milan where it was observed among others by the Italian mathematician and physician Girolamo Cardano, who noted that it genuflected before an archbishop.

When the elephant arrived at Vienna, the wife of an innkeeper holding several of her infants in her arms accidentally dropped one of the children before the feet of the advancing beast being led along the street. Tradition relates that the elephant gently recovered the child with its trunk and restored it to its mother. The child's father expressed his appreciation by carving the image of the beast on the front of his inn in the Graben, with the doggerel verse 'Zur Goldenen Krone'. The elephant was thirteen years of age at the time of its arrival in Vienna, and it died two years later. Its bones were fashioned into a chair and presented to Sebastian Hulstall by command of the emperor. The elephant was commemorated in 1554 in a lead medal by an artist who signed himself 'M. F.', and a sketch of it in black chalk survives in the Sloane Collection in the British Library.[22]

The young king Dom Sebastião of Portugal sent a second elephant as a gift to Emperor Maximilian II in 1563, although several historians, including Carolus Clusius and Francesco Guicciardini, claimed that the donor was the King of Spain. The elephant was transported via Zeeland and Antwerp to Vienna.[23]

In his *Memorias*, the monk Fray Juan de San Geronimo noted that in 1583 the King of Spain (who was then also King of Portugal, during the joint monarchy) acquired an elephant from Portugal. It arrived in Madrid at two o'clock in the afternoon of 9 October 1583, guided by a black horseman. The elephant paused before the king, looked at the sky, then trumpeted mightily. A week later it was installed in the gardens of El Escorial.[24]

In 1591 an elephant sent as a gift to King Henry IV of France was disembarked at Dieppe. The king was preoccupied with the siege of Noyon at the time and could not be concerned with domestic matters. He sent instructions for the beast's maintenance, however. When, by the following year, he had determined that its upkeep had proved too costly, he travelled to Dieppe to arrange to have the beast shipped across the Channel as a gift to Queen Elizabeth I of England.[25]

More than a century passed after Hanno's demise before Rome was to see another elephant. According to the popular diary of Giacinto Gigli, in 1655 'there was conducted in these days to Rome a female elephant, aged twenty-five years, and which also was pregnant, which had been trained to do various tricks with its trunk, moving it like a hand at its master's command.'[26]

As for the rhinoceros, not until 1684 was another seen in Europe. The English diarist John Evelyn noted that in that year such a beast was transported from India to London by merchants of the East India Company and sold for more than £2,000. After its arrival, it was paraded around the country for a year or more, and he had gone to see it. He reported that it was fed turnips, wheat and corn, of which it consumed one and a half pecks daily.[27]

A second rhinoceros was sent to London in 1739 by Humphrey Cole, an official of the East India Company. It was displayed on Eagle Street near Red Lion Square, where it was observed by Dr James Parsons, who published a paper about the animal in the *Philosophical Transactions* of the Royal Society.[28]

No wild life was recorded on the premises of the Vatican for at least four centuries after the death of Hanno. In the nineteenth century, Pope Leo XIII brought birds and beasts to the gardens, so that the sounds and smells of a menagerie again pervaded the hallowed precincts. Pope Leo XIII, the second pontiff exiled in the Vatican after the unification of the Italian States in 1870, had become homesick and longed for the countryside of his youth, around Carpentino in central Italy. Accordingly, he had a vineyard added to the Vatican gardens. Further to dispel the sense of imprisonment he felt had so strongly since his election to the holy office, he had the grounds planted with trees and flowers from far parts of the world to which he could no longer travel. He peopled the gardens with birds and beasts, domestic and exotic.

An ostrich and a gazelle shared the grazing areas with goats and deer, and a bald eagle and a large pelican were accommodated in the same aviary as the parrots. The story is told that one day the pelican succeeded in achieving its freedom and flew away towards southern Italy. After a tiring flight it alighted at last in the hunting preserve of King Umberto at Castel Porziano. A huntsman wandering in the preserve shot and killed it. The bird's strange appearance excited great attention. Unfamiliar with pelicans, his fellow huntsmen concluded that it must be a rare species which had probably flown in from the African coast; accordingly, the dead bird was carefully packed and sent off to King Umberto at the Quirinal Palace in Rome. There, amidst considerable consternation, it was recognized as being none other than the pope's pelican. There was nothing to be done other than to offer the dead bird to the exiled pontiff with the apologies of the king and his royal court. The pelican was neither accepted nor acknowledged at the Vatican. Pope Leo XIII maintained a dignified silence as the now much travelled dead bird was returned to the Quirinal.[29]

The rich ecclesiastical gifts brought to Rome by the mission of obedience of King Manuel I miraculously survived the passage of three centuries. Not only did most of them escape the sack of Rome in 1527, but subsequent upheavals in the Eternal City as well – until the late eighteenth century when Bonaparte conquered Italy.

Then, near the close of the century, following the capitulation of Milan and Mantua, French troops advanced towards Rome. Pope Pius VI hastily concluded the Treaty of Tolentino with Bonaparte's Directoire, and in compliance with the conditions of the peace, was required to pay a huge ransom, which the pontiff vainly attempted to raise. In his efforts to meet the exorbitant terms of the French conqueror, Pope Pius VI collected as much gold, silver and precious stones as he could from the great jewelled chalices and altar furnishings of the reigns of Innocent VIII, Julius II, Leo X, Paul III, Gregory XIII, Sixtus V and succeeding pontiffs. Many masterworks of the goldsmith's art were reduced to carcasses with the gold and gems removed, although the pontiff made every effort to preserve the remaining metal and cloth as historic relics.

Realizing that all that had been collected still fell far short of the weights required, the pontiff then decided to supplement the precious metals and gems from the only other source available. He ordered that all pearls and precious stones be detached from the mantles, cloaks, chasubles, stoles, altar frontals and other antique pontifical vestments and furnishings which could be spared from daily use. Included were vestments of rich and marvellous quality which had been preserved for centuries and maintained with great care in the wardrobes of the papal chapels.[30]

Among the oldest of the garments and altar furnishings were those which had been presented to Pope Leo X by King Manuel I. The very finest was the extremely large altar frontal executed in the most sumptuous needlework with images of Christ and the twelve apostles in gold work and embroidered with pearls and gems. Another was 'the capacious extraordinary red-glowing, golden, precious garment called a pluvial, suitable to the majesty of the pope, in which he [Pope Leo X] showed himself more imperially in public, and which he used in his papal offices. It was covered on the outside with pearls and orna-ments stitched on.' Thus it had been described by one of the observers at the time of the Portuguese mission's arrival in 1514.[31]

The prefect of the apostolic sacristy compiled an inventory of the vestments, noting that the pearls removed from them, including all sizes, weighed '50 Roman *libbre* and 7 ounces, and that the weight of the garnets, rubies, and other gems was slightly less than 1 *libbra*'. The pope ordered that the denuded ecclesiastical robes and accoutrements were to be carefully preserved and stored away by members of the Vatican staff to ensure that at least these remnants of the historical relics would survive for future generations.[32]

These efforts proved to be in vain. In February 1798, after Pope Pius VII had become a captive in the Vatican during the French occupa-tion of Rome, the commissioners of the Directoire of the Grand Republic of France descended upon the Vatican and ordered that the robes and altar furnishings be collected and brought into the Cortile del Belvedere. There they were placed upon the pavement and – while the Vatican custodians watched in despair – burned to ashes for the purpose of recovering the small amounts of gold and silver thread with which the cloths had been woven. Nothing survived of the Vatican treasures, for what was not confiscated and taken back to France was stolen and squandered by the French commissioners, even to the uten-sils of the papal kitchens.[33]

If nothing remained in Rome relating to the historic mission, what may have survived in Portugal? There was, to be sure, the illuminated manuscript stated to have been brought to King Manuel I as a gift from Pope Leo X. In writing about Francisco d'Ollanda, the historian Joaquim de Vasconcellos reported 'Leo X indeed sent a valuable illu-minated work to King Emanuel via Tristão da Cunha; it was not a bible but a Book of Hours [*Livro de Horas*]…'

Contemporary accounts relate that the king presented the volume to his privy chamberlain, his Armador-Mor, Dom Alvaro da Costa, requiring that it be entailed and passed down through succeeding generations of his family. As late as 1894, according to Vasconcellos, it was in the possession of the Duque de Albuquerque and later that of his brother, the Conde de Mesquitela. Vasconcellos noted also;

the aged Garcia de Resende, who like the last-named [Diogo Pacheco], remembered with enjoyment the happy days at the court of Leo X, when they had with Tristão da Cunha transmitted the splendid presents of their king, and, in return for the oft-sung and depicted white elephant and the cope which was destroyed during the [French] plunder of Rome, brought home a valuable illu-minated prayer-book.[34]

The volume did not come to notice again until 1882, when it was displayed in an exposition in Lisbon, in which it was described as a 'Book of the Hours of Our Lady'. In the late 1880s the Mesquitela family decided to sell the book. The decision was reported in an undated letter from Dr António da Costa to a certain Anselmo, believed to be Anselmo Ferreira Pinto. He described the volume as 'an artistic masterpiece, the work of the beginning of the sixteenth century, which was the gift of a pope who was named Leo X, to our king, who was called Manoel I, and given by the king to his Armador-Mor, D. Alvaro da Costa, his intimate associate and the founder of our house.' He proposed that the volume be offered for sale in London, hoping that it would be acquired by a major museum. In this connection he had already contacted several London antiquarian booksellers, including Henry Sotheran & Co. and Bernard Quaritch.[35]

The final disposition of the volume was reported in two letters from a certain José, a member of the Mesquitela family, written from London to his friend, Dr Fidelio de Freitas Branco in Lisbon. José reported that he had shown the work to several prospective purchasers but that the response was not very enthusiastic, and that it had become apparent that the value of the work had been greatly over-estimated by its owners. The volume was subsequently sold in France for 3109.5 *francs*, or over 8,000 *escudos*, a sum which was divided among eight Mesquitela heirs. No further trace of the volume has been found.[36]

The work was described in the Lisbon exposition of 1882 in the following words: '*No. 17 – Manuscript, parchment, octavo. At the head of the page, a gilt and coloured drawing of the Costa family crest set in a niche in the Manueline style. Illuminated initials, borders, and drawings in gold and colours. Bound in green velvet with silver catches. XVI century.*'[37] There appears to be no doubt that this volume was in fact the gift of King Manuel to Costa, but it may not have been the volume which had been sent by Pope Leo X to the Portuguese king. It is unlikely that the king would have disposed so quickly of a gift from the pontiff, particularly in the light of concessions requested and received by the Portuguese mission of obedience. Furthermore, it is doubtful that the family arms of the Costa family would have been featured upon such a gift, although they could have been part of a new cover or binding added after the presentation from the king.

Further investigation reveals that Tristão da Cunha and his associates returned to Lisbon from Rome with not one but two gift volumes. In a letter written to King Manuel I on 5 June 1514, a Neapolitan artist named Giovanni Marco [Joanne Marco] Cristiplocus described an illuminated manuscript which he was preparing for the monarch. This communication was followed by a second letter on the same subject written four days later. It is probable that the work was brought to Rome by Cristiplocus and given to Cunha to take back with him to Lisbon, where the king presented it to Costa.[38]

But what, then, of the illuminated manuscript which the pope sent to King Manuel? An item listed in the inventory made in 1522 of the King's Wardrobe and Library was described as a small volume bound in hand-tooled red leather with gilt embellishments. The entry specified that it was 'in printer's form [set in type] with portraits of the Roman Emperors. Begins with the printed words "Leo papa." It will be recalled that Pope Leo X employed agents to seek out classics buried in Italian family libraries and on the shelves of booksellers, and to purchase them for the papal library. One of the treasures brought to light was a manuscript of the *Annals* of Tacitus. Gian Angelo Arcimboldi had discovered the first five books of this precious codex at Corvey, and the pontiff purchased it for 500 gold *florins*. He entrusted the task of editing it to Filippo Beroaldo, and when the work was published in 1515 under the pope's imprimatur, rewarded him with the position of librarian of the Vatican library. The discovery and publication of this work was a great scholarly achievement of the time, and it is likely that the pope sent a copy of the *Annals* to the Portuguese king. This seems a strong candidate for the work described in the inventory of 1522. However, since it was not published until 1515, a year after Cunha's return to Lisbon, it cannot have been the illuminated manuscript volume unaccounted for. The contemporary description tells us that it was a breviary or Book of Hours. Manuel's library was totally destroyed during the earthquake of 1755, which levelled the palace at Almeirim on the left bank of the Tagus River south-west of Santarem. The possibility exists that this volume survived, that it has remained unidentified as the papal gift because it no longer retains a record of its papal association. Where it is, or what happened to it, remains unknown.[39]

The lone survivor in Portugal of the generous and continuing exchange of gifts between the king and Leo X, therefore, appears to be a carved marble chimneypiece said to have been sent to Manuel by the pontiff, probably with the returning mission in June 1514. Regrettably, no documentation of such a gift has come to light in either the Arquivo Nacional da Torre do Tombo in Lisbon nor in the Archivio Segreto Vaticano, and its provenance relies totally on tradition. [62]

The earliest known mention of the chimneypiece occurs in an account of the Portuguese mission published in a popular Portuguese periodical in 1854. The author was the distinguished diplomat and

[62]

writer, António Teles da Silva Camiñha e Meneses, Marques de Resende, perhaps a descendant of the Resende who accompanied the mission. He noted that in the exchange of gifts between the pontiff and the king, the former sent the Portuguese monarch 'a magnificent chimneypiece of white marble decorated with figures in relief, a work which was attributed by some to [Michelangelo] Buonarotti'.

[62] *facing page* Chimneypiece carved of white marble, traditionally claimed to be a counter-gift to King Manuel I sent to Lisbon in 1514 by Pope Leo X. In the Sala des Pegas of the royal palace at Sintra, Portugal.

[63] Details of the Hermes supporting the chimneypiece.

[64] Detail of the sculptured overmantel of the chimneypiece.

It was installed first in the royal palace at Almeirim. Within the course of the year following the earthquake, King José I ordered his prime minister, the Marquez de Pombal, to have the chimneypiece recovered from the ruins and transported to the royal palace at Sintra and to have it installed there in a small chamber which he designated, known as the 'Chamber of Caesar'. It was a room that the monarch was accustomed to use when he was at Sintra, and thereafter he often warmed himself before the hearth with its magnificent chimneypiece. Later, wrote Resende with sadness, 'after our misfortunes' (namely the Liberal Revolution), the chamber was converted into a pantry for the palace, and Resende saw the great fireplace at Sintra desecrated by having flat irons placed before it to be heated, and dishcloths stretched out upon it to dry.

The chimneypiece was next noted in the writings of the Marquis Patric Mac Swiney de Mashanaglass, who had made a thorough examination of Vatican records for his studies on the relations between Portugal and the Holy See. In a work published in 1898, he reported that among the gifts sent by Pope Leo X to King Manuel, 'outstanding above all others [was] a chimneypiece of white marble carved with admirable sculptures which were attributed to the magic chisel of Michelangelo'. He did not, however, provide documentation for his statement that it had been a papal gift to the Portuguese king.[40]

In 1898 the chimneypiece was removed from the Chamber of Caesar and built into the Sala des Pegas, or 'Chamber of the Magpies', where it is presently to be found.[41] The marble structure is enormous and consists of three major segments. The lowermost includes two finely chiselled pillars supporting a Doric entablature of magnificent proportions. Particularly notable are two venerable Hermes supporting the entablature on either side of the hearth. [63, 64] The middle portion is a finely carved panel in low relief depicting two warriors or knights on horseback facing each other with couched spears ready to charge, against a background of war trophies hanging from delicately fashioned festoons. The pediment, surmounted by an urn, features a winged cherub.[42]

Authorities have been divided for almost a century on the attribution of the work. After having made a minute examination of it, the Abbot de Castro asked, 'Who would say that he does not recognize the sublime and ingenious style of Michel Angelo Buonarotti?' When Albert Haupt first saw the chimneypiece, he attributed it to an unidentified Italian master of the first half of the sixteenth century. He wrote that at Sintra 'in one of the principal salons one encounters a work of greatest perfection of foreign sculpture in Portugal, a mantelpiece of white marble… We maintain that, without doubt, we have before us a work of superior quality of some Italian artist of the second quarter of the sixteenth century, and I have the opinion that those who consider it to be the work of Michel Angelo at first view will not find themselves in error.' Following a later visit, however, he was led to change his mind because of the festoons and acanthus leaves featured in the base, and attributed it to an unnamed artist of the Flemish school. Reinaldo dos Santos was convinced that it was the work of Nicolau Chanterene, executed in Estremoz marble quarried in Portugal. Chanterene was a sculptor in the service of King Manuel I and was described as a friend of Clenardo and the humanists of Evora.[43]

Modern art historians appear to be just as puzzled by the chimneypiece as were their earlier peers. It has been suggested that it was executed by a sculptor trained in a Florentine studio and produced at some time between 1490 and 1510. Among the Florentine masters of that period were Antonio Rosellini, Andrea Sansovino, Antonio Gagini and Giuliano da Sangallo. Gagini was one of the sculptors who assisted Michelangelo in the execution of the tomb of Pope Julius II. Sangallo was at work at the Vatican at the time of the arrival of the Portuguese mission.

Andrea Sansovino is another likely candidate, for he had been employed first by Pope Julius II and then by Pope Leo X. At the time of the mission's arrival, he was 'chief and master general of the *Fabbrica Loretana*' in charge of the works of sculpture for the ornamentation of the Santa Casa of Loreto, and periodically spent several days at a time in Rome. The late Professor Ulrich Middeldorf was in fact convinced that the chimneypiece had been his work and that of no other. 'I am very much taken with the piece,' he wrote,

and believe that it is by Andrea Sansovino. Its architecture resembles that of the drawing for a tomb of Leo X which I once published. This is the architecture of a man, who has grown up in the Quattrocento and does not yet handle the new classic style with ease. It is about the opposite of Giuliano da Sangallo's architecture. The delicate carving of the ornament, the elegant movement of the horsemen and the slightly clumsy complicated scrollwork of the finial have parallels in the Bassi and Sforza tombs. I have almost no hesitation with this attribution. This, of course, is a most important discovery, as we know little about Sansovino's activity in Rome. Strange, that in the accounts of Leo X in the Archivio Segreto Vaticano there should not be a mention of this work.[44]

The confusion among art historians could well be due to the fact that the chimneypiece may now lack some original parts and include extraneous elements that were added later to the original work. This can be readily explained by the fact that the chimneypiece had three separate installations and two removals and had also suffered serious damage from an earthquake. As noted, after the destruction of the palace at Almeirim, the chimneypiece was recovered from the rubble and it is reasonable to believe that parts of it had been damaged beyond repair and required replacement. Or, just as likely, components of other marble chimneypieces were recovered at the same time and used to assemble a complete one.

Replacement may have been made either from new pieces of marble or parts salvaged from other works, which would explain some of the chimneypiece's incongruities. For example, the vase surmounting the chimneypiece appears to be in the style of Louis XVI, although it could be of an earlier date. The putto has odd features and occupies an incongruous position above the scrolls. The battle scene is placed in an unorthodox position. Until such a time as documentation of the chimneypiece's origin can be found that would identify when, by whom and for whom it was made, its attribution as a papal gift relies entirely and tenuously on tradition. Thus even this apparently single survival of the great mission of obedience remains in question.

In Rome, the area and the street where once Hanno was domiciled continued proudly to bear the elephant's name for many decades, but later were re-named without any souvenir of its former presence. The inn called the 'Casa del Liofante' situated at the end of the Via Sistina, deriving its name from the inn sign featuring an elephant, became widely known as a shelter for travellers to Rome during the sixteenth century. The innkeeper was identified in contemporary records as a man named Francesco, who paid an annual rent or tax of sixteen *carlini* to the Compagnia di Sant'Angelo. By the end of the sixteenth century, however, with the re-naming of the street and of the Borgo, no trace of the inn was to be found.[45]

Although Raphael's mural of Hanno at the entrance to the Vatican was destroyed in the course of remodelling, the possibility remained that the epitaph might have been inscribed on a separate plaque and might have survived. It was long the practice in Rome to utilize discarded but unbroken marble tablets by using the blank reverse side and adding new inscriptions. A recent search of surviving memorials stored at the Vatican proved fruitless, and a prolonged and repeated search of the Vatican Library, Secret Archives, Pontifical Museums and Galleries, and the storerooms of the Fabbrica di San Pietro failed to bring to light any evidence of the elephant.

Then, inadvertently, this intensive search brought forth the casual comment from a young Vatican employee that a few years previously some curious bones believed to be those of a dinosaur had been recovered during an excavation in the Cortile della Libreria. Dinosaur? Well, perhaps... at the least they called for further investigation. With some persistence, the story was finally pieced together.

On 6 February 1962 a crew of workmen of the Sorveglianza Impianti Tecnici [buildings management] of the Vatican was engaged in enlarged a heating or air conditioning facility for the Library. This required excavating a section of the slope at the right side of the Cortile della Libreria near the corner of a flight of steps leading from the Vatican's museum wing. In the course of digging, the workmen brought forth fragments of bones. The digging was promptly interrupted and the fragments were carefully removed and preserved together with soil samples for future study. These were brought to officials of the Vatican Library, the project being on Library premises, and given into the care of the custodian of the Library's museum collections, the late Monsignor Guido Ferrari, OSB.

He arranged for the bones to be examined by an authority in Rome. The sixteen fragments were identified as one large tooth, four large pieces and eleven smaller bits of the mandible of a sizeable beast. [66a and 66b] The report stated further that they appeared to be from an *Elephas antiquus* or fossil elephant, and not a dinosaur after all. The fragments were returned to the Vatican on 8 May 1964 and placed in the custody of Professor Filippo Magi, head of the Vatican's Direzione degli Studi e delle Ricerche Archeologiche. Following the latter's retirement, they were stored with other collections of the Vatican museums.[46]

The discovery of bones came as no great surprise, for during the previous several decades geologists had unearthed a wealth of fossil remains in Rome and on Vatican hill. In a formation uncovered in the area between the Vatican's recently erected Pinacoteca and the ancient Leonine bastions, a cemetery of bones of large animals came to light. Included were bones of primitive elephants, bulls, horses, deer, rhinoceroses, hippopotami, beavers, hares, dogs, bears, and felines. Among the finds were even human remains, of *Homo Neanderthalis*.[47]

The bones found in the Cortile della Libreria in 1962 were not fossilized, however. Apparently no one associated them with the elephant Hanno at that time, and they remained forgotten until the present study brought them to light once more. Paleobiologists of the US Geological Survey and the National Museum of Natural History of the Smithsonian Institution confirmed that they were not fossilized, and that they belonged to a young male elephant less than ten years of

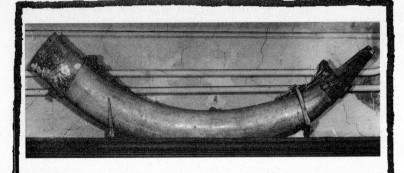

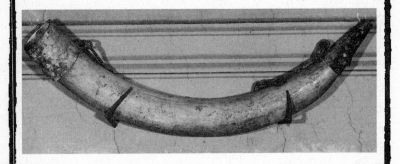

[65] Hanno's mortal remains: [a, d] The two tusks of Hanno with sixteenth-century decorated copper terminals and wrought iron hanging chains. In the Archivio Capitolare della Basilica di San Pietro, the Vatican. [b] Side view of a third or fourth tooth of the elephant Hanno; [c] Three larger fragments of the mandible – recovered in excavations in the Cortile della Libreria.

age. The tooth was identified as a lower cheek tooth of an Asian elephant or *Elephas maximus*. Elephants have a single tooth, or parts of two teeth, on each side of the jaw at any one time. As the tooth wears, it moves forward in the jaw and is eventually succeeded by another tooth moving in from the rear. The teeth differ from one another since they grow successively larger, and it is possible to estimate the animal's age from their size. Because one end of the tooth found at the Vatican was broken, its age could not be determined with complete accuracy, but it was determined as the third or fourth tooth. This fact, coupled with the degree of wear of the crown, identifies it as having come from an animal aged between five and ten years at most.[48] [65b & c]

In the early sixteenth century, the site from which the bones were recovered formed part of the Cortile del Belvedere. Since then the courtyard had been divided into three distinct sections: first, by the building, late in the sixteenth century, of the wing that now houses the Vatican Library and the Secret Archives; next, by the construction, in the eighteenth century, of the Braccio Nuovo for the Vatican Museums. Whether the remainder of Hanno's carcass survives under the courtyard is a matter of conjecture. It is possible that it may have been unearthed, and disposition made without being identified, at the time that the Braccio Nuovo with its two great staircases was constructed. Or it may still remain buried in the Cortile.

More recently, another part of Hanno's remains came to light in the Sala of the Archivio Capitolare of the basilica of St Peter. The discovery was made by the noted Vatican archaeologist, Professoressa Margherita Guarducci. Displayed on one of the Sala's walls, where they undoubtedly had been hanging for several centuries, are two tusks which have been identified as both having belonged to the same beast, a young Indian elephant. [65a & d]

The condition of the ends of the tusks reveals that they had not been sawn and taken from the animal in life, but removed from its skull after death. That the tusks are from the same animal is confirmed by their relative size: one measures 148 m. and the other 135 m. The internal dimension of the raw end of one is 015 m. and the other is 012 m. Both ends of each tusk are covered by decorative copper sleeves confirmed to be of sixteenth century Italian worksmanship, each attached to a wrought iron chain from which they are suspended.

A curious fact is that the tusks are omitted in some of the depictions of Hanno, yet are shown in reduced form in other representations. It suggests that there was a concerted effort among the artists who depicted the beast to make it appear more benign by underplaying this feature, which might be considered as implying ferocity. Because the tips of the tusks are covered with metal sleeves, it is not possible to determine whether in fact the tusks had been trimmed. It is not surprising that the tusks were preserved, however, for the value of ivory was considerable, and furthermore the pontiff undoubtedly wished to have some tangible souvenir of his pet. What is remarkable is that the tusks survived at the Vatican through the centuries, apparently without having come to prior scholarly or public attention.[49]

Perhaps one day the pope's elephant will be awarded a fitting memorial at the site of its burial where its bones were discovered, or elsewhere on the Vatican premises. Most appropriate would be the restoration of its epitaph to public view as a reminder of the elephant-diplomat which had become the symbol of the reign of Pope Leo X and had so delighted the pontiff and his court and the people of Rome almost five centuries ago.

Although the memory of the elephant was obscured and finally erased by the passage of the centuries, relics of its existence precariously survive: whether in the poetry of the sixteenth century seldom read, in sketches and paintings dispersed in art collections throughout the world, in occasional monuments now unexplained and unrecognized... the image of Hanno remains – vivid and curious as in its lifetime. And in the diaries and records of the courts of Lisbon and Rome that now lie buried in dusty and forgotten archives, Hanno's ghostly presence persists, a symbol of the golden age and the century of wonder.

ENDMATTER

APPENDIX 1

Additional Literary References

CHAPTER THREE : *The Rose and the Sword*
Following are translations of writings of poets of Rome commemorating the
arrival of the Portuguese mission of obedience, in addition to those already
included in the main text.

Joachim Cipellus

> *Manuel has arms, Pacheco a tongue*
> *The former shines in his strength,*
> *The latter in his eloquence.*
> *And while the learned Pacheco exalted him*
> *I felt that every royal virtue*
> *Was Manuel's alone,*
> *Hence I am hesitant as to whether*
> *The King is so distinguished*
> *Or Pacheco was just making an oration.*
> *Nor do I know whether his offspring and nephews*
> *Or the conquered Arabs, or the Indians or Africans*
> *Will say he is more to be praised than feared.*[1]

B. Blosio

> *The brave deeds and the pious acts of the Portuguese*
> *Fill the city and the world, and the ocean and the empire.*
> *No voice, no age, has ever refrained from praising the pious*
>   *and famous king [of Portugal].*
> *But after Pacheco spoke of these things in a sublime oration*
> *And depicted the great king as though making a [great] announcement*
> *The Father and the Father of the Fathers were amazed*
> *And their spirits were struck dumb. The praise of the king shone doubly:*
> *They praise the king on the one hand because of his famous deeds,*
> *And on the other because he commanded his praises*
> *To be sung by such an orator.*[2]

Pietro Curzio (P. Cursius Carpinen)

> *Glory of Kings, Star of Princes*
> *Ornament of Europe, Conqueror of India –*
> *You make (yourself) – a single Manuel – equal to all men.*
> *Were the truth known, kings do not make themselves more powerful by wars.*
> *There is no need to record this, because everyone*
> *Knows it [now] as well as your power.*
> *For a while your Pacheco explained these things in his sublime speech;*
> *Leo, by far the best of all popes, [told] the Senate;*
> *Thus the whole world was amazed by your victories*
> *Whether at the very thought of them,*

Or because Pacheco described them.
Glory of Kings, Star of Princes,
Ornament of Europe, Conqueror of India,
Because the rising sun worships the setting,
Because although the [Orient] sun is strong, it is weaker than the setting sun,
Because you achieve so many miracles worth celebrating
Forever and by all learned men.[3]

Lancellotus Politus

What is this work? For whom do I pray for words and seek them?
For whom? For great Manuel.
What could be said to be worthy of such a Prince?
Who could say things worthy of such a god?
Pacheco, you who delivered a noble and worthy speech,
You are worthy of Manuel, you are worthy of Leo.
Your virtue, great Leo, is unique;
And your acts, Manuel, are also unique.
The glory of Pacheco's speaking, however, is double
Since he is unique in genius and unique in eloquence.[4]

D. Dardanus

Spain increased the broad confines of the Empire
When Rome sent its imperial troops
When this Pacheco sang the praises of the King of Portugal
He brought back from there the lost art of eloquence.[5]
And lest this glory should be missing
From the arms of this western nation
She brought forth the rare honour of this genius
For recently, when Rome's Portuguese orator
Poured forth an abundant flood of eloquence
Venerable Rome with its sacred Senate was astounded
And sad Albula stopped with its waters thunderstruck.
The eloquence which the Tagus once drew from its mistress city
Let the Tiber now draw from the streams of western Tagus.[6]

Camillo Portio

Previously, to be sure, Manuel, King of Kings,
The glory of war and of arms were surrendered to you
And the praises and renown of warfare
Through which the might of Rome, mother of gods and men,
Once raised herself to the skies, was taken from us.
While you, having put civil wars aside, happily turned
The arms that now press upon wretched Europe
Against the fates of the infidels groaning with oppression;
You harass the Indians and the Ethiopians
And regions unknown to your kingdom.

And you cover with so many fleets the indignant waters of the sea.
Nevertheless, before this the shores of Latium
And the Laurentian sands were not lacking in brilliance
Where so many tongues flourished
Outstanding in their speech, ever accustomed to fly
Amid the plentiful tongues
Of men and to earn eternal glory and fame.
But after your orator Pacheco began to thunder grandiloquently
Relating, Manuel, your exploits and wondrous deeds,
He carried away the bystanders with the soul-flexing sweetness of his voice;
You are outstanding of eloquence, accustomed to soar through
The ample tongues of men, and merit both a name and eternal glory;
But after your orator Pacheco proclaimed your deeds with resounding voice
Manuel, repeating your wondrous achievements, and with the sweetness
Of his soul-bending voice taking in the bystanders
All were in wonderment; even the Muses in Latium were astounded,
That he might make his Tiber migrate to the bosom of the Mirata
To the gold-bearing waves of the Tagus and the ever-rich Douro.[7]

CHAPTER SIX : Epitaph of Hanno at the entrance to the Vatican
(See 31–34. For English translation see pp.145-6)

D. M.

MONTE SUB HOC ELEPHAS INGENTI CONTEGOR INGENS, QUEM
EX EMANUEL, DEVICTO ORIENTE, LEONI
CAPTIVUM MISIT DECIMO: QUEM ROMULA PUBES
MIRATA EST, ANIMAL NON LONGO TEMPORE VISUM,
VIDIT ET HUMANOS IN BRUTO TEMPORE SENSUS. INVIDIT
LATII SEDEM MIHI PARCA BEATI. NEC PASSA EST TERNOS
DOMINO FAMULARIER ANNOS: AT QUAE SORS RAPUIT
NATURAE DEBITA NOSTRAE, TEMPORA, VOS SUPERI
MAGNO ACCUMULATE LEONI.

VIXIT ANN. SEPTEM
OBIIT ANGINAE MORBO
ALTITUDO ERAT PALM. DUODECIMO.
IO. BB. BRANCONIUS AQUILANUS
A CUBICULO & ELEPHANTIS CURAE
PREFECTUS POSUIT.
LEONIS DECIMI PONT. ANNO QUARTO

RAPHAEL URBINAS QUOD NATURA ABSTULERAT
ARTE RESTITUIT.

In other versions, and presumably on the engraved epitaph from which they
were copied, 'MDXVI .VIII . IUNII .' followed the word 'POSUIT.'

Chapter Epigraphs

PAGE x : William Roscoe, *The Life and Pontificate of Leo the Tenth*. 6th edition, revised by his son, Thomas Roscoe. 2 vols. London: Henry G. Bohn, 1853, vol. II, p. 256.

CHAPTER ONE : Jacob Burckhardt, *The Civilization of the Renaissance*. Translated by S. G. C. Middlemore. Oxford: Phaidon Press, 1945, p. 113.

CHAPTER TWO : Malaspini Pasquale de'Marchesi di S. Margharita. *'De l'elefante mandato dal Re di Portogallo a Papa Leone.'*

CHAPTER THREE : Jacob Burckhardt, *The Civilization of the Renaissance*. Translated by S. G. C. Middlemore. Oxford: Phaidon Press, 1945, p. 177.

CHAPTER FOUR : William Roscoe, *The Life and Pontificate of Leo the Tenth*, 6th edition, revised by his son, Thomas Roscoe. 2 vols. London: Henry G. Bohn, 1853, vol. II, p. 391.

CHAPTER FIVE : [Joshua Sylvester], *The Complete Works of Joshua Sylvester; for the first time collected and edited; with memorial introduction, notes and illustrations, glossarial index, etc., etc.,* by the Reverend Alexander B. Grosart. Edinburgh: For private circulation [by T. and A. Constable], 1880, 'Du Bartas His Divine Weekes and Works,' p. 124.

CHAPTER SIX : Baron Ludwig von Pastor, *The History of the Popes from the Close of the Middle Ages*. Edited by Ralph Francis Kerr. London: B. Herder, Kegan Paul, Trench, Trubner & Co., Ltd., 1908, vol. VIII, p. 141.

CHAPTER SEVEN : Jacob Burckhardt, *The Civilization of the Renaissance*. Translated by S. C. G. Middlemore. Oxford: Phaidon Press, 1945, p. 113.

CHAPTER EIGHT : [Edmund Spenser], *The Complete Works of Edmund Spenser*. Introduction by William P. Trent. New York: Thomas Y. Crowell Company, 1903. 'Complaints,' (1591). 'The Ruines of Rome,' translated from *The Antiquities of Rome* by Joachim du Bellay, p. 652.

SOURCES AND NOTES

Abbreviations used below : AG : Archivio Gonzaga, Mantua / ANTT : Arquivo Nacional da Torre do Tombo, Lisbon / ASF : Archivio di Stato di Firenze, Florence / ASM : Archivio di Stato di Mantova / ASR : Archivio di Stato di Roma / ASV : Archivio Segreto Vaticano / BAA : Biblioteca de la Academia, Madrid / BAJ : Biblioteca de Ajuda / BL : Biblioteca Laurenziana, Florence / BAM : Biblioteca Ambrosiana, Milan / BAV : Biblioteca Apostolica Vaticana / BC : Biblioteca Colombina, Catedrale de Sevilla / BE : Biblioteca de Evora, Evora, Portugal / BN : Bibliotheque Nationale, Paris / BNC : Biblioteca Nazionale Centrale, Florence / BNM : Biblioteca Nazionale Marciana, Venice / BRM : Biblioteca del Real Monasterio di San Lorenzo, El Escorial, Madrid, Spain / UB : Universität-Bibliotek, Munich

CHAPTER ONE : The Golden Age

1. *'Gaudium magnum nuntio vobis. Papam habemus reverendissimum dominum Johannem de Medicis, Diaconum Cardinalem Sanctae Mariae in Domnica, qui vocatur Leo Decimus!'* Roscoe (3), vol. I, pp. 295–9, n. 212; Pastor (1) vol. VII, pp. 40–44; Chamberlain (1), pp. 209–13. 'Palle' is the Italian word meaning 'balls', and here refers to the seven orbs of the Medici family coat-of-arms.

2. Brosch, passim; Partner, pp. 3–23; Roscoe (3), vol. I, pp. 267–8, 289–93; Pastor (1), vol. VII, pp. 45–52, vol. VIII, pp. 142–4.

3. Pastor (1) vol. VII, pp. 33–5; Mitchell, pp. 13–17; Roscoe (3), vol. I, pp. 295–300; Young, pp. 295–6; Hibbert, 215–17.

4. Penni, p. 231; Cancellieri, *Solenni Possessi*, pp. 61–9; Hale, pp. 66–70; Chamberlain (1), pp. 213–17; Mitchell, pp. 60–61; Roscoe (3), vol. I, pp. 300–3; Pastor, Kerr tranls., vol. VII, pp. 35–43.

5. Wood, pp. 1–4, 1548–51. Dr Wood, head of the Chinese Department of the British Library, has assembled recent international scholarship to show the the *Description of the World* (1298) supposed to have been derived from Polo's travels, is based on Arabic and Persian sources. She concludes (p. 150) that 'Marco Polo himself probably never travelled much further than the family's trading posts on the Black Sea and in Constantinope…'

6. Diffie and Winius, vol. I, pp. 195–272; Boxer, pp. 30–64; Penrose, pp. 48–66; Parry, pp. 148–62; Rogers (2), pp. 3–6, 105–6; Runcinan, pp. 77–8. Peoples in the East were traditionally grouped according to their religion if it differed from that of the paramount power and treated as an autonomous community under its religious head. Such a group was described by the Persian word 'melet' or 'milet' meaning a nation.

7. Boxer, pp. 33–63; Diffie and Winius, vol. I, pp. 72, 94, 317–20, 424–30; Parry, pp. 258–61.

8. Sanuto, *Diarii*, Tomo VI, p. 168; ASV, Burchardi, *Diarium*, Tomo III, fols. 214, 391; Rogers (1), pp. 5–6; Pellizzari, pp. 118–29; Mac Swiney de Mashanaglass (2), pp. 24–5; Rogers (3), pp. 122–3; Picca, p. 142.

9. ASV, *Introitus et Exitus, Camera Apostolica*, Tomo I, fol. 181^v, Febbraio 27,

1506; Burchardi, *Diarium*, Tomo III, fol. 214; Grassi, *Diarium*, Tomo V, fol. 439; *Archivio dei Maestri dei Ceremoni Pontificiale*, Tomo 369, fol. 105.

10. *Bullarium Patr. Port.*, vol. I, pp. 9–10; Rebello da Silva, Tomo I, pp. 238–42; Castro, pp. 159–75; Mac Swiney de Mashanaglass, III, pp. 24–5; Rogers (1), pp. 3–6, 105–6; Rogers (3), pp. 12–3, 188; Picca, p. 142.

11. Muntz (3), pp. 1–11; Churchill, pp. 13–24, 163–226; Muntz (1), pp. 408–11; Muntz (3), pp. 326–7.

12. ASV, *Brevis Minutiae, 1513–1514*, No. 255; *Grand Encyclopedia*, vol. X, p. 924, Mac Swiney de Mashanaglass, III, pp. 106–7.

13. Hibbert, pp. 217–19; Roscoe (3), vol. I, pp. 269–84, 307–19, 364–5.

14. Partner, pp. 113–18; Chamberlain (1), p. 220; Roscoe (3), vol. I, pp. 303–4; Hibbert, pp. 218–25.

15. Fabronio, *Vita*, p. 206; Hale, pp. 247–50; Roscoe (3), vol. II, pp. 390.

16. Fabronio, *Vita*, ad not. 83; Chamberlain (1), pp. 217–18; Roscoe (3), vol. II, p. 392.

17. Mac Swiney de Mashanaglass, III, pp. 106–7; Andrade, pp. 119–23; Ciutiis, pp. 19–50; Ciacconio, *Vita et res*, p. 329; Roscoe (3), vol. I, p. 362; Pastor (1), vol. VII, p. 74.

18. ASV, *Brevis Leonis Minutiae, 1513–1514*, N. 255; *Grand Enciclopedia*, vol. X, p. 924; Roscoe (3) p. 362.

19. ANTT, *Collecção de Bullas*, Maço 29, No. 8; ASV, *Brev. ad Princeps*, Tomo V, fol. 33; Sanuto, Tomo XVIII, pp. 85–6; Andrade, p. 124; Ciutiis, pp. 28–9; S. Joanninensis, p. 99.

20. Partner, pp. 196–7; Oliveira Martins, *Historia*, Tomo II, Livro V, pp. 4–8; Pellizzari, pp. 118–24.

21. Boxer, pp. 228–31; Diffie and Winius, vol. I, pp. 172–4; Silva Rego, pp. 15–16.

22. ANTT, *Collecção de Bullas*, Maço 21, No. 12, 'Orthodox fidei nostra cura divina', 8 March 1514; Rebello da Silva, vol. I, pp. 217–34.

23. Giobbio, vol. I, p. 344; Pastor (1), vol. VII, pp. 68–73; Roscoe (1), vol. I, pp. 303–4.

24. ASV, *Nunziatura*, Garabai, Libro 35, cap. 31, fol. 402'; Rebello da Silva, Tomo I, pp. 209–10; Ciutiis, pp. 19–20; Mac Swiney de Mashanaglass, III, pp. 102–10; Cunha, p. 61.

25. Andrade, pp. 119–23; Ciacconio, p. 329; ASV, *Nunziatura*, Garabai, Libro 35, cap. 31, fols. 160–72.

26. Mac Swiney de Mashanaglass, III, pp. 106–7.

27. ASV, *Brevis Leonis Minutiae 1513–1514*, N. 255; Pastor (1), vol. VII, pp. 76–78; *Grande Enciclopedia*, vol. X, p. 924, Avery, p. 810.

28. Sanuto, Tomo XVIII, cols. 85–6; Andrade, p. 124; Ciutiis, pp. 28–9; AG, Letter from Postumo, 13 Marzo 1514; Joanninensis, p. 99.

29. Loisel, pp. 215–20.

30. Vilhena Barbosa, pp. v–vi; Lach (1), pp. 113, 167–8.

31. Loisel, pp. 197–203; Burckhardt, pp. 176–7; Lloyd, pp. 39–41, 47–8.

32. Loisel, pp. 36–119; Pliny the Younger, vol. III, Liber VIII, p. 31.

33. Popham, pp. 37–8; Loisel, pp. 162–3.

34. Popham, pp. 179–83; Loisel, pp. 168–72; Bourdignes, passim; Pico della Mirandola, vol. II, p. xxxii; Lloyd, p. 64.

35. Vilhena Barbosa, pp. iv–viii; Brito, p. 81.

36. ANTT, *Corpo Cronologico*, vol. II, fols. 20–40, 12 January and 19 January 1510.

37. Albuquerque, *Cartas*, vol. III, p. 317; ANTT, *Corpo Cronologico*, vol. II, fols. 20–40.

38. Albuquerque, *Cartas*, vol. III, p. 317.

39. ANTT, *Corpo Cronologico*, vol. II, fols. 20–40, Maço 35, Doc. 186, 1 Dezembre 1512, Maço 53, Doc. 262, 10 Dezembre 1512, Parte II, Maço 36, Doc. 12.

40. ANTT, *Corpo Cronologico*, Parte I, Maço 15, Doc. 5; Rebello da Silva, vol. I, pp. 238–42; *Centenario*, pp. 17, 60.

41. Valeriano (2), Libro 2, Introduction, fol. 21ᵛ; AG, *Est. Lett. B. 862*, Letter from Giovanni Piero Valeriano, 4 Marzo 1514.

42. Valeriano (2), fol. 21ᵛ; Matos, p. 72; Lach, vol. II, Book I, p. 136.

43. Ciacconio, vol. III, pp. 329, 377–85; Popham, pp. 185–6; Hartenfels (1), Part II, cap. 6, pp. 164–5.

44. Hartenfels (1), Parte II, cap. 6, p. 164; Pliny, vol. III, Liver VIII, p. 3.

CHAPTER TWO : The Road to Rome

1. Ciutiis, pp. 19–50; Andrade, pp. 119–32; Castro, pp. 159–75; Lanciani, p. 158; Cagnat, pp. 69–71.

2. Matos, vol. I, pp. 44–55; Oliveira Martins (1), Tom. II, pp. 9–15; Pellizzari, pp. 118–29; Goes, Parte III, capit. XXXIX, fols. 73ᵛ–74ᵛ, capit. LV, fols. 99ᵛ–100ᵛ.

3. ANTT, *Corpo Chronologico*, Parte I, Maço 94, Doc. 66; Rebello da Silva, Tom. I, pp. 238–42.

4. Rebello da Silva, Tom. I, pp. 238–42; Castro, pp. 162–3.

5. Rebello da Silva, Tom. I, pp. 238–42.

6. *New Catholic Encyclopedia*, vol. X, p. 148; Alvisi, pp. 402–6; Avery, p. 7.

7. ANTT, *Corpo Chronologico*, Parte I, Maço 15, Doc. 5; Rebello da Silva, Tom. I, pp. 238–42; Matos, pp. 44–7.

8. Pellizzari, pp. 133–7; Gregorovius (1), vol. III, pp. 182–3; Pastor (1), vol. VII, pp. 74–6; Hahn, pp. 44–5; Goes, Parte III, pp. 259–63; Paschini, pp. 409–13.

9. Rebello da Silva, Tom. I, p. 241.

10. BAV, *Cod. Barb. lat. 2273*, Novellus, fol. 11ʳ; ASV, *Nunziatura*, Garabai, *Compendio*, Libro 35, capit. 31, fol. 402ʳ; Ciacconio, vol. III, pp. 329, 377–85; Fabronio, 74–6; Maffei, vol. III, pp. 215–16, 234–6; Oliveira Martins (1), vol. II, pp. 9–15, 27; Pellizzari, pp. 115–40; Hartenfels (2), Part II, capit. 6, p. 164; Osorio (1), Libri 12, vol. III, p. 160; Oliveira Martins (1), vol. II, pp. 9–15; Sanuto, vol. XVI, col. 422, letter from Jeronimo Sernigi to Clemente Sernigi, Oct. 29, 1513, vol. XVIII, cols. 57–9; Castro, pp. 160–74; Schafer, Band III, pp. 81–9; Vilhena Barbosa, pp. v–vi; Rodocanachi (1), pp. 318–20; Popham, pp. 183–4; Cesareo (1), pp. 187–92; Hecksher, p. 170.

11. ASV, *Chron. V., Polit.*, 50, fol. 62; *Nunziatura*, Garabai, Compendio, fol. 402ʳ; Grassi, vol. VIII, fols. 101ᵛ, 171ʳ; vol. XIV, fol. 197; S. Joanninensis, p. 99; AG, letter from Guido Postumo in Rome, 13 Marzo 1514; Goes, (1566–67), Parte III, cap. XXXIX, fols 73ᵛ–74ʳ⁻ᵛ; cap. LV and LVI, fols. 99ᵛ–101ʳ; Vilhena Barbosa, pp. v–vi; Cesareo (1), pp. 133–4.

12. Goes (1566–67), Parte III, cap. LVII, fols. 102–4.

13. Sanuto, vol. XVIII, cols. 85–6.

14. Dickinson, pp. 40–65; Hulsen, pp. V–XIII; Ackerman (2), pp. 70–91; Masson, pp. 211–15; Morton, pp. 51, 58, 233, 238.

15. Paschini, pp. 211–20; A. Mercati, pp. 121–7; ASV *Fondo Borghese*, serie 1, vol. 566, *Diarium Paridi*, tome IV, fols. 113ᵛ–114ᵛ.

16. Pelli, p. 204; Boffito, pp. 555–61; Pagnini, pp. 211–14; Eisler, pp. 312–32.

17. Fabronio, pp. 74–6; Sanuto, vol. XVIII, cols. 57, 85–6; Guicciardini, vol. I, Libri XII, cap. 3, p. 335; Hutten, vol. I, p. 262; Valeriano, Liber II, Introduction, pp. 20–21; Carrington, p. 201; Serão, pp. 2–3, 32 n. 44; Rogers (3), p. 129; Pastor (1), vol. VII, p. 75; ASM Arch. Gonzaga, serie E, xxv3, busta 862, letter from Postumo to Marquis, 13 March 1514.

18. BAV, *Cod. Ottob. lat.*, parte 2, fols. 255, 263ʳ.

19. ASV, *Nunziatura*, Garabai, *Compendio*, Libro 35, cap. 31, fols. 915–16, 266ᵛ, 402ʳ; Grassi, vol. 12, fol. 24; vol. 51, fol. 50ʳ; BAV, *Cod. G. II, 37*, Tizio, *Hist. Senen.*, fols. 285ᵛ, 287ᵛ, 293; Sanuto, vol. XVIII, cols. 58–60; Valeriano, Liber II, pp. 25–26; Goes (1566–7), Parte III, cap. LV, fols. 99ᵛ–102ʳ, cap. LVI, fols. 101ʳ–102ʳ; Pastor (2), vol. IV, Part I, pp. 48–50; Melho, pp. 318–20; Rebello da Silva, Tom. I, pp. 234–8; Pico della Mirandola, vol. II, 'Examen vanitatis doctrinae gentium', p. xxxii. Pico della Mirandola commented upon Hanno's arrival in Rome and recalled another '*elephas me puero vectus in Italiam*', probably the one presented to Ercole d'Este by merchants of Cyprus and preserved in effigy at Belfiore.

20. Fabronio, pp. 161–4; Popham, p. 184; Cesareo (1), pp. 133–4; Pastor (1), vol. VII, p. 76; Andrade, pp. 212–14; Rebello da Silva, Tom. I, pp. 232–4, 238–42; Mitchell, pp. 76–7.

21. ASV, Grassi, *Diarorum*, vol. VIII, fols. 101ᵛ, 156, 161, 171ʳ, 176, 183; Hergensroether, fasc. I–VI, pp. 457, 474, 479, 506; Sanuto, vol. XVIII, cols. 139–40.

22. BE, *Cod. CX*, fols. 1–14, *Cod. CIII*, fols. 2–20 (C.82) *Cod. CV*, fols. 1–3 (C.203); BAV, Cod. Vat. lat. 2032, No. 6, 'Discorso di Diogo Pacheco'; [Pacheco], *Epistola Potentissimi*; Roscoe (1), vol. VI, pp. 184–92; ASV *Fondo Borghese*, serie 1, vol. 566, Grassi *Diarium*, tome IV, fols. 115ʳ⁻ᵛ.

23. ASV, Grassi, *Diarorum*, vol. XII, fol. 24; ASF, *Fondo Mediceo*, filza 107, letters from Balthassare Turini de Pescia to Lorenzo de'Medici, 20 Marzo and 26 Marzo 1514; Pastor (1), vol. VII, pp. 76–77; Roscoe (1), vol. I, pp. 361–4.

24. Gebhart, pp. 177–8; Picca, pp. 142–4; Ciutiis, p. 44; Sanuto, vol. XVIII, cols. 139–40; Roscoe (1), vol. I, pp. 262–64; Sanuto, vol. XVIII, cols. 58–9, 85–6; Dos Passos, pp. 266–8;

25. ASV, *Nunziatura*, Garabai, Compendio, Libro 35, cap. 31, fols. 915–16, 402ʳ⁻ᵛ, 403ʳ⁻ᵛ; 26. BAV, *Cod. Urb. lat. 1023*, Francia, fol. 340ᵛ; *Cod. Ottob. lat.*

2603, parte 2, fols. 255, 263ʳ; *Cod. Barb. lat. 2272*, Novellus, fol. 11ʳ.

26. ASV, *Brevis Leonis X, Sadoleto Brevia*, vol. II, Nr. 255, vp;. XXX, parte 2, fol. 268; ANTT, *Colleçcao de Bullas*, Maço 29, No. 3, Maço 34, No. 23; Rebello da Silva, Tom. I, pp. 250–53, 'Breve da Papa Leão X a el-Rei, 11 May 1514.'

27. Soman, pp. 58–59, 84–95. The Indian dogs sent by King Manuel I to Pope Leo X may have been of the Saluki breed, which traces its origin to ancient Egypt, and were used in India for the hunt during the Moghul period and thereafter. It is also possible that they may have been of the Shenkottah or Kombai breeds, both also used for hunting.

The Indian hens may have been jungle fowl, *Gallus gallus*, or pea fowl, *Pavo cristatus*, a bird indigenous to India and Ceylon. Pea fowl were already well known in Italy, however, and jungle fowl most probably were selected for their novelty.

28. Gebhart, pp. 177–8; Picca, pp. 142–4; Ciutiis, p. 44; Sanuto, vol. XVIII, cols. 139–40; Roscoe (1), vol. I, pp. 262–4.

29. Roscoe (4), vol. VI, pp. 169–99, 'Sadolet. Ep. Pont. Ep. No. 20'.

30. Muratori, p. 351; Guicciardini, vol. XII, p. 355ᵛ; ASV, *Brevia ad Principes*, Arm. 44, tome 5, fols. 64ʳ⁻ᵛ.

31. Giovio (1), p. 205; Giovio (2), p. 229; Goes, Parte III, cap. LVII, fols. 102ʳ, 104ʳ; Croce, vol. II, p. 44; Avery, p. 456.; Madelin, pp. 277–78; BA, *Ms. 12.72 – N 76.*, fols. 178ʳ–179ᵛ, '*Tratado que un criando do duque de Bragança escreveveo pera Sua Senhoria d'algunas notavees cousas que vio indo pera Rome, e de suas grandezas e indulgencias e grandes acontecimentos que las socerderam em espaço de sete años qui i esteve*' [Treatise that a servant of the Duke of Braganza wrote for His Lordship of some notable things that he saw while on their way to Rome, and of his greatness and indulgences and the great events that came to pass during the space of seven years in which [I] was there]; ASV, *Nunziatura*, Garabai, *Compendio*, Libro 35, cap. 31, fol. 402ʳ; Osorio (2), vol. III, Libris IX, pp. 263, 346; Osorio (1), pp. 143–45.

32. Goes, Parte III, cap. LVII, fols. 102ʳ–104ʳ.

33. Fabronio, p. 74; Sanuto, vol. XVIII, cols. 57–60; Brasio, pp. 51–87.

CHAPTER THREE : The Rose and the Sword
1. Ciutiis, p. 40n (Casanova); Roscoe (1), vol. VI, pp. 192–3.

2. Ciutiis, p. 42n. (Janus Vitalis); Roscoe (1), vol. VI, pp. 192–3.

3. BAV, *Cod. Vat. lat. 3419*, fol. 60ʳ, 'Epigrammi di Evangelista Maddaleni de' Capodiferro sul Baraballo, D. M. Elephanti ab Emmanuele Lusitaniae rege Leonis X pont. max. missi'; *Cod. Vat. lat. 3351*, 'E. F. de' Capodiferro,' fols. 164ᵛ–165ʳ; Tommasini, Seria Quarto, vol. X, parte I, p. 8.

4. Sereno, cols. Fiiiiʳ⁻ᵛ, Gᵛ, Giiʳ et seq., 'Joannis Capitonis Aretini Elegia ad eusdem Elephantem'; Roscoe (4), vol. V, pp. 264–7, Doc. LXXXIV, vol. VI, pp. 181–2; Avery, p. 62; Ciutiis, pp. 50–51; Giovanni Mercati, p. 43.

5. Ciutiis, pp. 50–51; Roscoe (4), vol. VI, pp. 183–4.

6. Pasquale, *Rime*, 'De l'elefante mandato dal Re di Portogallo a Papa Leone'. Cited in Faria, pp. vi–vii.

7. Vicente, pp. 27–28.

8. Gillet, vol. IV, pp. 401–5.

9. Gillet, vol. IV, p. 50.

10. Rebello da Silva, Tom. I, pp. 207–9; Pastor (1), vol. VII, pp. 77–8; Roscoe (3), vol. I, pp. 363–4; Silva Rego, pp. 5–7; Bull. Patr. Portug., Tome I, 2, 6, 20.

11. Giacchieri, pp. 85–8; *New Catholic Encyclopedia*, vol. X, pp. 723–4.

12. Rebello da Silva, Tom. I, pp. 242–43, 'Carta de Tristão da Cunha ao secretario de Stado, l5l4–Abril.'

13. Andrade, pp. 212–14.

14. Muntz (3), pp. 1–11; 'La rose,' pp. 326–27; Churchill, pp. 13–24; 'The Golden Rose,' pp. 523–4; Bulgari, passim.

15. ASV, *Introitus*, No. DLI, fol. 229, No. DLIII, fol. 146; Muntz (2), p. 105; Mac Swiney de Mashanaglass, III, p. 116.

16. Cancellieri (1), pp. 247–54; ASV, Grassi, *Diarorum*, vol. VII, fols. 107, 176, 182; *Archivio dei Maestri*, vol. CCLXXIII, fol. 82v; ASF, *Fondo Mediceo*, filza 107, 'Letera [sic] di Balthasare de Pescia a Lorenzo de' Medici, 20 Marzo 1514'.

17. ASV, Grassi, *Diarorum*, vol. VIII, fols. 107, 182, 183; *Archivio dei Maestri*, vol. CCLXXIII, fol. 86; Mac Swiney de Mashanaglass, III, pp. 116–19; ASF, *Fondo Mediceo*, filza 107, 'Letera di Balthasare de Pescia Turini to Lorenzo de'Medici, 26 Marzo 1514'; Roscoe (3), vol. V, p. 12.

18. ANTT, *Colleçcao de Bullas*, Maço 21, No. 3, Maço 29, No. 10; Rebello da Silva, Tom. I, pp. 244–8, 'Bulla do Papa Leao X dirigida a el-Rei, 29 Abril 1514'; *Providum universalis ecclesias*.

19. ANTT, *Colleçcao de Bullas*, Maço 34, No. 23, 'Si tua anima atque virtutis ornamenta'; Maço 29, No. 3, 'Consecrauimus more maiorum per Romanos Pontifices', Rebello da Silva, Tom. I, pp. 250–3.

20. ANTT, *Colleçcao de Bullas*, Maço 20, No. 13, 'Dum fidei constantiam'; Rebella da Silva, Tom. I, pp. 254–7; Rogers (3), p. 130.

21. Vasconcellos (2), pp. cxxxvii, xviii.

22. Mac Swiney de Mashanaglass, I, p. 34.

23. ANTT, *Colleçcao de Bullas*, Maço 22, No. 46, 'In Sacra Petri Sede', 14 setembro 1514; Rebello da Silva, Tom. I, pp. 269–71.

24. ANTT, *Colleçcao de Bullas*, Maço 29, No. 6, 'Praecelsae devotionis', 3 novembro 1514; Rebello da Silva, Tom. I, pp. 271–5; Silva Rego, pp. 15–17; Rogers (3), pp. 130–31.

25. Muntz (1), vol. VII, No. 4, pp. 408–11; vol. XXIII, pp. 281–92; Churchill, pp. 163–226; Lessing, pp. 103–37.

26. Raynauldus, vol. X, pp. 230, 523–30; Mondelli, *Decade II, Dissertat. VII*, parte II, pp. 99–103.

27. ASV, *Introitus*, fol. 178; Mac Swiney de Mashanaglass, I, pp. 34–5.

28. ASV, Grassi, *Diariorum*, vol. XI, fol. 220; ANTT, *Corpo Diplomatico*, vol. I, p. 309; Mac Swiney de Mashanaglass, I, p. 37.

29. ANTT, *Corpo Diplomatico*, vol. I, p. 309.

30. ANTT, *Colleçcao de Bullas*, Maço 20, No. 13, 'Dum fidei constantiam'; Mac Swiney de Mashanaglass, I, p. 37; Roscoe (4), vol. VI, pp. 202–4.

31. Resende, vol. XI, p. 255.

32. ANTT, *Corpo diplomatico*, vol. I, p. 315; Pastor (1), vol. VII, pp. 74–8; Rogers (3), pp. 29–31.

33. Brito, pp. 197–8; Andrade, pp. 130–32.

34. Brito, pp. 196–7; Andrade, pp. 129–32; A. Carneiro, pp. 196–8.

CHAPTER FOUR : The Elephant-Diplomat

1. ASV, *Diversorum*, vol. 69, fol. 67, 14 luglio 1522; ASR, *Archivio di San Spirito*, vol. 1458, cc. 24–5, vol. 1460, cc. 34–5; *Archivio di Sant' Angelo, Miscellanea*, No. 4, *Libri dei Rendiconti*, 1555; *Archivio della Santissima Trinità*, 'Piante antiche di case e liti, ecc. dell'Archiconfraternità', fasc. c. 92; *Archivio dei Raccomandati*, Arm. III, mazzo 1, No. 78; *Libri dei Istrumenti*, fols. 342–3; Lanciani (2); *Miscellanea Giovanni Battista de Rossi* (Parte Prima), pp. 239, 242; Adinolfi, pp. 50–51; Umberto Gnoli, pp. 99–100; Delli, p. 362.

2. Lach (1), Book II, pp. 532–3; Lach (3), vol. II, Book One, p. 138 fn. 78; Burrow, p. 353.

3. Valeriano (2), Liber II, Introduction, pp. 20–21; Lach, 'Asian Elephants', pp. 133–76.

4. Knight, vol. II, pp. 5, 12–13; Carrington, pp. 174–6, 201; Morewood-Dowsett, pp. 3–40; Murray, pp. 65–73; Gray, pp. 36–43.

5. Sanuto, vol. XVIII, p. 68; Gebhart, pp. 177–81; Picca, pp. 133–44; Loisel, pp. 135–59, 197–220; Rodocanachi (2), p. 102; Truc, pp. 115–16; Ackerman (2), pp. 41–72; Ackerman (1), pp. 70–91.

6. Burckhardt, p. 177; Albertini, p. 39, 'Sunt ibi nemora ferarum et avium cum viridariis et hortulis'; Ackerman (2), pp. 43, 143; Schaffer, p. 72.

7. Loisel, vol. I, p. 198, vol. II, pp. 149–53, 197–201; Rodocanachi (2), p. 97; Masão Finiguerra, vol. 3, pp. 256–7; Burckhardt, pp. 176–8.

8. Gebhart, pp. 180–81.

9. Truc, pp. 115–16; Hahn, pp. 44–5; Knight, vol. II, pp. 5, 12–13; Loisel, pp. 202–4, 219.

10. Campana, pp. 225–7; Jacobilli, p. 101, 'Memini audisse me a viro Fiorentino Leonem X pont. max. habuisse in delitiis chameleontem'.

11. Aretino, Act III, scene XII, pp. 94–5; Sartorelli, pp. 79–86; Avery, pp. 62–4.

12. Rivera, pp. 239, 245–56; Pansa (1), pp. 239–45; Pansa (2), pp. 4–7; Hergenroether, fasc. I, pp. 20, 126, 157, 619, 712; Rodocanachi (3), p. 70; Pastor (3), vol. IV, p. 505; ASV, *Breve del Leone X*, 26 febbraio 1514, 'Dilecto Filio Io. Baptistae Branconio Clerico Aquilano Cubiculario secreto et Familiari continuo commensali nostro'.

13. Torriggio, capit. XX, p. 72, 'Die Francesco Parisiano Gubernatore delle Elefante del nostro Signor Papa Leone'; Rodocanachi (3), p. 70n.

14. Ferrajoli, vol. XXXIV, fasc. III–IV, p. 389.

15. Communication to the author from Dr Sami K. Hamarneh, Curator Emeritus of Medical Sciences, National Museum of American History, Smithsonian Institution, 8 March 1977.

16. BAV, *Cod. Vat. lat. 8598*, 'Rotulus Papa Leo X, scutiferi'; Ferrajoli, fasc.

1, fol. 384, 389; Friedenberg, Band VI, Heft I, pp. 59–60; Ferrajoli, fasc. 1, p. 389.

17. ASF, *Fondo Mediceo*, filza 107, Letter from Balthasare Turini de Pescia to Lorenzo de' Medici, 8 Giugno 1514; Roscoe (2), vol. IV, pp. 142–9.

18. ASF, *Fondo Mediceo*, filza 107, letter from Turini de Pescia to Lorenzo de'Medici, 10 Giugno 1514.

19. ASF, *Fondo Mediceo*, filza 107, letter from Turini de Pescia to Lorenzo de'Medici, 16 Giugno 1514.

20. [Hutten], *Epistolae*, vol. I, pp. 212, 262.

21. Pastor (1), vol. VIII, pp. 139–49; Roscoe (3), vol. II, pp. 390–91; Pecchiai, pp. 387–93.

22. Gnoli (1), pp. 581–3; Gnoli (2), vol. I, p. 40, vol. II, pp. 639–42.

23. Ademollo, pp. 69–93; Borgatti, pp. 277–87.

24. Chamberlain, p. 225–6; Gnoli (1), pp. 581–3; Gnoli (2), pp. 637–8; Pastor (1), vol. VIII, pp. 151–4, 275; Cesareo (3), pp. 79–82.

25. ASV, *Indice Garampi*, vol. I; BAV, *Cod. Vat. 172, 5356*, 'Poema del Baraballo per il concorso di Settembre 1513 [*sic*]'; Ferraro, pp. 210–11; Ferrajoli, vol. XXXIX, fasc. I–II, pp. 565–71; Pastor (1), vol. VIII, pp. 154–6; Roscoe (3), vol. II, pp. 180–81, 462.

26. Romano, pp. 43–7; Lancetti, p. 336; Luzio (1), pp. 551–3, Letter from Fra Mariano to the Marchesa di Mantua, 29 January 1513; Cesareo (1), pp. 133–8, 190–94.

27. BAV, *Cod. Vat. 72, 5356*; Onori, pp. 1143–6; Gnoli (3), pp. 108–17; Cesareo (1), pp. 133–8; Cesareo (5), pp. 190–96; Lancetti, pp. 332–40.

28. Giovio (1), Liber Quattuor, pp. 97–8, 102; Giovio (2), p. 190.

29. Sanuto, vol. XIX, p. 74.

30. ASF, *Fondo Mediceo*, filza 107, fols. 50r, 59v, Lettera No. 32, Turini de Pescia to Lorenzo de'Medici, 8 Giugno 1514; Ciutiis, pp. 40–42n.

31. Giovio (1), Liber Quattuor, pp. 85, 102; Gnoli (3), pp. 108–17; Roscoe (3), vol. II, pp. 180–81; Roscoe (4), vol. VII, pp. 208–11.

32. Domenichi, pp. 220–21; Rodocanachi (2), pp. 121–2; Riviera, vols. XI–XIII, pp. 252–5; Pastor (1), vol. VIII, pp. 154–6; Roscoe (3), vol. II, pp. 180–81.

33. Colocci, pp. 64, 109; Roscoe (4), vol. VII, p. 210.

34. Gnoli (3), pp. 266–99; Avery, p. 4.

35. Beroaldo, *Carminum*, Liber III, fols. 45–53, 'Prologue in Comoediam habitam in coronatione Baraballi'; Ferrajoli, vol. XXXIX, fasc. III–IV, pp. 563–71, 'Epigrammo No. 63'; Avery, p. 129.

36. BNM, *Cod. Marciana lat. XII, 211*, c. 28, unpublished satirical verses about the papal elephant by Giovanni Francesco Filomuso, pseudonym of Giovanni Francesco Superchio of Pesaro, quoted in Rossi, pp. 228–9.

37. Beroaldo, Liber III, fols. 45r–51v.

38. Sereno, (Ia. Manius Philenus); Roscoe (4), vol. VI, p. 184.

39. Sereno, fols. 52–53; Giovio (2), p. 99; Roscoe (4), vol. VI, p. 195.

40. *BN, Ms. lat.* 5165, Grassi, *Diarorium*, vol. II, p. 627; Pastor (1), vol. VII, pp. 68–70, 96–8; Stigliano, pp. 169–75.

41. Luzio (1), pp. 571, 576; Reumont, Band III, p. 131; Passavant (1), pp. 163–4; Graf, pp. 187–95; Cesareo (1), pp. 134–5; Cesareo (5), pp. 190–95; Truc, pp. 116–17.

42. Giovio (2), p. 102; Pastor (1), vol. VIII, p. 155; Rivera, pp. 252–5.

43. Maes, Parte I, pp. 94–5; Cian, pp. 279–80; Pastor (1), vol. VIII, p. 155; Roscoe (3), vol. II, p. 181.

44. Cesareo (5), pp. 190–95; Cesareo (2), p. 201; Gnoli (3), pp. 181–2, 193–4.

45. Aretino, vol. II, p. 11; Avery, pp. 62–4. Donatus was a 4th-century writer of textbooks that continued so long in use that the word '*donat*' was used in the Middle Ages to mean 'textbook'. The author of these lines appears to be comparing Baraballo to a mere textbook writer who parodies or distorts from lack of real understanding, the ancient wisdom that he purveys.

46. Macchiavelli, vol. II, Chap. 6, 'The Golden Ass', p. 766; Avery, pp. 577–9.

47. Domenichi, p. 221; Rossi, pp. 22, 152, 155, 159; Giovio (2), pp. 51–2.

48. Passavant (2), vol. I, pp. 167–8; Vasari (1), vol. IV, p. 363, vol. V, p. 524, vol. VI, pp. 554–6; Odelscalchi, pp. 218–24; Avery, p. 89.

49. Domenichi, p. 201; Giovio (2), pp. 51–2; Rossi, pp. 152–5.

50. Gnoli (3), pp. 164–287; Gnoli (2), p. 41.

51. Cesareo (5), pp. 193–6; Gnoli (3), pp. 166–7.

52. Gnoli (3), p. 182.

53. Gnoli (3), 176–80.

54. Ferrajoli, vol. XXXIX, fasc. I–II, pp. 569–73; Gnoli (3), p. 181.

55. Gnoli (3), pp. 181–2.

56. Gnoli (3), p. 182; Avery, p. 508.

57. Philomathes, unpaginated; Matos, pp. 44–7; BAV, *Mss. Chigiana G. II–37*, Tiziano, 'Historiarum Senenentium', fol. 285^v.

58. Luzio and Renier, p. 76; Campori, pp. 7–9; Luzio (1), pp. 571–2; Avery, pp. 360–65, 880.

59. Luzio (1), pp. 571–2; Luzio and Renier, p. 137.

60. Luzio and Renier, pp. 76–7.

61. Luzio and Renier, p. 76 n. 3; Campori, pp. 7–9.

62. Luzio (2), p. 163.

63. Oberhuber, pp. 353–4; Franchini, p. 94; Bini, p. 34–6.

64. Ferino, pp. 262–5; Passavant (1839–58) p. 577; Shearman (1987), p. 215; Franchini, p. 94; Archivio di Stato di Mantova, *Fondo Gonzaga*, Busta n. 2923, copialettera 243, c. 18, Busta n. 863.

65. Roscoe (3), vol. II, pp. 5–12; Avery, pp. 623–4.

66. Sanuto, vol. XVIII, p. 59; Rodocanachi (2), p. 97; Pecchiai, pp. 356–9.

67. Sanuto, vol. XX, pp. 99–100; Popham, p. 184.

68. Rodocanachi (2), pp. 96–7.

69. ANTT, *Gavetaas 10*, Maço 4, No. 41; Robinson, p. 294, Item 146; Passavant (1), vol. II, p. 593.

70. BAV, *Ms. Urb. lat. 1641*, 'Giustizie Sixtus IV al Leo X', fols. 497^r–499^v.

71. BAV, *Ms. Urb. lat. 1641*, fol. 499^v; Shearman, pp. 152–55; Hibbert, pp. 219–22; Ciseri, pp. 11–44, 182–4; Marquand, pp. 37–8.

CHAPTER FIVE : The Ill-fated Rhinoceros

1. Albuquerque (1), vol. V, parte I, p. 420, vol. II, p. 132; Barros, Liv. 4, cap. I–III; Fontoura da Costa, pp. 9–10; Lach (1), Book I, pp. 169, 394–406; Avery, pp. 18, 92.

2. Fontoura da Costa, pp. 11–13; Albuquerque (1), vol. II, pp. 32–48; Castanheda, Liv. III, cap. C, CXXXIII–CXXXIV; Goes, parte III, cap. LXIV, pp. 406–9; Barros, Liv. 10, pp. 421–3; Correa, vol. II, pp. 373–4; Lach (2), pp. 394–406.

3. Albuquerque (2), vol. IV, p. 104, vol. VI, p. 196; Correa, vol. II, cap. XLVI, pp. 373–4; Albuquerque (1), vol. II, pp. 32–48, vol. III, pp. 99–101; Costa, pp. 15–18.

4. Albuquerque (1), vol. I, pp. 356, 359, 367, vol. IV, pp. 16–18; Correa, vol. II, cap. XLVI, pp. 373–4.

5. Correa, vol. II, cap. XLVI, pp. 373–6; Albuquerque (1), vol. I, pp. 356–9; Valeriano (3), Liber II, p. 27; Dodgson (2), vol. I, pp. 307–8.

6. Pliny, vol. III, Lib. VIII, p. 53.

7. Loisel, pp. 217–20; Gowers, pp. 288–9; Hahn, p. 45.

8. Castilho, Livro II, pp. 168–84, Livro III, pp. 270–74; Vilhena Barbosa, pp. vi–vii; Loisel, pp. 218–19; Dos Passos, pp. 259–66; Hahn, p. 45; ANTT, *Chanceleria de D. Manuel*, Maço 1498, Livro 32, fol. 30, 'Pagamentos para mantimento'; Casa forte, 'Livro dos Plantas e Monteas de todas os Fabricas das Inquisiçoes deste Reino e India ordenado por mandado do Illmo e Rev^{mo} Senhor Dom Francisco de Castro Bispo Inquisidor Geral e do Conselho Geral e do Conselho de Estado de Sua Magestade, Anno Domini 1634', pp. 33, 48.

9. Fontoura da Costa, pp. 19–26; Castilho, pp. 270–74; Goes, parte IV, cap. XVIII, fols. 23r–26r, 477–91; Loisel, pp. 218–19; Münster (1), p. 1086; Münster (2), pp. 1339–41; Schotius, vol. I, pp. i–xi, 1172–3; Brito, pp. 79–86; Vilhena Barbosa, pp. vi–vii; Clarke (1), pp. 2–3; Gesner, fol. cxxxi^r; Lach (3), pp. 158–72; 'Le rhinoceros', pp. 202–3.

10. BNC, *Cod. Strozziano 20, Cl–XIII 80*, 'Lettera scripta da Valentino Moravia germano a li mercanti di Nuremberg'; Gubernatis, pp. 289–92.

11. Dodgson (2), pp. 307–8; Fontoura da Costa, pp. 5–7; Panofsky, p. 192.

12. Dodgson (1), pp. 10–12; Dodgson (3), pp. 45–6; Gowers, pp. 288–9; Rookmaaker (2), pp. 20–22; Clarke (3), p. 7; Dembeck, p. 279.

13. Giehlow, pp. 60, 71; Huber, pp. 310–20; Massing, pp. 47–8.

14. Giehlow, pp. 59–61; Dodgson (1), p. 11.

15. Killerman, p. 86.

16. Penni, *La Victoria*, unpaginated; Matos, pp. 387–98; Gnoli (3), p. 72n.

17. Penni, unpaginated.

18. Philomathes, [See Chapter III, note 61]; [BC; Sander, fig. 800. (?)]

19. Fontoura da Costa, pp. 28, 42; Alcaçova Carneiro, pp. 198–9; ATNN, Nucleo Antigo, fols. 256^v, 259^{r-v}, 260^{r-v}, 261^r, 'Receita e despesa das obras que el Rey D. Manuel mandou fazer para sua casa, Anno de 1514'.

20. Fontoura da Costa, p. 28; Matos, p. 43; Alcaçova Carneiro, pp. 196–9.

21. Alcaçova Carneiro, pp. 198–9; Dodgson (3), pp. 50–51.

22. Carlos de Melho, pp. 320–21; Costa, p. 23.

23. Barillion, vol. I, p. 193; Goes, parte IV, cap. XVIII; Dodgson (3), pp. 50–51; Giovio (3), p. 50; Fontoura da Costa, p. 29; Avery, pp. 409–10.

24. Goes, parte IIIa, capit. XXXIX, fols. 73v, 74r–v, capit. LV–LVII, fols. 99v–104r, capit. LXIV, fols. 23r–26r; Giovio (3), pp. 31, 55; Ruffi, pp. 198–9; Delaunay, p. 146.

25. BA, *Ms. 51.5.1.*, fol. 164r, copy of a letter from King Francis I to King Manuel I written from Saint-Germain-en-Laye, undated. Cited by Matos, p. 46. Conflans is identified in the Académie's *Collection*, vol. I, p. 220, n. 1214, vol. II, p. 354, n. 5546, vol. V, p. 632, n. 17904, p. 675, n. 18140.

26. Belon, quoted in Sainen (1), pp. 222–3.

27. Giovio (3), p. 55; Giovio (4), p. Dii^v; Goes, parte IV, capit. XVIII, p. 491; Castilho, vol. II, pp. 172–3; Vilhena Barbosa, pp. vii–viii; Brito, pp. 85–6; Fontoura da Costa, pp. 54–5; 'Le Rhinoceros,' pp. 202–3.

28. Brito, p. 85.

29. Giovio (4), p. Dii^v; Giovio (1), Liber quartus, p. 207, Poem of 12 lines about the rhinoceros by Antonio Sanfelici; Goes, parte IV, capit. XVIII, p. 491; 'Le Rhinoceros', p. 203.

30. Goes, parte III^a, capit. LXXVIII, parte II, capit. XLII, fols. 75–7, parte IV, capit. XVIII, fols. 23r–26r; 'Chronique,' pp. 198–9.

31. Fabronio, p. 74.

32. ANTT, *Corpo diplomatico*, parte I, Maço 20, Doc. 84; Rebello da Silva, Tom. I, pp. 384–6; Gowers, pp. 288–9.

33. Giovio (3), p. 31; Castilho, p. 274.

34. Lacépède, 'Le Rhinoceros', p. 2.

35. Shufeldt, p. 371 n.

36. Fontana, pp. 29–30; BU, *Ms. Aldrov. 97*, 'Degli Animali', cc. 585^{r-v}, 586^r, 'Tavole degli Animali', vol. I, c. 91^r; Ms. 6, vol. I, 'Corrispondenza tra U. Aldrovandi e Francesco I^o', passim; *Catalogo dei manoscritti*, passim.

37. Olmi (2), p. 125, fig. 1; Avery, pp. 19–20.

38. Vasari (4), vol. 3, pp. 52–3; Champlin, vol. II, p. 106; Bryan, pp. 293–4; Benezit, vol. IV, pp. 385–6; Thieme and Willis, Band 24, pp. 500–2; Berenson, pp. 143–6; Holst, *passim*.

39. In a search for records relating to the disposition of the Lisbon rhinoceros, a comprehensive examination was undertaken of libraries and archives in Florence on behalf of the writer by Dott.ssa Letizia Strocchi of the Kunsthistorisches Institut di Firenze, with negative results. Among the repositories and records searched are the Archivio delle Gallerie di Firenze (*Mss. 70, 71, 76, 79, 82 and 98*); Archivio di Stato di Firenze (*Guardaroba Mediceo 1553 and 1561*, filze 28 and 36); bibliographical records of the Kunsthistorisches Institut, records of the Istituto e Museo di Storia della Scienza, Museo Zoologico della Specola, Commissione scientifica per la futura mostre Mediceo, and the Archivio della Soprintendenza per i Beni Artistici e Storici.

* Chapter title taken from Edmund Spenser's *The Faerie Queene*, Book VII Canto 6, Stanza 1, '*The ever-whirling wheele of Change, the which all mortall things doth sway.*'

1. Burckhardt, pp. 280–97; Pastor (1), vol.VII, pp. 4–6, 291–7; vol.VIII, pp. 445–52; Roscoe (3), vol. I, pp. 267–8; ASF, *Fondo Mediceo avanti Principato*, filza 107, Letter from Turini de Pescia to Lorenzo de'Medici, 8 Giugno 1514; Pastor (1), vol.VIII, p. 449 n.; Sanuto, vol. XVIII, p. 86.

2. Pastor (2), vol.V, pp. 224–5; Pastor (1), vol.VIII, pp. 449–50; Höfler, Band IV, Abt. 3, pp. 36–7, 56–7; Sanuto, vol. XVIII, p. 139, vol. XXI, pp. 338 et seq.; Wadding, vol. XIV, p. 323, marginal note; Reeves, pp. 438, 448; AG, letter of C. Agnello in Rome, 2 August 1516; ASV, Grassi, *Diariorum*, vol. XII, fol. 23.

3. Sanuto, vol. XII, pp. 474–5; Rossi, p. 227 n. l.

4. Dorland's, p. 594, 'Fistula'; Sanuto, vol. XXII, pp. 412, 443–4, vol. XXX, p. 466; Gualino, Anno VI, No. 3, pp. 25–9, No. 4, pp. 157–68; ASV, Grassi, *Diariorum*, vol. IV, fols. 139, 154; Rodocanachi (2), p. 101 fn.

5. Pastor (2), vol.V, pp. 224–5; Pastor (1), vol.VIII, p. 449–50; Rodocanachi (1), p. 125.

6. Sanuto, vol. XII, pp. 474–5. The interrogation of the clairvoyant friar was not recorded in the chronological indices of the Archivio di Sant'Angelo, the *Instrumenta Miscellanea*, nor in the *Schedario Garampi* of the Archivio Segreto. Communication from Monsignor Charles Burns, ASV, 28 October 1978; Pastor (2), vol.V, pp. 224–5; Pastor (1), vol.VIII, pp. 449–50.

7. Höfler, Band IV, Abt. 3, pp. 56–57; UB, Biblioteca Frisingensis, [Stephan Rosin], 'Exemplum literarum Domini Stephanus Rosin Caesarae Majestatis apud S. Sedem Sollicitatoris ad Reverendum principem D. Carolus Gurcensem 12 mai 1516'.

8. Muratori, p. 364; Sanuto, vol. XXII, pp. 315–16, 474–75; BAV, *Cod. Ottob. lat. 2602*, parte II, fol. 262, 'Diario di Branca Tedallini'; *Cod. Barb. lat. 3552*, fol. 27, [Anonymous], 'Diario', entry for 'Lunedi, XVI giugno 1516' quoted by Lefevre (2); Madelin, pp. 277–8; Hutten (2), pp. 245–7; Hutten (1), vol.VI, p. 246; Reumont, Band III, pp. 2, 81, 147, 857. At the time of the elephant's death, the pope's personal surgeon was Giacomo da Brescia, and his physicians were Maystro Francesco Dandini and Maystro Bartholomeo di Pisis.

9. BNM, *Manoscritti, Lettere particolare*, 'Come era morte il liofante del re di Portogallo mando a donar al Papa'; Sanuto, vol. XXII, p. 316; Gnoli (1), p. 583; Pastor (1), vol.VII, p. 76; Crowe and Cavalcaselle, pp. 355–7; Rossi, p. 227 n. 1; Winner, pp. 71–109; Hartt (1), pp. 67–94.

10. Reumont, vol. III, pp. 81, 147; Cancellieri (2) p. 62 n. 1; Suida, pp. 13–17; Lanciani (1), p. 272.

11. Cancellieri (2), p. 62; Reumont, vol. III, p. 857; BAV, *Cod. Ottob. lat. 2967*, fol. 94r, 'Epigrafo del elefante'. Neither the identity of the author of the manuscript nor of the epigram is known.

12. Giovio (1), pp. 205, 230; Beroaldo, 'Epitaphium Elephantis'; Paquier, p. 35.

13. Winner, pp. 71–75; Berlin, Staatliche Museen zu Berlin, Preussischer Kulturbesitz, Kupferstichkabinett, 'Der Elephant Hanno. Kopie nach verschollener Zeichnung von Raffael. Feder laviert. Stiftung Preuss., Kulturbesitz'; Tormo, pp. 141–3. Although several interpretations for the letters 'D. M.' prefixing the elephant's epitaph have been proposed, Tormo's suggestion that they were the initials of 'Deus Maximus' appears to be the most likely one.

14. Winner, pp. 72–5; Harvard University, Fogg Art Museum, Cat. No. 1955.17, Roman school, 16th century, 'Elephant and Two Attendants'.

15. BRM, *Libro de deseños o dibujos de Francisco de Hollanda*, fol. 31^v; Segurado, pp. 101–2; Tormo, pp. 141–3; Vasconcellos (2), pp. xxx–xxxv; Vasconcellos (1), pp. 42–3, 47.

16. Pliny, vol. III, Liber VIII, p. 3.

17. BAV, *Cod. Ottob. lat. 2603*, parte II, 'Diario de Branca Tedallini', fol. 270^r.

18. Burckhardt, p. 96; Gebhart, p. 184. The legend that the elephant Hanno had been gilded may derive from the oft-repeated account of the great festival of St John held at Florence in 1514, in which the body of a young boy had been gilded from head to foot resulting in his death 'because he could not breathe through his pores'. Actually no such breathing takes place.

19. Hutten (2), pp. 245–57; Hutten (1), vol. VI, p. 246; Scheil, p. 19.

20. Muratori, p. 364.

21. Sanuto, vol. XXII, pp. 315–16, 379, 412.

22. '*Fistula in natibus cum orificiis quinque*', Rossi, p. 227; Grassi, pp. 35–6; ASV, Grassi, *Diariorum*, vol. IV, cc. 139, 154, 176r–v, 177^{r-v}.

23. Valeriano (4), Libro II, pp. 55–6; Luzio (3); Pastor (1), vol. VIII, pp. 74–76; Roscoe (3), vol. II, p. 390.

24. Ferrajoli, vol. XXXIX, fasc. I–II, pp. 564–5, fasc. III–IV, pp. 563–7; Beroaldo, op. cit, 'Epigrammo No. 42. Elephas comestus a Gazoldo'.

25. Venice, Museo Correr, *Cod. Cigogna 2673*, cc. 240^v–241^r, 'Testamento del elefante'; Gregorovius (1), Band VIII, p. 238; Rossi (3), pp. 629–48; Pietro Romano, pp. 52–58; Angelo Romano, pp. 405–24.

26. Aretino, Atto terza, scena XII, pp. 94–5; Rossi (3), pp. 629–48.

27. Rossi (3), pp. 633–46; Aretino, pp. 94–5.

28. Rossi (3), pp. 640–48.

29. Tasso (1), p. 104, 'Il Conte o Vero l'Impresse'; Cesareo (6), p. 136; Romano, pp. 43–7, 52–8; Graf, pp. 196–8, 404–6; Avery, pp. 905–6.

30. Tasso (2), Canto XVII, p. 422.

31. Osorio, *Cancioneiro*, vol. I, pp. 23–5.

32. Osorio, vol. IV, p. 24; Resende, pp. 312–14.

33. Valeriano (3), pp. 25–7; Ferrajoli, vol. XXXIX, fasc. I–II, pp. 564–5.

34. Pasquale *Rime*, 'De l'elefante mandato dal Re di Portogallo a Papa Leone'; Rossi (3), pp. 636–48.

CHAPTER SEVEN : Remembrance and Reflection*

* Chapter title taken from Alexander Pope's *Essay on Man, Epistle I*, line 225, '*Remembrance and reflection how allied!*'

1. Vasari (3), vol. II, p. 904; Lugano, p. 260 n. 3, 261 n. 2; Odescalchi, pp. 218–24; BAV, *Cod. Barb. lat. 4410*, fol. 32r, 'Aquarello del poeta Baraballo sul-elefante'. According to S. Pierlasi, *Inventarium Codium mss. Bibliotheque Barberinae*, the identities of the author of the manuscript and of the artist are unknown. The writer gratefully acknowledges the assistance of Dr Deoclecio Redig de Campos who brought this drawing to his attention.

2. Passavant (2), vol. I, pp. 164–5; Passavant (1), pp. 163–4; Crowe and Cavalcaselle, vol. II, p. 502; Vasari (1), vol. IV, pp. 311–416, vol. V, p. 524, vol. VI, pp. 555–6; Vasari (3), vol. II, p. 1286; Hoogewerff, p. 256; Lasinio, fig. II, No. iv; *Enciclopaedia Italiana*, vol. XX, pp. 558–59; Vollmer et al, pp. 403–4.

3. Hoogewerff, p. 256; Winner, pp. 100–3; Nesselrath, pp. 53–4, 60, 66, 72, 79.

4. Vasari (3), vol. II, pp. 903–4; Vasari (1), vol. VI, pp. 555–6; Roscoe (1), vol. IV, pp. 238–44; Passavant (1), pp. 164–6; Crowe and Cavalcaselle, vol. II, pp. 355–6; ASV, Grassi, *Diariorum*, vol. III, p. 227.

5. Communication from Dr John Shearman, 19 January 1978.

6. Gusman, pp. 314–24; Hofmann, I, pp. 1–47; Lefevre (3), pp. 148–53, 264–8; Lefevre, (3), pp. 40–42, 51, 69–71; Lefevre (4), pp. 148–53, 264–8; Fischel, vol. I, pp. 123–4, 164–5, figs. 289a, 289b; Hare, vol. II, pp. 260–63.

7. Lefevre (4), pp. 149–51, 264–8; Lefevre (1), pp. 81–90; Vasari (3), vol. II, p. 1287; Lefevre (3), pp. 40–42.

8. Gotti, vol. I, p. 170; Lefevre (4), pp. 149–50.

9. Hülsen and Egger, Band I, fols. 19ᵛ, 24ʳ, 40ʳ.

10. Lefevre (2); Hofmann (1), Band IV, Tafel 2, Nos. 7219, 7133; Vasconcellos (1), vol. II, No. 2, pp. 42–3, 47; Segurado, pp. 101–2; Fischel, vol. I, pp. 123–4, 164–5, figs. 289a, 289b; Tormo, pp. 145–8.

11. Montini and Averini, pp. 12–13, 24–5, 30–36; Montini, pp. 4–7, 14; Redig de Campos (1), pp. 4, 14; Redig de Campos (2); Lefevre (2).

12. Montini and Averini, pp. 31–2; Montini, pp. 4–7; Redig de Campos (1), pp. 4, 15.

13. Mariani, p. 41; Lefevre (2); Montini and Averini, parte II, pp. 32–3, Tav. XXIX; Cermenati (1), pp. 105–23; Cermenati (2) pp. 308–31, *vide* p. 323; Hergensroether, Nos. 314, 2195, 2696, 9848, 11537; Toni, pp. 73–5; McCurdy, pp. 136–46.

14. Pedretti, pp. 530–31; Solmi, pp. 68–98; BAM, *Codex Atlanticus*, fol. 287ʳ; Solmi, pp. 186–201; Vasari (1), vol. IV, pp. 17–90.

15. Young, p. 364–72; Burckhardt, pp. 177–8.

16. D'Onofrio, *Obelischi*, pp. 230–37; BAV, *Cod. Barb. lat. 1926*, cc. 17–20; Colonna, *Hyperotomachia*, fols. b–c; BAV, *Cod. Chigi I. IV. 205*, cc. 337–41; Hecksher, p. 170.

17. Beltrami, pp. 1071–4; Beltrami, *Castello* (1885), pp. 213–14; Marangoni, pp. 274–81; Casati, pp. 106–7; Bassani, 'Raffaello', pp. 57–63

18. Gnoli (3), p. 118; Benevolo, pp. 61–73; Bruschi, pp. 3–18; Fasolo, pp. 33–60; Zander, pp. 19–32; Portoghesi, pp. 74–6.

19. Lang, pp. 427–30; Davidson, pp. 178–80.

20. Shearman (2), pp. 52–5.

21. Robinson, pp. 294–5, catalogued as 'Raphael P. II 590, Studies of Elephant'; Popham, p. 185.

22. Oxford University, Ashmolean Museum, Department of Western Art, *Cat. P II 655D*, School of Raphael, 'The Adoration of the Magi'.

23. Parker, K.T. *Catalogue of Drawings in the Ashmolean Museum* (Oxford), 1956), No. 590.

24. Campori, pp. 115–18; Ferrini Pagden, pp. 263–5.

25. Salerno, pp. 198–200; Antal, pp. 87–9.

26. Bierens de Haan, pp. 177–81.

27. Passavant (2), vol. III, pp. 190–211; Rackham, pp. 294–5; Robinson, pp. 294–5; Bierens de Haan, pp. 178–80.

28. Saxl, pp. 38–9; Winner, p. 106.

29. Müller and Singer, p. 422; Winner, p. 106.

30. Paris, The Louvre, Cabinet des dessins, Cat. 6104; Winner, pp. 103–4.

31. Ellesmere Collection, *Catalogue*, p. 51, Item 22; Hartt (2), vol. I, pp. 28–31, vol. II, Nos. 254, 275.

32. Borgatti, pp. 340–43, fig. 133.

33. Panza (1), pp. 23; Panza (2), pp. 145.

34. Fanti, c. I^r, 'Rota del Leonfante', Eisler (1), pp. 156–7; Winner, pp. 99–100.

35. Pasquilli [1518].

36. Hare, vol. II, pp. 293–4.

37. Giovio (3), pp. 31–2; Giovio (5), pp. 55–7. The first edition, published in Rome by Antonio Barre in 1555, was not illustrated.

38. Champion, p. 115; L'Eglise, pp. 87, fig. 4,

> *Longuement a vesçu et vivra la memoire d'Hercules*
> *que tant a de monstres surmontez*
> *Les peuples fiers et forts par moy France a domtez*
> *Furent, sont et seront ma perdurable gloire.*

39. Rabelais, Book Five, Chapter 30; Sainean (1), pp. 218–20; Sainean (2), vol. I, p. 22–3, 41; Solomon, pp. 498–501; Françon (1), p. 96; Françon (2), pp. 22–7; Françon (3), pp. 371–4.

40. Rabelais, Book Five, Chapter 30; Solomon, pp. 498–501; Sainean (1), pp. 218–19; Sianean (2) Book I, pp. 21–3, 41.

41. Dodgson (2), vol. I, pp. 307–8; Dodgson (3), pp. 45–9, 54–6.

42. Münster (1), vol. I, p. 1086; Münster (2), vol. V, pp. 1339–41.

43. Camerarius, pp. 9–14.

44. Gesner, pp. 953, cxxxi^r; Johnstonus, Caput II, art. XI, plate 38, pp. 66–7; Topsell, vol. I, pp. 460–68.

45. Cole, vol. I, pp. 337–56; Clarke (1), pp. 1–13; Clarke (4), pp. 16–27;

Pope-Hennessy, pp. 88–90; Dembeck, p. 279; Lach (3), pp. 163–72.

46. Dodgson (3), pp. 55–6; Giehlow, pp. 60, 71; Dodgson (1), pp. 10–12, fig. 12.

47. Clarke (2), pp. 113–14, fig. 2.

48. Ibid.

49. Arphe y Villafane, Book III, p. 8; Acunai, pp. 625–8; Palm, pp. 67–74.

50. Pope-Hennessy, vol. III, p. 117, fig. 168; Clarke (2), pp. 2–13; Clarke (1), p. 5.

51. Ibid.

52. Clarke (1), pp. 2–13; Spinazzola, pp. 143–6; Lach (3), pp. 163–72.

53. ANTT, Casa forte. *Leitura Nova*, 'Livro Octavo da Odiana;' Lisbon, Museo de Arte Antiga.

54. *Livro de Horas de D. Manoel I*, 16th c., unpaginated; Forjaz de Sampião, vol. I, pp. 272–8, 300–2; Santos, vol. III, pp. 302–4; *Grande Enciclopedia*, vol. XIV, pp. 889–91.

55. Cabrita, 'Pintura Mural de S. Pedro da Ribeira', unpublished manuscript, courtesy of the Comissão Nacional para as Comemorações dos Descobrimentos Portugueses; Santos, pp. 240–43; Espanca, pp. 366–7; Banha de Andrade, pp. 60–61.

56. Bassani and Fagg, pp. 90–109, 140–47, 234–8; Bassani, 'Additional Notes', pp. 41–5; 'Raffaello', pp. 57–63.

57. Bassani and Fagg, p. 117, 118–19; Bassani, 'Additional Notes', p. 43; Bassani, 'Raffaello', p. 57.

58. Bassani and Fagg, p. 235, item 82; Bassani, 'Additional Notes', pp. 43–4; Bassani, 'Raffaello', pp. 59, 62.

59. Bassani and Fagg, p. 235, item 85; Bassani, 'Additional Notes,' p. 43; Bassani, 'Raffaello', pp. 93.

60. Bassani, 'Additional Notes', pp. 41–5.

CHAPTER EIGHT : The Prey of Time★
★ Chapter title taken from Edmund Spenser's *Complaints*, (1591).

1. Rebella da Silva, Tom. I, pp. 375–8; ANTT, *Colleçcao de Bullas*, Gaveta 7, Maço 1, No. 6, 'Constanti fide', 30 Junho 1516; Rebello da Silva, Tom. II, p. 9; ANTT, *Colleçcao de Bullas*, Gaveta 7, Maço 21, No. 9, 'Vidimus quae super', 3 Maio 1518; Rebello da Silva, Tom. II, pp. 15–16; ATNN, *Colleçcao de Bullas*, Gaveta 7, Maço 29, No. 1, 'Exponi nobis super', 12 Junho 1518; Rebello da Silva, Tom. II, pp. 47–9; ATNN, *Colleçcao de Bullas*, Maço 31, No. 19, 'Etsi com recte', 20 Agosto 1521.

2. Pastor (1), vol. VII, pp. 328–60; Roscoe (3), vol. II, pp. 83–107.

3. Kuhner, pp. 138–43; Roscoe (3), vol. I, pp. 381–90; Chamberlain, pp. 236–44.

4. Valeriano (4), p. 74, 'Simia'; Gnoli (2), pp. 631–2; Roscoe (4), vol. IV, p. 94, vol. V, pp. 274–6; Valeriano (1), p. 26,

> Sermo cui titulus est Simia, ad Leonem X,
> Ecce aiunt, vere nunc Simia vana Leonem.
> Exagitat, viden' ut turba importuna poetae!

Quam primum nostro illuxit Leo Maximus orbi,
Hunc misere alligunt quocomque in Limine.

5. Partner, pp. 142–6; Gnoli (2), vol. II, pp. 50–55, 631–2, 638–9; Mitchell, pp. 79–86; Pastor (1), vol. VIII, pp. 184–90; Avery, pp. 535, 905.

6. Gnoli (2), vol. II, pp. 643–4; Pastor (1), vol. VIII, pp. 149–51.

7. Hibbert, pp. 229–30; Roscoe (4), vol. II, pp. 176–82, 376–8, 392; Pastor (1) vol. VII, pp. 92–3, vol. VIII, pp. 149–57; Paschini, vol. XII, pp. 431–2.

8. Guarico (1); Guarico (2); Guarico (3); Rodocanachi (2), p. 340; *Biographie Universelle*, vol. XXIII, p. 326; Brosch, pp. 97, 323; Sanuto, vol. XI, p. 776.

9. Pico della Mirandola (2), '*Iohannis Francisci Pici Mirandolae et Concordiae Comitis, Oratio ad Leonem X et concilium Lateranense de reformandis Ecclesiae moribus*', 'Annates' – The first year's revenue of a see or benifice, paid to the pope. Before the Reformation, it had been a source of complaint from the Roman Catholic Church in England, but it was a useful source of revenue for King Henry VIII thereafter.

10. Partner, pp. 212–15; Roscoe (3), vol. II, pp. 89–107; Pastor (1), vol. VIII, pp. 21–31, 37–40, 177–81 Chamberlain, pp. 236–46.

11. Hibbert, pp. 237–9; Pastor (1), vol. VIII, pp. 59–66; Roscoe (3), vol. II, pp. 369–73.

12. Gnoli (2), vol. II, pp. 47–50, 638–44; Roscoe (3), vol. II, pp. 372–3, 505–6; Pastor (1), vol. VIII, pp. 64–5; Roscoe (4), vol. XII, pp. 41–51.

13. Roscoe (3), vol. II, pp. 370–73, 504–6; Gnoli (3), pp. 309–29.

14. Pecchiai, pp. 5–8; Gnoli (3), pp. 378–83; Pastor (1), vol. VIII, pp. 65–70; Roscoe (3), vol. II, pp. 370–71.

15. Pecchiai, pp. 8–20; Symonds, vol. I, pp. 221–2, Kuhner, pp. 149–50.

16. Burckhardt, pp. 99–100; Symonds, vol. I, p. 222.

17. Pecchiai, pp. 21–9, 422–39; Young, pp. 341–61; Pastor (1), vol. VII, pp. 8–11; Symonds, vol. I, pp. 222–4, vol. II, pp. 523–30; Avery, pp. 250–53.

18. Burckhardt, pp. 77–9; Symonds, vol. I, pp. 222–4, vol. II, pp. 532–3; Gnoli (3), pp. 330–37; Gregorovius (1), vol. VIII, p. 644.

19. Penrose, pp. 66–7, 155–62; Parry, pp. 258–74; Boxer, pp. 228–43.

20. Pastor (3), vol. IV, parte I, p. 48; Redig de Campos (4), pp. 203–11.

21. Pope, Book II, lines 13–16, p. 231.

22. Popham, pp. 186–9.

23. Popham, pp. 186–87; Loisel, pp. 234–5.

24. Juan de San Geronimo, Tome VII.

25. Popham, pp. 186–91; Massing, 'Depiction', p. 47.

26. Gigli, p. 112.

27. Evelyn, passim.

28. Parsons, pp. 523–6, 537, 539; Clarke (2), pp. 113–14; Clarke (2) part II, pp. 113–14.

29. Pepper, pp. 59–60.

30. Baldassari, vol. I, pp. 175–6.

31. BAV, *Cod. Barb. lat. 2273*, Fr. Novellus, 'Vita Leonis X', fol. 11ʳ.

32. Baldassari, vol. I, pp. 175–80; Ciutiis, pp. 55–6.

33. Ciutiis, pp. 56–7 n. 2.

34.Vasconcellos (2), pp. XVIII–CXXXVII.

35. *Catalogo Illustrado*, vol. II, p. 316; Castilho, Livro IV, cap. III, pp. 499–502; ATNN, *Arquivo Mesquitela*, Draft of an undated letter from D. Antonio da Costa to Anselmo [Ferreira Pinto].

36.ATNN, *Arquivo Mesquitela*, Letters from José [?] to Dr Fidélio de Freitas Branco; Receipt from D. Bernardo da Costa for his one-eighth share of income from the sale of the book; *Conselho Nobilarchico de Portugal*, pp. 117–20, 'O Livro do Armeiro-Mor. O Sr. Conde de Mesquitella ra seu legitimo possuidor – Revalaçoes curiosas d'aquele titular'.

37. *Catalogo*, vol. II, p. 316, Item 17.

38. ATNN, *A. S. Gavetas da Torre do Tombo. Centro de Estudos Históricos Ultramarinos*, Livro XV, pp. 8–9, Livro IV, pp. 208–11.

39. ATNN, *Inventario de Guardaroba do el-Rei D. Manuel*, fol. LXXXIII; Roscoe (3), vol. I, pp. 356–8; Symonds, vol. I, p. 524; Roscoe (4), vol.VI, pp. 137–40; BL, *Fondo Mediceo avanti Principato*, Letter from Jacopo Sannazaro in Naples to A. Seripando, 10 October 1517.

40. Mac Swiney de Mashanaglass, I, p. 34; Teles da Silva Caminha e Meneses, pp. 219–22, 253–5, 261–3, 271–2, 274–5. Mac Swiney de Mashanaglass wrote:'*parmi lesquels on remarquiat surtout une cheminée de marbre blanc ornée d'admirables sculptures que l'on attribuait au magique ciseau de Michel-Ange.*'

41.José de Melo, pp. 136, 163–4; Lino, pp. 95–6, fig. XI, Appendix, pp. 21–2; Inchbold, pp. 138–9; ATNN, *Casa das Obras*, vol. 91, 'Almoxarifado dos Reais Paços de Sintra dos Annos de 1784 ate 1787'.

42. Lino, pp. 95–6, Appendix, pp. 21–2; Battelli (3), pp. 17–18, fig. 3; Haupt (1), Band I, p. 132.

43. Haupt (1), Band I, pp. 132–3; Haupt (2), pp. 131, 136; Watson, p. 122; Battelli (1), p. 254–8; Battelli (2), pp. 291–3; Huntley, pp. 69–71; Middeldorf, pp. 107–15; [Anon.], 'Andrea Sansovino', *Civiltà*, Anno 82, vol. IV, 1931, pp. 415–29, Anno 83, vol. I, 1932, pp. 15–29, 224–36; Avery, pp. 834, 839. An exhaustive search for references to the chimneypiece in the Arquivo Nacional da Torre do Tombo included *Leitura Nova, Livros dos Extras*, vol. I; *Colleçcao Especial*, Caixa 37; *Nucleo Antigo*, vols. 705, 756, 776, 789, and 871; *Cartas Missivas*, Maços 1–14; *Corpo Chronologico*, Parte I, Maços 9–119, Parte II, Maços 34–53, and Parte III, Maços 1–14, all with negative results.

44. Letter from the late Ulrich Middeldorf to the writer, 16 October 1978. For Sansovino's drawing for the tomb of Leo X, see G. H. Huntley, *Andrea Sansovino* (Cambridge: Harvard University Press, 1935), p. 72.

45. ASR, *Archivio di Sant'Angeli al Corridori, Miscellanea,* No. 4; *Libri dei Rendiconti di Verzellino Bucca*, 1555; *Archivio della Santissima Trinità de' Pellegrini*, Piante antiche di case, fasc. 2, c. 92; Archivio dei Raccomandati del Salv., Arm. III, mazzo 1, No. 78; *Libri degli Istrumenti 1511–1546*, fols. 342–43; Adinolfi, pp. 50–51 n. 1; Gnoli, U., pp. 99–100; Rodocanachi (2), p. 319 n. 2, 320 n. 5.

46.The recovery of the bones in the Cortile della Libreria was first brought to the writer's attention in June 1977 by Carlo Salerni of the staff of the Servizio della Floreria Vaticana.

47. d'Ossat (2), p. 37; d'Ossat (1), pp. 421–34.

48. The elephant's tooth and jawbone fragments were made available to the writer for study by Dott. Rag. Walter Persegati, then Secretary-General of the Vatican's Monumenti, Musei e Gallerie Pontificie, and he also assisted in locating the precise site from which they had been recovered. The tooth and fragments were identified by Dr Frank C. Whitmore, Jr. of the Paleontology and Stratigraphy Branch of the U. S. Department of the Interior working at the Smithsonian Institution.

49. Guarducci, pp. 47–68.

APPENDIX : Additional Literary References
1. Ciutiis, p. 40n (Jo. Ja. Cipellus).
2. Ciutiis, p. 41n (Blosius); Roscoe (1), vol. VI, p. 193.
3. Ciutiis, p. 41n (P. Cursius Carpinem); Roscoe (1), vol. VI, pp. 193–4.
4. Ciutiis, pp. 4ln–42n (Lancellotus, Politus); Roscoe (1), vol. VI, pp. 194–5.
5. Ciutiis, p. 42n. (Dardanus).
6. Ciutiis, p. 42n. (Dardanus).
7. Ciutiis, p. 42n. (Porcio).

BIBLIOGRAPHY

Documents and Manuscripts

Archivio Segreto Vaticano

Johannis Burchardi, *Diarium...*, Tomus III, fols. 214, 391; Fondo Borghese, serie I, vol. 566, *Diariorum Paridi*, Tome IV, fols. 113ᵛ–114ᵛ, 115ʳ⁻ᵛ.

Introitus et Exitus Camera Apostolica, Tomus I, fol. 181ᵛ, Febbraio 27, 1506, No. DLI, fol. 229, No. DLIII, fol. 146; a mense Aprilis per totum Martium 1515, fol. 178;

Paridi de Grassi, *Diarorum*, Tomus III, fol. 227; Tomus IV, fols. 139, 154, 176ʳ⁻ᵛ, 177ʳ⁻ᵛ; Tomus V, fol. 439; Tomus VII, fols. 107, 176, 182; Tomus VIII, fols. 101ᵛ, 107, 182, 156, 171ʳ, 176, 183; Tome XII, fol. 24, Tomus 51, fol. 50ʳ, Tomus XIV, fol. 197; Tomus XI, fol. 220;

Archivio dei Maestri dei Ceremoni Pontificiali, Tomo CCLXXIII, fol. 82ᵛ, 86; Tomus CCCLXIX, fol. 105;

Brevia ad Principes, Arm. 44, Tomus V, fol. 33, 'Saepe egimus'; fol. 64ʳ⁻ᵛ, Brief Leo X to Manuel, May 11, 1514 written by Sadoleto.

Nunziatura di Portogallo Nr. 2, Estevan de Garabai, *Compendio Historial d'España*, libro 35, cap. 31, fols. 160–72, 266ᵛ, 402ʳ⁻ᵛ, 403ʳ⁻ᵛ, 915–916; '*Ex libro IX de rebus gestis Emmanuele Regis Lusitaniae, auctore Hieronimo Osorio Episcopi Silveni*'.

Brevis Leonis Minutiae 1513–1514, Sadoleto, *Brevia*, Tomo II, Nr. 255, Tomus 30, parte 2, fol. 268;

Breve del Leone X, 26 Febbraio 1514, 'Dilecto Filio Io. Baptistae Branconio Clerico Aquilano Cubiculario secreto et Familiari continuo commensali nostro';

Chron. V, Polit., Tomus 50, fol. 62;

Osorio, *De rebus*, Tomus III, Libris IX, pp. 263, 346;

Diversorum Cameralium, Tomus 69, fol. 67, 14 July 1522;

Indici Garampi, Serie Abbazie, Tomo I;

Arquivo Nacional da Torre do Tombo, Lisbon

Collecçao De Bullas, Maço 20, No. 13, 'Dum fidei constantiam'; Maço 22, No. 46, 'In Sacra Petri Sede', 14 September 1514; Maço 29, No. 6, 'Praecelsae devotionnis', 3 November 1514; Maço 34, No. 23, 'Si tua anima atque virtutis ornamenta'; Maço 36, N. 28; Maço 29, N. 3, 'Consecrauimus mors mairorum per Rom anos Pontificies'; N. 8, N. 10; Maço 21, No. 3, N. 12, 'Orthodoxe fidei nostra cura divina'; Gaveta 7, Maço 1, No. 6, 'Constanti fide'; Maço 21, No. 9, 'Vidimus quae super', 3 maio 1518; Maço 29, No. 17, 'Exponi nobis super', 12 Junho 1518; Maço 31, No. 19, 'Etsi com recta', 20 Agosto 1521;

Corpo Chronologico, Tome II, fols. 20–40, 12 January and 19 January 1510; Maço 15, doc. 5; parte I, Maços 9–119, Parte II, Maços 34–53, Parte III, Maços 1–4; Maço 35, doc. 186, 1 Dezembre 1512; Maço 53, doc. 262, 10

Dezembre 1512, Parte II, Maço 36, Documento 12; Parte I, Maço 94, Doc. N. 66; Parte I, Maço 15, doc. n. 5;

Cartas Missivas, Maços 1–4, Maço 3, doc. 72, 30 July 1512;

Corpo Diplomatico Portuguez. Relaçoes com a Curia Romana, Tomo I, p. 315, 309; part I, Maço 20, doc. 84;

Chancelaria de D. Manuel, Maço 1498, Livro 32, fol. 30, 'Pagamento *para mantimento*';

Casa forte, 'Livro dos Plantas e Monteas de todas os Fabricas das Inquisiçoes deste Reino e India ordenado por mandado do Ill.mo e Rev.mo Senhor Dom Francisco de Castro Bispo Inquisidor Geral e do Conselho Geral e do Conselho de Estado de Sua Magestade, Anno Domini 1634', pp. 33, 48;

Casa forte, Leitura Nova, 'Livro Octavo da Odiana';

Núcleo Antigo, fols. 256v, 259^{r-v}, 260^{r-v}, 261^r, 'Receita e despesa das obras que el Rey D. Manuel mandou fazer para sua casa, Anno de 1514'; vols. 705, 756, 776, 789, 871;

Arquivo Mesquitela, draft of an undated letter from D. António da Costa to Anselmo [Ferreira Pinto]; letters from José (?) to Dr Fidélio de Freitas Branco; receipt from D. Bernardo da Costa for his 1/8 share of income from the sale of the book;

Conselho Nobilarchico de Portugal, fols. 117–29, 'O Livro do Armeiro-Mor. O Sr. Conde de Mesquitela era seu legitimo possuidor – Revalaçoes curiosas d'aquele titular';

A. S. Gavetas da Torre do Tombo. Centro de Estudos Historicos Ultramarinos, Livro XV, fols. 8–9; Livro IV, fols. 208–11;

Inventario de Guardaroba de el-Rei D. Manuel, fol. LXXXIII;

Casas das Obras dos Paços Reais, Tomo 91, A'lmoxarifado dos Reais Paços de Sintra dos Annos de 1784 até 1787;'

Leitura Nova, Livros dos Extras, Tomo I;

Collecçao Especial, Caixa 37.

Archivio Gonzaga, Mantua

Est. Serie E, XXV, 3, Busta 862, letter from Guido Postumo, 13 March 1514; letter from Giovanni Piero Valeriani, 4 March 1514; letter from C. Agnello in Rome, 2 August 1516.

Archivio di Stato di Firenze

Fondo Mediceo Avanti Principato, letters from Baltassare Turini de Pescia to Lorenzo de' Medici, filza 107, No. 1, 20 March 1514, 26 March 1514, fols. 50^r, 59^v; filza 107, No. 32, 8 June 1514, No. 34, 10 June 1514, No. 38, 16 June 1514;

Guardaroba Mediceo 1553, 1561, filze 28, 36;

Archivio delle Gallerie di Firenze, Mss. 70, 71, 76, 79, 82, 98.

Archivio di Stato di Roma

Archivio di S. Spirito, Tom. 1458, cc. 24–25, vol. 1460, cc. 34–35;

Archivio di Sant'Angeli al Corridori, Miscellanea, Tom. 4, 'Libro dei Rendiconti di Verzellino Bucca, 1555';

Archivio della Santissima Trinità de' Pellegrini, 'Piante antiche di case e liti, ecc. dell'Archiconfraternità', fasc. 2, c. 92;

Archivio dei Raccomandati del Salv., Armad. III, mazzo 1, No. 78;

Libri degli Istrumenti 1511–1546, fols. 342–3.

Biblioteca Ambrosiana, Milan

Leonardo da Vinci, *Codice Atlantico, fol. 287*.

Biblioteca Apostolica Vaticana

Cod. Barb. lat. 2273, Fr. Novellus, 'Vita Leonis X', fol. 11^r;

Mss. Chigiana G.II.37, Sigismondo Tizio, 'Historiae Senenses', fols. 285^{r-v}, 287^v, 293;

Cod. Vat. lat. 2032, No. 6, 'Discorso di Diogo Pacheco;'

Cod. Urb. lat. 1023, Fra Gratia de Francia, fol. 340^v;

Cod. Ottob. lat. 2603, parte 2, 'Diario de Sebastiano de Branca de Talini [sic]', fols. 255, 263^r; parte 2, fol. 262, 270^r;

Cod. Vat. lat. 3419, fol. 60^r, 'Epigrammi di Evangelista Fausto Maddaleni de'Capodiferro sul Baraballo, D.M. Elephanti an Emanuele Lusitaniae rege Leonis X pont. max. missi;'

Cod. Vat. lat. 8598, 'Rotulus Papa Leo X, Scutiferi;'

Cod. Vat. lat. 172, 5356, 'Poema del Baraballo per il concorso di Settembre 1513 [sic]';

Cod. Urb. lat. 1641, 'Giustizie Sixtus IV al Leo X', fols. 497^r–9^v;

Cod. Barb. lat. 3552, fol. 27, [Anonymous], 'Diario', entry for Lunedi, XVI giugno 1516;

Cod. Ottob. lat. 2967, fol. 94^r, 'Epigrafo del elefante';

Cod. Barb. lat. 4410, fol. 32^r, 'Aquarello del poeta Baraballo sull-elefante'.

Biblioteca da Academia da Historia, Madrid

Ms. 12.7.2 – N. 76, fols. 178^r–9^v, 'Tratado que um criando do duque de Bragança escreveveo pera Sua Senhoria d'algunas notevees cousas que vio indo pera Roma, e de suas grandezas e indulgencias e grandes acontecimentos que laa socederam em espaco de sete anos qui i esteve.'

Biblioteca de Ajuda, Ajuda

Ms. 51.5.1, fol. 164^r, Copy of a letter from King Francis I at Saint-Germain-en-Laye to King Manuel I, undated.

Biblioteca de Evora

Cod. CX, fols. 1–4; Cod. CIII, fols. 2–20 (C. 82); Cod. CV, fols. 1–3 (C. 203).

Biblioteca del Real Monasterio di San Lorenzo, El Escorial, Madrid

Libro de deseños o dibujos de Francisco de Hollanda, fol. 31^v.

Biblioteca Laurenziana, Florence

Fondo Mediceo, letter from Jacopo Sannazaro in Naples to A. Seripando, 10

October 1517.

Biblioteca Nazionale Centrale, Florence
Cod. Strozziano 20, CL–XIII 80, 'Lettera scripta da Valentino Moravia germano a li mercanti di Nuremberg'.

Biblioteca Nazionale Marciana, Venice
Cod. Marciana lat. XII, 211, c. 28, unpublished verses by Giovanni Francesco Filomuso [Giovanni Francesco Superchio];
Ms. Lettere particolare, 'Come era morte il liofante del re di Portgallo mando a donar al Papa'.

Bibliothèque Nationale, Paris
Ms. lat. 5165, P. de Grassis, *Diarorum,* vol. II, f. 627.

Biblioteca Riccardiana, Florence
Cod. 1910, fols. 140ᵇ–3ᵇ.

Museo Correr, Venice
Cod. Cicogna 2673, (c. 1516), fols. 240ᵛ–41ʳ, 'Testamente del elefante'.

Biblioteca Universitaria, Bologna
Museo Aldrovandiano, Ms. Aldrov. 97, 'Degli Animali', cc. 585ʳ⁻ᵛ, 586ʳ; 'Tavole degli Animali', Tomo I, c. 91ʳ; *Ms. 6,* Tomo I, 'Corrispondenza tra U. Aldrovandi e Francesco Iº', passim.

Universitats-Bibliothek, Munich
Biblioteca Frisingensis, [Stephen Rosin], 'Exemplum literarum Domini Stephanus Rosin Caesarae Majestatis apud S. Sedem Sollicitatoris ad Reverendum principem D. Carolum Gurcensem, 12 mai 1516'.

Museu Nacional de Arte Antiga, Lisbon
Livro de Horas de D. Manuel I, unpaginated.

Printed Works

Académie des Sciences Morales et Politiques [Paris]. *Collection des ordnances des rois de France: Catalogue des Actes de François Iʳ.* Paris: Imprimerie Nationale, 1887–1908.

Ackerman, James S. (1). 'The Belvedere as a Classical Villa', *Journal of the Warburg and Courtauld Institutes,* vol. XIV, 1951, pp. 70–91.

— (2). *The Cortile del Belvedere. Studi e Documenti per la Storia del Palazzo Apostolico Vaticano.* Vatican City: Biblioteca Apostolica Vaticana, 1954.

Acunai, Luís Alberto. 'Un tesoro de arte colonial. La casa de Juan Vargas em Tunja', *Boletin de Historia y Antiguedades* (Bogotá), 1951, pp. 625–8.

Ademollo, A. *Alexander VI, Giulio II e Leone X ne Carnevale di Roma.*

Documenti Inediti 1499–1520. Florence: C. Ademollo L. C., Editori, 1886.

Adinolfi, Pasquale. *La Portica di S. Pietro ossia Borgo nell' Età di Mezzo.* Rome: Stab. Tip. di Marco, Lorenzo Aureli e C.ᵃ, 1859.

Albertini, Francesco. *Opusculum de Mirabilibus Novae et Veteris Urbus Romae.* Rome: n.p., 1510.

[Albuquerque, Afonso de] (1). *Cartas da Affonso de Albuquerque seguido de documentos que as elucidem…* Edited by Bulhão Pato and Lopes de Mendonça. Lisboa: Typ. de Academia Real das Sciencias de Lisboa, 1884–1903.

— (2). *The Commentaries of the Great Affonso Dalbuquerque.* Translated and Edited by W. de G. Birch. London: Hakluyt Society, 1875–83.

[Alcáçova Carneiro, Pero de]. *Relaçoes de Pero de Alcáçova Conde da Idanha sempo que sele seu pai António Carneiro servirem ad Secretarios (1515–1568).* Revised and annotated by Ernesto de Campos de Andrade. Lisbon: Imprensa Nacional, 1937.

[Aldrovandi, Ulisse]. *Catalogo dei manoscritti di Ulisse Aldrovandi a cura di Lodovico Frati con la collaborazione di Alessandro Ghigi e Albano Sorbelli.* Bologna: N. Zanichelli, 1907.

Alvisi, Edoardo. *Cesare Borgia Duca di Romagna. Notizie e Documenti Raccolti e Pubblicati.* Imola: Tip. d'Ignazio Galeati e Figlio, 1878.

Andrade, Antonio Alberto Banha de. (1). *Mundos Novos de Mundo. Panorama da difusão, pela Europa, de noticias dos Descobrimentos Geográficos Portugueses.* 2 vols. Lisbon: Junta de Investigaões do Ultramar, 1972, vol. II.

— (2). *Historia de um Fidalgo Quinhentista Português Tristão da Cunha.* Lisbon: Instituto Historico Infante Dom Henrique, 1974.

— (3). *Subsidios para a História da Arte no Alentejo.* (Published by the group of friends of Montemor-o-Novo). Lisbon: 1980.

'Andrea Sansovino a Loreto', *La Civiltà Cattolica*, Anno 82, vol. IV, 1931, pp. 415–29; Anno 83, vol. I, 1932, pp. 15–29, 224–36.

Antal, F. 'Observations on Girolamo da Carpi', *The Art Bulletin*, vol. XXX,, No. 2, June 1948, pp. 87–9.

Aretino, Pietro. *La Cortegiana.* Edited by Enrico Sampietro. Bologna: Grafiche Mignani, 1967.

Armellini, M. *Un censimento della città di Roma sotto il pontificato di Leone X.* Rome: Tipo di Roma del cav. A. Befani, 1882.

Arphe y Villafane, Joan de. *Varia Commensuraçion para la Esculptura y Architectura.* Seville: En la imprenta de Andrea Pescioni y Iuan de Leon, 1585.

Avery, Catherine B. *The New Century Italian Renaissance Encyclopedia.* New York: Meredith Corporation, 1972.

Baldassari, Msgr. Pietro. *Relazione della avversità e patimenti del glorioso Papa Pio VI negli ultimi tre anni del suo pontificato.* Rome: Tipographia Poliglotta della S. C. Propaganda Fide, 1889.

[Barillion, Jean]. *Journal de Jean Barillion (1515–1516).* Edited by P. de Vaissière. Paris: Société de l'Histoire de France, 1897.

[Barros, João de] (1). *Década Quarta da Asia de João de Barros.* Completed by Annibal Fernandes. Madrid: Na Impressao Real, 1615.

— (2). *Asia de João de Barros. Segunda Década.* Lisbon: Agencia Generale da

Colonias, 1777.

Bassani, Ezio and William B. Fagg. *Africa and the Renaissance: Art in Ivory*. New York: The Center for African Art and Prestel-Verlag, 1988.

Bassani, Ezio (1). 'Antichi avori Africani nelle collezioni Medicee', *Critica d'Arte*, 1975, No. 143, pp. 69–80; No. 144, pp. 8–23.

— (2). 'Additional Notes on the Afro-Portuguese ivories', *African Arts*, vol. XXVII, No. 3, 1994, pp. 34–5.

— (3). 'Raffaello al Tropici', *Critica d'Arte*, in press.

Battelli, Guido (1). 'A Chaminé de Sansovino no Paço de Sintra', *Illustraçao Moderna*, 6°. ano, Nr. 49, January–February 1931, pp. 254–8.

— (2). 'Chaminées Italianas da Renascença', *Illustraçao Moderna*, 6°. ano, Nr. 50, March–April 1931, pp. 291–93.

— (3). *Andrea Sansovino nell'Arte Italiana della Rinascenza in Portogallo*. Florence: Depositaria Libreria Internationale Seeber, 1936.

Bedini, Silvio A. (1). 'The Papal Pachyderms', *Proceedings of the American Philosophical Society*, vol. 125, No. 2, April 1981, pp. 75–90.

— (2). 'Metti che un Giorno al Papa Regalino un Elephante', *Airone*, No. 67, Novembre 1986, pp. 158–69.

— (3). 'E un Frate Marcio' su Roma Lanciando Maledizioi', *Airone*, vol 68, Dicembre 1986, pp. 153–63.

Belluzzi, A. and M. Tafuri. 'Giulio a Roma', in *Giulio Romano* (Exhibition catalogue). Milan: 1989.

Belon, Pierre. *Les Observations du plusieurs Singularitez et Choses Memorables*. Paris: G. Cavellat, 1555.

Beltrami, Luca (1). 'Nel Castello Sforzesco la "Sala dell'Elefante" e la "Sala Negra". Nuove indagini e nouvi documenti', *La Lettura* (Milano), 1902, pp. 1071–4.

— (2). *Il Castello di Milano sotto il Dominio degli Sforza MCCCCL–MDXXXV*. Milan: Colombo e Cordani, 1885.

Benevolo, Leonardo. 'Saggio d'interpretazione storica del Sacro Bosco', *Quaderni dell'Istituto di Storia dell'Architettura* (University of Rome), Nos. 7–8–9, Aprile 1965, pp. 61–73.

Benezit, E. *Dictionnaire critique et documentaire des Peintres, Sculpteurs, Dessinateurs et Graveurs...* Nouvelle Edition. Paris: Librairie Grund, 1976.

Berenson, Bernhard. *The Florentine Painters of the Renaissance. With an Index to Their Works*. New York: G. P. Putnam's Sons, 1909.

Beroaldo, Filippo, jun. *Ad Augustum Carminum Augustum Trivultum cardinalum...* Rome: Ant. Baldus, 1530. Libri III.

Bini, I. 'L'elefante Annone protogonista di una grande ambasceria a papa Leone X', *Gazzetta di Mantova*, 5 November 1976, pp. 34–5.

Biographie Universelle. Paris: Michaud Frères, 1811–62.

Bofitto, Giuseppe. 'L'occhiale e il cannochiale del Papa Leone X', *Atti dell' Accademia Reale delle Scienze di Torino*, vol. 62, 1897, pp. 555–61.

Borgatti, Mariano. *Castel Sant Angelo in Roma*. Rome: La Libreria dello Stato, 1929.

Bourdignes, Jehan de. *Chroniques d'Anjou et du Maire...* Angers: Impr. de

Cosnier et Lachese, 1842.

Boxer, Charles R. *The Portuguese Seaborne Empire 1415–1825*. New York: Alfred A. Knopf, 1969.

Branca Tedallini, Sebastiano de. *Diario romano dal 3 maggio 1485 al 6 giugno 1524*. Edited by P. Piccolomini. Città di Castello: Lapi, 1907.

Brasio, Antonio. 'Embaixada do Congo a Roma em 1514?' *Studia. Revista Semestral*, vol. 32, June 1971, pp. 51–87.

Brito, Gomes de. 'Os pachidermes do Estado d'El Rei D. Manuel', *Revista de Educaçao e Ensino* (Lisbon), vol. IX (1894), p. 81.

Brosch, Moritz. *Papst Julius II*. Gotha: F.A. Perthes, 1878.

Bruschi, Armaldo. 'L'abitato di Bomarzo e la Villa Orsini', *Quaderni dell'Istituto di Storia dell'Architettura*, Nos. 7–8–9, Aprile 1965, pp. 3–18.

Bryan, Michael. *Biographical and Critical Dictionary of Painters and Engravers. A New Edition Revised…* by George Stanley. London: H. G. Bohn, 1849.

Bulgari, Constantino G. *Argentieri, Gemmari e Orafi d'Italia. Notizie storiche raccolta dei loro contrasegni con la riproduzione gráfica dei punzioni individuali e dei punzioni di stato*. Rome: L. del Turco, 1958–9.

Burckhardt, Jacob. *The Civilization of the Renaissance in Italy*. Oxford: Phaidon Press, 1945.

Burrow, T. *A Dravidian Etymological Dictionary*. Oxford: Clarendon Press, 1961.

Cabrita, Teresa. 'Pintura Mural de S. Pedro da Ribeira'. Unpublished manuscript. Courtesy of the Comissão Nacional para as Comemorações dos Descobrimentos Portugueses, Lisbon.

Cagnat, René. 'Les dernieres decouvertes. La première representation connu du mode d'embarquement de l'elephant au IIe siécle de notre ere', *L'Amis des Monuments et des Arts*, vol. XIV, No. 78, (ND) pp. 69–71.

[Camerario, Joachim]. *Symbolorum et Emblematum ex Animalibus Quadrupedibus Desumtorum Centuria Altera Collecta a Ioachimo Camerario…* Nuremberg: Excudebat P. Kaufmann, 1595.

Camion, Pierre. *Paris au temps de la Renaissance. Paganisme et Reforme fin du Regne de François I^r au Henri II*. Paris: Calmann-Lévy, 1936.

Campana, Augusto. 'Il Cameleonte di Leone X', *Strenna dei Romanisti*, vol. XI, 1950, pp. 225–7.

Campori, Giuseppe (1). 'Notizie inedite di Raffaello da Urbino tratte da documenti dell'archivio Palatino da Modena', *Atti delle R. R. Deputazione di Storia per le Provincie Modenesi e Parmensi*, vol. I, 1863, pp. 115–18.

— (2). *Notizie e documenti per la vita di Giovanni Santi e di Raffaello Santi*. Modena: G. T. Vincenzi e nipoti, 1870.

Cancellieri, Francesco (1). *Descrizione storico critico delle Sale Regie e delle Cappelle Paolino e Sistina del Vaticano e del Quirinale. Part e Descrizione delle Cappelle Pontificie e Cardinalizie nelle Feste di tutto l'Anno*. Rome: Presso Luigi Perego Salvioni, 1790.

— (2). *Storia de'Solenni Possessi de'Sommi Pontefici detti Anticamente Processi o Processioni dopo la Loro Coronazione della Basilica Vaticana alla Lateranense*. Rome: Presso Luigi Lazzarini, 1802.

Carrington, Richard. *Elephants. A Short Account of Their Natural History, Evolution, and Influence on Mankind.* New York: Basic Books, 1959.

Castanheda, Lopes de. *Historia de Discobrimento e Conquista da India pelos Portugueses.* Lisbon: Na Typographia Rollandiana, 1832.

Casati, Carlo. *Vicende Edilizie del Castello di Milano.* Milan: Libreria Editrice di G. Brigola, 1870.

Castilho, Júlio de. *A Ribeira de Lisboa. Descrição Historica da Margem do Tejo desde a Madre de Deus até Santos-o-Velho.* Lisbon: Imprensa Nacional, 1893.

Castro, José de. *Portugal em Roma.* Lisbon: União Grafica, 1939.

Catalogo Illustrado da Exposição Retrospectiva de Arte Ornamental… celebrada em Lisboa em 1882. Lisbon: Imprensa Nacional, 1882.

Centenario do Descobrimento da America. Memorias da Commissão Portuguesa. Lisbon: Typographia da Academia Real das Sciencias, 1892.

Cermenati, Mario (1). 'Leonardo a Roma nel Periodo Leoniniano', *Nuova Antologia,* Anno 54, Sesta seria, vol. CCII, fasc. 1136, 16 Maggio 1919, pp. 105–23.

— (2). 'Leonardo a Roma', *Nuova Antologia,* Anno 54, Sesta seria, vol. CCII, Luglio–Agosto 1919, pp. 308–31, vide p. 323.

Cesareo, Giovanni Alfredo (1). 'Pasquino e la Satira sotto Leo X. I due archipoeti', *La Nuova Rassegna,* Anno II, 1894, pp. 133–8, 187–92.

— (2). 'Papa Leone e Maestro Pasquino', *Nuova Antologia,* Seria Quarta, vol. 75, 1898, p. 201.

— (3). 'Buffoni, parasiti e cortegiani alla corte di Leone X', *Nuova Rivista Storica,* Anno VII, Genniao–Aprile 1923.

— (4). *Pasquino e la Satira in Roma. Pasquino nel Cinquecento (Il Pontficato di Leone X).* Rome: Tipografia Agostiniana, 1936.

— (5). *Pasquino e pasquinate nella Roma di Leone X.* Rome: Nella Sede della Deputazione, Biblioteca Vallicelliana, 1938.

— (6). 'Pasquino e Pasquinato nella Roma di Leone X. La formazione di Mastro Pasquino', *Miscellanea del R. Deputazione Romana di Storia Patria,* 1938, pp. 190–5.

Chalderia, Francesco. *Rerum et Regionum Indicarum per Serenissimum Emanuelem Portugallie Regem Partarum Narratio Uerissima.* Roma: M. Silber, 1514.

Chamberlain, E. R. (1). *The Bad Popes.* New York: The Dial Press, Inc. 1969.

— (2). *The Sack of Rome.* London: B. T. Batsford, Ltd. 1979.

Champlin, John Denison, Jr. *Cyclopedia of Painters and Paintings.* New York: Empire State Book Co., 1927.

'Chronique de Damien de Goes', *Le Magazin Pittoresque,* 1855, vol. XXIII, pp. 198–9.

Churchill, Sidney J. *The Goldsmiths of Rome Under the Papal Authority. Their Statutes Hitherto Discovered and a Bibliography. Papers of the British School at Rome.* London: Macmillan & Co., Ltd., 1907.

[Ciacconio, Alfonso]. *Vita et res gestae Pontificum Romanorum et S.R.C. Cardinalium an initio nascentis Ecclesiae usque ad Clementem IX P.O.M. Alphonsi Ciaconii Ordinis Praedicatorum − et aliarum opera descriptae −*

cum uberrimis notis – an Augustino Oldoino Societatis Iesu recognitae… Roma: Cura et sumptibus Philippi et Ant. de Rubeis, 1677.

Cian, Vittorio (1). 'Gioviana', *Giornale Storico della Letteratura Italiana*, vol. XVII, 1900, pp. 279–80.

— (2). 'Pasquino e pasquinate nella Roma di Leone X', *Miscellanea della R. Deputazione Romana di Storia Patria.* Rome: Nella Sede della Deputazione alla Biblioteca Vallicelliana, 1938.

Cimino, Rosa Maria, 'Un elefante alla corte dei Papi', *Atti della Accademia delle Scienze di Torino*, Classe II, vol. 118 (1983–4), pp. 72–93.

Ciseri, Ilaria. *L'Ingresso Trionfale di Leone X in Firenze nel 1515.* Florence: Leo S. Olschki Editore, 1990.

Ciutiis, Comte Salvatore de. *Une ambassade portugaise à Rome au XVIe siècle. Memoire lu au IVe Congrès Scientifique International des Catholiques à Fribourg (1897).* Naples: Etablissement typographique Michele d'Auria, 1899.

Clarke, T. H. (1). 'The Iconography of the Rhinoceros from Dürer to Stubbs. Part I. Dürer's Ganda', *The Connoisseur*, vol. 184, No. 739, September 1973, pp. 1–13.

— (2). 'The Iconography of the Rhinoceros from Dürer to Stubbs. II. The Leyden Rhinoceros', *The Connoisseur*, vol. 196, No. 743, January 1974, pp. 113–13, fig. 2.

— (3). 'A European Rhine Hunt', *The Times* (London), 25 October 1975, p. 7.

— (4). *The Rhinoceros From Dürer to Stubbs – 1515–1799.* London: Sotheby Publications, 1986.

Clough, Cecil H. 'A manuscript of Paolo Giovio's *Historiae sui Temporis Liber VII.* More Light on Ludovico degli Arrighi', *The Book Collector*, Spring 1989, pp. 27–59.

Cole, F. J. 'The History of Albrecht Dürer's Rhinoceros in Zoological Literature', in *Science, Medicine and History; Essays on the Evolution of Scientific Thought and Medical Practice Written in Honor of Charles Singer*, edited by E. Ashworth Underwood. Oxford: Oxford University Press, 1933.

Colleccion de Documentos Inedites para la Historia de España. Madrid, 1845. vol. VII, p. 368.

[Colocci, Angelo]. *Poesie Italiane, e Latine di Monsignor Angelo Colocci con Piu Notizie Intorno alla Persona di Lui, e Sua Famiglia, Raccolta dall'Abate Francesco Lancellotti.* Iesi: Presso Pietropaolo Bonelli Stampatore Pubblico Vescovile e del Sant'Uffizio, 1772.

Colonna di Stigliano, Fabio. 'L'elefante di Leone X e il Poeta Baraballo', *Roma, Rivista di Studi di Vita Romana*, Anno 1, No. 5, Maggio 1923, pp. 169–75.

Correa, Gaspar. *Lendas da India.* Lisbon: Typ. da Academia Real das Sciencias, 1858–64.

Croce, Benedetto. *Poeti e Scrittori del Pieno e del Tardo Rinascimento.* Bari: Gius. Laterza & Figli, 1958.

Cruciani, F. *Il teatro del Campidoglio e le feste romane del 1513.* Milan: Il Polifilo, 1968.

Crowe, Joseph A. and Giovanni B. Cavalcaselle. *Raphael: His Life and Works, With a Particular Reference to Recently Discovered Records and an Exhaustive Study of Extant Drawings and Pictures*. London: J. Murray, 1882–5.

Dacos, Nicole. *Le logge di Raffaello. Il tesoro di Lorenzo il Magnifico*. 2 vols. Florence: Sansoni, 1973–5.

D'Amico, John. *Renaissance Humanism in Papal Rome. Humanists and Churchmen on the Eve of the Reformation*. Baltimore: The Johns Hopkins University Press, 1983.

Davenport, Frances Gardiner. *European Treaties on the History of the United States and Its Dependencies to 1648*. Washington: Carnegie Institution of Washington, 1917.

Davidson, Colin. 'Bomarzo', *Architectural Review* (London), September 1954, pp. 178–80.

Delaunay, Paul. *La zoologie au seizième siécle*. Paris: Hermann, 1963.

Delicati, F., Armellini, M. *Il Diario di Leone X di Paride de Grassi*. Rome: Tipo della Pace di F. Cuggiani, 1884.

Delli, Sergio. *Le Strade di Roma*. Rome: Newton Compton editori, 1975.

Delumeau, J. *Catholicism between Luther and Voltaire: a new view of the Counter-Reformation*. London: Burns & Oates, 1977.

Dembeck, Hermann (Hermann Hartwig, pseud.). *Animals and Men*. Translated from the German by Richard and Clara Winston. Garden City, N.Y.: The Natural History Press, 1965.

Denker Nesselrat, C. *Raffaello nell'appartamento di Giulio II e Leone X*. Milan: 1993. 'La Loggia di Raffaello', pp. 52–4.

Dickinson, G. *Du Bellay in Rome*. Leiden: E. J. Brill, 1960.

Diffie, Bailey W. and George D. Winius. *Foundations of the Portuguese Empire 1415–1580*. Minneapolis: University of Minnesota Press, 1977.

Dodwell, H. H., ed. *The Cambridge History of India*. Cambridge: Cambridge University Press, 1929. vol. V, British India.

[Dodgson, Campbell] (1). *The Dürer Society, Fourth Series*. Introductory Notes by Campbell Dodgson. London: n.p., 1901.

— (2). *Catalogue of Early German and Flemish Woodcuts Preserved in the Department of Prints and Drawings in the British Museum*. London: The British Museum, 1903.

— (3). 'The Story of Dürer's Ganda', in *The Romance of Fine Prints*, edited by Alfred Fowler. Kansas City, Mo.: The Print Society, 1938.

Domenichi, Lodovico. *Facetie, Motti, et Burle, di diversi signori et persone private*. Venice: Appresso Domenico Farri, 1584.

Dorland's Illustrated Medical Dictionary. Philadelphia: V. B. Saunders, 1974.

Dos Passos, John. *The Portugal Story: Three Centuries of Exploration and Discovery*. Garden City, N.Y.: Doubleday and Company, Inc., 1969.

d'Ossat, Gioacchino de Angelis (1). 'Storia geologica della Campagna Romana', Roma: *Rivista di Studi e di Vita Romana*, No. 9, fasc. 7, 1931, pp. 421–34.

— (2). *La geologia del Monte Vaticano*. Vatican City: Biblioteca Apostolica Vaticana, 1953.

Du Bellay, Joachim. *Les antiquitez de Rome*. Paris: Droz, 1947.

Eisler, Robert (1). 'The Frontispiece to Sigismondo Fanti's "Triompho di Fortuna"', *Journal of the Warburg and Courtauld Institutes*, vol. X, 1947, pp. 156–7.

— (2). 'The Polar Sighting Tube', *Archives International d'Histoire des Sciences*, vol. 3, No. 6, 1949, pp. 312–32.

[Ellesmere Collection]. *Catalogue of the Ellesmere Collection. Part II. Drawings by Giulio Romano and Other Sixteenth-Century Masters*. London: Sotheby & Co., Ltd., (5 December 1972).

Encyclopedia Britannica, The New. Chicago/London: Encyclopedia Britannica, Inc. 1974, vol. 14 (Portugal).

Encyclopedia Italiana di Scienze, Lettere ed Arti. Rome: Istituto della Enciclopedia Italiana, Treccani, 1933.

Erffa, H. M. von. 'Das Program der Westportals des Pisaner Dom', *Mitteilungen des Kunsthistorischen Instituts in Florenz*, Dezember 1965, p. 92.

Espanca, Tulio. *Inventário Artístico de Portugal-Distrito Évora*. Lisbon: 1975. Vol. I, pp. 366–7.

[Evelyn, John]. *The Diary of John Evelyn*. Edited by William Bray. London: O. Newnes, 1818.

[Fabroni, Angelo]. *Leonis X. Pont Max. Vita Auctore Angelo Fabronio Academiae Pisanae Curatore*. Pisa: Escudebat Alexander Landius, in aedibus auctoris, 1797.

[Fanti, Sigismondo]. *Triompho di Fortuna di Sigismondo Fanti*. Venice: n.p., 1526.

Faria, Antonio de Portugal de. *Portugal e Italia. Ensaio de Diccionario Bibliographico*. Leorne [I. Erma]: Typographia de Raphael Giusti, 1898.

Ferino Pagden, Sylvia. 'Quattri studi di elefanti', in *Giulio Romano*, by Ernst H. Gombrich et al. Milan: Electa, 1989.

Ferrajoli, Alessandro (1). 'Ruolo della Corte di Leone X (1514–1516)', *Archivio della R. Società Romana di Storia Patria*, vol. XXXIV, fasc. III–IV, 1911, p. 389.

— (2). *Il Ruolo della corte di Leone X (Rotulus familiae Leonis X)*. Rome: R. Società Romana di Storia Patria, 1911.

— (3). *Il ruolo della corte di Leone X (1514–1516)*, edited by V. De Caprio. Rome: Bulzoni, 1984.

Ferraro, Monsignor Salvatore. *Memorie Religiose e Civili della Città di Gaeta*. Naples: R. Tipografia Francesco Giannini & Figli, 1903.

Fischel, O. *Raphaels Zeichnungen*. Berlin: Gebr. Mann, 1913.

[Fontana, Felice]. *Saggio del Real Gabinetto di Fisica e di Storia Naturale di Firenze*. Rome: Nella Stamperia di Giovanni Zempel, 1775.

Fontoura da Costa, A. *Les deambulations du Rhinoceros (Ganda) de Modofar, roi de Cambay, de 1514 a 1516*. Lisbon: Division de publication et bibliothèque Agence Générale des Colonies, 1937.

Forjaz de Sampaio, Albino. *Historia da Literatura Portuguesa Illustrada*. 4 vols. Paris/Lisbon: Aillaud & Bertrand, 1929–42.

Fowler, Alfred, ed. *The Romance of Fine Prints*. Kansas City, Mo.: The Print

Society, 1938.

Franchini, Dario A. et al. *La Scienza a Corte. Collezionismo eclettico natura e immagine a Mantova fra Rinascimento e Manierismo.* Rome: Bulzoni, 1979, pp. 94–5.

Françon, Marcel (1). 'Sur le Rhinoceros du Cinquième Livre', *Les Amis de Rabelais et de la Deviniere,* Année 1964, vol. II, Bulletin No. 3, p. 96.

— (2). 'Mentions du rhinoceros par Rabelais', *La lingue straniere,* Anno XIII, No. 2, Marzo–Aprile 1964, pp. 22–7.

— (3). 'Two Notes on "Gargantua and Pantagruel"', *The Modern Language Review,* vol. LIX, No. 3, July l964, pp. 371–4.

Friedenburg, Walter. 'Ein Rotulus Familiae Papst Leo's X', *Quellen und Forschungen aus italienischen Archiven und Bibliotheken, herausgegehen von Konigl. Preussischen Historischen Institut in Rome,* Band VI, Heft I, 1903.

Fulvio, *Antiquitates.* Translated by Ferrucci. Rome: Avperrime aeditae, 1588

Gebhart, Émile. *La Renaissance Italiene et la philosophie de l'histoire.* Paris: Librairie Léopold Cerf, 1887.

Gherardi da Volterra, Jacopo. *Appendice 3°. Il Diario della 1517.* Edited by Paolo Piccolomini. Città di Castello: Coi Tipi della Casa Editrice S. Lapi, 1904.

[Gesner, Conrad]. *Conradi Gesneri medici Tigurini Historiae animalium liber primus de quadrupedibus viviparis…* Zurich: Apud Christ. Froschoverum, 1551–87.

Giacchieri, Capt. Pietro. *Commentario sugli Ordini Equestri Esistenti negli Stati di Santa Chiesa.* Rome: Stamperia di Propaganda Fide, 1852.

Giehlow, Karl. 'Beitrage zur Entstehungsgeschichte des Getbuches Kaisers Maximilian I', *Jahrbuch d. Kunsthistorischen Sammlungen d. allerh. Kaiserhauses* (Vienna), 1899, Band XX, pp. 60, 71.

Gigli, Giacinto. *Diario Romano (1608–1670).* A cura di Giuseppe Ricciotti. Rome: Tuminelli Editore, 1930.

Gillet, Joseph E., ed. *Propalladia and Other Works of Bartolomé de Torres Naharro.* Bryn Mawr: University of Pennsylvania Press, 1943–61.

Giobbio, Msgr. A. *Lezioni di diplomazia ecclesiastica dettate nella Pontificia Accademia dei nobili ecclesiastici.* Roma: Tipografia Vaticana, 1899.

Giovannoni, Gustavo. 'Un'opera sconosciuta di Jacopo Sansovino in Roma', *Bollettino d'Arte del Ministero della P. Istruzione,* Anno XI – MCMXVII, pp. 64–81.

[Giovio, Paolo] (1). *Pauli Iouii Episcopi Nocerini Elogia Virorum bellica virtute illustrium veris imaginibus supposita, quae apud Musaeum spectantur.* Florence: In officina Laurentii Torrentini Ducalis Typographi, 1551.

— (2). *De vita Leone decimi pont. max.* Florence: Ex officina Laurentii Torrentini, 1551.

— (3). *Dialogo dell'impresse militari et amorose; de Monsignor Giovio vescovo di Nocera, con un ragionamento di Messer Lodovico Domenichi, nel medesimo soggetto.* Venice: Appresso Gabriel Giolito de'Ferrari, 1557.

—. (4). *Gli Elogi Vite Brevamente Scritte d'Huomini Illustri di Guerra Antichi e Moderni.* Translated by M. Lodovico Domenichi. Venice: Appresso Francesco

Bindoni, 1558.

— (5). *Dialogo dell'Imprese Militari et Amorose di Monsignor Giovio, Vescovo di Nocera; Et di S. Gabriel Symeoni Fiorentino. Con un ragionamento di M. Lodovico Domenichi, nel medesimo soggetto.* Lyons: Appresso Guglielmo Rouillio, 1574.

— (6). *The Worthy Tract of Paulus Jovius, Contayning a Discourse of Rare Inventions, Both Militarie and Amorous called Impresse. Whereunto is Added a Preface Contayning the Arte of Composing Them, With Many Other Notable Devices*, By Samuel Daniell. London: S. Wate[rson], 1585.

Gnoli, Domenico (1). 'Raffaello alla corte di Leone X', *Nuova Antologia*, Serie 3, vol. XIV, 16 Aprile 1888, pp. 577–97.

— (2). 'Secolo di Leone X. Le Lettere', *Rivista d'Italia*, vol. II, 1898, pp. 625–50; Vol. III, 1899, pp. 39–55.

— (3). *La Roma di Leone X. Quadri e Studi Originali Annotati e Pubblicati a Cura di Aldo Gnoli.* Milan: Editore Ulrico Hoepli, 1938.

Gnoli, Umberto. *Topografia e Toponomastica di Roma Mediovale e Moderna.* Rome: Staderini Editore, 1939.

— (2). *Alberghi ed Osterie di Roma nella Rinascenza.* Spoleto: C. Moneta, 1935.

Goes, Damião de. *Chronica do Feliçissimo Rei Dom Manuel.* Lisbon: Francisco Correia, 1567.

[Goes, Damião de]. *Chronica do Serenissimo Senhor Rei D. Manoel Escritta por Damião de Góes, e novamente dada á luz, e offercida ao Illustrissimo Senhor D. Rodrigo Antonio de Noronha, o Menezes...* Lisbon: Na officina de Miguel Manescal da Costa, 1749.

'Golden Rose, The', *The Tablet*, vol. 72, No. 2526, (October 6, 1888), pp. 523–4.

Gotti, Aurelio. *Vita di Michelangelo Buonarotti narrata con l'aiuto di nuovi documenti.* Florence: Tipografia della Gazzetta d'Italia, 1875.

Gowers, Sir William. 'Early Rhinoceros in Europe', *Country Life*, vol. 111, February 1, 1952, pp. 288–9.

Graf, Arturo. *Attraverso il Cinquecento.* Turin: Ermanno Loescher, 1888.

Grande Encyclopedia Portugueso e Brasileira. Lisbon: Editorial Enciclopedia, Lda., 1935– .

[Grassi, Paride de]. *Il Diario di Leone X di Paridi de Grassi dai Volumi Manoscritti degli Archivi Vaticani della S. Sede.* Edited by Mons. Pio Delicati and Mariano Armellini. Rome: Tipografia della Pace di F. Cuggiani, 1884.

Gray, Denis D. 'A School for Elephants', *International Wildlife*, vol. 8, No. 1 (January–February 1978), pp. 36–43.

Gregorovius, Ferdinand (1). *Geschichte der Stadt Rom im Mittelalter. Vom 5. bis zum 16. Jahrhundert.* Stuttgart: J. T. Cotta, 1875–81.

— (2). *Storia della città di Roma nel Medio-Evo.* Rome: Casa Editrice Nazionale, 1902.

Grosart, Rev. Alexander B., ed. (See Sylvester, Joshua).

Gualino, Dr. Lorenzo. 'La Fistola di Leone X', *Bollettino dell'Istituto Storico Italiano dell'Arte Sanitaria*, Anno VI, No. 3, pp. 125–9; Anno VI, No. 4, pp. 157–68.

Guarducci, Margherita, 'Antichi Elefanti in Vaticano', *Atti della Pontificia Accademia Romana di Archeologia, Rendiconti*, serie III, vol. LI–LII, (1978–9, 1979–80) [1982], pp. 47–68.

Guarico, Luca (1). *Tractatus astrologicus.*Venice: C.T. Navo, 1542.

— (2). Guarici Neapolitani. *Geophonensis Civitatensis Ep. astronomi ac astrologi Opera omnia.* Basle: n.p. 1544.

— (3). *Alli giovani ingegnosi.Trattato di Astrologia judiciaria sopra la natività degli huomini et donne composto per Luca Guarice...* Rome: Per M.Valerio Dorico, et Luigi, fratelli Bresciani, 1550.

Gubernatis, Angelo de. *Storia dei Viaggiatori Italiani nelle Indie Orientali.* Leghorn: Coi Tipi di Franc.Vigo, Editore, 1875.

[Guicciardini, M. Francesco]. *La Historia d'Italia di M. Francesco Guicciardini gentilhuomo Fiorentino: Nuovamente con somma diligenza ristampata, & da molti errori ricorretta. Con l'agiunta de'sommarij a libro per libro: & con le annotazioni in margine delle cose piu notabili: Fatte dal Reverendo Padre Remigio Fiorentino.* Venice:Appresso Nicolo Bevilaqua, 1563.

Gusman, Pierre. 'La Villa Madama prés Rome', *Gazette des Beaux-Arts*, Series 3, vol. 29, 1903, pp. 314–24.

Haan, J. C. J. Bierens de. *L'oeuvre gravé de Cornelis Cort graveur Hollandais 1533–1578.* La Haye: Martinus Nijhoff, 1948.

Hahn,Emily. *Animal Gardens.* Garden City, N.Y.: Doubleday and Company, Inc., 1967.

Haidacher, A. *Geschichte der Papste in Bildern. Eine Dokumentation zur Papstgeschichte von Ludwig Freiherr von Pastor.* Heidelberg: 1965.

Hale, John R. *Renaissance Europe. Individual and Society, 1480–1520.* New York: Harper & Row, 1971.

Hare,Augustus J. C. *Walks In Rome.* 2 vols. Philadelphia: David McKay, n.d. 17th edition.

[Hartenfels, Georg Christoph Petri von] (1). *Elephantographia Curiosa, seu, Elephanti Descriptio, Juxta Methodum et Leges Imperialis Academiae Leopoldino-Carolinae Naturae Curiosorum Adornata, Multisque Selectis Observationibus Physicis, Medicis et Jucundis Historiis Referta cum Figuris Aeneis.Authore D. Georgio Christophoro Petri ab Hartenfels.* Erfurt: Imprensis Authoris,Typ. J. H. Groschii, 1715.

— (2). *Elephantographia.* Leipzig & Erfurt:Typis & imprensis Joh. Mich. Funckii, 1723.

Hartt, Frederick (1). 'Raphael and Giulio Romano and Notes on the School of Raphael', *The Art Bulletin*, vol. XXVI, 1944, pp. 67–94.

— (2). *Giulio Romano.* 2 vols. New Haven:Yale University Press, 1958.

Haupt, Albrecht (1). *Die Baukunst der Renaissance in Portugal.* Frankfurt am Main: Heinrich Keller, 1890.

— (2). *Arquitetura da Renascenca em Portugal.* Lisbon: J. Rodrigues & Ca. [1924].

Heckscher,William S. 'Bernini's Elephant and Obelisk', *The Art Bulletin*, (Vol. no. XXIX) September 1947, p. 170.

Hergenroether, Jos. S.R.E. Cardinal. *Leonis X. Pontificis Maximi Regesta*

Gloriosa Auspiciis Leonis D. P. PP. XIII Feliciter Regnantis... Freiburg im Breislau: Sumptibus Herder, 1884.

Hofmann, Theobald (1). *Raffael in seiner Bedeutung als Architekt.* Dresden: In Kommission der Gilbers'chen Verlagsbuchhandlung, 1900.

— (2). *Raffael in seiner Bedeutung als Architekt. I. Villa Madama zu Rom.* Dresden: Gilbers, 1901.

Höfler, Constantin. 'Analecten zur Geschichte Deutschlands und Italiens. II. Italienischen Zustande gegen Ende des 15. und im Anfange des 16. Jahrhunderts', *Abhandlungen der III. Klasse der k. Bayerischen Akademie der Wissenschaften,* Band IV. Munich, 1845. Abt. 3, pp. 36–7, 56–7.

Holst, Christian von. *Francesco Granacci.* Munich: Bruckmann Verlag, 1974.

Hoogewerff, G. I. 'Documenti in parte inediti, che riguardano Raffaello ed altri artisti contemporanei', *Pontificia Accademia di Archeologia. Rendiconti,* Serie 3, vol. 21, 1945–6.

Huber, Eduard von. 'Die malerfamilie Burgkmair', *Zeitschrift des historischen Vereins für Schwaben und Neuburg,* vol. I, 1874, pp. 310–20.

Hülsen, Christian. 'Römische Antikengarten des XVI. Jahrhunderts', *Abhandlungen der Heidelberger Akademie der Wissenschaften Stiftung Heinrich Lanz. Philosoph.-historische Klasse, 4. Abhandlung,* 1917, pp. v–xiii.

Hülsen, Christian and H. Egger, eds. *Die Römischen Skizzenbucher von Maarten van Heemskerk.* Berlin: J. Bardi, 1913.

Huntley, G. Hayden. *Andrea Sansovino, Sculptor and Architect of the Italian Renaissance.* Cambridge, Mass.: Harvard University Press, 1935.

Hutten, Ulrich von (1). *Opera quae extant omnia. Collegit edidit variisque annotationibus illustravit Ernestus Josephus Herman Munch.* Berlin: Sumtibus J. C. Reimer, 1821–27.

— (2). [Attributed to]. *Epistolae obscurorum virorum aliaque aevi decimi sexti monimenta rarissima. Die Briefs der Finsterlinge an Magister Ortuinus von Deventer.* Leipzig, J. C. Hinrichssche Buchhandlung, 1827.

— (3). *Epistolae Obscurorum Virorum: The Latin Text With an English Rendering, Notes, and an Historical Introduction by Francis Griffin Stokes.* London: Chatto & Windus, 1909.

Inchbold, A. C. *Lisbon & Cintra, With Some Account of Other Cities and Historical Sites in Portugal.* London: Chatto & Windus, 1907.

Joanninensis, S. *In Miceam Monarchium Pentatheucus ad div. Clementem Medicem Pont. Max. VII.* Ancona: n.p., 1524.

Jacobilli, Lodovico. *Biblioteca Umbriae, sive de scriptoribus provinciae Umbriae.* Foligno: n.p., 1658.

Johnstonus, Joannes. *Historia Naturalis.* Amsterdam: Ionnem Iacobi Fil. Schipper, 1657.

José de Melo, Antonio Maria, Condé de Sabugosa. *O Paço de Cintra, Deseñhos de Sua Magestade a Rainha a Senhora Dona Amelia.* Lisbon: Imprensa Nacional, 1903.

Juan de San Gerónimo, Fray. *Memorias. Colleçcion de Documentos ineditos para la historia de España.* Madrid: n.p., 1845.

Killerman, S. *Dürers Pflanzen-und Tierzeichnungen und ihre Bedeutung für die*

Naturgeschichte. Strassburg: J.H.E. Heitz, 1910.

Knight, C. *The Menageries. Quadrupeds Described and Drawn from Living Subjects.* The Library of Entertaining Knowledge. London: Nattali and Bond, 1847, vol. II, pp. 5, 12–13.

Kuhner, Hans. *Encyclopedia of the Papacy.* New York: Philosophical Library, 1958.

Lacépède, Bernard Germain Etienne de la Ville-sur-Illon, Comte de and Baron Georges Léopold Chretien Frederic Dagobert Cuvier. *La Ménagerie du Museum National d'Histoire Naturelle ou les Animaux Vivants, Peints d'âpres nature, sur velin, par le citoyen Marechal, peintre du Museum, Et gravées au Jardin des Plantes… Avec une note descriptive et historiques pour chaque animal, par les citoyens Lacépède et Cuviers, membres de l'Institut.* Paris: Chez Miger, Patris, Grandcher et Dentu, An X (1801).

Lach, Donald F. (1) *Asia in the Making of Europe. Volume I. The Century of Discovery.* Chicago: University of Chicago Press, 1965.

— (2). *India in the Eyes of Europe. The Sixteenth Century.* Chicago: University of Chicago Press, 1968.

— (3). *Asia in the Making of Europe. Volume II. A Century of Wonder. Book One: The Visual Arts.* Chicago: University of Chicago Press, 1970.

— (4). 'Asian Elephants in Renaissance Europe', *Journal of Asian History*, vol. I, No. 2, 1967, pp. 133–76.

Lancetti, V. *Memorie intorno ai poeti laureati.* Milan: A spese di Pietro Manzoni, 1839.

Lanciani, Rodolfo (1). *The Golden Days of the Renaissance From the Pontificate of Julius II to that of Paul III.* Boston: Houghton Mifflin Co., 1906.

— (2), 'Notas Topographicas de Burgo Sancti Petri Saeculo XVI ex Archivis Capitolino et Urbano', *Memorie della Pontificia Accademia Romana di Archeologia*, Serie 3, vol. I, parte 1, 'Miscellanea Giovanni Battista de Rossi' (Parte Prima). Rome: Tipografia Poliglotta Vaticana, 1923.

Lang, S. 'Bomarzo', *Architectural Review* (London), June 1957, pp. 427–30.

'La rose d'or pontificiale', *Le Magazin Pittoresque*, Année IX, 1841, pp. 326–7.

[Lasinio, Carlo]. *Ornati delle Loggie del Vaticano.* Rome: Niccola de Antoni, [18?].

'Le rhinoceros du roi Emmanuel, Son triomphe et sa mort', *Le Magazin Pittoresque*, vol. 23, 1855, pp. 202–3.

Lefevre, Renato (1). 'La fontana dell'elefante', *Capitolium*, Nos. 3–4, 1951, pp. 81–90.

— (2). 'Attualità critica dell'Elefante Annone', *L'Osservatore Romano*, 24 Aprile 1957.

— (3). *Villa Madama.* Rome: Isitituto Poligrafico dello Stato, 1964.

— (4). *Villa Madama.* Rome: Editalia, n.d.

L'Église, Fernand de. 'Les entrées de souvrains d'âpres l'estampe', *L'Amateur d'Estampes*, vol. IX, No. 3, 1930, p. 87, fig. 4.

Lessing, Julius. 'Die Schwerter des Preussischen Krontresors', *Jahrbuch der Konigl. Preussischen Kunstsammlung* (Berlin), vol. XVI, 1895, pp. 103–37.

Lino, Raul. *Quatro Palavras sobre os Paços Reais da Vila de Sintra*. Lisbon: Ediçao de Valentim de Carvalho, L.ᵈᵃ, 1938.

Lloyd, Joan Barclay. *African Animals in Renaissance Literature and Art*. Oxford: Clarendon Press, 1971.

Loisel, Gustave. *Histoire des ménageries de l'antiquité à nos jours*. 3 vols. Paris: Octave Doin et fils et Henri Laurens, 1912.

L'Orte Botanico di Roma. With an Introduction by Cesare d'Onofrio. Rome: Palombi, 1975.

Lowry, Bates. 'Notes on the *Speculum Romanae Magnificentiae* and Related Publications', *The Art Bulletin*, vol. XXXIV, pp. 46–50.

Lugano, P. 'Le Tarsie di Fra Giovanni da Verona alla Camera della Segnatura nel Palazzo Vaticano', *Rivista Storica Benedettina*, Anno 3, vol. III, 1908, p. 260 n. 3, 261 n. 2, p. 262.

Luzio, Alessandro (1). 'Federigo Gonzaga ostaggio alla corte di Giulio II', *Archivio della R. Società Romana di Storia Patria*, vol. IX, 1887.

— (2). 'Isabella d'Este ne' primordi del papato di Leone X e il suo viaggio a Roma nel 1514–1515', *Archivio Storico Lombardo*, Anno XXXIII, fasc. XI, vol. 5, 30 settembre 1906, p. 163.

— (3). 'Una nuove storico di Leone X', *Corriere della Sera*, 15 Ottobre 1906.

Luzio, Alessandro and Rodolfo Renier. 'La coltura e le relazioni letterarie di Isabella d'Este Gonzaga. II. Le relazione letterarie', *Giornale Storico della Letteratura Italiana*, vol. XXIV, 1899, p. 76.

[Macchiavelli, Niccolò]. *Macchiavelli; The Chief Works and Others Translated by Allan Gilbert*. Durham, N. C.: Duke University Press, 1965.

McCurdy, Edward. *The Mind of Leonardo da Vinci*. New York: Dodd, Mead & Co., 1940.

— *The Notebooks of Leonardo da Vinci Arranged, Rendered into English and Introduced*. New York; Reynal & Hitchcock, 1939, p. 1177.

Mac Swiney de Mashanaglass, Marquis Patric. (1) *Le Portugal et le Saint-Siege. I. Les epées d'honneur envoyées par les Papes aux Roix de Portugal au XVIᵉ siécle*. Memoire lu au IVᵉ Congres Scientifique International des Catholiques a Fribourg. Paris: Alphonse Picard et fils, 1898.

— (2). *Le Portugal et le Saint-Siege. III. Les roses d'or envoyées par les Papes aux Rois de Portugal au XVIᵉ siécle*. (1904). Paris: Alphonse Picard et fils, 1905.

Madelin, Louis, ed. 'Le journal d'un habitant français de Rome au XVIᵉ siécle (1509–1540). Etude sur le Manuscript XLIII–98 de la Bibliothèque Barberini', *Melanges d'archeologie et d'histoire*, vol. XXII, 1902, pp. 277–8.

Maes, Constantino. *Curiosità di Roma*. Rome: Stabilimento Tipografico dell'Editore E. Perino, 1885.

Maffei, Giovan Pietro. *Le Historie delle Inde Orientali. Tradotte di Latino in lingua Toscana, da M. Francesco Serdonati Fiorentino*... Venice: Appresso Damian Zenaro, 1589.

Malaspina, Pasquale de' Marchesi di S. Margharita, *Rime*. Rome: Dorico, 1533. 'De l'elefante mandato dal Re di Portogallo a Papa Leone'.

Marangoni, Guido. 'Il "Portico dell'Elefante" nel Castello Sforzesco di Milano', *Rassegna d'Arte* (Rome/Milan), 1920, pp. 274–81.

Mariani, Valerio. *Il Palazzo Massimo alle Colonne*. Rome: Editrice 'Roma', n.d. [193?].

Marquand, Allan, 'A Memorial of the Entry of Leo X Into Florence', *The Burlington Magazine*, vol. XX, No. CIII, October 1911, pp. 36–8.

Marucci, V., Marzo, A. and Romano, A., eds. *Pasquinate romane del Cinquecento*. Rome: Salerno Editrice, 1983.

Massing, Jean Michel. 'Rhinoceros', in *Circa 1492. Art in the Age of Exploration*. Edited by Jay A. Levenson. New Haven: Yale University Press, 1991, p. 300.

—— 'Hans Burgkmair's depiction of native Africans', *RES*, vol. 27, Spring 1995, pp. 39–52.

Masson, Georgina. *The Companion Guide To Rome*. Fifth edition. London: Collins, 1974.

Matos, Luís de (1). 'Natura Intelletto e Costumi dell'Elefante', *Boletim Internaçional de Bibliografia Luso-Brasileira*, vol. I, 1960, pp. 44–55.

—— (2). 'Forma e natura e costumi del Rinoceronte', *Boletim Internaçional de Bibliografia Luso-Brasileira*, vol. I, No. 3, Julho–Setembro 1960, pp. 287–98.

Melho, Francisco Manuel Carlos de, Conde de Ficalho, ed. *Coloquios dos Simples e Drogas da India por Garcia da Orte*. Lisbon: Imprensa Naçional, 1891.

Mendonça, Henrique Lopez de. *Estudos sobre Navios Portuhuenzas nos Seculos XV e XVI*. Lisbon: Typographia da Academia Real das Sciencias, 1892.

Mercati, Angelo. 'Raffaello da Urbino e Antonio da Sangallo "Maestri delle Strade" di Roma sotto Leone X', *Rendiconti della Pontificia Accademia di Archeologia*, Anno 1, 1923, pp. 121–7.

Mercati, Giovanni. 'Un indice di libri offerti a Leone X', *Il Libro e la Stampa*, Anno II, Serie nuovo, fasc. 2–3, Marzo–Giugno 1908, pp. 40–45.

Middeldorf, Ulrich. 'Giuliano da San Gallo and Andrea Sansovino', *The Art Bulletin*, vol. XVI, No. 2, June 1934, pp. 107–15.

Mitchell, Bonner. *Rome in the High Renaissance. The Age of Leo X*. Norman, Okla.: University of Oklahoma Press, 1973.

Mondelli, Francesco Ant. *Qual sia della Stocca d'Ore l'origine?* Bologna: n.p., 1792.

Montini, Renzo U. and Riccardo Averini. *Palazzo Baldassini e l'Arte di Giovanni da Udine*. Rome: Istituto di Studi Romani, Editore, 1957.

Montini, Renzo U. 'Palazzo Baldassini oggi sede dell'Istituto "Luigi Sturzo"', *Capitolum*, Anno XXXII, No. 2, pp. 4–7, 14.

Morewood-Dowsett, J. *Elephants Past and Present*. London: Macmillan and Co., Ltd., 1939), pp. 3–40.

Morton, H.V. *A Traveller in Rome*. New York: Dodd, Mead and Co., 1957.

Müller, Hermann Alexander and Singer, Hans Wolfgang. *Allgemeines Kunstler-Lexikon. Leben und Werke der beruhmtesten bildenden Künstler*. Frankfurt am Main: Literarische Anstalt Rutten & Leoning, 1896.

Münster, Sebastian (1). *Cosmographia Universalis Lib. VI in quibus, iuxta certioris fidei scriptorum traditionem describuntur omnium habitabilis orbis partium situs*. Basel: Henrichus Petri, 1550.

—— (2). *La cosmographie universale, contenant la situation de toutes les parties du monde, avec leurs proprietez et appartenances.* Basle: H. Pierre, 1556.

Muntz, Eugène. (1) 'Les epées d'honneur distribuées par les Papes pendant les XIVe, XVe, et XVIe siècles', *Revue d'Art Chretien*, New series, vol.VII, No. 4, 1889, pp. 408–11; vol. XXIII, 1890, pp. 281–92.

— (2). *Les Arts à la cour des Papes.* Paris: Ernest Leroux, ed., 1898.

— (3) 'Les roses d'or pontificiales', *Revue de l'Art Chretien*, 44e année, serie 5, Tome XII, No. 1, Janvier 1901, pp. 1–11.

Muratori, L. A. *Raccolta degli Storici Italiani del cinquecento al millecinquecento. Il Diario Romano di Jacopo Gherardi da Volterra. Appendice 3°. Il Diario della 1485–1517.* Edited by Paolo Piccolomini. Città di Castello: Coi Tipi della Casa Editrice S. Lapi, 1904.

Murray, Neil. *The Love of Elephants.* London: Octopus Books, Ltd., 1976.

Nesselrath, Christiane Denker. 'La Loggia di Raffaello', in *Raffaello Nell' Appartamento di Giulio II e Leone X: Monumenti, Musei e Gallerie Pontificie.* Milan: Electa, 1993.

New Catholic Encyclopedia. The. New York: McGraw-Hill Book Company, 1967.

[Nilakantha]. *The Elephant Lore of the Hindus. The Elephant-Sport of Nilakantha.* Translated from the original Sanskrit with an Introduction, Notes and Glossary by Franklin Edgerton. New Haven: Yale University Press, 1931.

Nozing, Jacob Schrenck von. *Augustissimorum Imperatorum.* Innsbruck: Excudebat Ioannes Agricola, 1601.

Oberhuber, Konrad. 'Putti sull' elefante, stucco nella volta della camera delle Aquila', in Ernst H. Gombrich et al, *Giulio Romano.* Milan: Electa, 1989.

Odelscalchi, E., 'L'arte dell'intaglio e della tarsia e Fra Giovanni da Verona a proposito d'una recente pubblicazione', *Rivista Storica Benedettina*, Anno I, 1906, pp. 218, 224.

[Oliveira Martins, Joaquim Pedro de] (1). *Obras Completas de Oliveira Martins. Historia de Portugal.* Edited by Dr. J. Franco Machado. Lisbon: Viuva Bertrand & Ca. 1886; Guimarae & C^a. Editores, 1951.

— (2). *Historia de Portugal.* Lisbon: Viuva Bertrand & C^a, 1886.

Olmi, Giuseppe (1). *Ulisse Aldrovandi Scienza e Natura nel Secolo Cinquecento.* Trento: Università di Trento, n.d.

— (2). *Osservazione della natura e raffigurazione in Ulisse Aldrovandi.* Trento: Università di Trento, n.d.

Onori, L. 'L'Elefante Annone e il Poetà Baraballo', *La Lettura* (Milan), Anno X, Dicembre 1910, pp. 1143–6.

Osorio, Jerónymo (1). *De rebus Emmanuelis regis Lusitaniae.* Olysippone: Apud Antonium Gondisaluum, 1571, pp. 345–7.

— (2). *De rebus Emmanuelis, Lusitaniae Regis Invictissimi, Virtute et Auspicio Domi Forisque Gestis.* Coimbra: Ex Typis Academico-Regin, 1791.

— (3). *The History of the Portuguese, During the Reign of Emmanuel...* Now first translated into English by James Gibbs. London: For A. Miller, 1752.

Osorio, João de Castro (1). *O Além-mar na Literatura Portuguesa.* Lisbon: Ediçoes Gama, 1948.

—, compiler (2). *Cancioneira de Lisboa.* 3 vols. Lisbon, 1956.

Paccagnini, G. *Il Palazzo del Tè*. Milan: A. Fattorini, 1957.

Pace, Giovanni Maria. 'Il barrito di Annone', *La Reppublica* (Rome), 8 January 1989.

[Pacheco, Diogo]. *Epistola Potentissimi ac Invictissimi Emanuelis Regis Portugallie y Algarbioru & De Victoriis nuper in Affrica habitis. As S. in xpo patrem y dum nostrum dum Leone X. Pont. Max.* Rome: Marcellus Silber, 1513.

[Pacheco, Diogo]. *Emmanuelis Lusitan: Algabior: Africae Aethiopiae Arabiae Persiae Indiae Reg. Invictiss. Obedientia.* Rome: Eucharius Silber, 1514.

Palm, Erwin Walter. 'Dürer's Ganda and a XVI Century Apotheosis of Hercules at Tunja', *Gazette des Beaux-Arts*, vol. XLIX, No. 48, November 1956, pp. 67–74.

Panofsky, E. *The Life and Art of Albrecht Dürer*. Princeton: Princeton University Press, 1955.

Pansa, Giovanni (1). 'Le relazioni di Raffaello con G. B. Branconio…', *Arte e Storia*, Serie V, vol. XXX, No. 8, 15 Agosto 1911.

— (2). 'Raffaello d'Urbino e Giambattista Branconio dell'Aquila', *Arte e Storia*, vol. XXXIX, 1920.

Parry, John H. *The Age of Reconaissance*. New York: The New American Library, 1964.

[Parsons, James], 'A Letter from Dr. James Parsons, M.D., F.R.S., To Martin Folkes, Esq.; President of the Royal Society, containing the Natural History of the Rhinoceros', *Philosophical Transactions of the Royal Society of London*, No. 470, 21 April 23 June 1743, pp. 523–6, 537, 539.

Partner, Peter. *Renaissance Rome 1500–1599. A Portrait of A Society.* Berkeley, Cal.: University of California Press, 1976.

Partridge, Loren and Starn, Randolph. *A Renaissance Likeness: Art and Culture in Raphael's Julius II.* Berkeley, Cal.: University of California Press, 1979.

Paschini, P. (1). 'Da Ripetta a Piazza del Popolo', *Roma*, vol. III, 1925, pp. 409–13.

— (2). *Roma nel Rinascimento.* Volume XII of the series *Storia di Roma*, Istituto di Studi Romani. Bologna: Licinio Cappelli, 1940.

Passavant, Johann D. (1). *Raphael of Urbino and His Father Giovanni Santi.* London: Macmillan and Co., 1872.

— (2). *Raffaelle d'Urbino e il padre Gio. Santi.* Translated into Italian by G. Guasti. Florence: Successori Le Monnier, 1882–1889.

Pastor, Baron Ludwig von (1). *The History of the Popes From the Close of the Middle Ages.* Volume VII. Edited and translated by Ralph Francis Kerr. London: B. Herder, Kegan Paul, Trench, Trubner & Co., 1908.

— (2). *The History of the Popes From the Close of the Middle Ages.* Volume IV. Translated by Frederick Ignatius Antrobus. St. Louis, Mo.: B. Herder & Co., 1923.

— (3). *Storia dei Papi dalla fine del Medio Evo.* Volume IV. Translated into Italian by Angelo Mercati. Rome: Descles & C^i. Editori Pontifici, 1945.

Pecchai, Pio. *Roma nel Cinquecento.* Volume XIII of the series *Storia di Roma*, Istituto di Studi Romani. Bologna: Licinio Capelli, 1948.

Pedretti, Carlo, 'Spigolatura nel Codice Atlantico', *Bibliothèque de Humanisme et Renaissance, Traveaux et Documents* (Geneva), Tome XXII, 1960, pp. 530–31.

Pelli, Giuseppe Bencivenni. *Saggio Istorico della Real Galleria.* Florence: n.p., 1779.

Pellizzari, Achille. *Portogallo e Italia nel secolo XVI. Studi e ricerche storiche e letterarie.* Naples: Società Editrice F. Perrella E. C., 1914.

Penni, Giovanni Giacomo (1). *Croniche delle magnifiche & honorate Pompe fatte in Roma per la Creatione & Incoronatione di Papa Leone X Pont. Max.* Rome, 27 July 1513.

[— (2)]. *La Victoria de lo Serenissimo ed invictissimo Emanuele Re de Portgallo, ec. hauta novamente contra Mori: e la presa de Azamor e de Almedina e altre terre nel regno de Marrochia. In Rima. Forma e natura de lo Rinoceronte stato condutto in Portogallo dal Capitano de larmata del Re e altre belle cose condutte dalle insule novamente trovate.* Rome: In casa de Mastro Stephano Guilireti, 3 luglio 1515. *J. J. de Pennis faciebat Rima.*

Penrose, Boise. *Travel and Discovery In the Renaissance 1420–1620.* Cambridge, Mass.: Harvard University Press, 1967.

Pepper, Curtis G. *The Pope's Back Yard.* New York: Farrar, Straus & Giroux, 1966.

Philomathes [pseud.]. *Natura Intellecto & costumi de lo Elephante cauato da Aristotele Plinio e Solino: & alcuni exempli de esso Elephante; insieme con un Capitulo de defectiui de natura in Rima.* Rome: Stefano Guillery, (Manuscript, n.p., n.d., unpaginated; c. 1514.

Picca, Paolo. 'Dall'antico "Vivarium" al moderno Giardino Zoologico', *Nuova Antologia,* 1.° Gennaio 1911, pp. 133–49. Figure 20.

Pico della Mirandola, Giovanni Francesco (1). *Opera Omnia.* Basle: Sebastian Henrichum Petri [1601].

— (2). *Discursus Epistolares Politico-Theologici.* Frankfurt: n.p., 1610.

Pierlasi, S. *Inventarium Codicum mss.* Roma: N.D.

Pliny the Younger. *Natural History.* Translated by H. Rackham. Cambridge, Mass.: Harvard University Press, 1967.

Pope, Alexander. *Dunciad.* In *The Complete Poetical Works of Alexander Pope.* Boston/New York: Houghton Mifflin Company, 1931.

Pope-Hennessy, Sir John. *Italian High Renaissance and Baroque Sculpture.* New York: Phaidon Press, 1972.

Popham, A. E. (1). 'Elephantographia', *Life and Letters,* vol. V, No. 27, August 1930.

Popham, A. E. and Johannes Wilde. *The Italian Drawings of the XV and XVI Centuries.* London: Phaidon Press, 1949.

Portoghesi, Paolo, 'Nota sulla Villa Orsini di Pitigliano', *Quaderni dell'Istituto di Storia dell'Architettura,* Nos. 7–8–9, Aprile 1965, pp. 74–6.

Rabelais, François. *The Histories of Gargantua and Pantagruel.* Translated by J. M. Cohen. Harmondsworth: Penguin Books, 1955.

Rackham, Bernard. *Catalogue of Italian Maiolica.* London: Victoria and Albert Museum, 1940.

Ramusio, G. B. *Navigazione e Viaggi*. 2 vols. Turin: N.P. 1979.

Rapp, Francis. *L'Église et la vie religieuse en Occident a la fin du Moyen Age.* Paris: Presses Universitaires de France, 1971.

Ray, John. *Synopsis Animalium*. London: O. Newnes, 1818.

Raynauldus, O. *Annales Ecclesiastes*. Luques: n.p., 1755.

Rebelo da Silva, Luís Augusto. *Corpo Diplomatico Portuguez Contendo os Actos e Relações Politicas e Diplomaticas de Portugal com as Diversas Potencias do Mundo desde o Seculo XVI até os Nossos Dias.* Publicado de Ordem da Academia Real das Sciencias de Lisboa. Lisbon: Typographia de Ordem da Academia Real das Sciencias, 1897.

Redig de Campos, Dioclecio (1)... *L'Illustrazione*, vol. III, 1932, pp. 33–36.

— (2). 'Notizie di Palazzo Baldassini', *Bolletino del Centro di Studi per la Storia della Architettura*, 1957, No. 10, pp. 4, 14.

— (3). 'Palazzo Baldassini', *L'Osservatore Romano*, 26 February 1956.

— (4). *I Palazzi Vaticani*. Bologna: Casa Editrice Licinio Cappelli, 1967.

Reeves, Marjorie. *The Influence of Prophecy in the Later Middle Ages*. Oxford: Clarendon Press, 1969.

[Resende, Garcia de]. *Chronica de Dom João II. Miscellanea. Conforme a edição de 1622.* Lisbon: Escriptorio, 1902.

Reumont, A. von. *Geschichte der Stadt Röm*. Berlin: R.V. Decker, 1870.

Rivera, Luigi. 'Raffaello e varie memorie attinenti all'Abruzzo e a Roma (con documenti inediti del sec. XVII)', *Bolletino del R. Deputazione Abruzzese di Storia Patria*, vols. XI–XIII, 1922.

Robinson, Sir J. C. *A Critical Account of the Drawings by Michelangelo and Raffaelle in the University Galleries, Oxford.* Oxford: Clarendon Press, 1870.

Rodocanachi, Emmanuel Pierre (1). *Le Chateau Sainte-Ange. Traveaux de Defense, Appartements des Papes, Sieges, Prisonniers, Executions, le Tresor.* Paris: Librairie Hachette et Cie, 1909.

— (2). *La première Renaissance. Rome au temps de Jules II et de Leon X.* Paris: Librairie Hachette & Cie, 1912.

— (3). *Histoire de Rome. Le pontificat de Leon X (1513–1521).* Paris: Librairie Hachette et Cie, 1931.

Rogers Francis M., ed. (1). *The Obedience of a King of Portugal.* Translated, with commentary, by Francis M. Rogers. Minneapolis: University of Minnesota Press, 1958.

— (2). 'Victory at Azemour', *Miscellanea de Studos a Joaquim de Carvalho*, No. 5, 1960, pp. 445–56.

— (3). *The Quest For Eastern Christians. Travel and Rumor in the Age of Discovery.* Minneapolis: University of Minnesota Press, 1962.

Romano, Angelo. (1.). 'Il testamento dell'elefante attribuito a Pietro Aretino', *Filologia e Critica*, Anno XIII, fasc. 3, Settembre–Dicembre 1988, pp. 405–24.

— (2). *Periegesi Aretiniane. Testi, Schede e note Biografiche intorno a Pietro Aretino.* Rome: Salerno Editrice, 1991.

Romano, Francesco Maria Torriggio. *Historica narratione della chiesa parrochiale et archiconfraternità del Santissimo Corpo di Christo posto in S. Giacomo*

Apostolo in Borgo. Roma: Per Lodovico Grignani, 1649.

Romano, Pietro. *Pasquino e la Satira in Roma: Pasquino nel Cinquecento. (Il Pontificato di Leone X).* Rome: Tipografia Agostiniana, 1936.

Rookmaaker, L. C. (1). 'Captive Rhinoceros in Europe from 1500 until 1810', *Bijdragen Tot de Dierkunde,* Allevering 43, Nummer 1, 1973, pp. 39–44.

— (2). 'Two collections of rhinoceros plates compiled by James Douglas and James Parsons in the eighteenth century', *Journal of the Society of Bibliography of Natural History,* vol. I, 1978, pp. 20–22.

— (3). *Bibliography of the Rhinoceros. An Analysis of the Literature on the Recent Rhinoceros in Culture, History and Biology.* Rotterdam: Balkema, 1983.

Roscoe, William (1). T*he Life and Pontificate of Leo the Tenth.* 4 vols. Philadelphia: Printed at the Lorenzo Press of E. Bronson, 1806.

— (2). *Vita e pontificato di Leone X di Guglielmo Roscoe...* Tradotta e corredata di annotazioni e di alguni documenti inediti dal Conte Cav. Luigi Bossi Milanese... 12 vols. Milan: Dalla Tipografia Sonzogno e Comp., 1817.

— (3). *The Life and Pontificate of Leo the Tenth.* 4 vols. Second Edition, Corrected, with Notes by Henke, Translated from the German Into English. Heidelberg: Printed for Joseph Engelmann, 1828.

— (4). *The Life and Pontificate of Leo the Tenth.* Sixth edition, revised by his son Thomas Roscoe. 2 vols. London: Henry G. Bohn, 1853.

Ross, D. H., ed. *Elephant – The Animal and Its Ivory in African Culture.* Los Angeles, 1992.

Rossi, Vittorio. (1). 'Un elefante famoso', *Intermezzo,* vol. I, 1890, pp. 629–48.

— (2). *Pasquinate di Pietro Aretino ed anonimo per il conclava e l'elezione di Adriano VI.* Palermo: n.p., 1891.

— (3). *Dal Rinascimento al Risorgimento.* Florence: G. C. Sansoni, 1930. (testament – vol. 2 pp. 223–42).

Ruffi, Antoine de. *Histoire de la ville de Marseille, contenant tout ce qui s'y est passé de plus memorable depuis sa fondation, durant le temps qu'elle à este republique, & soubs la domination des Romains, Bourguignons, Visigoths, Ostrogoths, roys de Bourgongne, vicomtes de Marseille, comtes de Provence, et de nos roys tres-chrêtiens...* Marseille: Par C. Garcin, 1642.

Sainean, L. (1), 'L'Histoire naturelle dans l'oeuvres de Rabelais', *Revue du seizieme siécle,* vol. III, 1915, pp. 222–23.

— (2). *La langue de Rabelais.* Paris: E. De Boccard, Editeur, 1922.

Salerno, Luigi, 'Disegni inediti di Tiziano e lo studio d'Alfonso d'Este', *Commentari, Rivista di Critica e Storia dell'Arte,* Anno 3, No. 3, 1954, pp. 198–200.

Sampião, Albino Forjaz de. *Historia da Literatura Portuguesa Illustrada.* Paris/Lisbon: Aillaud & Bertrand, n.d.

Santarem, Visconde de and Luís Augusto Rebelo da Silva. *Quadro elementar das relaçoes politicas e diplomaticas de Portugal.* Paris: J. P. Aillaud, 1842–60.

Santos, Luis Reis. *Estudos de Pintura Antiga.* Lisboa: n.p., 1943.

Santos, Reynaldo dos. *Oito Seculos de Arte Portuguesa Historia e Espirito.* Lisbon: Imprensa Naçional de Publicidade, 1970.

[Sanuto, Marino]. *Diarii di Marino Sanuto*. 58 vols. in 35; Venice: A Spese degli Editori, 1881–7.

— *I Diarii di Marino Sanuto (MCCCCXLVI–MDXXXIII)*... pubblicati per cura di Renaldo Fulin, Federigo Stefani, Nicolo Barozzi, Guglielmo Berchet, Marco Allegri, auspice la R. Deputazione Veneta di Storia Patria. 58 vols. Venice: F. Visenti, 1879–1903.

Sartorelli, Gabriele. 'Un Amico di Raffaello', *Nuova Antologia*, No. 2085, September 1974, pp. 79–86.

Saxl, F., 'The Classical Inscription in Renaissance Art and Politics', *Journal of the Warburg and Courtauld Institutes*, vol. IV, 1940–41, pp. 38–9.

Schafer, Heinrich. *Geschichte von Portugal*. Hamburg: F. Perthes, 1836–54.

Schaffer, K. N. *Die Ausgaben der Apostol Kammer unter Benedikt XII...* 1914.

Schiel, Gustav. *Die Tierwelt in Luther's Bildersprache in seinen reformatorisch-historischen und polemischen deutschen Schriften*. Bernburg: n.p., 1897.

Schottus, A. *Hispaniae illustratae seu rerum urbiumque. Hispaniae, Lusitaniae, Aethiopiae et Indiae scriptores varii. Partim editi nunc primum, partim aucti da ementalqueati, quorum seriem se quem post praefationem pagina exhibet Tomis aliquot divisi, opera et studio doctorum hominum*. Frankfurt: Apud Claudius Marnium et haeredes Iohannis Aubrij, 1603.

Segurado, Jorge. *Francisco d'Ollanda*. Lisbon: Edit. Excelsior, 1970.

[Serao, M. Francesco]. *Opuscoli di Fisica Argomentato. I. Descrizione dell'Elefante*. Naples: Per Giuseppe de Bonis, 1766.

[Sereno, Aurelio]. *Theatrum Capitolinum Magnifico Juliano institutum per Avrelium Serenum Monopolitanum et de elephante carmen eiusdem*. Rome: In aedibus Mazochianis imperante diuo Leone X Pont. Maximo pontificatus sui anno secundo, anno domini 1514.

Shearman, John (1). 'The Vatican Stanze: Functions and Decoration', *Proceedings of the British Academy*, vol. LVII, 1971, pp. 369–424.

— (2). 'The Florentine Entrata of Leo X, 1515', *Journal of the Warburg and Courtauld Institutes*, vol. 38, 1975, pp. 152–5.

— (3). 'Alfonso d'Este's Camerino', in *Il se rendit en Italie – Etudes offertes à André Chastel*. Paris: 1987.

Shufeldt, R. W. 'Scientific Taxidermy for Museums (Based on a Study of the United States Government Collections)', *Annual Report of the Board of Regents of the Smithsonian Institution, Showing the Operations, Expenditures, and Condition of the Institution for the Year Ending June 30, 1892. Report of the U. S. National Museum*. Washington, D.C.: U. S. Government Printing Office, 1893, p. 371n.

Silva Rego, Antonio de. *Le Patronage Portugais de l'Orient Aperçu Historique*. Translated from the Portuguese by Jean Haupt. Lisbon: Agencia Geral do Ultramar, 1957.

Solmi, Edmondo (1). 'Il Trattato di Leonardo da Vinci sul linguaggio "De vocie"', *Archivio Storico Lombardo*, Serie quarta, Anno XXXIII, fasc. XI, 30 Settembre 1906, pp. 68–98.

— (2). *Leonardo (1452–1519)*. Milan: Longanesi & Cie, 1971.

Solomon, Richard, 'A Trace of Dürer in Rabelais', *Modern Language Notes*, vol. LVIII, No. 7, November 1943, pp. 498–50l.

Soman, W. Z. *The Indian Dog*. Bombay: Popular Prakashan, 1963.

[Spenser, Edmund]. *The Complete Works of Edmund Spenser. With an Introduction by William P. Trent*. New York: Thomas Y. Crowell Company, 1903.

Spinazzola, Vittorio, 'Di un rinoceronte marmoreo del Museo Nazionale di Napoli', *Bollettino d'arte*, vol. VII, 1913, pp. 143–6.

Stephens, Henry Morse (1). *The Story of Portugal*. New York: G. P. Putnam's Sons, 1891.

— (2). *Albuquerque*. Oxford: Clarendon Press, 1892.

[Stokes, Francis Griffin, ed.]. *Epistolae Obscurorum Virorum: The Latin Text With an English Rendering, Notes, and an Historical Introduction by Francis Griffin Stokes*. London: Chatto & Windus, 1909.

Suida, W. E. *Raphael*. Oxford: Phaidon Press, 1948.

[Sylvester, Joshua]. *The Complete Works of Joshua Sylvester; for the first time collected and edited; with a memorial introduction, notes and illustrations, glossarial index, etc., etc., by the Reverend Alexander B. Grosart*. Edinburgh: Printed for private circulation [by T. and A. Constable], 1880.

Symonds, John Addington. *Renaissance in Italy*. 2 vols. New York: Charles Scribner's Sons, 1898–1900.

[Tasso, Torquato] (1). *I Dialogi di Torquato Tasso*. A cura di Cesari Guasti. Florence: Felice Le Monnier, 1839, 'Il Conte o Vero l'Impresse'.

— (2). *Jerusalem Delivered*. Introduction by Robert Weiss. London: Centaur Press, 1962.

Teles da Silva Caminha e Meneses, Marques de Resende, Antonio, 'Embaixada de El-Rei D. Manuel ao Papa Leão X', *O Panorama, Journal Litterario e Instructivo*, Terço da Terceira Serie, vol. XI, 1854, pp. 219–22, 253–5, 261–3, 271–2, 274–5.

Thieme, Ulrich and Fred C. Willis. *Allgemeines Lexikon der Bildenden Kunstler von der Antike bis zur Gegenwart Begrundet von Ulrich Thieme und Felix Becker*. Leipzig: Verlag E. A. Seeman, 1921.

Tommasini, Oreste. 'Evangelista Maddaleni de' Capodiferro accademico… e storico', *Atti della R. Accademia dei Lincei*, Anno CCLXXXIX, Seria Quarta, vol. X, Parte I, 1893, p. 8.

Toni, Giambattista de. *Piante e gli Animali in Leonardo da Vinci*. Bologna: Nicola Zanichelli, 1922.

Topsell, Edward. *The Historie of Four-Footed Beasts and Serpents and Insects*. London: Printed for E. Cotes for George Sawbridge, 1658.

Tormo, Elias. *Os desenhos das antigualhas que vio Francisco d'Ollanda pintor Português (…. 1539–1540…)*. Publicados con notas de estudio y preliminares, del Prof. E. Tormo. Madrid: Relaçiones Culturales, 1940.

Torriggio, Francesco Maria. *Historica Narratione della Chiesa Parocchiale et Archiconfraternità del Santissimo Corpo di Christo Posto in S. Giacomo Apostolo in Borgo*. Rome: Per Lodovico Grignani, 1649.

Truc, Gonzague. *Leon X et son siécle*. Paris: Éditions Bernard Grasset, 1941.

Valeriano, Giovanni Piero (1). *Poesie*. Ferrara: n.p., 1550.

— (2). *Hieroglyphica, sive de Sacri Aegyptiorum aliarumque gentium literis,*

Commentarium Libri LVIII cum duobus alijs ab eruditissimo viro annexis. Basle: Palma Ising, 1556.

— (3). *Hieroglyphica, sive de sacris Aegyptiorum aliarumque gentium literis, Commentariorum Libri LVIII cum duobus alijs ab eruditissimo viro annexis.* Frankfurt: Sumptibus Antonij Hierati, escudebat Erasmus Kempffer, 1614.

— (4). *De Literatorum infelicitate.* Amsterdam: Apud Cornelium Joannis, 1647.

— (5). *La Infelicità dei letterati... aggiuntovi dialogo del Valeriano sulle lingue volgari.* Milan:Tipografia Malatesta, 1829.

Van Gulik, G. and Eubel, C. *Hierarchia Catholica Medii et Recentioris Aevi,* edited by L. Schmitz-Kallenberg. Monasterii: Sumptibus et Typis Lub, Regensbergianae, 1923, vol. III.

[Vasari, Giorgio] (1). *Le Vite de' piu eccellenti pittori, scultori, ed architettori scritte da Giorgio Vasari pittore Aretino con nuove annotazione e commenti di Gaetano Milanesi.* Florence: G. C. Sansoni, 1906.

— (2). *Lives of the Most Eminent Painters, Sculptors, and Architects.* Translated by Gaston Du C. de Vere. London: P. L. Warner, 1912–14.

— (3). *Lives of the Most Eminent Artists, Sculptors, and Architects.* Translated by Gaston Du C. de Vere. NewYork: Harry N. Abrams, Inc., 1979.

Vasconcellos, Joaquim de (1). 'Os desenhos de Francisco de Hollanda', *O Archeologo Português,* vol. II, No. 2, Fevereiro 1896, pp. 42–43, 47.

— (2). *Francisco de Hollanda. Vier Gespräche über die Malerei geführt an Röm 1538.* Vienna:Verlag von Carl Graeser, 1899.

[Vicente, Gil]. *Four Plays of Gil Vicente.* Edited by A. F.G. Bell. Cambridge: Cambridge University Press, 1920.

Vilhena Barbosa, Ignácio de. *Apontimentos para a Historia das Collecções e dos Estudos de Zoologia em Portugal.* Lisbon: Typ. de Christovão Augusto Rodrigues, 1885.

Vollmer, H., B. C. Kreplin, J. Muller, I. Scheewe, H. Wolff, C. Kellner. *Allgemeines Lexikon der Bildenden Kunstler von der Antike bis zur Gegenwart.* Leipzig:Verlag von E. A. Seeman, 1928.

Wadding, Luke. *Annales Minorum.* Grottaferrata: Quaracchi, 1933.

Watson, Walter Crum. *Portuguese Architecture.* London:Archibald Constable and Company, 1908.

Winner, Matthias (1). 'Raffael malt einen Elefanten', *Mittelungen des Kunsthistorischen Instituts in Florenz,* Band XI, Heft II–III, November 1964, pp. 71–109.

— (2). 'Raffael als Elefantenzeichner', *Stil und Uberlieferung in der Kunst des Abendlandes, Akten des 21. Internationalen Kongresses für Kunstgeschichtes in Bonn 1964,* Band III, pp. 164–66. Berlin:Verlag Gebr. Mann, 1967.

Wood, Frances. *Did Marco Polo go to China?* London: Secker & Warburg, 1995.

Young, G. F. *The Medici.* New York: Random House, Modern Library Edition, 1933.

Zander, Giuseppe, 'Gli elementi documentari sul Sacro Bosco', *Quaderni dell'Istituto di Storia dell'Architettura,* Nos. 7–8–9, Aprile 1965, pp. 19–32.

INDEX

FOR THE BEST IN PAPERBACKS, LOOK FOR THE

In every corner of the world, on every subject under the sun, Penguin represents quality and variety—the very best in publishing today.

For complete information about books available from Penguin—including Puffins, Penguin Classics, and Arkana—and how to order them, write to us at the appropriate address below. Please note that for copyright reasons the selection of books varies from country to country.

In the United Kingdom: Please write to *Dept. EP, Penguin Books Ltd, Bath Road, Harmondsworth, West Drayton, Middlesex UB7 0DA.*

In the United States: Please write to *Penguin Putnam Inc., P.O. Box 12289 Dept. B, Newark, New Jersey 07101-5289* or call *1-800-788-6262.*

In Canada: Please write to *Penguin Books Canada Ltd, 10 Alcorn Avenue, Suite 300, Toronto, Ontario M4V 3B2.*

In Australia: Please write to *Penguin Books Australia Ltd, P.O. Box 257, Ringwood, Victoria 3134.*

In New Zealand: Please write to *Penguin Books (NZ) Ltd, Private Bag 102902, North Shore Mail Centre, Auckland 10.*

In India: Please write to *Penguin Books India Pvt Ltd, 11 Panchsheel Shopping Centre, Panchsheel Park, New Delhi 110 017.*

In the Netherlands: Please write to *Penguin Books Netherlands bv, Postbus 3507, NL-1001 AH Amsterdam.*

In Germany: Please write to *Penguin Books Deutschland GmbH, Metzlerstrasse 26, 60594 Frankfurt am Main.*

In Spain: Please write to *Penguin Books S. A., Bravo Murillo 19, 1° B, 28015 Madrid.*

In Italy: Please write to *Penguin Italia s.r.l., Via Benedetto Croce 2, 20094 Corsico, Milano.*

In France: Please write to *Penguin France, Le Carré Wilson, 62 rue Benjamin Baillaud, 31500 Toulouse.*

In Japan: Please write to *Penguin Books Japan Ltd, Kaneko Building, 2-3-25 Koraku, Bunkyo-Ku, Tokyo 112.*

In South Africa: Please write to *Penguin Books South Africa (Pty) Ltd, Private Bag X14, Parkview, 2122 Johannesburg.*